Buddha and
Early Buddhism

These articles have been published in the Indian Historical Quarterly and the details of the articles are given below for reference:

Issue	Year of Pub.	Page Nos.	Page Nos. in the present book
Vol. 33 (1-4)	1957	295-304	1-8
Vol. 6 (1-4)	1930	537-544	9-16
Vol. 6 (1-4)	1930	665-678	17-30
Vol. 20 (1-4)	1944	319-333	31-44
Vol. 7 (1-2)	1931	365-366	45-46
Vol. 6 (1-4)	1930	717-726	47-54
Vol. 7 (3-4)	1931	654-656	55-58
Vol. 9 (1-2)	1933	46-48	59-62
Vol. 12 (1-4)	1936	1-20	63-80
Vol. 10 (1-4)	1934	274-287	81-92
Vol. 32 (1-4)	1956	338-340	93-96
Vol. 9 (1-2)	1933	585-587	97-100
Vol. 10 (1-4)	1934	737-760	101-120
Vol. 29 (1-4)	1953	35-49	121-134
Vol. 30 (1-4)	1954	167-177	135-144
Vol. 33 (1-4)	1957	129-138	145-154
Vol. 8 (3-4)	1932	781-784	155-158
Vol. 32 (1-4)	1956	129-135	159-164
Vol. 1 (1-2)	1925	234-244	165-172
Vol. 11 (1-4)	1935	710-740	173-198
Vol. 3 (3-4)	1927	689-715	199-218
Vol. 16 (1-4)	1940	639-646	219-224
Vol. 21 (1-4)	1945	163-183	225-246
Vol. 32 (1-4)	1956	265-269	247-252
Vol. 32 (1-4)	1956	141-147	253-258
Vol. 13 (1-4)	1937	624-628	259-262
Vol. 12 (1-4)	1936	282-286	263-266
Vol. 37 (1-4)	1961	111-125	267-278

Facets of Buddhist Thought and Culture : 1

Buddha and Early Buddhism

Collection of Articles from the Indian Historical Quarterly

Vol. 1

Compiled by
Dr. Mahendra P. Mittal

Introduction by
Prof. S. R. Bhatt

Originals
(an imprint of Low Price Publications)
Delhi-110052

Distributed by
D.K. Publishers Distributors (P) Ltd.
4834/24, Ansari Road, Darya Ganj,
New Delhi-110002
Phones: 3278584, 3278368, 3261465,
e-mail: dkpd@del3.vsnl.net.in
visit us at: www.dkpd.com

Articles first published in the Journal from 1925-1963
First published as a book
With an Introduction 2002
ISBN 81-7536-268-5

Published by
Originals
(an imprint of Low Price Publications)
A-6, Nimri Commercial Centre,
Near Ashok Vihar Phase-IV,
Delhi-110052
Phones: 7401672, 7452453
e-mail: lpp@nde.vsnl.net.in
visit us at: www.lppindia.com

Printed at
D K Fine Art Press P Ltd.
Delhi-110052

PRINTED IN INDIA

Introduction*

Prof. S.R. Bhatt

"Caratha bhikkhave Cārikam
Bahujanahitāya bahujana sukhāya lokānukampāya
Atthāya, hitāya, sukhāya
Devamanussānam"

> "O Monks! Move around for the well-being of every one, for the happiness of every one, showering compassion on the entire world; for the good, for the welfare, for the happiness of divine and human."
>
> Vinaya pitaka I. 23.

The advent of Śākyamuni, the Buddha, initially the light of India and Asia, and now of the entire world, has been a significant event in the history of world culture and civilization. Born in a princely family with all maternal prosperity and physical comforts, he was awakened by the pain and suffering, finitude and evanescence of the mundane life. After intensive study, deep reflections and profound meditation he gained insight into the nature of reality and the phenomenal world. Having attained enlightenment, he did not remain self-centred. He was not contented with his own emancipation and longed for the liberation of the suffering humanity. He showed to the humanity the sure path of Nirvāna, a way to eradicate suffering and to escape from the labyrinth of the cycle of birth and death (*bhava cakra*), which consisted of a symbiosis of wisdom and conduct, ethics and meditative practice. He realized the 'Four Noble Truths', practiced them in the form of 'Noble Eight-fold Path' in his own life and subsequently enlightened people about it. That is why he was regarded as a great healer, a liberator

---

* In preparing this write-up the author is indebted to Prof. P.V. Bapat and Prof. K.S. Murty whose works he has freely consulted.

(*bheṣajya guru* or *tāyin*). In the words of Rhys Davids, "He was the greatest, and wisest, and best of that long line of reformers who have tried to infuse new strength into the religious life of India" (Buddhism, p.83).

II

The Buddha has been one of the finest products of Indian culture, He was an inheritor of an old tradition as well as a creator of a new outlook. In his own words, "Even so have I, O Monk, seen an ancient way, an ancient road, traversed by the supremely enlightened ones of the olden times (Samyutta Nikāya II, p. 106-7). The Buddha was a well-read and well-versed person with a critical bent of mind and subtle logical acumen. He was well-steeped in the Vedic lore and drew his ideas and inspirations from it. He was fully exposed to the rich and varied cultural milieu of his time. The point to be noted is that he was not born in an intellectual void and his ideas did not grow in a cultural vacuum or in isolation. In fact they sprang up as resurgent thoughts protesting against the distortions in the Vedic lore which crept in later on in the vast temporal canvas of Indian history. It should be made clear that the Buddha did not condemn the Veda but only those aberrations which were violative of Vedic spirit and about which even the Upaniṣads raised their voice. The protest against violence in sacrifice can be cited as an example, as it is expressed in the Bṛhadāraṇyaka or Muṇḍaka Upaniṣad. Of course, the Buddha was more vocal and emphatic.

It will be pertinent to state that at the time of the birth of the Buddha there was no existence of what we now call as 'Hinduism'. The word 'Hinduism' is a late coinage. It has been a name assigned to later Brāhmaṇic tradition but initially it meant 'Indian'. Indian culture was known as 'Zendu' in some parts of Asia and the word 'Hindu' is derived from this. What we now call as Hinduism, Buddhism, Jainism etc. are distinct phases of the same pluralistic Indian culture. They possess the same spiritual genus and as species they differ only in emphasis. They share the same stock of culture, have common source of ideas, beliefs and practices, and therefore, inspite of shift in emphasis they have no cleavages. They are like different branches stemming from the same root. Perceptive and unbiased western indologists like Macnicol, Mr. and Mrs. Rhys Davids, Mrs. Stevension and many others apart from several Indian scholars have very categorically avered this fact and have adduced evidences in support.

It can be said in the words of Dr. S. Radhakrishnan that, "Buddha did not feel that he was announcing a new religion. He was born, grew up and died a Hindu. He was restating with a new emphasis the ancient ideals of Indo-Aryan civilization "(Foreword to "2500 years of Buddhism," P. 68, Government of India, Publication Division). Dr. S. Mukherjee in his paper on Buddhism in "The cultural Heritage of India" states, "It will not be incorrect to say that every Hindu is a Buddhist. Buddhism has permeated the entire religious and philosophical thought of India and percolated into the deepest recesses of the religious mentality of the present-day Hindus" (Ed. Haridas Bhattacharya, vol. I p.575, Calcutta, 1958). It was not for nothing that long before Varāha, Agni and other Purāṇas accepted Buddha as an Avatāra of Viṣṇu, the most significant Mahāyāna Buddhist text "Laṅkāvatāra Sūtra' itself identified the Buddha with Viṣṇu and Rāma. In the Hindu tradition all honours due to other incarnations of Viṣṇu were also accorded to the Buddha. He was worshipped along with Viṣṇu or Śiva or as Viṣṇu or Śiva, by offering flowers, food, cloths, incense, prayers etc. The Paurāṇic pantheon and mythology were adopted in Buddhism and all Hindu gods and demi-gods were made to be engaged in the services of the Buddha. The 'Gīta Govinda' of Jayadeva, the temples in Bihar, Orissa, Nepal etc. are eloquent testimony to this absorption of Buddhism in the broad Hindu fold.

III

The Buddha was a great social reformer. He was opposed to the caste system and social heirarchy. He accepted the vocational distinctions prevalent in the society but accorded equal status to all the *varṇas*. He declared, "*Ime cattāro vaṇṇā samasamā honti. Samano Gotamo cātuvaṇṇim suddhim paññāpeti*" i.e. "All the our *varṇas* are exactly the same. One who is a śramāṇa gotama recognises all as equally pure." (Dīgha Nikāya I, 99-100).

The Buddha was not ill-disposed towards the Brāhmaṇas and, in fact, longed to be a brāhmaṇa in the next birth. The history of Buddhist thought in India testifies the fact-that most of the prominent Buddhist thinkers were brāhmaṇas. Of course, there were fierce verbal exchanges between Buddhist and non-Buddhist scholars and votaries but Śaiva-Vaiṣṇava conflicts were also there not only in words but also physically. The Buddha explicitly said that one becomes a brāhmaṇa or a śudra not by birth but by deeds. Notwithstanding all this it must be emphasised that the Buddha, like the Vedic and Upaniṣadic thinkers, was a great champion of egalitarianism and democratic mode of thinking and living. Oecumenistic outlook was deeply ingrained in him. This gave rise to Buddhist syncretism which enabled Buddhism to co-exist with other national cultures of Asia.

IV

Buddhism, like any other system of philosophical thought in India, has its springs and moorings in the Vedic and Upaniṣadic thought. As H. Zimmer has rightly remarked, "The Buddha remained within the sphere of India's traditional philosophy." (Philosophies of India, p. 530-1, New York, 1951). The Nāsadīya Sūkta of the Ṛgveda explicitly refers to *sat* (from which *Satkāryavāda* evolved) and *asat* (from which *Asatkāyavāda* evolved which culminated in the theory of *pratītya-samutpāda*) and proposes to transcend the two view points (an idea which got formulation as *madhyama pratipad*). In the Chāndogya and the Bṛhadāraṇyaka Upaniṣads the doctrine of '*Nāmarūpa*' and the distinction between *paramārtha* and *vyavahāra* have been clearly propounded. The Maitrāyaṇi Upaniṣad advocates the ideals of '*Nirātmā*' and '*Śunya*' as the *summum bonum* of life (Chapter VI) The Yoga Vāśiṣ-tha Rāmāyana (II, 5, 6,7 and 16) avers the same. The same advocacy is found in the Mahābhārata, Śāntiparva, 191, 23. The idea of *nissvabhāvatā* of all empirical objects is expounded in the Bṛhadāraṇyaka. Of course, credit goes to the Buddha in giving these ideas the most effective formulation. A.E. Gough in "Philosophy of the Upaniṣads" (p. 187) remarks that "Buddhism is the philosophy of the Upaniṣads with Brahman left out". Prof. K.S. Murty writes that: Marya Falk and other "Conclusively demoustrated' (in D.L. Snellgroves words) "the origin of Buddhist religious experience in the general context of the upanishds." (Forward to Bodhi-Raśmi). The Vedāntic and the Buddhist thoughts are so very akin that some Buddhist thinkers were regarded as 'crypto-vedāntins' and some Vedāntic thinkers were regarded are crypto-Buddhists: The Purāṇas and some later Vedāntic thinkers have opined that conceptually the Brahman of Vedānta and the 'Śunya' of Mādhyamika are the same. The idea of Brahman as the source and sustenance of the entire universe is similar to the idea of *Bhūtatathatā* and *Dharmakāya* in Mahāyāna Buddhism. D.T. Suzuki in "Outlines of Mahāyāna" ably demonstrates this. Hajime Nakamura, a great authority on Buddhism and Vedānta opines that, "the realization of Nirvāṇa can be explained as taking refuge in the true self of one's own. On this point the Buddha's assertion is very similar to that of the Upaniṣads and of Vedānta philosophy. But the latter's self (Ātman) was rather metaphysical whereas the Buddha's self was genuinely practical. (Buddhism in the Modern World (eds) H. Dumoulin and J.C. Malarado p. 18, New York and London, 1976). The same is reiterated by Josquin pérez-Remón in his book" Self and Not-self in Early Buddhism (Mouton, the Hague, 1980, pp. 304-5). Th. Stcherbatsky in his "The conception of Buddhist Nirvāṇa" (p.63) writes that there is but little difference between Buddhism and Vedanta."One need not multiply citations in support from erudite Buddhist scholars on this point. We have to properly understand and appreciate the concepts of *nairātmya* and *anātma* in the specific context in which they have been expounded, keeping in view the *Buddhavacana* and the later developments in the Mahāyāna.

V

The history of Indian philosophical thoughts evinces an intense exchange of ideas (*vāda*), both constructive and critical, between and among various systems of thoughts including Buddhism. It goes to the credit of Buddhism and Nyāyā to develop an elaborate method of *vāda* for this purpose and we have many subtle and sophisticated works written on the topic. The debates in the form of *pūrvapakṣa* and *uttarapakṣa* or *siddhānta* among Indian thinkers belonging to different schools of thought have been very fierce but illuminating which have resulted in mutual corrections and mutual enrichment. There have been mutual borrowings and thus improvement in ideas. For example, the well-known four *Brahmaviharās* professed and practiced by the Buddha are derived from the Yoga Sūtras of Pātanjali. It is indisputable that the Buddha was initiated in the yogīc practice by Ālara Kālām and Udraka Rāmaputra. The Buddhist vipassanā is only a specific form of varieties of Yoga systems available to us. The Buddha immensely contributed to the propagation and refinement of Yoga. There is a close affinity between the Sānkhya philosophy and teachings of the Buddha not only with regard to the analysis of suffering and the way to its eradication but also about the structure of reality and transcient nature of matter. The idea of *paramāṇu* is shared by the Buddha with the Vaiṣeśikas. In epistemology the concepts of '*Āpta*', *svaprakāśa*, *svataḥ prāmāṇya* etc. are common to Buddhism and Mimāṃsā. The fact is that all the Indian philosophical systems developed in mutual give and take and no one single system should be approached in isolation from the rest. Mutual borrowing is the healthy attitude and it has been inculcated in the Indian mind right from the Vedic times.

VI

The Brāhmaṇic and Śrāmaṇic traditions have their basis in the Vedic thought and both were prevalent and significantly interacting well before the advent of the Buddha on the scene. The contribution of the Buddha was to purge the Brāhmaṇic tradition of its ritualistic stereotypes, sacrificial violence and other impurities. He founded a religious order i.e., *Saṁgha* and gave a new turn to the institution of *saṁnyāsa*. For entry into the *Saṁgha* three vows were to be undertaken. But this apart there were certain rules and regulations of the monastic life which were to be followed. There were positive and negative prescriptions and one who is to be initiated in the *Saṁgha* was taught about these by the preceptors. Those who transgressed the rules were given suitable punishments. Pātimokkhasutta and several other pāli treatises deal with them in detail. The functioning of the *Saṁgha* was democratic. The authority of the *Saṁgha* was supreme and binding on all the inmates. As admission to the Samgha was simple so was exit from it. A monk was always at liberty to return to his household life. In the beginning women were not admitted in the *Saṁgha* but later on they were also initiated in the order but with a different code known as Bhikkhunīpātimokkha. Separate bhikkhuni samghas were established. The monks and nuns were required to lead an ascetic life of unwordliness and they were asked to spend most of their time in meditation in the monastery.

VII

The Buddha was a wise and a practical person fully knowledgeable of human psychology. He not only discerned the inner cravings of human heart and intellect, he also knew the logic and language in which he was to communicate with them. So he gave his discourses in the language in which people were conversant. But later on Buddhist scholars took recourse to Sanskrit or mixed Sanskrit. Geographical distances also required resorting to Sanskrit which was perhaps the *Lingua franka* at that time. The story of two brāhmaṇa brothers of Puruṣapura (present Peshawar in Pakistan) recorded in the Cullavagga testifies the need to put the *Buddhavacanas* in *chāndasa* i.e. Vedic Sanskrit. Among the followers of the Buddha brāhmaṇas were quiet prominent and they preferred to use Sanskrit. Another reason could be the ease with which subtle and sophisticated ideas were to be expressed and communicated and Sanskrit was handy for this job for the scholiasts.

VIII

The Buddha was not in favour of believing in a Creator-God, nor did he like any cult or hero worship. He did not claim divinity or divine powers in him. This is the general impression about him. However, subsequently in the course of time he was deified and his worship started. Large size images of the Buddha were constructed. The Pauraṇic pantheon and mythology were accepted wholesale and complicated religious symbolism was developed. The same Pauraṇic Yakṣas, Yakṣiṇis, Dikpālas, Devatās, Nāgas, Kubera, Indra, Brahmā,

Prajāpati, Gandharvas, Apsarās, Rakṣaśas, Piśacas etc. found a place in the Buddhist mythology. Supernatural powers were ascribed to the Buddha. This was more so in the later Buddhism. One thing is definite that the Buddha was a spiritualist and not a materialist. His silence on the question of the existence of God is to be interpreted as his non-acceptance of the idea of God.

IX

It is a widespread opinion that Buddhism got extinct in or was banished from India, the land of its origin and development. It is perhaps not a correct way of looking at the situation. Buddhism was an offshoot of Indian culture and not an upstart movement originating *de novo*. So the Indian psyche accepted and imbided the ideas propagated by the Buddha as something worthwhile. It was quite natural therefore that Buddha's teachings got assimilated in the mainstream Indian culture. The interfusion was so deep and pervasive that there was no need for its separate existence in India. All aspects of 'Hindu culture' became Buddhistic by the acceptance of the main doctrinal and practical tenets of Buddhism. As Prof. S. Mukherjee has opined in the paper referred to earlier, Buddhism may not exist in India as a separate sect (of course now it does as a result of its revival by Dr. Ambedkar), but Hinduism is Buddhism and Buddhism is Hinduism. The so-called decline of Buddhism is a mistaken view. It is assimilation and absorption of something which is our own and not something alien. As Dr. S. Radhakrishnan has stated, "The Buddha left his foot prints on the soil of India and his mark on the soul of the country." India is Buddhistic through and through, whether we believe it or not. It is not a matter of argumentation but of feeling.

Buddhism is alive in the deepest recesses of the Hindu mind and it cannot be extinct so long as Hinduism is extant. One has not to see the legacy of Buddhism in the national emblems in the form of *Dharma Cakra* or *siṁhanāda*, or in the sectarian followers, but one has to look for it in the very cultural ethos of the country, in our modes of thinking and ways of living. If one wants to see cleavages and chasms one is free to do so but this does not seem to be a healthy approach. There have been vested interests to take such a stance but there have also been sane non-divisive approaches.

X

While concluding this write up it may be said that the Buddha is one of the most revolutionary thinkers and the holiest persons ever lived on the earth. He has been a beacon light not only for India or Asia but for the entire world. His advocacy of pursuit of *Prajñā* and practice of *Karuṇā*, his vision of self-sameness with everyone (*Parātma Samatā*), and zealous longing for eradication of suffering of others as one's own (*Parātma Parivartana*) cross all barriers of race, creed, country and even humanity. His benevolent teachings of universal compassion and cosmic goodwill, his emphasis on the noble virtues of *Maitrī*, *Karuṇā, Mudita* and *Upekṣā* known as *Brahmavihāras* (i.e. living and working for totality), all these have a significant message for the present-day distracted humankind suffering from exhaustion of spirit and languishing in the narrow and rigid confinements of ego-centricism, parochalism and disasterous materialistic consumerism. In the present times our traditional cultures are facing terrible danger of extinction under the perverting impact of the so-called modernisation which is divisive, depriving and destructive. For the first time since their inception such a large scale threatening situation has arisen. We have not so far cared to share a common platform to meet the challenge in a decisive and global way, may be due to ignorance, negligence, self-centeredness or bewitchment with modernism etc. A time has come for the beginning of a cultural renaissance for which the teachings of the Buddha can play a vital and pivotal role. A renewal of cross-cultural interactions under their banner will not only help and contribute to mutual understanding, mutual empathy and mutual enrichment, it will also consolidate our common spiritual roots and resources. It will enable us to appreciate the spiritual, holistic and integral perspective as against the divisive and diachotomous world-view. If the humanity looks back to its hoary past to discern whatever is true, good and beautiful, whatever is living and beneficial in it, the wisdom of those times will help us more intimately and more truly to our mutual well-being. The present volume, which is the first in the series of four volumes consisting articles published in the Indian Historical Quarterly, may be a right step towards this goal.

Contents

Chapter - 1

The Day of Buddha's Conception and Birth

Biswadeb Mukherjee

The *Mahāpadāna Sutta* and *Acchariyabhutadhamma Sutta* represent the earliest systematic expositions of the Bodhisattva conception developed out of still earlier legends. In the *Mahāpadāna Sutta*, the legend has been told with reference to Vipassi Buddha, and the identical events have been recorded, with wearisome re-iteration, in the case of the other Buddhas. We are not concerned with the whole of this legendo-doctrinal exposition, but the following passages may be quoted here:-

1. "Now Vipassi, brethren, when as Bodhisattva ceased to belong to the hosts of the Tusita heaven, descended into his mother's womb mindful. That, in such a case, is the rule"[1]

2. "It is the rule, brethren, that whereas other women bring forth after bearing either nine or ten months, the mother of a Bodhisattva brings not forth till she has borne the child ten months."[2]

As pointed out by Rhys Davids, such legends of the fore-runners of the historical Buddha were constructed in imitation of the then adopted beliefs as to the life of Gotama. This canonical description, in identical form, also recurs in another sutta, the *Acchariyabhutadhamma Sutta* where, of course, Gotama the Buddha is the central figure of the story. In this sutta the events have been characterised as wonderful and marvellous and not as a 'rule' (Dhammatā), as has been done in the *Mahāpadāna Sutta*. The constantly repeated refrain "Ayam ettha dhammatā" stated in connection with every event narrated in the latter sutta indicates that these events were already old, and popular enough to gain recognition as

---

1. *Sacred Books of Buddhists*, vol. II, p. 8.
2. *Ibid.*, p. 11.

"Dhammatā". In both these Suttas 10 months' period of gestation has been noted, though nothing has been recorded as to the day marking the beginning and end of this period. Neither Pūrṇimā nor any other day is hallowed by its association with the conception and birth of the Buddha. Again '*Ta pen ching*'[1] and '*Wei chen Yu fa ching*'[2] the Chinese versions of the *Mahāpadāna Sutta* and the *Acchariyabhutadhamma Sutta* of the Sarvāstivāda Āgama, record the descent of *Pú Se* (Bodhisattva) from the Tuṣita heaven along with many other legendary details but remain silent as to the days of the conception and birth. The omission of such an important element, the time element, in the Āgama and Nikāya, when considered against the mention of other events comparatively less significant, tempts one to surmise that the early Buddhists had not yet developed any tradition regarding the auspicious moment when the 'garbhavakrānti' and 'janma' should take place.

Concerning the stages of evolution of the tradition the main sources of our information may be divided into two categories:-

1. The *Chinese Sūtras* which preserve the early Sarvāstivādin tradition.

2. The *Sanskrit Buddhist texts*, namely *Mahāvastu* which presents us with the Lokottaravādin tradition, and *Lalitavistara* which contains a different Sarvāstivādin tradition, the exact nature of which is uncertain.

The earliest text belonging to the first groups is *Hsiu Hsing Pen Ch'i Ching*. It was translated in the later Han dynasty. As the text was translated in the 2nd century A.D., it may be reasonably held to have been composed in the 1st century A.D. Two portions of this text bearing on our problem are quoted here:-

1. *Neng Pú Se* (Śākyamuni Bodhisattva) changed himself into a rider on a white elephant and entered into the womb on the 8th day of the 4th month".[3]

2. On the fulfilment of the 10th month the body of the prince attained completion. On the 8th day of the 4th month the queen went out (for a stroll). She was passing under the Min tree which was in full bloom.[4] It further states that when the Bright Star (Ming Hsing) was coming out, the queen was delivered of the child.

The 2nd sūtra belonging to this group is *T'ai Tzu Sui Ying Pen Ch'i Ching* of the Wu period. As to the time of conception it only states

---

1. Akanuma, Comparative Catalogue, p.3; Taisho vol. 1, p.1ff.
2. Akanuma, *Ibid.*, p. 170; Taisho, vol. I p. 469ff.
3. Taisho vol. III, p. 463b.
4. *Ibid.*, pp. 463c.

that the Bodhisattva entered the womb when the queen was sleeping at day time. However about the time of birth this sūtra is more explicit and clearly states that the Bodhisattva was born on the night of the 8th day of the 4th month when the Bright Star appeared.[1]

Last comes the *Kuo Ch'u Hsien Chai Yin Kuo Ching* translated in the Liu Sung dynasty. It states that the Bodhisattva descended into his mother's womb on the 8th of the 4th month when the Bright Star appeared, and after a full ten month the Bodhisattva was born on the 8th of the 2nd month when the sun was in the ascension.[2]

Before entering into the analysis of these sources, we should first try to determine what is really meant by this 4th month. Some are of opinion that the 4th month here stands for the 4th month of the Christian calendar and therefore is identical with the month of April.[3] But it is difficult to see eye to eye with this view. The *Hsiu Hsing Pen Ch'i Ching*, being a translation of the 2nd century A.D. it may be reasonably held to present faithfully the Indian text of the first century A.D. or B.C. and it is unlikely that at such an early period it would be influenced by the Christian calendar. Therefore we may be justified in holding that the Chinese sūtras have preserved some Indian tradition, and the 4th month in question really refers to the 4th month of some Indian calendar. So it would be worthwhile making an investigation into the ancient Indian calendar here.

The Indian year is traditionally divided into the following six seasons, each consisting of two months:

1. Śiśirakāla of the two months of Māgha and Fālguna.
2. Vasantakāla of the two months of Caitra and Vaiśākha.
3. Grīṣmakāla of the two months of Jaiṣṭha and Āsāḍha.
4. Varṣākāla of the two months of Śrāvana and Bhādra.
5. Śaratkāla of the two months of Āśvina and Kārttika.
6. Hemantakāla of the two months of Agrahāyaṇa and Pauṣa.

According to the *Bṛhatsaṃhitā* the year commenced from the winter season which comprised the two months of Māgha and Phālguna[4]. In another place Varāhamihira further points out that according to an earlier work the Uttarāyaṇa commences from the time when the sun touches the star Dhaniṣṭhā.[5]

---

1. *Ibid.*, p. 473b-c.
2. *Ibid.*, pp. 624a; p. 625a.
3. Dr. P.C. Bagchi, *Twelve years of the Wandering Life of Buddha.*
4. Jogesh Chandra Roy, *Amāder Jyotish* O' *Jyotishi*, p.52.
5. *Ibid.*, p. 51.

Now the star Dhaniṣṭhā is associated with the two houses of the zodiac, Capricorn (Makara) and Acquaris (Kumbha). This means that as soon as the Sun touches Dhaniṣṭhā in Capricorn the year commences. This can take place only in the month of Māgha. Thus from two different sources of evidence we can conclude that according to Varāhamihira, the year commenced from the month of Māgha when the Sun remains in the house of Capricorn. If this tradition is followed, the 4th month will be the month of Vaiśākha. Now Veḍāṅgajyotiṣa also holds that the year starts from the month of Māgha[1]. Thus, there was prevalent a calendar from the 6th century B.C. according to which Vaiśākha was the 4th month and evidently the Buddhists followed this tradition when they held that Buddha was born on the 8th day of the 4th month.

On the basis of the conclusion reached above we may have the following tabular representation of the information contained in the Chinese Sūtras:

Conception	*Gestation period*		*Birth*
Hsiu Hsing Pen Chi Ching— 8th Vaiśākha	10 months.	8th	Vaiśākha
Tai Tzu Suī Ying Pen Chi Ching— ...		8th	Vaiśākha
Kuo Ch'u Hsien Chai Yin Kuo Ching— 8th Vaiśākha	10 months.	8th	Phālguna

From the above chart it is apparent that the earliest tradition suffers from inconsistency. We cannot reject the tradition of the gestation period of ten months, for its genuineness is proved by the sūtra literature, and if this tradition is accepted, we cannot place both the conception and birth on the same day of the same month, for to do so a gestation period of twelve months is necessary. Consequently we meet with a conscious attempt to do away with this discrepancy in the other two sūtas. *T'ai Tzu Sui Ying Pen Ch'i Ching* has partially gained by remaining silent as to the time of conception and the period of gestation, while clearly stating that Buddha was born on the 8th Vaiśākha. On the other hand *Kuo Ch'u Hsien Chai Yin Kuo Ching*, has fully solved the problem by changing the date of birth from the 8th Vaiśākha to the 8th Phālguna and maintaining the old traditions of conception and gestation.

Let us now turn to sources of the second category. In the *Kulapariśuddhiparivartta*[2] of Lalitavistara it has been stated:

1. *Ibid.*, p. 27-28. For this discussion I am indebted to Dr. Sudhakar Chatterjee.
2. Lefmann edition, p. 25.

न खलु पुनर्मार्षा कृष्णापक्षे बोधिसत्त्वो मातुः कुक्षावक्रामति। अपि तु शुल्कपक्षे एवं पञ्चदश्यां पूर्णायां पूर्णिमायां पुष्यनक्षत्रयोगे पोषधपरिगृहीताया मातुः कुक्षौ चरमभविको बोधिसत्त्वोऽवक्रामति॥ But at the end of this Parivartta an earlier and shorter account of the contents of the whole chapter has been given in verse, but neither Purṇimā nor any other day has been brought into connection with the conception.[1]

Contrarily the *Garbhavakrāntiparivartta*[2] begins with the following sentences:- इति हि भिक्षवः शिशिरकालविनिर्गते वैशाखमासे विशाखनक्षानुगते ऋतुप्रवरे वसन्तकालसमये......त्रिभुवनज्येष्ठो लोकमहितो व्यवलोक्य ऋतुकालसमये पञ्चदश्यां पूर्णमास्यां पोषधगृहीताया मातुः पुष्यनक्षत्रयोगेन बोधि-सत्त्वस्तुषितवरभवनाच् च्युत्वा स्मृतः संप्रजानन् पाणडुरो गजपोतो भूत्वा...जनन्या दक्षिणायां कुक्षाववक्रामद् अवक्रान्तश्च स दक्षिणावचरोऽभून्न जातु वामावचरः॥

Here the legend is in a more fabricated form. Not only the '*Puṣyanakṣatra*' and '*Pañcadaśyām*' have been mentioned but also the month of Vaiśākha has been brought into association with the moment of conception of the Bodhisattva. This means that the Bodhisattva's conception occurred in Vaiśākha on the fullmoon day when the moon was in conjunction with the star Puṣyā. But this can never happen in the month of Vaiśākha, for in order to have the full moon of that month, the moon must be on Libra while Puṣyā is associated with Cancer. Here evidently is a confusion. On the other hand, in the account of the Suddhāvāsakāyikā gods' meeting with king Suddhodana,[3] all such data connected with the auspicious moment of conception have been omitted. Here, in apprising the bewildered king of what had really happened the Suddhāvāsakāyikā gods describe the descent of the Bodhisattva from the Tuṣita heaven into queen Māyā's womb in the form of an elephant, along with other legendary details, but nothing has been said regarding the moment of conception.

In the *Janmaparivartta*[4] we come across the following line:-

स परिपूर्णानां दशानां मासानाम् अत्ययेन मातुर्दक्षिणपार्श्वान्निष्क्रामति स्म।

Here the ten months' period of gestation has been noted though nothing is said as to the day of birth.

When we compare the *Fang Kuang Ta Chuang Yen Ching* i.e. the Chinese translation of the *Lalitavistara* in the T'ang period, we get almost an identical picture. In the *Sheng Chu P'in* (Kulapariśuddhiparivartta) it has been stated: "The Bodhisattva does not descend into his mother's womb in the Kṛṣnapakṣa; in the Śuklapakṣa when the moon is in unison with the Puṣyā star, (he descends).[5]

1. *Ibid.*, pp. 27ff.
2. *Ibid.*, p. 54-55.
3. *Ibid.*, p. 56.
4. *Ibid.*, p. 83.
5. Taisho, vol. III. p. 543a.

Here, unlike the Sanskrit version, Pūrṇimā has been omitted. However the *Ch'u T'ai P'in* account of this problem is identical with the *Garbhavakrāntiparivartta* passage.[1] Here *Yueh Yuan* or full moon day has been expressly mentioned. The Chinese translation also tallies with the *Janmaparivartta* account, and the birth at the end of full ten months has been mentioned.

There are, thus, three traditions:-

1. The early Sarvāstivādin tradition (Chinese sūtras) connects the sacred day of 8th Vaiśākha with the conception, as well as with the birth, of the Bodhisattva. But ultimately the tradition of birth on 8th Vaiśākha seems to have been given up and changed to 8th Phālguna in order to reconcile the tradition of the gestation with the tradition of the conception on the 8th Vaiśākha.
2. The second tradition, preserved in the *Kulapariśuddhiparivartta*, holds that the Bodhisattva was born on the full moon day when the moon was in the star Puṣyā.
3. The third tradition holds that Bodhisattva was conceived on the Vaiśākha Pūrṇimā, and as the earlier tradition of the gestation period of ten months is followed, the birth, though not expressly mentioned, automatically falls on the full moon day of Phālguna.

On the other hand in the Mahāvastu[2] we meet with the following tradition:- न खलु बोधिसत्त्वा कालपक्षे मातु कुक्षिं ओक्रामन्ति ॥ अथ खलु पूर्णमास्यां पुष्यनक्षत्रयोगयुक्तायां रात्र्यां बोधिसत्त्वा मातुः कुक्षिमवक्रामन्ति ॥

Here in a clear and succinct way, the conception has been placed in the month of Māgha and as the ten months period of gestation finds a place in the Bodhisattva idea of the Lokottaravādins, the birth may be placed in the month of Agrahāyaṇa. This account tallies in toto with the tradition preserved in the *Kulapariśuddhiparivartta* of the Sanskrit version of the *Lalitavistara*, and in part with its 7th century A.D. Chinese translation. Again both the *Garbhavakrāntiparivartta* (Sanskrit and Chinese versions) and *Mahāvastu* agree in associating Pūrṇimā and Puṣyā nakṣatra with the conception. It should be also noted here that the passages in *Mahāvastu* and *Kulapariśuddhiparivartta* of the *Lalitavistara* are almost identical in expression and clearly indicate the borrowing of one text from the other.

Now the problem is whether the Sarvāstivādins or the Lokottaravādins are responsible for introducing the elements of Pūrṇimā and Puṣyānakṣatra in the legend. We have seen that these two

1. *Ibid.*, p. 548c.
2. Senart. p. 8.

elements are conspicuous by their absence in the Chinese translations of the Sarvāstivādin sūtras of the 2nd and 3rd centuries. Whereas some passages of the Sanskrit *Lalitavistara* and its Chinese translation of the 7th century A.D. expressly mention them. Evidently Pūrṇimā and Puṣyānakṣatra did not find favour with the early Sarvāstivādins. On the other hand *Mahāvastu* was composed some time between 2nd century B.C. and 4th century A.D. and the said passage, though there is no definite proof to show to which stage of evolution it belongs, at least it cannot be proved to be of later origin. Again the early Sarvāstivādin tradition was never expressly rejected, while the later tradition, as found in the Sanskrit *Lalitavistara* and Chinese translation of the 7th century A.D., betrays confusion in itself. The confusion arises out of placing together the Vaiśākhamāsa, Pūrṇimā and Puṣyānakṣatra. From the above discussion it is reasonable to surmise that with the Lokottaravādins originated the tradition of पूर्णायां पुणभास्यां पुष्यनक्षत्रयोगयुक्तायां which constitutes an inconsistent and foreign element in the Sarvāstivādin legend. As it appears, the early Sarvāstivādin tradition is not totally wiped out and the month of Vaiśākha is retained in later legends, and consequently it is on this fragment of the early tradition that the Lokottaravādin idea was engrafted. Hence the rise of the tradition of the Bodhisattva's conception of the full moon day of Vaiśākha.

It is difficult to ascertain whether the Sarvāstivādins or the Lokottaravādins are to be held responsible for this engraftment of foreign elements. As we already know the Sarvāstivādins never openly disapproved of their own tradition. On the other hand we also know that the Mahāyānists recast the *Lalitavistara* in order to bring it in line with their speculations. It may be, therefore, suggested here that in course of recasting the text they, accepted the Lokottaravādin tradition while rejecting that of the Sarvāstivādin, as in Buddhological speculations they had more affinity with the former.

However there is no reason to regard this Pūrṇimā tradition as authentic. The passage dealing with the time of conception, as already pointed out, cannot be shown as belonging to the later period of evolution of the Mahāvastu. If we tentatively place this passage in the first century B.C., it appears that two different traditions about the time of the conception were prevalent round about first century B.C., that is the tradition of Pūrṇima followed by the Lokottaravādins and the tradition of the 8th day of Vaiśākha accepted by the Sarvāstivādins. This hints at the lack of an earlier tradition common to both the schools. This fact when considered along with the silence of the Sūtras on this particular problem, proves that the Buddhists themselves had lost all authentic information as to the day of the Bodhisattva's birth and conception, and therefore it was possible that different traditions appeared regarding the day of the Bodhisattva's conception and birth.

Once the Pūrṇima element was introduced, it gradually made its way into the legend of the Theravādins, and in the account of the *Nidānakathā*, the conception is explicitly stated to have taken place on the full-moon day. According to the *Nidānakathā*[1] on the full-moon day of the month Āsāḷha (June to July) the Bodhisattva entered into the womb of queen Māyā and was borne by the Queen for ten months like oil in a bowl. Thus the *Nidānakathā* account corresponds with the traditional date of his birth on the full moon day of Vaiśākha (April to May). It should be noted that this date of the birth is identical with the date of conception given in the *Lalitavistara*.

It is also clear from the study of the legends that the connection of Pūrṇimā with the birth is never explicit but always implicit. It is the conception and not birth that is stated to have occurred on the full-moon day and it is only as a result of mathematical calculation that the birth came to be associated with this day. The Buddhists on the whole seem to be more concerned with the auspiciousness of the moment of conception than with that of the birth. This seems quite natural on their part, for what they were really interested in, was the descent of the Bodhisattva into this world, and as it was the conception, and not the birth, that really stood for this momentous event, it was the moment of conception that the Buddhist naturally wanted to invest with sacredness. Hence when the Buddhists attached importance to Pūrṇimā, they thought of it in connection with the conception.

To sum up, the Buddhists of the Sūtra period had no idea either as to the day when the Bodhisattva was conceived in the womb of his mother, or as to the time of his birth. All authentic informations seem to be lost and his facilitated and growth of mainly two different traditions round the traditionally sacred days of the Pūrṇimā and the 8th day (of Vaiśākha or Phālguna). As to the tradition of Pūrṇimā it appears to have been introduced by the Lokottaravādins and first came to be connected with the conception of the Bodhisattva. The conception was thought to have taken place either on the full moon day of Māgha (*Mahāvastu*) or on the full moon day of Vaiśākha (*Lalitavistara*) and the date of birth varied accordingly, following the earlier tradition of the gestation period of ten months. It is only in the late account of the *Nidānakathā* that the conception has been connected with the full-moon day of Āsāḷha and consequently the day of birth with the Pūrṇimā of Vaiśākha.

---

1. E.J. Thomas, *The Life of Buddha*, p. 31.

Chapter - 2

The Origin of Buddhism*

Manoranjan Ray

So general an interest has been shown in Buddhism and it has been brought so near to us as a result of enthusiasm and sometimes of superficiality, that to many minds it appears a little in the abstract, divested of those marvellous and singular traits and of those popular and Indian elements which are liable to shock the western observer. But my work as an Indianist imposes on me a contrary pre-occupation. Happily for me you have acquired here sufficiently serious habits of thought, you value history and the investigation of the links of successive transformations, sufficiently for me to venture to ask you to make your patience equal to the test to which I shall put it.

I shall not, however, claim to be able to describe in an hour all the sources of Buddhism; I wish only, in the light of a number of characteristic facts, to set it in the true environment from which it has drawn its sap.

I

To avoid excessive obscurity I must remind you at the outset how the religious tradition of India presents itself.

On the one hand there is the Vedic tradition which continues from the hymns of the Ṛg-veda into the mystic and liturgic literature of the Brāhmaṇas wherein the religious ceremonies have been elaborated and explained, and then of the Upaniṣads which are especially devoted to speculation. By their language merely, not to speak of other characteristics, these works must be placed at the source of literary development; but leaving out of consideration the fact that archaisms have been artificially preserved by scholars many differences in regard

---

* The translator gratefully records his indebtedness to Mr. Ernest Lerouk, publisher of Paris, for giving him the necessary permission to print this translation. Sincere thanks are also due to the learned editor of the IHQ., for obtaining the permission for the translator.

to date are disclosed within this long series. Above all, this literature is essentially sacerdotal and ritualistic—less the reflection of the common religious life than the work of a class of privileged priests strong in their liturgical influence, and proud of the sacred song of which they were the custodians. And on this carefully guarded teaching it was only slowly and progressively that the action of beliefs which grew up and became transformed and mingled exerted itself behind the screen of a supposed immutability.

On the other hand comes the literature of the Epic poetry and the Law Books. In these we find a crowd of gods and divine heroes, new or renewed by their unforeseen importance, also new ideas and new legends. This literature obviously draws on living and popular sources. Yet whatever may have been its beginnings, the epic literature had reached us only in a much altered form. In practical life as well as in its books the sacerdotal class took advantage of its twofold privilege, religious and literary; it extended its authority over different sects and systems; and under the nominal supremacy of the Vedas it has presented them to us in the form of an orthodoxy which is uncompromising only on the subject of the pre-eminence of the brahmins. For the period of religions history which extends from the earliest times down perhaps to the neighbourhood of the Christian era, the Mahābhārata remains an almost unique mine of information, and it is not the less precious on that account. But how shall we attain an approximately clear vision in a long drawn out past, across a confused mass of cults and doctrines, among the contradictions of interpenetrating theories, joined together by editors always prejudiced in one direction and yet yielding as time goes on to inspirations of different kinds. Still therein exist with something of animation, the complications of reality and the traces of beliefs whose reactions and conflicts during a definite period the woof of Hindu life.

Thus we have the two currents of information, the ritualistic and the speculative tradition of the Brāhmaṇas, and the epic tradition of the Mahābhārata. By the ideas which they represent they appear to me like two parallel strata of the same rather than of two successive periods. But one anticipates the information of the other and they have mutual influences, which obscure all realities. More than anything else it is the uncertainty of chronology that disturbs our investigation. The relative dates of the works are often doubtful and always insufficient; and in a century like India where scarcely exists any work which can strictly be said to be the production of a single author, the ideas transmitted through a book may be much older than its composition, and an encyclopaedia like the Mahābhārata is composed of fragments whose antiquity is as uncertain as the interpolations are obvious.

Buddhism offers a twofold advantage: it has chronology, and it contains writings independent of the influences of brāhmaṇic orthodoxy. It can scarcely be doubted that Buddha preached towards the close of the 6th century B.C.; and it can no longer be doubted that his doctrines and legends were soon completed in their main outlines in such forms as are accessible to us.

Under these circumstances, you see well enough how much we ought to study those teachings which, referring directly to the comparisons of different doctrines, make up in some measure the absence of positive chronology, and how many of those comparisons of which Buddhism furnishes the material are of special importance by marking definite dates within the age. For a long time I have been trying to open this mine of information by analysing various episodes which constitute what I have called the "Legend of Buddha." I shall not conceal from you that I adhere to my first theory in its main import. Still less must I conceal it from myself that by attaching too much importance to the system of mythologic interpretation then in vogue I then made some mistakes in my theory; I have offended beyond reason, I think, the intellectuals who are rightly prejudiced against certain ecstasies of comparative mythology. Above all, there I have neglected to show clearly under what impulse and by what mechanism the doctrines which Buddhism professes and the stories which clash from the very fact of its origin were put together. To-day we are better prepared to solve this problem of juxtaposition. If I return to this subject it is not from obstinacy or egoism; and if there is pleasure for an old worker in uniting together the fragments of his researches under certain leading ideas you will pardon him perhaps when he thinks that the meeting in this hospitable house gives him a favourable opportunity for it.

II

The Buddha, also known as Gautama or Śākyamuni, is certainly a historical and real personality; but he is also by tradition the hero of stories which are mythical in origin and character. This point I would like to make clear to you by an instance against which, I think, some futile objections have been raised.

The critical moment in the life of the Buddha and of all the imaginary Buddhas after him comes up, when having recognised the insufficiency of learning in which he was initiated and having found that the mortifications fruitlessly exhausted his strength, he sits at the foot of the prophetic Tree of Knowledge where the light of Absolute Truth is to be revealed to him—the light which is technically called "Bodhi". But he will only obtain that light after having resisted the assaults of Māra. Māra, the chief of the gods of sensuality, sees his dominion menaced by the sacred doctrine which will spring up among mankind, and he makes one supreme effort for averting the danger. He leads to the conflict the whole army of demons, all the monstrous battalions of the legend; and armed with the most formidable engines they all fall on the Wise Man in thunder and lightning which shake the whole universe. But the Saint remains undisturbed in his luminous serenity, and Māra at last retires vanquished and forelorn.

Painted in the crudest colours and illustrated with the coarsest representations in some accounts, this contest is also otherwise presented, in a calmer outline and from a moral aspect, in a dialogue where Māra tries in vain to dissuade Gautama from his resolution by showing to him the easier path of worldly life and of sacrificial rites. Some descriptions of this severe conflict make up a scene of temptation where Māra whose effort is foiled before the virtue of the Saint despatches, though without better success, his daughters, Thirst, Voluptuousness and Concupiscence. In short, a number of stories dispersed throughout the Buddhist scriptures represent Māra as approaching sneakingly the Buddha or some one of his disciples under various disguises, suggesting to one or the other thoughts contrary to the sacred doctrine, and then fleeing away as soon as he is unmasked. These interventions, however, almost always tend to frighten rather than to seduce.

Now it may be asked: which of these two versions is more in conformity with the original?

The old atmospheric duel between darkness and the hero of light abounds in the Vedic hymns and pervades the whole Indo-European mythology; and in various transformations it continues into Epics and more recent religions. I detect in the Buddhistic scene only one of its variant representations. I thought and I think still, that under the surcharges and amidst the inconsistencies of a modernised version, it is only this origin that accounts for the form that the episode has received, and also for the bizarreries which require explanation. Others, on the contrary, have liked to see in Māra only a disguised tempter; all the paraphernalia of the Epic scene are (to them) mere fanciful embellishments of the imagination of the pious, zealous to adorn, and ready to materialise the spiritual grandeur of the Master.

The word Māra means the "Destructor"; it is connected with the causative sense of the verb "Mar", "to die", and is ultimately another name of Death. But in the Buddhist literature Māra has another name still and another aspect. He is called Kāma, "Lust," or "Desire."

That there is a close connection in the doctrines of Buddhism between these two aspects cannot be lost sight of. For, on the one hand, founded on the belief in transmigration, Buddhism preaches, above all, to give the means of escaping from the cycle of re-births and consequently of escaping from death. "Māra"; and, on the other hand, its moral teachings rest on the fundamental idea that it is the destruction of the bonds of lust by which we are rivetted and attached to life, the suppression of "Thirst" or "Desire", of Kāma in short, which alone assures this deliverance. Taken in this light Māra and Kāma are fundamentally one and the same; and one can rightly say that there is a complete allegory, strictly conforming to the principles of the system.

But can it be said that Māra is an original creation of Buddhism? It might also have utilised for its end a tradition bequeathed to it by the past, and of which it was necessary to reconcile the discordances. We can only decide (between two hypotheses) by going to the very origin of the conception of Māra. He is, besides an interesting figure in religion, a veritable Satan, with whom some believe to recognise a close resemblance of the Satan of our Christian tradition. Doubtless it is worthwhile to sketch out his history.

III

Māra is a personal existence, a personality in Buddhism. Though he is not unknown in the more ancient literature, it is in the Buddhist scriptures that his name becomes traditionally established. Side by side, Buddhist texts mention Mṛtyu, and it cannot be overlooked that from their peculiar traits and characteristic epithets both prove to be the one and the same.

Now, Mṛtyu, the spirit of Death, is a familiar figure in old sacerdotal tradition of the Brāhmaṇas and the Upaniṣads which I have just now mentioned to you. There he is armed with bonds (pāśa) which are also the distinctive weapons of Māra; and like Māra in Buddhism he is frequently characterised by such epithets as "Pāpam" "the evil" or "the wicked one." Often "Pāpam", is identical with Mṛtyu. And though at the beginning, this "Evil" especially refers to death, the physical catastrophe of man, it soon takes a moral meaning: a notion of sin comes to be attached to Mṛtyu.

The transition from the brāhmaṇic "Mṛtyu-Evil" to the Buddhist "Māra-Desire", the source of all Evil, is scarcely noticeable: as Māra is a synonym of Mṛtyu, so "Kāma" is often equivalent to "Pāpam." "Pāpam" sometimes vaguely denotes a wicked spirit: and it is no doubt by these steps that Mṛtyu has come to be identified with "Vṛtra", the Vedic enemy of the divine Indra. Also the Buddhists call Māra by the name of Namuci, the other demon of Darkness and as such identical with Vṛtra. In this point also the parallelism subsists.

The horror of death and the solicitude to extend longevity to the furthest limit always appear in the hymns as well as in liturgic works with an intensity which can be expected from such a universal sentiment. But it is well known that the hymns do not profess that belief in transmigration of souls, which afterwards gained an undisputed ascendancy in India. It is in the liturgic literature that the doctrine is introduced and becomes established; and as soon as it takes roots people talk of the victory over death or recurrent deaths (mṛthu or punarmṛtyu). In order to increase the value of some rite or mystical secret it becomes often conventional to represent the deliverance from death as the prize of the contest where Mṛtyu is struck down and defeated.

Is not such a representation suggested by the demoniacal aspect of Mṛtyu as identified with Pāpam, Vṛtra and Namuci? The fact is that from the ancient stratum of Hindu tradition a parallel scenery was spontaneously deduced in a very customary manner. When the question is of justifying a ritual or of exalting its efficacy, the Brāhmaṇas or Upaniṣads invariably imagine a contest between the Devas and the Asuras, between the spirits of light and darkness where the observance of that ritual had determined the victory. It is verily in such a contest as to whom will be assured the privilege of immortality that in remembrance of the old myth of the conquest of ambrosia, the gods and demons are thus confronted. And is it not exactly for such an immortality that the Buddha fights under the Tree of Knowledge? A parallel scene invokes thus the phraseology of the sacerdotal school in a condensed, but in a similarly stereotyped fashion; and there, as in other coincidences, the method exhibits succinctly a complete efflore-scence of vivid narratives of which the popular imagination as is exemplified by the Vedic hymns and the Epic songs has largely multiplied the analogies.

The whole terminology; elements and up-keep of this mythic contest not to speak of the inspiration which brought then into play were existing before Buddhism; and it was not therefore any chance metaphor that it draw upon. The Brāhmaṇic Mṛtyu—Pāpam is anterior to the Buddhist Māra—Kāma, and these representations of titanic combats existed much before Mṛtyu was identified with Kāma. Thus Buddhism received the heritage before it could put in parables the rôle of Kāma which is after all a subsequent creation.

It is verily the army of infernal legions and not as one would say, a symbolic army of passions and vices, that assail the Buddha in the primitive version of the story, and, therefore, the texts, as to prevent all misapprehensions, deliberately represent them as an army of Mṛtyu, that is to say, of Māra, considered not in a moral aspect but in his original character as the spirit of death and destruction. Moreover, the texts which are held as the most authoritative and which are invoked to prove a later origin of this myth, make certain allusions in the mythical combat, which have often been overlooked. Buddhism is not a miraculous religion; it does not create myths; and it has not invented a scene wherein it sought to imprint a moral meaning so apparently in conflict with it.

It may, no doubt, appear at first quite natural that the zeal of the disciples has introduced miracles into the lift of Gautama in order to satisfy their overdrawn fancies to glorify a great name. Popularity requires legends: one does not deny it. This would sufficiently explain the situation if we had to deal with a few accidental and incoherent data. But the fact is otherwise, and we have before us a definite type, the theoretic Buddha, whose superhuman traits is connected and harmonised within the unity of a more ancient cycle.

How is it with Buddhism, which assumes rationalistic aspects and excludes the name of God, has so quickly and easily dressed up in mythical disguises and a thoroughly divine halo the personage of its founder, real and recent. Such is the prime question which the episode of Māra lays before us and which I must pause to consider.

Is there no *via media* wherein all the discordant factors unite?

Chapter - 3

Origin of Buddhism

Manoranjan Ray

Continuation of the Chapter 2

IV

Gautama has repulsed the assaults of Māra, and has become the master of the Tree of Knowledge; but these are merely the preliminaries of his task. It still remains for him to enter by one final decisive effort of meditation into possession of the absolute truth, into that illumination which will make him the Buddha. This second phase of the scene is not less instructive than the first. The saint reaches that stage progressively as a result of ecstatic concentration. He has to pass through the four stages of meditation, by which from deep and calm reflection he at last rises to that absolute indifference, superior to all sentiments of pleasure and pain, and in fact, beyond all consciousness. This is the self-same road which leads to the salvation of all. Now, properly speaking, this theory no more appertains to Buddhism than the legendary adventure which it embellishes. Not only all this mystic construction is familiar to the Yoga, but by the conception of the soul which the theory takes for granted, it is as logical in that system as it is illogical in Buddhism which denies the soul. The traditional Buddhist formula preserve some expressions which have their true significance only in the language of the Yoga; and in fact, it is from the Yoga that Buddhist has received its four kinds of contemplation or dhyānas.

You know and you may have even seen here many representations of those strange ascetics, who, calm and absorbed, their body almost naked and covered with ashes, and living on coarse food got from private charity, draw the curiosity of the traveller and the veneration of the mob on the Indian road side. They are sometimes designated by the name of Yogin. It is rather an incorrect mode of speaking. Really, however, the Yogins are the followers of the Yoga system. But what is the Yoga?

The Hindus categorise and classify in excess. Thus, from the period of the organisation of their literature, they have stereotyped the forms of six systems of philosophy, to which, in their anxiety to subordinate everything to the Brāhmaṇic organisation they have, in spite of contradictions often irreconcilable, uniformly assigned a "patent" of vedic orthodoxy. By the side of the idealistic pantheism of Pūrvamimāṃsā elaborated by priestly tradition, by the side of its living antithesis Sāṃkhya with its realism and the dualism of its two co-eternal principles, the Yoga has a prominent place in that list, the other system of which I can omit for the present.

It is admittedly towards the 2nd century B.C. that the Yoga received its classic form in the sūtras or Rules of Patañjali. Essentially it is a method of concentration and of ecstasy, though it does not disdain physical means. It prescribes, for example, studied modes of sitting of which we can sometimes distinguish eighty-four: and we are assured by a well-informed commentator that this number is merely a charitable reduction made by the god Śiva of the original 8,400,000 bodily postures. Then, there is the progressive suppression of the respiration, and industrious fixing of the vision with an insistence which leads to hypnotic sleep. The successive teachers outbid each other in multiplying and elaborating these processes. But less complicated at the origin they were sought to serve the purpose of a very pure moral discipline and of a high and refined ideal of contemplation. The Yoga presumes to procure for its followers various miraculous powers, and then, in a higher stage, the gift of perfect indifference with respect to pleasure or pain and that absolute deliverance from re-birth which is the common object of every doctrine in India. The Yoga conceives this deliverance, so to speak, as retraction of the soul in its eternal isolation by which it escapes all contamination of matter and activity. It is exactly the ideal of the Sāṃkhya also; the difference lies only in the respective ways and means—gnosis, for the Sāṃkhya, and for the Yoga, aversion to all earthly things and mystic ecstasy. From old date the two systems appear as one in their theoretical basis; but they are not the less distinct in their first inspiration and in their sources. Really one great distinction separates the two. The Yoga recognises and invokes the intervention of God for whom there is no place at all in the Sāṃkhya. There is accordingly much scope of independence between the two; they could and they *did* yield to different tendencies and had recourse to different combinations. Besides, I think it is agreed on all hands that the definite texts of the two systems bear, for all times, the mark of a prolonged evolution.

By looking for the Yoga within its classic texts it can be quickly perceived that the theory of the four meditations is far from being the only point of contact between it and Buddhism. Truly speaking, moral perfection is the only important thing in Buddhism, because it alone can lead to salvation. Why then does it so emphatically claim for the most learned and virtuous of its followers, those prerogatives, marvellous even to the absurd, which resemble so closely the magical powers which the Yoga extols? It is not by accident that by following the example of the Yoga, Buddhism classifies saints in four orders, according as they are more or less advanced in their ways; that on both sides the same metaphor of "bhūmi" or "earth" made prominent by the identity of certain fantastic names is used to mark the stages of religious progress. I shall not, however, enter into detail. What is significant, above all, is the common inspiration which is the very sap of the two doctrines. Both have the same conditions for salvation: absolute detachment, destruction of all desires. So it is not surprising that the eight aṅgas of the Buddhistic "ways", the two enumerations, at the same time diverse and similar, culminate in the same final term "Samādhi", concentration or ecstasy. Somewhat abstruse and uncertain in their chronological inferences, though these coincidences are not decisive in any way, at any rate we get here an important hint which it may by useful to try to make it more precise.

V

On account of its ancient process of divisions and sub-divisions the origin or Yoga is lost in the remotest antiquity. It springs from superstitious and mixed practices of magic an asceticism which are invariably developed in all rudimentary religions. From its beginnings up to its scholastic organisation the Yoga has passed through diverse destinies in accordance with the changes of history. Side by side with the Sāṃkhya speculation and the popular cults, it is also associated with that stratum of religious life which, as I have indicated to you just now, issues directly from deep sources but obscured for a long time by the partial tradition of the sacerdotal class and its ritualistic literature it made its appearance later on through the epic chants in the literary documents.

The Yoga occurs in a predominating perspective in the Mahābhārata. You remember the celebrated episode which under the name of the Bhagavadgītā (or Song of the Blessed) has gained an immortal popularity in India and has aroused such an enthusiastic admiration in the West. And you also recall the strange setting: the two rival armies stand face to face in the field of battle where they will be engaged in mortal combats. Just at the moment of rushing into the conflict where he is to play the decisive rôle, Arjuna, the hero of the Pāṇḍavas, foreseeing the slaughter of his brethren, cannot overcome his pity, and his arm begins to quiver. Then Kṛṣṇa, the God-hero who has consented to assure him the victory by acting as his charioteer, consoles him and brings him back to the fight. He explains to him that all the apparent slaughters are quite negligible in the eyes of the wise who know that life is indestructible, and in essence one and universal and that it is becoming to the wise to have a transcendental indifference over these miserable contingencies. The doctrine which is taught there with system appears in a more or less developed form in twenty other places of the Mahābhārata; and, in fact, it is the system which inspires and dominates the entire epic at least in its definitive form. It is the Yoga: not the pure and technical Yoga but a Yoga more living, which supports the religion of Viṣṇu-Nārāyaṇa as combined with the cult of Kṛṣṇa; a system which rests on the speculative theories of the Sāṃkhya philosophy but pretends at the same time to absorb the orthodox pantheism by attributing Godhead in the supreme Brahman. Ladies and gentlemen, this is the Viṣṇuvite Yoga of the sect of the Bhāgavatas—a name which through the Bhāgavata-purāṇa has penetrated even our contemporary comedies and has found its way in "le monde oú l' on s'ennuie."

Evidently, this system is struggling amidst diverse and even contradictory inspirations which it tries to gather into a coherent unity. It exalts alternately the power of sacrifice and the virtue of gnosis, the supreme necessity of morality and abstinence, the incomparable results of devotion, the complete resignation, the bhakti towards Viṣṇu or Kṛṣṇa; it glorifies the practice of sacrifice and repose, it admits the absolute authority of the Sāṃkhya and does not fear to add to the twenty-five categories which form its frame-work, a twenty-sixth where it inserts, as if the matter fitted perfectly well, the contradictory notion of God transfigured in universal Brahman. Here is a singularly expressive instance of the mentality of the Hindus very little capable of solid concatenation but powerfully intuitive and mystic.

Whatever it may be, the system, very remarkable since it dominated the spirit of the epic, has its two poles in the Viṣṇuism and in the Yoga. Side by side, the Buddhist tradition with its succession of sages descending at intervals from heaven to instruct the people of the earth—another form of the idea of Viṣṇuvite Avatāras with its Mahāpuruṣa Cakravartin very akin to Viṣṇu-Nārāyaṇa, and with the scattered traits of the marvellous legend of Gautama, is certainly moving in an atmosphere which we may call Kṛṣṇaite. This cannot be left out of view, though opinions may vary as regards their respective importance, dates and interpretation of facts. More or less altered and deformed a certain Viṣṇuvite heritage floats on the current of Buddhism. Now, the question may be "how"? and "why"?. If Buddhism is connected with certain ties with the Yoga, it is the Viṣṇuvite Yoga connected intimately with the general movement of sects and beliefs that gives us the explanation in this respect; and it is there, evidently, that we must look to.

VI

Buddhism in its simplest form preaches salvation to be acquired by abnegation, by the destruction of concupiscence—that chain which ties man to the miseries of existence. There it is on identical grounds with the Yoga. The Bhagavadgītā again and again extols that impassiveness which is free from all actions and the bitter fruits which actions inevitably carry in rebirths. The two systems readily attribute to knowledge (vidyā) and gnosi (jñāna) an efficacy which is not, truly speaking, in the strict reasoning of either, but which is manifest in the positive power recognised on both sides in Samādhi or total intuition. The two doctrines express the knowledge of the highest truth by the same verb "budh" "to know" which assumed two forms exactly equivalent, "bodhi" and "buddhi". From beginning to end they agree in the same notions and in the same forms of expressions. A blissful but a very vague state of being definitely frees people from transmigration in effect in this life, in fact after death. From both sides it receives the same names "Śānti," and "Nirvāṇa." But Nirvāṇa has been variously interpreted. In my opinion its importance and originality in Buddhism have been made too much of. Etymologically the word has merely the idea of peace and blissfulness. Outside Buddhism, the word occurs only in the Yoga circle. The negative presumption of Buddhism and its theories which deny the soul incline us to believe that it is the Yoga, and not Buddhism, which was invited that fascinating word and introduced it in the language of religion. Undoubtedly Buddhism would not have created a term which, in order to harmonise it with its nihilism, it often applies in etymological juggleries to distort its logical interpretation.

The Mahābhārata speaks somewhere of one Ṛṣi Mudgala thus: "Gaining power by means of contemplation and obtaining the supreme Buddhi he reaches an immutable perfection which is called Nirvāṇa". It only remained to substitute "bodhi" for "buddhi", so that the whole thing breathing of the Yoga inspiration might be applied to the Buddha and Buddhism with faultless precision.

It is clear that the god Viṣṇu-Kṛṣṇa and Master Gautama the teacher are little alike. And it is therefore, all the more remarkable that both are honoured by the same title "bhagavat" "blessed"; and it is certainly not without significance that the name occurs in the religion of the Viṣṇuvite Yoga, the sect of the Bhāgavatas, that is to say, the worshippers of Bhagavat. Speaking theoretically the Buddha is a man; Viṣṇu-Kṛṣṇa is not only a god but he is the very exposition of Brahman, the universal soul. Still the gulf between the two is not so insuperable as it at first appears; and there are more bridges than one joining the two shores.

It must not be forgotten that the Viṣṇuvite Yoga, leaving out the secondary influences which were brought to bear upon it, results essentially from a fusion of the Yoga founded on the atheism of the Sāṃkhya and the popular devotion to Viṣṇu-Kṛṣṇa. And this original contradiction re-acted from both sides in opposite directions. As a distinct self-sufficient system the Yoga recognises a god who is however given the name the Īśvara, doubtless abbreviated from the modest title of "Yogeśvara," "the master or the lord of the Yoga." But no active rôle is assigned to him who is defined merely as a superior type of those puruṣas or "spirits" which the Sāṃkhya recognises in infinity. His only function is to help his followers in their religious lives: the devotion and abandonment to Īśvara is the sure and ready means of attaining perfection. Thus says Patañjali : 'He has in him the power of omniscience ; not being limited in time he is the master of all principle". Evidently this adventitious god is influenced from opposite directions by two currents occasioned and maintained by original diversities. The theoretical system, of itself, tends to diminish his importance and reduces him to a category less incompatible with its premises. On account of his association with popular religion he has only preserved a timorous existence, feeble and attenuated; from the negative tendencies of the Yoga with which they are fusioned, the Bhāgavatas preserve in their ways of expression, some inequalities and inconsistencies which astonish us at the first sight. The very Viṣṇu-Kṛṣna who receives homages as hyperbolic, sometimes has the simple title of "Yogaeśvara" or "Yogīśvara" which is also attributed to persons human or reputed as such, and in any case, of an inferior rank. Even the epithet "bhagavat" is not originally a divine name; it is the respectful denomination, used in antique expressions, for the religions preceptor. Though ultimately raised to the supreme godship, Kṛṣṇa is at first presented with the traits of a human hero; and though he receives that title, and, in spite of his apotheosis, it is as a semi-divine master that he appears in the Bhagavadgītā.

Inversely, in Buddhism the stories clash with doctrinal affirmations. Though the Buddha is only a man in theory, the legend repeatedly transforms him into a Being with supernatural powers. He is the Mahāpuruṣu—a title which under the converging action of the Sāṃkhya terminology and the Vedic tradition, is frequently attributed to Viṣṇu-Nārāyaṇa. It might be as well said of Gautama as of Kṛṣna. "If a leaf, a flower, a fruit or a little of water is offered to me in devotion, I welcome the gift of the virtuous man". How many examples there are in Buddhist legends of a poor and insignificant offering which, because it is made to a Buddha, is recompensed by immediate deliverance—a prompt promotion to the supreme dignity of the Buddha: It is a just the thing without the word "bhakti", the supreme devotion perhaps closely allied to the word "bhagavat" which in all cases enlivens and penetrates so curiously the cult of Viṣṇu-Kṛṣna; it is the *Praṇidhāna*, that prayer to Īśvara which Patañjali extols and which in a sense scarcely altered is consecrated by the terminology of Buddhism.

The God of the Bhagavatas receives in his turn the characteristic epithet of the Sage of Buddhism. It is under the title of the Buddha as having the perfect knowledge of all things that the supreme spirit which, as I pointed out to you, the Yoga of the Epic adds to the twenty-five categories of the Sāṃkhya, is presented on several occasions in opposition to the individual spirit which is still on the road towards light. It is undoubtedly a question of doctrinal expositions which may be relatively late. I shall however presently show that the verb *budh* and its derivatives play such an ancient and significant rôle in Yoga, that this coincidence does not appear to be a negligible thing.

VII

It is here, in spite of the conclusions to which it leads, that the conditions under which the literary tradition presents itself to us appear unfavourable and confusing; we are not only unable to date precisely the composition of the books which are the sources of our information but we see clearly that they reflect the ideas of different ages. But we must not exaggerate the difficulties to justify the deductions, a little hazy perhaps but not the less certain; which we arrive at.

The affinities are undeniable. Though Buddhism had some slow circumstantial re-actions on the Viṣṇuīsm and the Yoga, no one will certainly pretend to assert that the latter two sprang from the former. Buddhism is undoubtedly the borrower. But the question may very well be put whether the borrowings are haphazard, accidental or deliberate.

The answer resides in the facts themselves, and particularly in the decisive fact that between the two religious systems separated by so much of divergences and having no idea of mutual connexion, the agreement runs on two parallel lines in doctrines and legends.

As regards legendary embellishments, the more that deification of a master who is human in all respects is inconsistent with the moral tendencies of Buddhism the more it is natural to think that its constituents have been received from outside: (in fact) it is the past reappearing under a new varnish which one has sought to cover up.

Buddhism is not a miraculous religion which spontaneously crystallises traditional myths around its creed. It has not moreover whimsically appropriated extraneous spoils; it does not exactly reproduce or copy, even for the purpose of distinguishing, any of the recountings which constitute its proper foundations. The legends present variants similar in nature and in general significance but quite different in details. The family appearance is apparent, but immediate filiation cannot be admitted; and consequently the theory of accidental borrowings is excluded. And yet such are the doctrines, tendencies and the common denominations as cannot be merely accidental.

Between Buddhism and Viṣṇuism the Yoga supplies the connecting link; this is what gives us the *via media*. As in its scholastic: formula it has preserved a perplexing and illogical theistic idea; from its association with the popular Viṣṇuism it has also carried into Buddhism its effects—titles, creeds and myths—which are no less strange and logically no less repugnant to the new sect. From the time to which these movements of ideas carry us backward, Viṣṇuism was complete in adapting kṛṣṇa. However enthusiastic his cult might have been form that time, the souvenir of his supposed human origin prepared the tradition to be re-fastened on to a sage, even more authentic, and more near (in time). The Yoga under the influence of the Sāṃkhya tended to bring on the earth the divine privileges; everything was favourable to make the passage smooth.

VIII

In short, if there had not existed a religion made up of the doctrines of the Yoga, the legends of Viṣṇu and the devotion to Viṣṇu-Kṛṣṇa worshipped under the name of Bhagavat, Buddhism would not have come into existence, or in any case it would have appeared to us in a different aspect. The sect of the Bhāgavatas satisfies all these postulates. Does it then amount to say that it had necessarily existed before Buddhism, and exactly as it is represented in the Mahābhārata? This is what I never intend to affirm.

We have noticed the connexions but the differences also are not without their significance.

In the great Epic the Bhāgavatas preach a Yoga system which avowedly accepts the dogmas of the Sāṃkhya as a philosophical basis. On the other hand, they rely on brāhmaṇic pantheism, identifying their God Viṣṇu-Kṛṣṇa with the "ātman", the universal soul of the Upaniṣhad. These are the two points in which Buddhism radically differs from it.

The most essential dogma of the Sāṃkhya system is the dualism in which the eternal spirit or rather spirits, *puruṣas*, are placed in opposition to the equally eternal *prakṛti*, of the active and sensible reality. The latter is based on a combination in different degrees of the three "guṇas" or qualities—the three elements which are its constituents. Now, *puruṣa, prakṛti* and *guṇas*, are all unknown to Buddhism. It admits neither the dualism nor the substantial existence; it even expressly rejects "the doctrine of the reality of effects," that is to say, the Sāṃkhya. If some eminent critics have thought that they have discovered some affinities between the Sāṃkhya and Buddhism, it is because of their not having distinguished, as it is necessary, the Sāṃkhya from the Yoga, or because of having concluded rather hastily from some secondary notions and tendencies which govern the entire mentality of the Indian people. Buddhism may use certain expressions and formulas of the Sāṃkhya, and yet, for all that, far from being a direct emanation it shows in its turn an avowed opposition or at any rate an utter independence.

On the other hand, Buddhism teaches an extreme phenomenalism, and accordingly nothing is permanent in its estimation; it views events as a chain of successions which are not unified by any personality or substance. Its fundamental "dogma" is the "an-ātma." As it ignores the ontologic construction of the Sāṃkhya, does not its emphatic negation of the soul likewise tell against any association with the Vedic brāhmaṇism? It must be remembered that unlike the Bhāgavatas engulfed in orthodoxy, Buddhism denies the authority of the vedas and is based on a system irrevocably heretic and dissident.

The moral tendencies of the Yoga when transported in a metaphysical domain could easily give rise to the nihilism of Buddhism. By rejecting all egoistic considerations and denying any importance to sensible objects and by the force of repeating always that one should consider then with their cortège of pleasure and pains, as if they are not existent, the human and especially the Hindu mind can easily come to deny all objective existence. Speaking logically, this negation of personality does not well accord with the notions of responsibility and recompense and prolonged punishment through transmigration. Like other popular doctrines it is yet on these notions that Buddhism is founded. One can scarcely imagine that this destructive metaphysic united by Buddhism in such a paradoxical alliance may spring up from any other source than those moral representations transformed in speculative dogmas.

In any case it must be observed that the Yoga system from which Buddhism comes out was not inseparably blended with the Sāṃkhya or the Vedic pantheism. Before the Viṣṇuvite Yoga received its definite formulas transmitted to us by the Epic, Buddhism appears already as an independent lineage; it corresponds to an epoch or environment where the Yoga and Viṣṇuism already associated were yet in a more fluid state, and if I say so, more plastic. Its theoretical and legendary variations prove this fact.

I have already told that the Yoga, the Sāṃkhya and the popular cults belong to the same stratum of religious life which is quite different in its origin from the Vedic tradition. These systems have only gradually been reunited to it, by the continuous action of the sacerdotal class who after their absorption transformed it into a sovereign instrument for rule. When Buddhism was founded the work, which has blended together in different proportions the diverse floating elements, in the cadre of multitudinous sects, was undoubtedly yet unachieved. In opposition to these syntheses preserved in books, it followed in its own manner the evolution of the Yoga; or better still, it experienced a re-action of independence against the synthesis which was on its way to be effected, and against the brāhmaṇic influence whose work this synthesis was. It is easy to understand how Buddhism could attain an independent growth.

IX

Asceticism has always been held in high estimation in India. It received at an early date a particular organization and was adopted by numerous orthodox and non-orthodox confraternities. In their observances, preferences of rites and ceremonies, or speculative theories, there are often only minute differences. In that country of castes with individual instincts, these endless divisions and subdivisions have facilitated the combination of the most whimsical doctrines; the sacerdotal learning has transmitted to us the standard rules of that religious life. Even in detail these rules coincide with those imposed on the Buddhist mendicant.

The monks were grouped in local communities even before Buddhism; and its originality appears to have consisted in curtailing the macerations and, as one would say, in drawing a line of *via media* between wordly relaxation and the terrible mortifications of the penitent. And here even it came under the inspiration of the Yoga. Among other things, Buddhism is essentially a monastic order evolved out of this moving mêlée.

Thus it is that it unites so much of traditional matter with the great personal influences of its founder, and that its theoretical doctrines are so much involved in legends which by their nautre are so foreign to it; nay, it even unites some tendencies which are themselves contradictory. To look there for a system perfectly well-balanced, co-ordinated and logically deducted, coming out of the spontaneous reflexion of one great thinker, would be as absurd as to regard the laws of castes as a juristic system drawn up in the solitude of a cabinet.

The memory of such a beginning has not faded away without leaving some traces behind. Gautama begins his religious career by going to two masters Ārāḍa Kālāma and Udraka Rāmaputra and asking for instructions. The little that we know of their instructions suffices to understand that they were two Yogins professing the doctrines of the Yoga. We learn from a testimony which after all may have some value that the former preached a Yoga which excluded the theories of the *guṇas* and was therefore already similar to Buddhism by their common opposition to the Sāṃkhya.

Is not it from a persistent recollection of this origin that some two hundred years after the death of the Buddha, the inscriptions of Aśoka, the most ancient Buddhist documents dated with certainty, has called the faithful Buddhists by the names of "Yuta" and "Dharmayuta" (Yukta and Dharmayukta)? In the language of religion "Yoga" is used in the sense of "exertion". Is it merely by chance that the king calls the faithful by a name derived from Yoga as "those who exert themselves", "who devote themselves with exertion to religion? Under the influence of these very ideas made prominent in the Yoga by the importance which it attributes to "viriya" or "energy", the word *Parakrama* "courage" or "heroism" is with insistence applied by Aśoka to the religious practice. And in the single inscription where the Buddha is expressly alluded to the title of Bhagvat invariably accompanies the mention of the Saint.

The sect of the Jains was at first considered as an offshoot of the nascent Buddhism; but now it passes as anterior to it. It has grown up almost at the same time and very nearly from the same source whence Buddhism has come out; and like Buddhism it converges on the Yoga and has borrowed some inspirations and legendary categories from Kṛṣṇaism. It also resembles Buddhism in several doctrinal formulas and in the characteristic title of its saints. But in spite of all these the divergences are numerous and important. The declaration of the Buddhist faith is expressed in a triple formula; and similar is the case with Jainism; but while the Buddhists take refuge in the Buddha, the Law and the Church, the Jains use the names of truth, wisdom and virtue. Jainism organizes a monastic life, but it greatly exaggerates the importance of austerities, and far from denying the existence of soul, it attributes it to all creatures however humble; its principal theories are also those of the Sāṃkhya.

Thus one can judge as is verified by so many examples how religious divisions easily occur in India and how the logic dogmas occupies very little importance at the outset. In religious and social organisation sects and systems suffer parallel destinies. In both the accidental variations, the local divergences and the flimsy disagreements were often sufficient to multiply divisions: general ideas and original views were rare. Even as regards Buddhism its expansion need not create much illusion as regards its origin.

To conclude, Gautama was a Yogin brought up in the practices of a Yoga system which received its final religious form in the cult of the Viṣṇu-Kṛṣṇa; the Bhāgavatas of the Mhābhārata give us a similar type though somewhat more advanced and more definite. The Buddha no doubt preached some particular doctrines; above all, he wielded a personal influence which was apparently very great. He was inspired by an intense feeling of charity. Founder of an order, he was also a teacher of mankind. Around the monastic fraternity the laity grouped in abundance and they showed a religious ardour which is nowhere more vehement than in India. The futility of mere speculation did not satisfy them; and the two courses—instruction and legend—were adopted in the tradition; but these two had been already existing side by side when the sect was really constituted; their common sources are lost in the vanishing perspective of antiquity. Hence these two tendencies have received according to circumstances unequal impulses in the lives of different followers and have been nourished by particular predelections. They could unite only because they were contemporary in origin and were already reconciled in a society which produced the Master. Thus it is, thanks to the contribution of the monks with their discipline and of the faithful with their devotion and stories, that they have passed into the newborn religion as a result of necessary adaptations but of the same impulse.

What Buddhism appears to have innovated, amidst its negations tempered by agnosticism, accounts for its success much less than the nobleness of its moral doctrine which it has received from the Hindu tradition. Thus also its success in India though brilliant has been ephemeral. It is perhaps a curious thing which can be cursorily noted that the same cause which compromised Buddhism in the country of its birth also helped it abroad. It repudiated the Vedic orthodoxy; in India it declined and then was eclipsed by the beliefs which coming out of the same origin and imbued with the same principles could have the support of the brāhmaṇic class of which they accepted the directions and exploited the patronage; on the other hand, it could spread more easily abroad because it was more free from the scruples which put the brāhmaṇas on guard against broadcast communication of their doctrines and the contamination of the barbarians; it was less indissolutely tied to the ground.

Whatever it may be, our curiosity naturally turns to the beginnings, often humble and always obscure, of memorable creations. Please excuse me for detaining you so long in the windings and obstacles of those ways which are, alas! like those leading to the source of large rivers.*

Chapter - 4

Was the Buddha a Theist?

L.B. Keny

The preachings of Gautama the Buddha are perhaps India's few of the greatest gifts to the world. In the cultural history of the East, the doctrine of this preacher has had a similar effect on the religious and philosophical thought, as the teaching of Jesus has had in the West. He was born in an age when India was in great need of earnest leaders to divert the attention of the people of the place from superstitious and ritualistic ceremonials and wasteful sacrifices.

For a period of about fortyfive years, Gautama and his followers went from place to place, preaching their philosophy to the peoples of Aṅga, Magadha, Vajji, Malla, Kāsi, Kosala, Cedi, Vatsa, Matsya, Śūrasena, Kuru, Pañcāla, Sivi, Daśārṇa, Assaka and Avanti. They had no occasion, it seems, to stir outside the limits of the middle country, due to the great and insistent demand over there.[1]

Studying perfectly well the thoughts of his age, Gautama knew that the two extreme paths followed by the people of the time for a religious life viz. self-indulgence and self-mortification, were wrong. The perfect way was the middle path.[2] He moreover, understood and so preached, the four truths of the world about sorrow, the cause of sorrow, the extinction of sorrow, and the path leading to the extinction of sorrow.[3]

The Buddha knew and was convinced that the earth was a vale of misery, and the world nothing but a mass of pain. Birth is sorrow. Decay is sorrow. Sickness is sorrow. Death is sorrow. To be conjoined to things which we dislike, to be separated from things we like,—that also is sorrow. Not to get what one wants,—that too is sorrow. Conflict, in short, is the root cause of all the miseries of man in the world.

---

1. Law, *Geography of Early Buddhism*, p. xv.
2. *Mahāvagga*, I, 6, 17; *Majjhima Nikāya*, II, Araṇa-Vibhaṅga Sutta, p. 230.
3. *Majjhima Nikāya*, I. Sabbāsava Sutta, p. 9; Mahāhatthipadopama Sutta pp. 184-85.

After finding out the sorrow of this world, the great "knower", knowing as a great logician that every effect has a cause, started to search for its cause. With a search in the right direction he knew that the very desire to live or the craving for existence is the cause of the sorrow or miseries of this world. "There is no fire like desire..." states the *Dhammapada.*[1] Cravings and desires bind the soul, as if in chains, and reduce it to a servitude from which it would fain escape. This thirst or desire that leads to re-birth, accompanied by pleasure and lust, is the real cause of suffering or sorrow upon this earth.

The simple principle of cause and effect that governs the whole universe applies to the events of human life also. The Buddha accepts the already established principle of *karma* and rebirth. According to the law of *karma*, the "doing" of a man cannot die,[2] but must necessarily lead to its legitimate result. "Evil doers," according to the *Dhammapada*, "go to hell, righteous people to heaven."[3] One is thus rewarded or punished in the next world in agreement with his deeds in this world. Man is for ever fashioning himself. He can never escape the consequences of his deeds. As he acts so shall he be. So when a man dies, he is reborn according to the *karma* (doing) of his previous birth. In other words, the outward condition of the soul is, in each new birth, determined by it actions in the previous birth. It is, thus, the craving that leads from re-birth to re-birth, accompanied by lust and passion; it is the craving for the gratification of the passions, the craving for continued existence, the lust for present delight, that is the chief cause of sorrow. The thirst that leads to rebirth is the real cause of suffering. He is a thoughtless man who "runs from life to life like a monkey seeking fruit in the forest."[4] Existence cannot continue without the clinging to life, just as fire cannot continue without fuel.[5]

Knowing the cause of suffering, Gautama the Buddha, speaks about the cessation of suffering, which ceases with the annihilation of this very craving, the forsaking of, complete deliverance from it, is the real path of the cessation of this sorrow.

And what is the true path that leads to the cessation or annihilation of this sorrow? It is the noble Eight-fold path—path that consists of (i) right belief, (ii) right aims, (iii) right speech, (iv) right action, (v) right mode of livelihood, (vi) right effort, (vii) right

---

1. *Dhammapada,* XVIII, 251.
2. *Mahābhārata,* Śāntiparva, 348, Cf. *Gautama Dharma Śāstra,* XIX, 5. *Vaśiṣṭha Dharma Śāstra,* XXII, 4.
3. *Dhammapada,* IX, 126; Cf. *Dīgha Nikāya,* III, Aggañña Suttanta, pp. 83-97.
4. *Dhammapada,* XXIV, 334.
5. Cf. *Saṁyutta Nikāya,* II, 12, 53.

mindfulness, and (viii) right meditation.[1] It is this middle path alone that leads to *Nirvāṇa*, "salvation or emancipation" which "knows neither disease nor death, neither sorrow nor impunity,'[2] it is that 'eternal deliverance' from which it is wholly impossible to fall.[3] Nirvāṇa is, according to the *Dhammapada,* "an unchangeable place,"[4] where there being no rebirth there is no suffering.

The doctrine of *karma*, as we find in Buddhism,[5] is one of the basic points of the philosophy of the earlier Upaniṣas and Sāṃkhya school,[6] e.g. in the *Chāndogya Upaniṣad* we find that man, indeed, is reborn pure by pure deeds, and is reborn evil by evil deeds.[7] The *Praśna Upaniṣad* also states that in consequence of good work (*puṇya*) one goes to the good world (heaven); in consequence of evil (*pāpa*) to the evil world (hell); in consequence of both, to the world of men.[8]

The Buddha clearly states in the Kukkura-vatika-Sutta of the *Majjhima Nikāya*, that "creatures are the heirs of their own actions,"[9] and that what they do, determines what they pass to.[10] "My action", says he "is my possession: my action is my inheritance: my action is the matrix which bears me: my action is the race to which I belong: my action is my refuge: whatever deed I do, whether good or bad., I shall become heir to it".[11] Even the words of Raṭṭhapāla, in the Sutta of his name, describing the state of a king hereafter and stating that "he passes hence to fare hereafter as his deserved,"[12] go to corroborate the same, viz., the Buddha's belief in the *karma* theory.

The *karma* theory again, is itself the cause of the transmigration of the soul. They being thus interrelated as cause and effect cannot be

1. *Mahāvagga*, I, 6. 18; *Dīgha Nikāya*, I, Mahāli Sutta. p. 157; Kassapa Sīhanāda Sutta. p. 165; II, Mahā-satipaṭṭhāna Suttanta, pp. 311-12; *Majjhima Nikāya*, II, Araṇa vibhaṅga Sutta, p. 231.
2. *Majjhima Nikāya* I, Ariyapariyesana Sutta. p. 166.
3. *Ibid.*, I, Mahāsāropama Sutta. p. 197.
4. *Dhammapada*, XVII, 225.
5. 'Buddhism' during the time of its preacher, was not a religion as such but merely an order. It is a misnomer to call it by the above term especially when talking about the period of Gautama himself.
6. Keith, *The Sāṅkhya System*, p. 26.
7. *Chāndogya Upaniṣad*, III, 14, 1; Cf. *Bṛhadāraṇyaka Upaniṣad*, III, 2, 13; IV, 4, 5; *Kaṭha Upaniṣad*, V, 13; *Kanṣītaki Brāhmaṇa Upaniṣad*, 1, 2; Cf. *Bhagavad Gitā*, XVIII, 12.
8. *Praśna Upaniṣad,* III. 7.
9. *Majjhima Nikāya*, I, p. 390.
10. *Ibid.*
11. *Aṅguttara Nikāya*, III, 57, 2 and 8; Cf. Radhakrishan, *Gautama the Buddha*, p. 16; "The Teaching of the Buddha by Speech and by Silence", *Hibbert Journal*, XXXII, p. 349.
12. *Majjhima Nikāya*, II, 73; *satto pana gacchati yena kammam.*

independent as Rhys Davids supposes.[1] "Buddhism," says the scholar, "swept away from the field of its vision the whole of the great soul theory......[2] "The ignoring of the soul", he continues, "is the most important fact in the comparative study of Buddhism."[3] But the absence of the word 'soul' *ātmā* as such, in the Piṭakas,[4] does not prove the disbelief of the Buddha in the same. According to the theory of *karma*, on the other hand, one is rewarded or punished in the next world in agreement with his deeds in this world. Who is to be rewarded or punished in the next world if the soul is not there? The material body can never reach the next world, it being prone to destruction. The law of *karma*, thus, cannot be of any effect without the existence of the soul immortal. When asked by Kūṭadanta: "Does the venerable Gotama admit that he who celebrates such a sacrifice, or causes it to be celebrated, is reborn at the dissolution of the body, after death, into some state of happiness in heaven?" "Yes O Brāhmaṇa, that I admit",[5] was the calm reply of Gautama.

Life, according to the theory of transmigration, is a long chain of existence; and the Buddha preached to the people to escape from this chain, to attain to a condition that will be outside the circle of this change, outside the reach of the causes of change, and which will contain within itself the element of finality. The only such condition is, according to the Buddha, that state of mind in which the craving and desire shall have ceased; no new link will then be formed in the chain of existence; the *karma* will cease to influence; and there shall be no more birth.[6] This state is Nirvāṇa. In the words of Kassapa "the state of Nirvāṇa is a state of rest, but that rest cannot be found as long as we live under the empire of senses and passions. That rest excludes existence, birth, old age and death; the great mental attainments alone lead thereto.[7]

We would not like to go into details about the exact meaning of the term 'Nirvāṇa', not only because it has been already explained by innumerable scholars in different ways, but also because the short space at our disposal does not allow it. Nirvāṇa in its fullest and

---

1. *Lectures on the Origin and Growth of Religion*, (Hibbert Lectures, 1881) pp. 83, 91, 93-94.
2. *Ibid.*, p. 29; Cf. Kern, *The Manual of Buddhism*, p. 11.
3. *Ibid.*, p. 30; Cf. Ray, "Origin of Buddhism", *IHQ.*, Vi, p. 665.
4. *Ibid.*, p. 91.
5. *Dīgha Nikāya*, I, Kūṭadanta Sutta, p. 143; (Tr. by Rhys Davids).
6. Cf. *Dīgha Nikāya*, II, Mahā Satipaṭṭhāna Suttanta, p. 307; III Dasuttara Suttanta, p. 275.
7. *Vide* Bigandet. *The Life and Legend of Gautama the Buddha of the Burmese*, p.143.

strictest meaning, is nothing but a perfect union of the soul with the Divine or Brahmā.[1] Therefore it can never be possible here in this world. The union with Brahmā cannot be but spiritual, though perfectly real. A material body can never be perfectly united with a spiritual being as Brahmā is. The bodies have an end but the soul is permanent and indestructible.[2] Therefore the human body cannot obtain this perfect union with the Divine. How can the human soul, still bound to the body in this life, be perfectly united with the Supreme in this world? It is only after death, when the soul is separated from the body, and is thus free, that the perfect union with Brahmā is possible. The soul is the only element in our body which comes directly from Brahmā and so through which alone, we can approach Brahmā.[3] The Tevijja Sutta of the *Dīgha Nikāya* clearly states "that the Bhikkhu who is free from anger, free from malice, pure in mind, and master of himself should, after death, when the body is dissolved, become united with Brahmā,......such a condition of things is in every way possible".[4] With a man attaining Nirvāṇa "what binds him to being is cut".[5] It is only after the dissolution of the body that one is reborn in some happy state in heaven.[6]

But finding the state of perfect Nirvāṇa in the next world, as seen above, it is very strange to find references in several passages of Buddhist literature to the Nirvāṇa in this world.[7] This Nirvāṇa of this world is not the perfect Nirvāṇa, viz. the union of the soul with Brahmā, as we have seen before. The Nirvāṇa of this world is simply the freedom from all the wordly desires[8] and end of all pain.[9] On being asked by Ānanda to explain the occasions on which the colour of the skin of a

1. *Taittiriya Upaniṣad*, II, 1-5; *Dīgha Nikāya*, I, Brahmajāla Sutta, pp. 34-36; cf. Schrader, "On the Problem of Nirvāṇa, *Journal of the Pāli Text Society,* 1905, p. 169; Radhakrishan, *Indian Philosophy*, I, p. 451; Radhakrishan, *Gautama the Buddha*, pp. 25-26.
2. *Bhagavad Gitā*, II, 18; Cf. *Mahābhārata,* Śāntiparva, 12887.
3. Barua, *History of pre-Buddhistic Indian Philosophy*, p. 66.
4. *Dīgha Nikāya,* I, p. 252; Cf. *Majjhima Nikāya*, I, Māra Tajjaniya Sutta, p. 336; Vallabha, *Anubhāṣya, p. 244.*
5. *Ibid.*, I. Brahmajāla Sutta, p. 36: *ucchinnabhavanettiko.*
6. *Ibid.*, II, Janavasabha Suttanta, p. 212; Sakka Pañha Suttanta, p. 271; Pāyāsi Suttanta, p. 357; III Udumbarika Sīhanāda Suttanta, p. 52; *Majjhima Nikāya,* I, Bhaya-Bherava Sutta, pp. 22-23; Cūla-Dhamma Samādāna Sutta, pp. 307-309; II, Raṭṭhapāla Sutta, p. 73 etc.
7. *Ibid.*, Mahāparinibbāna Suttanta, p. 153; III, Udumbarika Suttanta, pp. 55-56; *Majjhima Nikāya*, I, Mahā Sīhanāda Sutta, p. 71; Ariyapariyesana Sutta pp. 172, 175; Cūlahatthipadopama Sutta, p. 177; Potaliya Sutta, p. 307; Tevijja Vacchagotta Sutta, p. 482; Mahā Vacchagotta Sutta, p. 496; II, Mahā-Sakuladāyi Sutta, p. 22; *Aṅguttara Nikāya*, III, 6, 55 etc.
8. *Dhammapada* IX. 126; Cf. Rhys Davids, *op. cit.*, 1881, pp. 99, 100, 206.
9. *Majjhima Nikāya*, I, Sammā-Diṭṭhi Sutta, p. 47: *diṭṭhe...dhamme dukkhassa antakaro hoti*; Cf. Sekha Sutta, pp. 357-58.

Tathāgata becomes clear and bright, the Buddha replies" "On the night......on which a Tathāgata attains to the supreme and perfect insight [in this world], and on the night in which he passes finally away in that utter passing away which leaves nothing whatever to remain" [hereafter].[1] Similarly the Cakkavatti-Sīhanāda-Suttanta refers to a state of happiness here and rebirth in the heavenly worlds.[2] The Buddha himself argues that one who does not know happiness here, cannot state that the soul is happy in the next world.[3] There is success both in this world and in the next.[4] It is, thus, only when one attains to Nirvāṇahood in this world, that he can obtain the perfect Nirvāṇahood in the other world. The second one is simply the continuation of the first.[5] Thus Buddhism in the words of Nariman, "sees in salvation or Nirvāṇa the supreme bliss and in the conception of Arhatship, which is already in this life a forestate of the coming Nibbāṇa, the end and goal of all suffering."[6]

As can be seen in the Tevijja Sutta of the *Dīgha Nikāya*, a Brahman cannot be united with Brahmā or the Supreme in the next world, it first he does not become like Brahmā in this world.[7] By himself becoming Brahmā, as the *Bhagavadgītā* also, states, a yogin attains Brahmā's bliss.[8] The Mahā-sāropama Sutta of the *Majjhima-Nikāya* describes both the "temporary Deliverance," here and the "eternal Deliverance" hereafter.[9] "Those who go hence," according to the *Chāndogya Upaniṣad*, "without here having found the soul (ātman=Brahm) and those real desires (*satya kāma*)—for them in all the worlds there is no freedom. But those who go hence having found here the soul and those real desires—for them in all worlds there is freedom."[10]

Transmigration, which is being given so much importance in the teachings of the Buddha, is a punishment, and so the cause of so much misery and fear. And the Buddha aimed at the destruction of this misery which was itself the outcome of the falling of man into the chain of re-births. Both Nirvāṇas are the effect of the same cause viz.,

---

1. *Dīgha Nikāya*, II, Mahāparinibbāna Suttanta, pp. 134; 136.
2. *Ibid.*, III, p. 66; Cf. Aggañña Suttanta, pp. 83, 84, 93, 95-97; *Jātaka*, II. p. 430.
3. *Ibid.*, I, Poṭṭhapāda Sutta, p. 192.
4. *Ibid.*, I, Sigālovāda Suttanta, p. 181; Cf. *Majjhima Nikāya* II. Brahmāyu Sutra. p. 143.
5. Elliot, *Hinduism and Buddhism*, I, p. 223.
6. *The Literary History of Sanskrit Buddhism*, p. 3.
7. *Dīgha Nikāya*, I, pp. 247-48.
8. *Bhagavadgītā*, V, 24.
9. *Majjhima Nikāya*, I, pp. 196-97.
10. *Chāndogya Upaniṣad*, VIII, 1, 6.

the destruction of the miseries of this world which are the craving for existence and the overcoming of the temptations which lead to the whirlpool of transmigration.

It was only the knowledge of god that could surely exempt a person from transmigration. "Whoever knows Brahmā" as the *Śvetāśvatara Upaniṣad* says, "will not be reborn at all."[1]

A double mistake, therefore, seems to have been committed by most of the scholars, western and eastern, in calling Buddhism, an atheistic or an agnostic religion.[2]

To call Buddhism a religion is the first mistake. It was not a religion as such[3] during the time of the Buddha, though it was raised to that status much later. At the early stage it "was a form of faith for ascetics only, not a religious creed for all people."[4] The *Majjhima Nikāya* describes the Buddha as "the founder of a saving creed, not religion.[5] The Soṇadaṇḍa Sutta of the *Dīgha Nikāya* also describes him as "the head of an order of a school, as the teacher of a school, the acknowledged chief of all the founders of sects."[6] He followed the ancient religion of the land, and by following its principles he was finally led to the creation of a monastic order. He never established a new religion.[7]

To call the Buddha as 'agnostic' or an 'atheist' is the second and very common mistake committed by most of the authors that have written on Buddhism.

During that time the spirit of speculation was fully at work. Moral life suffered, since metaphysical subtleties and theological discussions absorbed the energies of people. "It was" as Radhakrishan states, "an age of speculative chaos, full of inconsistent theologies

---

1. *Śvetāśvatara Upaniṣad*, III, 7; Cf. *Chāndogya Upaniṣad*, I. 9, 3.
2. Elliot *op. cit.*, I, p. 105; Keith, "The Buddha as a Master Mind", *Indian Culture*, V, p. 236; Rhys Davids, *Hibbert Lectures 1881, op.* 147; Barua, *History of pre-Buddhistic Indian Philosophy*, p. 215; Dutt, *A History of Civilization in Ancient India*, p. 281.
3. Cf. Monier Williams. "Buddhism in its Relation to Brahmanism" *JRAS.*, XVIII, p.130; Jayaswal, "Hāthigumphā Inscription of the Emperor Khāravela,"*JBORS.*, III, p. 447; Ball "Wanted a Philosophy of life Buddhism "*Buddhistic Studies*, p. 563, (ed. by Law).
4. Law, *Some Kṣatriya Tribes of Ancient India*, p. 68; Radhakrishan, *Gautama the Buddha*, p. 21; cf. Monier-Williams, *op.cit.*, pp. 129-30; Sankalia, *The University of Nalanda*, p. 21.
5. *Majjhima Nikāya*, II, Mahā Sakuladāyi Sutta, p. 3.
6. *Dīgha Nikāya*, I, p. 116.
7. Cf. *JRAS.*, 1894, p. 588; Havell, *Aryan Rule in India*, p. 56; *Majjhima Nikāya*. I, Cūḷa Saccaka Sutta, p. 234.

and vague wranglings."[1] And the Buddha is charged as being an agnostic or atheist only because he does not say or discuss or describe anything definite about God or about His mysteries and existence.

"Every system of thought," in the words of Sir Sarvapalli Radhakrishan, 'embodies and reflects the tendencies of the time, and cannot be understood unless we realise the point of view from which it looked at the world, and the habit of thought which made it possible.[2] At the very outset "the fact that Buddha felt that he was in possession of truth and could lead men on to it, militates against the view of agnosticism. If he did not know the truth," continues the learned philosopher, "he would not have considered himself to be a Buddha or the enlightened."[3]

Very often questions were being proposed to the Buddha about the fundamental mysteries of the universe, and he gave no answer. Such discussions would not conduce to knowledge, peace, or freedom from passion he said. But nowhere, in early Buddhist literature, do we find any reference to doubts about the existence of God, much less any clear statement denying God's existence.[4] This does not mean in the least, that he did not know God or other things spiritual.[5] "Though Buddhism and the Upaniṣads," says Radhakrishan, "refuse to see ultimate reality of substance or being in the changing sequence, the difference at most is that while the Upaniṣads assert a reality beyond change or becoming, Buddhism adopts a suspense of judgement on this question." "In no sense," continues the author, "is this healthy non-commital attitude to be construed into a denial of an ultimate being."[6] "If the Buddha declined to define the nature of this absolute," says the same author, "or if he contented himself with negative definitions, it is only to indicate that absolute being is above all determinations."[7] The Buddha avoided the discussion as it was not profitable in any way, for fostering the real spirit of his doctrine. "Those who believe that Buddha's silence was a cloak for nihilism, do not seem to rate highly his courage or character."[8]

---

1. *Indian Philosophy*, I, 353.
2. *Ibid.*, I, p. 352.
3. *Ibid.*, I, p. 465; Cf. *Gautama the Buddha*, pp. 34-35.
4. Cf. Rhys Davids "Silence and Emphasis in Buddhism," *Hibbert Journal*, XXXII, p. 129.
5. Cf. *Dīgha Nikāya*, I, Poṭṭhapāda Sutta, p. 188; *Majjhima Nikāya*, I, Cūḷa Mālumkyā Sutta, p. 431; Aggi Vaccagotta Sutta, p. 486; Radhakrishan, *op.cit.*, I, pp. 564-65.
6. Radhakrishan, *Indian Philosophy*, I, p. 379; cf. p. 464.
7. Radhakrishan, *Gautama the Buddha*, p. 46.
8. Radhakrishan, "The Teaching of Buddha by Speech and by Silence.' *Hibbert Journal*, XXXII, 351.

Gautama knew more than what he told his disciples, as several passages of the Nikāyas clearly show.[1] In the *Saṃyutta Nikāya*, for example, he has frankly admitted that he did not reveal all the truths he knew. We find therein that he took a few *śiṃśapā* leaves and urged that as those did not exhaust the leaves of the whole forest, even so the truths he knew had announced were not all the truths that he had learned.[2] He even knew of things transcendental and the way that led to the state of bliss in heaven.[3]

Now Nirvāṇa, the very gist of the Buddha's doctrine, and which is the perfect knowledge of the Supreme, or the union of the soul with Brahmā, as we have already seen, cannot be possible without the very existence of Brahmā.

We have also seen that the Buddha never looked upon himself as an innovator, but only a restorer of the ancient way i.e. the way of the Upaniṣads. The Māgandiya Sutta of the *Majjhima Nikāya* clearly states that the happiness of Nirvāṇa, which is the final goal of the doctrine, was preached even before the Buddha, by the wanderers of old or their teachers and even the teachers of the teachers.[4] The Buddhists believed in six previous Buddhas—Vipassi, Sikhi, Vessabhu, Kakusandha, Koṇāgamana and Kassapa; Gautama was the seventh;[5] and the Buddha himself talks of the four noble truths as forming a part of the teaching of the previous Buddhas and he had admitted that he himself was only their discoverer and not inventor.[6] The *Milindapaṇho* further corroborates this by quoting these words of the Buddha himself: "Now I perceived, O, breathern the ancient way, the ancient path along which previous Buddhas walked."[7] And it was not necessary for him, therefore, to enter into fresh discussions about God. The belief in God was one of the common beliefs of the times. As mentioned in the Kaṇṇakatthala Sutta of the *Majjhima Nikāya*, when king Prasenajit of Kośala asked the Buddha: "Does Brahmā exist?" the latter replied: "Why ask such a question?" King Pirasenajit thereupon continued, "Does he, or does he not, return to life on earth?" And the Buddha replied that a malign Brahmā does; a benign Brahmā does not."[8]

---

1. *Dīgha Nikāya*, I, Mahāli Sutta, p. 15; Poṭṭhapāda Sutta, pp. 187-88; *Majjhima Nikāya*, I, Cūla Mālumkyā Sutta, p. 431.
2. *Saṃyutta Nikāya*, IV, 6, 31; Cf. Radhakrishan, *Indian Philosophy*, I, p. 466.
3. *Majjhima Nikāya*, I, Mahā Sīhanāda Sutta, p. 73.
4. *Majjhima Nikāya*, I, p. 509.
5. *Dīgha Nikāya*, II, Mahāpadāna Suttanta p. 2 Cf. Radhakrishan. "The Teaching of the Buddha by Speech and by Silence", *Hibbert Journal*, XXXII, p. 349.
6. *Therigāthā*, 487-93; Cf. Radhakrishan, *op. cit.*, XXXII, p. 343.
7. *SBE.*, XXX, pp. 13-14; cf. *Dīgha Nikāya*, III, Cakkavatti Sīhanāda Suttanta, pp. 58, 77.
8. *Majjhima Nikāya*, II, p. 132.

The first reply of the Buddha to king Prasenajit's blunt question about the existence of Brahmā, viz. "Why ask such a question?" clearly shows that the query was out of date at the time. Everybody believed in the Supreme Being. As the same Sutta mentions later on this Brahmā is the same as the 'adhideva.'[1] And it was, again, due to this very belief that the king, taking the existence of Brahmā for granted, asked the second question: "Does he or does he not return to life on Earth?" Readers might take this second question of the king to the Buddha to disprove the common belief of the existence of the Supreme Brahmā. But the second question of the king does not refer to Brahmā, the Supreme, but the Brahmā of this world, viz. the man who has attained to Brahmahood here. This is confirmed by another passage of the Aggañña Sutta of the *Dīgha Nikāya*. On being told that only the Brāhmaṇas are genuine children of Brahmā, born of his mouth offspring of Brahmā, created by Brahmā and the heirs of Brahmā, the Buddha says: "Surely...the Brāhmaṇas have quite forgotten the past when they say so. On the contrary," as he continues further, "the wives of Brāhmaṇas are known to be fertile, are seen to be with child, bringing forth and nursing children. And yet it is these very womb-born Brāhmaṇas who say that...Brāhmaṇas are genuine children of Brahmā, born from His mouth; His offspring, His creation, and His heirs! By this they blaspheme Brahmā."[2] Without his belief in Brahmā the Buddha would not have uttered the above words as a reproach to the Brāhmaṇas.

On the contrary, had Gautama been an atheist, he had to state his negation of God, as it was something uncommon in those days. No one asked the Buddha to prove the doctrine of rebirth as it was assumed as part of the common belief.[3] In the same way there was no need to explain the existence of God, it being a common belief of the times.

Gautama believed in the law of '*karma*', as we have seen before. By believing in the law of *karma*, he definitely believed in the fruit of the sins and virtuous actions after man's death. A deed of a person cannot be declared as a sin or a meritorious action unless there existed a moral law; and for the universal idea of sin and good deeds, as the Buddha had, there ought to have been in existence a universal moral law according to which man's actions should be judged and sanctioned. Even a king who did not obey the universal law went to terrible hell,[4]

---

1. *Ibid.*
2. *te Brahmānaū cétc'evana abbhācikkhanti: Dīgha Nikāya,* III, p. 82; cf. Grimm. "Brahman and Dhamma". *The Mahā-Bodhi,* XXX. p. 401.
3. Cf. Hewitt. "Notes on the Early History of Northern India," *JRAS.*, 1888 pp. 362-63; Radhakrishan, *op. cit.,* I p. 361.
4. *Mahābhārata*, Śāntiparva, 2555.

for according to the Buddha even a rājā who was a world-monarch was bound by Dhamma.[1] Can there be a law without a law giver? Can there be a universal law without a universal law-giver? That law giver is the Brahmā of the Buddhist literature, the Ātman of the Upaniṣads i.e. God, who has power to impose sanctions on the breakers of the law even in the other world, according to the law of *karma*. The absoluteness of the moral law which the Buddha assumes does require a central spirit about which he seems to be silent. Thus in the law of *karma* itself "there is," as Radhakrishnan states. "the implication of the existence of the Highest."[2]

The Buddha has repeatedly mentioned that the source of all world miseries was the lack of knowledge. It was the lack of understanding and insight into the four holy truths.[3] And one has, therefore, to try to get as near to wisdom and goodness as one can by eliminating ignorance.[4] It is by the vision acquired through wisdom that the cankers of a *bhikkhu* are eradicated.[5] "Tranquil is his thought, tranquil are his word and deed, who," according to the *Dhammapada*, "has been freed by 'true knowledge,' who has become a tranquil man."[6] The Aggañña Suttanta again, repeats the same thought when it says that a Bhikkhu, an Arhant, gets perfect happiness when he has the 'perfected knowledge.'[7] The ascetic, according to the Mahāli Sutta, got his final happiness, only when there arose in him 'knowledge of emancipation.'[8] Thus, the very ultimate goal of the preaching of the Buddha viz. Nirvāṇa, which is the complete dissolution of rebirth or the union of the soul with Brahmā, is the result of the perfect knowledge, which is, according to the Buddha, the "knowledge of the four noble truths."[9]

But what is this knowledge which is styled as 'true' or 'perfected' or 'the knowledge of emancipation', or 'of the four noble truths'? What is this 'clear intellect' that is being prayed for in the Upaniṣ ads?[10] What is this knowledge that frees one from the quality of darkness and ignorance and makes one competent to unite with the Supreme?[11]

---

1. *Aṅguttara Nikāya*, III, 2, 14.
2. Radhakrishan *op. cit.*, I, p. 355; Cf. p. 460; Radhakrishan, *Gautama the Buddha*, p. 31.
3. *Saṃyutta Nikāya*, II. 12, 2-15; Dahlke, *Buddhist Essays*, p. 18.
4. Cf. *Dīgha Nikāya*, III, Dasuttara Suttara p. 274.
5. *Majjhima Nikāya*, I, Nivāpa Sutta, p. 160.
6. *Dhammapada*, VII, 90, 91, 96.
7. *Dīgha Nikāya*. III, p. 83; Cf. *Majjhima Nikāya*, I, Mahāvacchagotta Sutta, p. 490.
8. *Ibid.*, I, p. 158; Cf. Maitra-Fick, *Social Organisation in North East India in Buddha's Time*, p. 78.
9. *Ibid.*, II, Mahā-Parinibbāna Suttanta, pp. 90, 122.
10. Cf. *Śvetāśvatara Upaniṣad*, IV, 1 and 2.
11. Cf. *Mahābhārata*, Śāntiparva, 12884, 12888.

This is the same knowledge as the knowledge of the Supreme who is "the highest repository of truth."[1] Brahmā is, to them who knows.[2] "He who knows Brahmā, attains the highest"[3] or in other words, himself becomes Brahmā.[4] It is only after having acquired the knowledge of Brahmā that one is free from sin like snake from its skin.[5] And one who possesses this knowledge, as is clearly stated in the *Kaṭha Upaniṣad*, reaches his goal from which he is born no more.[6] The *Mahābhārata* seems to be more explicit about this when it says that those who do not wish to know the Supreme Being, are constrained to pass through numberless births and deaths;[7] but one who truly knows Him, is not born again, but goes to Him.[8]

But this knowledge is possible only through the Grace of the Supreme Being to be known.[9] It is Brahmā Himself who leads one across to the shore beyond ignorance.[10] This ignorance is, e.g. to take all the creatures of the universe as permanent beings, while in fact they are transient; they are becomings.

We find several passages in Buddhist literature where the Buddha refers to the world of Brahmā,[11] which is incorporeal[12] and so reached, at the body's dissolution after death;[13] and which cannot exist without the existence of Brahmā. The Saṅgītī Suttanta of the *Dīgha Nikāya* describes three happy rebirths, one of which is of Brahmā group.[14] In the Tevijja Sutta again, the Buddha clearly says: "Brahmā I know......and the world of Brahmā, and the path which leadeth unto it. Yes, I know it even as one who has entered the Brahmā-world, and has been born within it."[15] Even the description of Brahmā appears in

1. *Muṇḍaka Upaniṣad*, III, 1, 6: *satyasya paramam nidhanam.*
2. *Sutta Nipāta*, 656: *Brahmā Sakko vijānatan ti* (P.T.S. p. 123).
3. *Taittirīya Upaniṣad*, II, 1: *brahmavidāpanoti param.*
4. *Muṇḍaka Upaniṣad*, III, 2; Cf. *Bṛhadāraṇyaka Upaniṣad*, IV. 4, 23. *Bhagavadgītā*, VII, 2, 18; XIV, 2; XVIII, 55.
5. *Praśna Upaniṣad*, V, 5; Curiously enough the same simile is reproduced with Sutta Nipāta, Uragavagga, Uragasutta no.2.
6. III, 8.
7. *Mahābhārata*, Anuṣāsanika Parva, 1056.
8 *Ibid.*, Bhīṣma Parva, 1002.
9. *Kaṭha Upaniṣad*, II, 23; *Śvetāśvatara Upaniṣad*, III, 20; *Bhagavad-gītā*, XVIII, 56, 58 and 62.
10. *Praśna Upaniṣad*, VI, 8; VII, 2 and 18.
11. *Dīgha Nikāya*, I Kevaddha Sutta, p. 220; II Mahāgovinda Suttanta,p. 250; III, Pātika Sutta, p. 26; *Majjhima Nikāya*, I, Ākankheyya Sutta, p. 34; Mahā Sīhanāda p. 72; Ariya Pariyesana Sutta, p. 168; Māra Tajjniya Sutta, p. 337; Mahā Sakuladāyi Sutta, pp. 18-19.
12. *Majjhima Nikāya*, I, Apaṇṇaka Sutta, p. 410.
13. *Ibid.*, II, Makhādeva Sutta, p. 76.
14. *Dīgha Nikāya*, III, p. 218.
15. *Ibid.*, I, p. 249; *brahmānam piaham...pajānāmi brahmalokañca brahmaloka gāmininca paṭipadam yathā paṭipannoca brahmalokam uppanno tañca pajānāmīti;* Cf. *Majjhima Nikāya*, I. Māra Tajjaniya Sutta p. 337; II, Subha Sutta, p. 27.

the Kevaddha Sutta which says that He is "Brahmā, the Great Brahmā, the Supreme, the Mighty, the All-seeing, the Ruler, the Lord of all, the Controller, the Creator, the Chief of all, appointing to each his place, the Ancient of days, the Father of all that are and are to be."[1] The Aggañña Suttanta describes Him as the Eternal Youth.[2] This description is akin to those of the Āraṇyakas and the Upaniṣads where He is described as the Lord of beings, the Father and Friend of all living creatures, the Eternal, the All-pervading. Omnipresent, the Source of beings, the "Peaceful, Immortal, unaging, fearless and Supreme," "the origin of the past, the present, the all", and the Being or existent.[3] "This similarity of the conception about the idea of God, between the Buddhist and the Āranyaka-Upaniṣadic literatures, clearly shows the earlier belief of God being also admitted by the Buddha.

In the Brahmajāla Sutta, the Buddha, while stating some of the low arts of the recluses and the Brāhmaṇas for earning their livelihood by wrong means, mentions "the worship of the Great One as one of them.[4] Some may not understand here as to why the Buddha condemns this way of making money if he had not faith in God. But on the contrary, his condemnation for this type of money-making at the cost of a sacred cause, viz. the belief in God, clearly shows his belief in that 'Great One', that Supreme One, who reveals himself to the recluse,[5] and the *Dhammapada* is a further corroboration to this when it says: "With self well-subdued one obtains the Lord who is difficult to be obtained."[6]

Some scholars attempt to prove the theistic element of the faith by identifying the Brahman of the Veda with the Dhamma of the Buddha or with Nirvāṇa itself:[7] But just at the outset, Dhamma which led one to Nirvāṇa[8] and thus which was a means, could not be the same as the Nirvāṇa which was the end. About the identification of Nirvāṇa and Brahmā, Nirvāṇa may objectively be taken to be Brahmā Himself who is the supreme *ānanda* and the cause of all *nirvāṇa*.[9] But subjectively

---

1. *Ibid.*, I. p. 221; Cf. III, Tāṭika Suttanta, p 29.
2. *Ibid.*, p. 97; cf. II. pp. 241, 246.
3. *Bṛhadāraṇyaka Upaniṣad*, II, 5, 15 and 19; *Muṇḍaka Upaniṣad*, I, 1, 6; *Kaṭha Upaniṣad*, II, 18; *Śvetāśvatara Upaniṣad*, III, 2; *Maitri Upanisad*, V, 1; VI, 17; *Praśna Upaniṣad*, V, 7; *Kauṣītaki Upaniṣad*, I, 1, 3 and 6; *Chāndogya Upaniṣad*, VIII, 7, 1; Cf. Barua. *History of Pre-Buddhistic Indian Philosophy*, p. 65.
4. *Dīgha Nikāya*, I, p. 11.
5. *Dīgha Nikāya*, I, Kevaddha Sutta, p. 221.
6. *Dhammapada*, 160; *attanā nāthan labhati dullabham*.
7. Cf. Grimm, 'Brahman and Dhamma' *The Mahā-Bodhi*, XXXV, p. 446; Bhagavat, *Patna University Readership Lectures*, 1924-25, pp. 178-79; Radhakrishan, *Gautama the Buddha*, p. 39.
8. Bhagavat, *op. cit.*, p. 160.
9. *Taittirīya Upaniṣad*, II, 7.

considered, 'nirvāṇa' is 'ānanda' itself felt by the blessed in Heaven or the world of Brahmā, or by whatever name one denominates it. "It was", as Schrader puts it, "the Buddha and no one else who made the doctrine of *anattā* a moral principle, and that not by denying the Absolute One, but presupposing it as the true self, the only reality."[1]

But we cannot, for these reasons, conclude that in the *Saṃgha* of the Buddha there were not atheists and agnostics in later times. The misinterpretation of the life and doctrine of the Buddha by some of his later disciples, and by modern (at times atheistic and agnostic) scholars, have thrown great darkness over the person of Gautama and over the meaning of his enterprises.

India has ceased to be the centre of her ancient glory any more, but she still holds, and proudly too, the soil in which the great doctrine of the Buddha was nurtured. Her reputation as the cradle of Buddhism continuing the ancient philosophical truths of India's religion, remains unshaken.

1. Schrader "On the Problem of Nirvāṇa", *JPTS.*, 1904-5, P. 163.

Chapter - 5

The "Webbed finger" of Buddha

Ananda Coomaraswamy

Discussing this subject in I.H.Q. for December 1930, Mr. Banerjea defends the view of Foucher, that the *jālalakkhaṇa* originally referred to lines on the palms of the hands and soles of the feet, and that through the misinterpretation of a technical device of the sculptors (intended to prevent the fractures of the fingers of stone images), it later came to be regarded as implying a webbing or membrance connecting the digits. There is much to be said for this view, but against it may be cited the facts (1) that the palms and soles of the Buddha, as Mahāpuruṣa, were said to have been marked with a *cakka*, and are so represented in very many sculptures of an early date, and it is not likely that another *lakkhaṇa* referred to other lines in the same places, and (2) as pointed out by Stutterheim, in a discussion on the problem in Acta Orientalia, VII, 232 ff., (overlooked by Mr. Banerjea), the word *jāla* is employed by Kālidāsa in the *Śakuntalā*,[1] with unmistakable reference to the thin lines of rosy light which may be seen between the fingers when they are in contact, and the hand is held up against the light. These two objections make it very difficult to accept the Foucher-Banerjea interpretation *in toto*.

My solution would be to accept the definite statement of Buddhaghosa, that the *jālalakkhaṇa* did not refer to a webbing between the figures (and Mr. Banerjea is probably right in saying that Buddhaghosa deliberately begins with this statement, having in view the already existing image with this physical peculiarity indicated), but that the fingers were 'of one measure" (*ekappamāṇā*) "like the latticed window made by carpenter" (*vaḍḍhakinā-yojitajāla-vātapāna*), in other words, that the fingers were straight and regularly formed; another *lakkhaṇa* tells us that they were long.

---

1. Incidentally, it may be noted, that the "hand" described by Kālidāsa is evidently the *padmakośa hasta* of the works on *Abhinaya*, and that this *padmakośa* hand would certainly have been employed by the actor at this point in playing the part.

Buddhaghosa's reliability has already been demonstrated in so many cases once considered unintelligible or mistaken (e.g. in the matters of the *hatthi nakhakaṃ ālinda*, or that of the officiating of the king's eldest son as Pariṇayaka, where his interpretations have been shown to be correct. In the present case, his explanation gains plausibility from the fact of its correspondence with the usage of *jāla* in the Śakuntalā; in the simile of the window we meet with the same idea of lines of light seen between parallel opaque bands, fingers or wooden rods as the case may be. The *jāla*, then, does not imply "webbing" or any abnormality, but simply a perfection of form demonstrated by the appearance of the reddish lines of light that may be seen between the parallel fingers when the hand is held up to the light. But observe that such lines are only in fact regularly disposed (like the spaces between window bars) and evidently seen when the fingers are regular (*ekappamāṇā*) as well as delicate and long (which other *lakkhaṇas* require); if the joints are swollen, there will be places where the fingers are too closely pressed together to allow of the passage of any light at all, and other spaces where the fingers are not quite in contact, and only clear daylight can be seen between the fingers. Hence the *jālalakkhaṇa* implies after all nothing but a perfection of form of the fingers, such as might be looked for in the hand of the Mahāpuruṣa. If, as seems probable, a later misinterpretation arose, originating it the sculptor's device, this is only a parallel to what happened in the case of *uṇhīsa-sīsa* which originally meant "destined to wear a royal turban", and later came to be regarded (perhaps also by misinterpretation of images) as "having a cranial protuberance". It is not together surprising that a later age should have thus interpreted as miraculous abnormalities what had once been simple and intelligible matters; for the tendency to develop the miraculous elements in the Buddha legend is a well-recognised one in the corresponding literature.

Thus, I am on the side of Foucher and Banerjea as to the fact of misinterpretation based on the sculptor's device; but on the side of Stutterheim as to the original meaning of the word *jāla* as used in the *lakkhaṇa* lists.

Chapter - 6

The "Webbed Fingers" of Buddha

Jitendra Nath Banerjea

According to authoritative Buddhist tradition, Śākyamuni Gotama, when he was born, was endowed with 32 signs[1] of great men which prognosticated his future career. One of these signs is variously described in Pali and Sanskrit Buddhist Texts, as *Jāla-hatthapādo* (*Mahāpadāna-Suttanta*, Rhys Davids, *Dīgha Nikāya*, vol. II, p. 17), *Jālāṅgulihastopādaḥ*[2] (*Lalitavistara*, p. 106, ed. by Lefmann) and *Jālāvanaddha-hastapādaḥ* (*Mahāvyutpatti*, p. 6). This sign has been rendered into English by Prof. Grünwedel as 'his fingers and toes have a web between.'[3] Dr. Rhys Davids, however, translates the *Jāla-hatthapāda* of the *Mahāpadāna-Suttanta* as 'with hands and feet like a net' and adds the following foot-note to it: "Like a lattice, says the commentary, and explains this to mean that there is no 'webbing' between fingers and toes, but that these are set in right lines, like the meshes of a net."[4]

---

1. One who has these signs on his body is destined by fate. according to early Buddhist tradition, to be either a ruler or a saviour of mankind. A detailed list of these signs 'which probably date back to mythological origin and were originally attributed to Devas' is given in the following works among others: *Dīgha* vol. XI. 17-19; *Ibid.*, III, 142; *Suttanipāta*, 1040 sq.; *Dhammapada*, 352; *Milindapañha*, 10; *Lalitavistara*, pp. 105f.; *Mahāvyutpatti*, pp. 5f. This is with slight variations here and there occurs also in Siamese, Ceylonese, and Chinese traditions about the person of Buddha noticed by the scholars named Alabaster (*The Wheel of the Law*), Spence Hardy (*Manual of Buddhism*), and S. Beal (*Romantic History of Buddha*).
2. In Dr. R.L. Mitra's edition (Bibliotheca Indica Series, p. 121, the reading is *Jāṅglikahastapādaḥ*. He translates it thus: 'his fingers and toes joined with webs,' and adds this note 'the web is noticed only at the root of the toes and the fingers, the skin between them rising slightly in a thin web' (*Lalitavistara*, translation, Bibliotheca Indica edition, p. 143 and 170).
3. *Buddhist Art*, p. 161.
4. *Dialogues of the Buddha*, pt. II, p. 14. Cf. the commentary: *jālahatthapādo ti na cammena paṭibaddha aṅgulantaro. Ediso hi phaṇahatthako purisadosena upahato pabbajjaṃ pi na labhati. Mahāpurisassa pana catasso hatthaṅguliyo pañca pi pādaṅguliyo ekappamāṇā honti, tāsaṃ pana ekappamaṇattā jālalakkhaṇam aññamaññaṃ paṭivijjhitvā tiṭṭhanti, ath'assa hatthapādā sukusalena vaḍḍhakinā yojitajālavāta-pānasadisā honti, tena vuttaṃ jālahatthapādo ti.*

Now, the artists of the Gupta period are supposed by practically every scholar interested in Indian art to have portrayed this feature of the webbed fingers in many of the numerous images of Buddha fashioned by them. Dr. A.K. Coomaraswamy refers to the 'webbed fingers' as one of the characteristic features of the Buddhas of the Gupta period.[1] He further remarks, while describing the Mankuwār image, 'the fingers are webbed, as in several other early Gupta Examples.'[2]

But, are the fingers really webbed? The correct answer to this question can only be ascertained, if we put under close observation a few well preserved Buddha specimens of the Gupta period. We may refer first to the unique and interesting Mankumār image mentioned above.[3] Its left hand rests upturned on the lap, while the right hand is raised in the *abhayamudrā* with the palm spread outwards, fingers not being set close to one another, but placed slightly apart. It appears, however, that there is the suggestion of a thin continuous web at the back of the palm, joining, as it were, each finger with the other. But though at the first sight, this is apparent, the case is really not one of 'webbing'. The Gupta artist, in order to safeguard the preservation of these free-standing slender fingers, not only left the intervening space near the back of each uncarved, but the part of the stone-block in between the outspread palm and the upper arm was not chiselled away. However, a consummate master of his art as he was, he showed a fine edge along the top of the fingers in order to give a beautifying effect to his image. This finely carved line carried over one finger tip to the other[4] led the art-critics of the modern age to describe it a webbing. But that it was far from the original intention of the artist can be proved if we compare with the image jut described, the two beautiful mental images, one, the famous copper Buddha of Sultangunj, now in the art gallery of the Birmingham Museum, and the other, a bronze Buddha in the collection of the Boston Museum, both of the fifth century A.D.[5] The right hand of the latter is unfortunately broken, but its left hand, holding the hem of the garment with fingers, one

1. *History of Indian and Indonesian Art*, p. 74 & f. n. 2.
2. *Ibid.*, p. 241.
3. *Ibid.*, pl. XLIII, fig. 162. The image is inscribed and dated in the year 448-49 A.D.
4. In very rare cases, the upper one or one and a half digits of the fingers are carved in the round while in the lower section they are joined one with the other by means of this so-called 'web.'
5. Coomaraswamy, *op. cit.*, pl. XLI, 160 and pl. XL,159. Regarding the Boston Buddha, the learned author says that the typically Gupta bronze of figure 159 said to have been found in Burma is probably of Indian origin'; *op. cit.*, p. 171.

detached from the other, is well preserved. Both the hands of the former, however, are whole, the right one being in the usual *abhaya* pose, while the left one is holding the hem as above, but in a different manner. The fingers of the only remaining hand of the Boston image do not seem to show the slightest suggestion of 'webbing', while those of the Sultangunj Buddha, especially the right hand ones, just suggest the so-called webbed connection in their lower ends.[1] The fact appears to be that the casters of these metal images relied on the durability of the material in which they worked and had thus no necessity for completely joining the fingers of their image by means of the so-called 'web' for their safety. The greyish Chunar sandstone on which the stone artists of the Gupta period worked, was, however, from the point of view of durability, much inferior to metal and thus their choice of the material led them to adopt this peculiar device. This observation of ours will explain why even the portion between the chest and the top section of the upper arm beneath the armpits of the Mankuwār image which is fully in the round (unique in the case of a seated Buddha type of the Gupta age) and which had a halo (now almost gone) behind its head and shoulders only, is left uncarved by the skilful artist. Need I be more explicit and say that this was done only for giving a greater protection to the detached arms of the image and not for indicating a possible web between these two sections of Buddha's body?[2] In the case of the other seated figures of Buddha and Bodhisattva at Sārnāth, which are in very high relief, their back always resting on the *Prabhābalī*, generally rectangular in shape, the artists were in no fear of any sudden damage to the arms. A remark may be made in this connection, with regard to the left palms of some of the Gupta Buddhas shown holding the hem of the garment in a partially closed fist. When the fingers are slightly apart, they appear, at first sight, connected with the 'web'. But on close observation, it can be seen that this supposed connection is not really the 'web' which it looks like. The Gupta artist merely left the portion of the stone inside the bent palm unscooped and the fingers were shown in very high relief their inner side resting on the unscooped block. But usually their first digits were carved in much higher relief than the remaining portion, and it is this feature which gives it the specious appearance of the web.

---

1. The original image could not be observed. But from the plate, it seems that the fingers of the two hands are trated in a different manner, the detachment in the case of those in the left seems to be more marked than in the case of the others in the right.
2. It can on no account be suggested that these uncarved portions near the back are edges of garments, for had the case been so, at least a trace of it, however slight, would have been left on the arms along the line.

Our suggestion about this peculiar feature of a good many of the Gupta Buddhas is corroborated by an interesting peculiarity of the early Mathurā ones. Dr. Vogel, while describing the Kaṭrā Bodhisattva-Buddha, writes, "The hand (in the *abhaya* pose) is connected with the back-slab by means of a projection carved with decorative pattern"[1] (really a lotus?). This is nothing but a different manner of ensuring the safety of the fore-arm, palm and the fingers of the image, on the part of the Mathurā sculptors.

To elucidate our point further a reference may be made to some typical mediœval Viṣṇu images. The four-armed *Sthānaka-mūrti* of Viṣṇu in the Mathurā Museum[2] has his front hands hanging down, the right hand being in the *varada* pose with a lotus mark in the centre of the palm. The back of the palm rests on a full-blown lotus the stalk of which rises from the double petalled *padma* (*viśvapadma*) of the pedestal on which Viṣṇu stands. The left hand holding the *Śaṅkha* is also in a pose suggestive of *varada* and the back of its palm rests on a lotus as described above. It may not be quite apparent in the plate, but a close observation of similar *Sthānakamūrtis* of Viṣṇu in any of the museums will prove that the fore-man, which is slightly tilted forward thus making an angle with the upper arm, is by this lotus device (which is itself attached to the *prabhāvalī* by the portion of the original stone here ornamentally carved in the shape of a tapering cylinder) joined to the back slab for its proper preservation. The fingers also resting on the lotus blossom were thus saved from possible damage. There are very few stone images there, which have their fingers free and outstanding and completely set apart, one from another.

If we refer to the Gandhāra Buddha images we find that our contention is supported by their evidence in a peculiar manner. The hands are usually in the *dhyāna* or *dharmacakra* pose in the case of the seated images; where these are in the *abhaya* pose, they are almost invariably never thrust much forward from the body of the image and the fingers are usually set very close. Similar observation can be made with regard to the standing Buddha images from Gandhāra.[3] But wherever the fore-arms were made out of slabs other than the main one out of which the torso and other parts of the image were carved,

1. *Mathura Museum Catalogue*, p. 47, pl. VII. The standing Buddha no. A 4 in the Mathurā Museum also possesses this peculiarity; *ibid.*, p. 49, and pl. XVa.

2. *M.M. Cat.*, p. 101 and plate XVIII.

3. But compare Grümwede, *op. cit.*, p. 169, fig. 117, where the fingers are set apart, but the fore-arm with the hand in the *abhayamudrā* is folded up and practically attached to the upper arm and the torso, thus minimising the possibility of damage to the palm and fingers.

they were the very first to get damaged during the dilapidation of the monasteries and *stūpas*.[1] But in this conception, an interesting reference may be made to a broken hand which was discovered by Dr. D.B. Spooner in the course of his excavations at Sahri Bahlol. He wrote about it: "Thus the hand shown in fig. 9 of plate XXXV is remarkable for the well defined webbing between the fingers, one of the physical characteristics of the Buddha figure[2]......." It is needless to point out that the learned author misinterpreted the evidence at his disposal. The only conclusion that can be made from this fragmentary piece is that in very rare instances the Gandharān artists partially adopted the device so frequently used by the Gupta artists in carving the hands of the images; the hand, in this particular instance, however, could never have been the hand of a Buddha, because there are clearly marked bracelets on its calf, and thus might possibly have belonged to a Bodhisattva image.[3]

A few more references to the Buddha images of the Gupta period may be deemed necessary for further strengthening my hypothesis. If we study closely some typical Buddha specimens where other poses of the hand such as *dharma-cakra, dhyāna* and *bhūmisparśa* are shown, we find that this 'webbed connection' of the fingers is absent whether the palms are attached to the body or the fingers are set close together (as in *bhūmisparśa* and *dhyāna-mudrās*). The delicately beautiful Buddha in the Sārnāth Museum[4] has his hands in the *dharmacakra* pose; it seems that this *mudrā* in the early stages of its representation in the Indian art of the Gupta period was a combination of two distinct poses of the hand, viz., *vyākhyāna* or *chin* and *jñāna*,[5] the right hand

---

1. *A.S.I.A.R.*, 1906-7, P. 115: "As in the case of large Buddha figures, the hands of the larger Bodhisattvas also were not carved out of the same block as the main body of the figure, but were from the beginning carved separately and added to the finished statue" (Spooner). In this manner, the artist was no doubt 'saved a great labour of cutting away the vast amount of superfluous stone', but he decidedly impaired the durability of his images. The indigenous Mathurā and Gupta artists, on the other hand, surmounted this difficulty in a thoroughly artistic and at the same time practical manner.
2. *A.S.I.A.R.*, 1906-7, pl. XXXV, fig. 9. For 'webbing' in the fingers of a few Bodhisattva images in the Ind. Mus., see the foot-note above.
3. Cf. the seated Bodhisattva with the hands in the *dharmacakramudrā*, *ibid.*, pl. XXXIII (b).
4. D.R. Sahni: *Sarnath Museum Catalogue*, p. 70-1, pl. X; also reproduced in Coomarswamy, *op. cit.*, pl. XLII, 161.
5. Referred to under these names in iconographic literature, compiled at a comparatively late period; cf. T.A.G. Rao, *Element of Hindu Iconography,* vol. I, pt. I, pp. 16-17, pl. V. figs. 15&16. Might this combined representation of the *mudrās* in many early Buddhas specially of the Gupta period as well as in many Buddhas of the mediaeval eastern school of sculpture symbolise the attainment of the *bodhijñāna* first and then the expounding of the same to the various beings? In Gandhāra, we do not see this manner of representing the *dharmacakra* (cf. *A.S.I.R.*, 1906-07, pl. xxxII(b); this is the usual manner here).

being in the *vyākhyāna* and the left in the *jñāna* pose. Now, the right hand of our specimen shows traces of the so-called 'webbing'; while the left hand does not. The peculiar position of the fingers in the former needed this sort of protection, whereas that of the latter did not. Again, if the Gupta artist really interpreted the *jāla-hattha-pāda* of the texts as webbing of the fingers and toes, then why did he not depict the so-called 'fine net-like membrance' on the back of the toes of his images? Further, the Gupta sculptors, curiously enough, did almost always omit one of the most importance *lakṣaṇas* invariably met with in earlier and later images of the Buddha, viz. the *urṇā*. Is it not strange that they have particularly selected a characteristic which as interpreted by Buddhaghoṣa would be impossible to be shown in plastic or pictorial representations without marring their beauty or give it a plastic shape after completely misinterpreting it?

I may add here a words with regard to the correct interpretation of the *Jāla-hattha-pāda* and its variants in the early and late texts. The Buddhist commentators correctly interpreted this characteristic. Who was then responsible for this misinterpretation?[1] We may refer here to the English rendering of the Siamese, Sinhalese and Chinese texts by eminent scholars. Alabaster quotes Burnouf's rendering of this sign as "His toes and fingers are marked with lines forming a net-work."[2] The Siamese way of describing this sign is, "The palms and soles are exquisitely marked and the fingers set so close that no drop

---

1. From Buddhaghoṣa's manner of introducing his explanation of this interesting *lakṣaṇa*, we find that he was afraid that people might misinterpret it on account of the various meanings of the word *jāla* and so he begins *na cammena patibaddha aṅgulantaro*. The *jālāvanaddhahastapādaḥ* in the late compilation *Mahāvyutpatti* and *jālabaddhavajrāñgulipāṇipādatalatā* in Hodgson's list collected from the Nepalese literature of late date, prove that the learned commentator was quite justified in his apprehension. It may be argued that the wrong rendering of the term was in vogue during the time of Buddhaghoṣa himself. But, them, Dharmapāla who was possibly two centuries later than Buddhaghoṣa, gives its correct interpretation (see p. 725, f.n. 2) and we can infer that even as late as the 7th cent. A.D. the misinterpretation did not take place. If it be still insisted that it actually happened during the earlier commentator's time it may be answered that Buddhaghoṣa was an Indian of the 5th century A.D. (cf. Kern. *M. of Buddhism*, p. 125) and thus could certainly have seen some of the Gupta Buddhas, if not any of the Gandhāra ones, bearing the peculiarity discussed in this paper. He saw the danger of its misconstruction by the pious but uncritical worshippers of the images, and hastened to give the correct significance of *mahāpuruṣa-lakṣaṇa*. If is very likely, if not certain, that this suspicious appearance of the palms of the Buddha images led to the change in the meaning of this sign in a much later period.

2. Albaster, *The Wheel of the Law*, Appendix, p. 313.

of water can pass between them"[1]; the Sinhalese: "The palms and soles appeared like richly ornamented windows."[2] Beal, on the other hand, renders the Chinese translation of this sign from the Sanskrit original, thus: "The fingers and toes severally connected with a fine net-like membrane".[3] The fact is that the word *jāla* had, among various meanings, both the senses of a net and a latticed window.[4] Buddhaghoṣa skillfully uses both these senses in explaining the significance of the term *Jālahatthapāda* and he is certainly right. The word *Jālāṅgulihastapādaḥ* of *Laitavistara* can, without any great stretch of imagination, be very well explained as 'the fingers and toes marked with *Jālas* or uniform and parallel lines as are to be found in the meshes of a net or the lattice of a window'.[5] This seems to be a very obvious interpretation; that it was so long misunderstood by well-known scholars was perhaps partly due to the Gupta sculptures and

---

1. *Ibid.*, p. 113. He adds this curious note to it: "It is added that this peculiarity arose from 'his having steadily established himself in the four elements of benevolence, *Saṇgkhrihawatthu*'. These are the Sanskrit *Saṅgrahavastuni*, defined as almsgiving, agreeable speaking, kind acts, unity in that which is for the general good." *Ibid.*, p. 206.
2. Sp. Hardy, *Manual of Buddhism*, p. 368.
3. S. Beal, *Romantic History of Buddha*, p. 55.
4. Cf. Varāhamihira's *Bṛhatsaṃhitā*, (Vizianagram Sans. Series), ch. 57, v, I *Jālāntarage bhānau* etc. and Utpala's comment on it.
5. We may refer here to another interesting explanation of this term given by Dr. Stede in his Pāli-English Dictionary, p. 116 (*jāla*), on the authority of the commentary of *Vimāna-vatthu*:

"having net-like hands and feet (one of the 32 marks of a *Mahāpurisa*, probably with reference to long nails, *Dīgha*, II, 17 (see *Dial*, II, 14, note 3); cf. *Jālitambanakhehi, Vimānavatthu* 81, 16 (explained at *Vim. Vat. Aṭṭhakathā* 315: *Jālavantehi abhilohita-nakkeh. Tena Jāli (v. l. jāla-) hatthatan Mahāpuria-lakkhaṇan tambanakhetan anuvyañjanañ ca dasseti.*" But why Dr. Stede uses the expression 'with reference to long nails, is not clear. The passage in the *Vimānavatthu* is *so maṃ mudūhi pāṇīhi ti muduhatthataṃ mahāpuṅsalakkhaṇaṃ vadati. Jālavantehi etc.* Here two of the 32 greater marks viz. *muduhatthata* and *jalihatthata* and one of the 80 lesser ones viz. *tambanakhata* are mentioned. There is not the slightest reference here to another lesser sign viz. *tuṅganakhata*. Then, why should it be referred to, to explain *jālihattha* when the sense of the latter is obvious? Dhammapāla like Buddhaghosa clearly lays down that *jāli* means 'covered with net-like lines', and by his use of the single word *jālavanta*, makes himself perfectly clear; it it never *jilabaddha* or *jālanddha* with him, as in the texts of a much later period.

Reference may be made here to Varāhamihira's mention of *dāmanibhābhiś cāḍhyāḥ (Bṛhatsaṃhitā*, ch. 60, *Puruṣalakṣaṇa*, v. 47) in the course of his enumeration of the marks on human palms, and Utpala's comment on it. The latter writes, *dāmanibhābhī rajjvābhābhiś cāḍhyā īśvarā bhavanti*. There can be no doubt that the characteristic significance of the words *jāla, jāli* or *jālavanta* of the early Pāli tests and their commentaries are referred to here, though in a slightly different manner.

partly to the equivocal significance of the term *jāla*. But the blame for it can on no account be laid at the door of the artists; certainly it was not their fault that 'a simple craftsman's device' misled generations of art-critics of the modern age.

For the purpose of ascertain in the true significance of the 'webbed fingers' of Buddha, I examined several times very closely not only the Buddhas and Bodhisattvas of different periods in the collection of the Indian Museum, but also the images of various other gods and goddesses there. This close inspection has convinced me that there is a danger of our misunderstanding many such 'simple craftsman's device', one of which is the subject-matter of the present paper, if we study images only from their reproductions in the publications on Indian art and the museum catalogues. However excellent the reproductions might be, there is always just the chance of some detail, perhaps very simple from the image maker's point of view, but extremely important from that of the study of the images themselves, being not prominently shown there or, assuming a peculiar appearance which is far removed from its real character.[1]

I may mention here that an interesting Sanskrit text *Samyak-Sambuddhabhāṣita-Pratimālakṣaṇa* by name brought by my friend and colleague Dr. P.C. Bagchi of the Calcutta University from the Durbar Library, Nepal, which is being edited by me, though containing many interesting and important details about the Buddha Pratimā is silent about this so-called "webbed fingers."

---

1. "To refer to a typical case: The excellent reproduction of the Sārnath Buddha with his lands in the *dharmacakra mudrā* in Dr. Coomaraswamy's famous book *History of Indian and Indonesian Art* leaves us in some doubt as to whether the palms are connected with the chest by a portion of the original stone block left there purposely by the artist. But my study of a Sārnath Buddha in the Indian Museum (S. 49, Cat. II, p. 26) with his hands in the said pose led me to find out that the right palm which is in the *Vyākhyāna* pose and about 1 ½ inch away from the right breast of the figure, the left one in *jñāna* pose practically resting on the left breast, is joined with the torso in a manner just referred to. I am sure that this is almost invariably the case with the other Gupta Buddhas with their hands in the same pose. Similar is the case with the mediæval Buddha figures in the collection of the Indian Museum, whatever the poses of their hand might be—*abhaya*, *varada*, or *dharmacakra* (the last really being a combination of the *vyākhyāna* and *jñāna*?).

One observation more about the presence of the so-called webbed fingers in Gandhāra art. Exhibits No.s 9 (4945, r.h. *abhaya*, l.h. holding lotus), 10 (4946, r.h. *abhaya*, l.h. holding a vase) in the Gandhāra room, Indian Museum, show their r.h. fingers connected together by 'a thin membrane' (certainly it would appear so in reproduction) resting on hexagonal wedgeshaped stone thus connecting the back of the palm with the torso, but leaving the lower portion of the palm and the calf thoroughly detached; in one case the wedge is absent. The figures are those of the celestial Bodhisattvas. Gandhāra Buddhas no.s 4905 and 12 in the same room bear the same peculiarity in a slightly modified manner.

Chapter - 7

The "Webbed Fingers" of Buddha

Jitendra Nath Banerjea

Dr. Coomaraswamy, writing "on the Webbed-Fingers of Buddha" (in *I.H.Q.*, June, 1931 pp. 365-66) refers to an article on 'Le *jālalakṣ aṇa* in *Acta Orientalia* (vol. VII, 232ff.) in which the writer, Dr. Stutterheim seeks to prove that the *"jālalakṣaṇa"* means 'the thin lines of rosy light which may be seen between the fingers when they are in contact, and the hand is held up against the light.' For this interpretation Stutterheim relies on the well-known verse of the *Abhijñāna-śakuntala*

प्रलोभ्यवस्तुप्रणयप्रसारितो विभाति जालग्रथिताङ्गुलिः करः ।
अलक्ष्यपत्रान्तरमिद्धरागया नवोषसा भिन्नमिवैकपङ्कजम् ॥

laying much stress on the words *vibhāti* and *iddharāga*, and the simile of the fingers with the petals of a half opened lotus. Dr. Coomaraswamy disagreeing with my view and that of Mons. Foucher about the original significance of *jālalakṣaṇa* preferred the interpretation of Stutterheim. I am afraid I cannot accept the interpretation.

In explaining the word *Jālagrathitāṅguli*, the force of the word *grathita* should not be overlooked and the whole expression should be interpreted in relation to the poetical comparison of the boy's fingers with the petals of a *partially* opened lotus-flower in the early dawn. Drs. Böhtlink and Roth correctly take note of these points in their respective translations of this verse and refer to the fingers as joined. When the poet purposely makes this comparison, we are to understand that he had in his mind the idea about the jointure of the fingers, especially at their lower ends. The expression *iddharāga* refers to another of the *Cakravarti-lakṣaṇas*. Rāghavabhaṭṭa, while commenting on this verse of Kālidāsa, quotes this form the *Puruṣalakṣaṇa* in the *Sāmudra*:—

अतिरक्तः करो यस्य ग्रथिताङ्गुलिको मृदुः ।
चापाङ्कुशाङ्कितः सोऽपि चक्रवर्त्ती भवेद ध्रुवम् ॥

In this verse, as many as four auspicious signs, viz., *raktarkara, grathitāṅgulikara, mṛdukara* and *cāpāṅkuśāṅkitakara,* are mentioned; king Duṣyanta sees only two of these—and these, the first and the second are the only two that are visible form a distance—and Kālidāsa naturally refers to these very same in a manner particularly befitting one of the foremost poets of India.

Again, the early Buddhist texts refer to this sign as *Jālahatthapādo* (*Mahāpadāna* and *Lakkhanasuttāntas*), *jālāṅgulihastapādo,* (*Lalitavistara*), and as *jāla* (*Mahāvastu*—this work does not give us the full names of all these 32 *lakṣaṇas* and simply refer to them in a curt manner); the *Mahābhārata* also describes this *lakṣaṇas* as *Jalapādabhujan* (xii, 143, 36; this term most likely connotes the same thing as *Jātahastapāda*) while enumerating the characteristic signs of Nara and Nārāyaṇa, the two gods and *Mahāpuruṣ as* at the same time. The *Jālalakṣaṇa* of the toes can certainly not be explained in a manner in which Stutterheim interprets the same in the case of the fingers. 'The feet held up against the light' and thin lines of rosy light infiltrating through the interstices of the toes in contact with one another', would indeed be a curious explanation of the term *jālāṅgulipāda* or *jālapāda*! I need hardly point out that it would be quite unjustifiable to explain the *lakṣaṇa* in different ways—once in its relation to the fingers and secondly in connection with the toes.

It appears that in Kālidāsa's time, the adventitious sense of this sign as 'webbing of the fingers' (to the poet this was partial) has already been introduced. So I modify my previous statement that the misinterpretation of the term did not take place till a period much later than the 5th century A.D. Buddhaghosa and Dharmapāla refer to the original interpretation of the term in the sense of regular parallel lines on the fingers and toes of the palms and soles, whereas the poet refers to the other meaning (the poet is naturally silent about the toes, for king Duṣyanta sees the extended hand of Sarvadamana and does not look at his feet). That the sense of 'webbing' had made its appearance as early as the closing years of the 14th century A.D. is proved by the *Madhyamāgama* text (Taisho ed.; vol, I, p. 393) translated into Chinese by the Kashmerian Gautama Saṅghadeva in 397-8 A.D.; here, this sign was rendered into Chinese in the following manner—the feet and the hands of the Mahāpuruṣa are netted like those of the *haṃsarāja*—the golden mallard.' (I am indebted to Dr. P.C. Bagchi the Calcutta University, for this reference).

Dr. Coomaraswamy is definitely of opinion that Buddhaghosa in his explanatory note on this *lakṣaṇa* means the same thing as was according to Stutterheim meant by the poet Kālidāsa. But, in the comment of Buddhaghosa, which was quoted by me in full in my first article, there is nothing that could justify us in drawing the above conclusion. The commentator begins with the statement that this *lakṣ -aṇa* does not mean that the fingers were joined by a web, and that this kind of webbing between the fingers will define a peculiar kind of inauspicious hand, in shape like that of the hood of a snake (*phaṇahatthako*), which will be a fault in the figure of the man (*purisadosa*). Then he refers to the *four* (not *five*, evidently leaving out the thumb which being in a much lower plane than the other four fingers cannot have its lines touching those of the others) fingers of the hand and five toes of the feet which are of uniform or regular size (*ekappamāṇa*), their unformity or regularity being indicated by the auspicious sign of the *jālas* which remain touching each other (*aññamaññaṃ paṭivijjhitvā tiṭṭhanti*). Lastly, he uses the simile of the lattice of a window. All this, if it means anything, can only mean 'the fingers and toes are marked with *jālas* or uniform and parallel lines as are to be found in the lattice of a window'.

Dr. Coomaraswamy's other objection against this interpretation of the *lakṣaṇa* 'that the palms and soles of the Buddha, as Mahāpuruṣa, being marked with a *cakka* and so represented in very many sculptures of an early date, there can be no reference to another *lakkṣaṇa* in the same places' can be met by saying that the palms of the hand and especially the soles of the feet are marked by more than one auspicious characteristic; that these of many of the Buddha images (specially of the Mathurā ones belonging to the Saka-Kuṣāṇa period, and the mediœval ones) bear not only the *cakka,* but also *nandipāda triśūla, svastika* (and some mediæval ones, *dhvaja, yugmamīna, padam* and such others in addition; cf. the inscribed Buddha image set up by Dattagala, now in the Indian Museum) on them; that these symbols are carved on the palms (rarely) and soles, and not on the fingers and toes; that the reference in the case of this *lakṣana* is to the lines *on the fingers and toes* (in some texts, cf. *Lalitavistara*); that these could not be shown there by the artist 'in plastic or pictorial representations without marring their beauty'; that a good many of the 32 major signs as well as most of the 80 minor ones could not be plastically or pictorially represented in Buddha figures.

Chapter - 8

On Some Tibetan names of the Buddha

F. Otto Schrader

Every Sanskrit scholar acquainted with Tibetan and the Tibetan mania for etymological translations must have been puzzled by the two most frequent names of the Buddha in that language, viz., *saṅs-rgyas* and *bcom-ldan-ḥdas*. Are they translations of a Sanskrit compound, such as सम्यक्संबुद्धः, or of two uncompounded terms as, e.g. बुद्धो भगवान् or, if not, what is their origin? There are, of course, in Tibetan literature explanations for both of them, but I have seen none, either by a Tibetan or by an Indian or Western or Japanese scholar, which completely answers the question as to their Sanskrit original. I therefore venture to offer my own explanation of these terms.

There can be no doubt, to begin with, that either term is indeed, as Tibetan scholars hold, and *abbreviated compound*. The parts of either are also, excepting *saṅs*, easily recoignisable, but less so is the reason for which they were compounded.

Saṅs means, according to three explanations quoted in his *Dictionary* by Sarat Chandra Das, either 'fully awakened [from the slumber of Avidyā]' or 'purified [from all the sins arising from Avidyā]' or 'liberated [from the beginning]'. Now, as there is no other term in Tibetan which could be regarded as a direct translation of the title बुद्धः and as it is unthinkable that no direct tranlation of it should have been attempted, we have first of all to ask whether *saṅs.pa* may not actually means 'awakened' or 'awaked'. That this is so, we learn form Jäschke who (on p. 458a of his *Dictionary*) states that in the *Dzanglun* the word is once connected with *ra.ro.ba.las* 'from intoxication' and another time with *gzim.pa.las* 'from a deep sleep'. Associating herewith, as we can hardly avoid to do, the phrase *ḥtshoṅ-rgya. bar.ḥgyur.ba* 'become a Buddha' we arrive at the conclusion that there must have once been in Tibetan by the side of *ḥtshaṅ.ba, tshaṅs* 'to press into, to stuff' and *saṅ.ba.saṅs* 'to do away with, remove, cleanse' (e.g., in *sñun.saṅs* 'the disease is removed') a now obsolete present *ḥtshaṅ.ba* 'to awaken' or 'to awake' with its still existing perfect *saṅs*. The latter in *saṅs-rgyas,* then, undoubtedly does mean बुद्धः Why, then, was the Buddha not simply called *saṅs-pa*? Because of the well known pedantic anxiety of the Tibetans to translate with absolute accuracy. The translators here, as elsewhere now and then, had become aware of the insufficiency of a literal translations. An extreme case of this kind is the translation of वातायनेषु in *Buddhacarita,* III 18, by *rluṅ.brgyod.skar.khuṅ-rnams.su* where the Tibetan word for 'window', viz., *skar.khuṅ* (star-hole) has been added to the literal translation of the Sanskrit वातायनम् (wind passage), because *rluṅ.brgyod* had not in Tibetan the conventionally restricted meaning of वातायनम्। *Saṅs.pa* means 'awakened' in quite a general sense, as also 'removed, cleansed, purified'. and it lacks the *positive* sense conveyed by the term बुद्धः Therefore, to make good for this want and coin a technical term recognizable as such in Tibetan, the addition to *saṅs.pa* of *ye.śes.rgyas.pa* or *śes.rab.rgyas.pa* 'wide (perfect) in wisdom (प्रज्ञा)' or', was deemed necessary, and thus the compound *saṅs.ye.śes.rgyas* was created and further abbreviated in the same way as many other frequently used compounds. The result was that *saṅs.rgyas* practically ceased to be felt as a compound and was freshly compounded with *rdzogs.pa* (a synonym of *rgyas.pa*) and other 'prepositions' in *mṅon.par.rdzogs.par.saṅs.rgyas.par.* =अभि-सं-बुद्धः and *yaṅ.dag.par.rdzogs.paḥi.saṅs.rgyas*=सम्यक्-सं-बुद्धः.

An altogether analogous case is *bcom.ldan.ḥdas* 'the victoriously consummated' (Schiefner) or 'he who, sated with conquest, has passed beyond' (Sarat Chandra Das). If *bcom* means भगः 'success, victory' (S. Ch. Das), then *bcom.ldan* means of course भग-वान्, and the translation of this term alone, and not of a double term of which it was a part, can have been intended. This is also admitted by भगवान् only being given as the Sanskrit euivalent of *bcom.ldan.ḥdas*. For what purpose then, was *ḥdas.* [*pa*] added? Because *bcom-ldan* by itself does *not* mean भगवान् but 'victorious, triumphant [over enemies]' and thus, without an additional lable, must be understood as an epithet of kings rather than of ascetics. And there can be but little doubt that *ḥdas* is nothing but the remainder of a current expression shortened by composition, viz., of *myaṅ-ḥdas* (being itself a contraction of *ṁya.ṅan.las.ḥdas.pa*) 'which is now the usual, non-literal, Tibetan version of निर्वाण (Jäschke), but really means 'one who has passed away from suffering', i.e., 'attained Nirvāṇa.

Among the terms which did not require an additional lable, because they are clearly an individual designation, is *de.bzin.gśegs.pa* 'gone (or come) like those (or that one)', the Tibetan equivalent of

Kānāibaḍśī Inscription
By the courtesy of
Bangalore Sahitya Parishat

तथागतः. It is another question whether this Tibetan translation, which follows the usaual traditional explanations, is in accordance with the original meaning of the term. I think it is not. To my mind तथागतः in primitive Buddhism was just as little used in the literary sense as it is in non-Buddhist Sanskrit where it is (as early as, and probably earlier than, the *Ṛgveda-Prātiśākhya* synonymous with तथाभूतः, तथागुणः, एवंरुपः एवंगतः meaning 'of such qualities (kind, nature, condition).' But as a Buddhist religious term the word had, of course, from the beginning a more definite meaning (comp. तथात्वम्, तथता of later Buddhism), viz. 'being in such a condition [as is most desirable]' = 'the ideal man, the perfect man.' That this original meaning of तथागतः was still remembered even when it had already been obscured by scholastic sophistry, is shown by several passages in the Nikāyas such as the one of the *Aggañña-Sutta* translated by Mrs. Rhys Davids (though, curiously, with a foot-note explaining तथागतः as 'the thus-come' or 'thus-gone') as follows (*Buddhism,* p. 236): "............because such names as these, belonging to the Norm (dhamma), or to the Highest; and again, One with the Norm, or the Highest, are tantamount to Tathāgata."

Note—The author wishes to state that the usual method of tranliterating Tibetan, as applied by the editor to the above paper (the manuscript of which has the Tibetan words in the native script) is not the one recommended by him. For the latter (which in his opinion is also preferable to Professor Liebich's recent suggestions on pp. 238 ff. of his *Kṣīrataraṅgiṇī*) he begs to draw attention to his review of Jaschke's *Tibetan Grammer*, new edition, in Orientalische Literaturzeitung, 1931, columns 760-762.

Chapter - 9
Pre-Canonical Buddhism

A. Berriedale Keith

Even a cursory examination of the laws of evidence suggests that it is most improbable that we shall ever attain any accurate knowledge of the doctrines actually taught by the Buddha. In such matters we are compelled to argue from analogy, and it is of course notorious that, though we can fix the date of the founder of the Christian religion with far greater accuracy than we can that of the Buddha, there exists the utmost divergence of opinion as to the meaning and purpose of his teaching. Or again, though we have exact historical information about Socrates, the account of his teaching given by Zenophon and Plato is very divergent, and there has prevailed, without any prospect of final settlement, a controversy as to what Socrates actually taught. Plato himself left written records of considerable extent, and yet the criticisms which were obviously directed against him by Aristotle are such as to render it very difficult to explain how they came to be made. It is hardly possible to accuse Aristotle of mere misunderstanding of his great predecessor, and it is impossible to assume that he deliberately misrepresented him. In more modern times we are all familiar with the disputes which have arison as to the interpretation of the philosophical works of Kant and Hegel.

In these circumstances it seems practically impossible to accept as coming from the Buddha himself any special set of the remarkably varying doctrines which we find current later. It is true that it has been suggested that in the Pāli Canon we have a record actually formed within perhaps a century after the death of the Buddha.[1] A century of course is a very long time, but it is very doubtful whether we can accept the evidence in favour of the view that the Nikāyas

1. *Cambridge History of India*, I, 191 ff.

are to be referred to a period about half way between the death of the Buddha and the accession of Asoka, as suggested by the late Professor Rhys Davids. He admitted that the evidence was conclusive that the Nikāyas were put together out of pre-existing material, and that none of them has any claim to represent directly the views of the Buddha. But his opinion as to their date rests on wholly unsatisfactory evidence. He believed the tradition of the commentators that the *Kathāvatthu* was composed by Tissa at the time of the Council alleged to have been held there in the eighteenth year of Asoka's reign.[1] It is unfortunate that no inscription has yet been found to attest to the truth of this Council, and various explanations, none very convincing, have been adduced to prove that it ever existed. But apart from this no one perhaps will nowadays believe that the *Kathāvatthu* is just what we should expect for a book composed in Asoka's time. It is extremely significant that a profound student and expert in the Pāli literature, Mrs. Rhys Davids,[2] now sees in the Piṭakas compilations of a later period, ranging from the reign of Asoka till the last century B.C., and she admits that there was an indefinite amount of editing. It is indeed clear that, whatever view we take of the date of the compilation of the Piṭakas, we have not, and we cannot have, the slightest certainty as to the nature of the Buddha's teaching. All that we can do is to indulge in the legitimate, if somewhat useless, exercise of conjecturing what part of the doctrines which pass later as Buddhist is most likely to have been his own, having regard to the fact that there must have been something striking in his teaching to secure the success which he attained, and which made the Buddhists prosper while many other teachers, of whose existence the Buddhist texts give us assurance, passed completely away. It is not improbable that we may see his decisive service in his teaching of an attractive moral ideal within the capacity of his hearers to understand and carry into practice. We have some idea of the doctrines of his contemporaries; the materialism of Ajita Kesakambalī, and the denial of the reality of human activity which marked the views, otherwise divergent, of Pūraṇa Kassapa, Pakudha Kaccāyana and Makkhali Gosāla were little calculated to attract a substantial following, and there seems to be truth in the tradition that the Buddha rejected the extreme asceticism which could, after all, have attractions only for a select few. We may believe, or at least wish to believe, that the Buddha did teach the doctrine

---

1. Cf. Keith, *Buddhist Philosophy,* pp. 18, 19.
2. *Pathak Commemoration Volume*, p. 58.

which Mrs. Rhys Davids would wish to ascribe to him, of the possibilities of man's becoming something more and more. Unquestionably her method in her researches is sound. If there were traces of such a doctrine in the texts of the Pāli Canon which teach a much less attractive creed, we might well argue that thus we were recovering the truth. The difficulty so far is that, despite much ingenuity, the evidence assembled is so far from convincing that it may be feared that the real teaching of the Buddha has escaped us for good. It is possible also that there were other elements in the Buddha's teaching. He may have asserted a claim to be more than a mere human teacher, and have claimed for his teaching higher authority than its inherent reasonableness.[1] We cannot on this point prove anything. All that we hear of his super-normal character may be the figment of later tradition.

Quite a different question presents itself, when we give up the unscientific attempt to ascribe any definite doctrine to the Buddha and confine ourselves to the perfectly legitimate question of the development of Buddhist doctrine, without concerning ourselves with the insoluble question how far it can be carried back to the bUddha. Can we trace a definite development of doctrine? Was a system of pluralism developed by the scheme of antithesis into a monism, and then did it pass over into idealism? Is there truth in the doctrine found in the Tibetan sources of three successive Dharmacakrapravartanas? Are Pudgalanairātmya, Śūnyavāda, and Vijñānavāda three consecutive stages of Buddhist thought,[2] or are they three distinct developments of ideas current in unsystmatic form in early Buddhist circles?[3]

The systems which we have are relatively late in date, and they show very different appreciations of ideas which were no doubt strongly held in early Buddhism. The *anātmavāda* is interpreted in very different ways, and is treated as perfectly consistent with the holding of opinions which might well be deemed an *ātmavāda*. Thus the Sāmmitīyas professed the doctrine of the impredicable *pudgala*, and the Anatta-lakhaṇasutta indicates the possibility of such an interpretation of the *anātman* doctrine, making it a doctrine asserting the principle of *skandhas*, but not a *skandhamātratāvāda*.[4] That such views should be held indicates that the thinkers who adopted them were not very hostile to the idea of something which might be deemed some kind of soul. The Mahāyāna view, which recognises an

1. Keith, *Buddhist Philosophy*, pp. 27 ff.
2. Stcherbatsky, *IHQ.*, X, 739-60.
3. Schayer, *Archiv Orientální*, VII, 121-32; *OLZ.*, XXXVIII, 401-15.
4. Mrs. Rhys Davids, *Sokya or Buddhist Origins*, pp. 126 ff.

originally undefiled and radiant consciousness (*ādiśuddha prabhāsvara ekacitta*) would of course decline to be held to admit an *ātmavāda*, though the similarity of this *citta* to the *ātman* of Brāhmaṇical speculation is decidedly strong. The Yogācārins, accepting the principle of individual store consciousness (*ālayavijñāna*), declined to admit the charge of being personalists in doctrine. When we have all these views claiming to be compatible with the doctrine of *anātman*, it seems wholly impossible to ascribe to the Buddha the belief in an infinite number of separate evanescent entities in a state of beginningless commotion but gradually tending to quiescence, and to an ultimate absolute annihilation of all lie. It would be justifiable to do so only (1) if we could prove *a priori* that this view explains how the other doctrines came into being as logical developments thence, and (2) if we could stablish that this was the sole-doctrine currnet when the Nikāyas were compiled. But in fact no such proof is posible. It is quite impossible to prove that the Mahāyāna *dharmanairātmya* is derived as a further step from the *pudgalanairātmya* of the Hīnayāna. It may be argued[1] that āgārjuna merely applied the Hīnayāna assertion of the unreality of the self to the things of the outer world and thoughts also, but it is a fair rejoinder that to the Hīnayāna also both things and thoughts were unreal; the idea of a chariot is no moe real than the chariot itself. We have a distinct doctrine which does not grow out of the Hīnayāna.

Moreover, we have abundant evidence that a very different doctrine was widely current when Buddhism arose, the conception of the Brahman, of the final reality as reality, thought and bliss. Professor Jacobi[2] has called attention to the interest of those passages in which the elements are presented in an order leading from the more gross to the more refined. We find also that, in addition to those who believed in the orthodox five elements, earth, water, air, fire and ether, the Jains knew of people who added the soul to the series, and we have ample evidence from Pāli, Sanskrit, Tibetan and Chinese sources of the existence in Buddhist thought of a doctrine, the Ṣaḍdhātusūtra, which made personality consists of these five elements andconsciousness. Thevalue ofthisevidenceisgreat,precisely because the series will not fit into the traditional systems. Vasubandhu has to seekto work it in by declaring that the Sūtra merely enumerates the fundamental constituents of the individual (*maulasattvadravya*), so that it passes over the derived material constituents (*bhautikarūpa*)

1. Masuda, *Der individualistische Idealismus der Yogācāra-Schule*, pp. 20 ff.
2. *Die Entwicklungsgeschichte der Gottesidee bei den Indern*, pp. 12 ff., 41.

and the derivative mental phenomena (*caitasika*). Moreover he has to assert that *ākāśa* is *rūpadhātu.*[1] On the other hand,Buddhaghosa[2] holds that the sixfold division is to be equated to the sixteen *dhātus*, earth, air and fire being equal to the *phoṭṭhabbadhātu*, water and ether to the *dhammadhātu*, and consciousness to the *sattaviññāṇadhātu*. This treatment of *dhammadhātu* is most unsatisfactory, for Buddhaghosa himself explains the *dhammadhātu* as comprising twenty elements, three *arūpiṇo dhammā*, 16 *sukhumarūpa* including among them water and ether, and the *asaṅkhata*, while the *Dhammaaṅgaṇi* includes as *dhammadhātu* nothing but the *arūpiṇo dhammā*, which is the view of the Sarvāstivādins also. It is plain that the series of six *dhātus* as recorded is older than the scholastics, and what is essential is that it points to a definite gradation in which consciousness emerges as one of six essential elements, but more subtle than any other. This is clearly an earlier view that the Theravādin as regards not only consciousness but ether. The Theravāda has advanced to the view that ether belongs to derived matter, while the Sarvāstivādins take it out of contingent reality into the sphere of tone of their three *asaṃskṛtas*. But the six *dhātu* list suggests that we have a relic of a view which made consciousness the source whence the elements were derived, each less subtle than the preceding.

There is, of course, other evidence in the Pāli records of the existence of such aview ofthe primacy of consciousness.The orthodox doctrine repudiates the idea that *citta* should be taken by the unlearned as the soul, since it is in a state of constant arising and passing away in comparison with the relatively enduring character of the body made of the four elements.[3] But the *Visuddhimagga* (p, 554) reveals to us a very different aspect of consciousness as the relatively abiding element which transmigrates, passing from one existence into another just as a man swings himself across a ditch by using a rope tied to a tree, an idea which is certainly tobe compared with the *Bṛhadāraṇyaka* simile of the process of reincarnation of the *ātman* to the passage of a caterpillar from one straw to another. We have further the Mahāsāṅghika doctrine of a consciousness, originally pure, defiled by adventitious impurities,[4] which is well known to Mahāyāna texts, and which, as has been shown, is equally known to the Nikāyas, where the *Aṅguttara* (i. 10) has *pabhassaram idaṃ cittaṃ taṃ ca kho āgantukehi upakileśehi upakiliṭṭham*. Moreover, there

1. *Abhidharmakośa*, I, 49 ff.
2. *Visuddhimagga*, pp. 487 f.
3. Mrs. Rhys Davids, *Buddhist Psychology*, pp. 13 f.
4. Masuda, *Early Indian Buddhism*, p. 30.

are various canonical passages where we have explanations of Nirvāṇa which echo the ideas of the Upaniṣads regarding the ultimate reality. From these passages we gain, as Mr.Kimura points out,[1] the conception of Nirvāṇa as the eternal reality of cosmic existence which cannot be expressed in positive terms, and must merely be indicated by negations. It is perfectly clear that in the early Buddhist circles the idea of the ultimate reality, as something akin to the Brāhmaṇical conception of the absolute, was in circulation. From these early speculations in Buddhist schools we may see a natural development direct to the absolute which is developed in the Mahāyāna, and to the consciousness theory of the Vijñānavāda. These two ideas are not ultimately very deeply opposed; the latter emphasises the absolute as consciousness, the former contents itself with an absolute in relation towhich it considers that all empirical things lack reality. The essential point is that it is quite unnecessary to attempt to show that the Mahāyāna and the Vijñāna-vāda develop from Pluralism.

In the same way it is easy to see that the doctrine of *anityatā* is not the whole doctrine of early Buddhism or one that we need trace to the Buddha himself on the score of its universal acceptance. The fact is that the Pāli Abhidhamma differs from the classification of Vasubandhu in the *Abhidharmakośa* in that it treats as *rāpadharmas* the four *saṃskṛtalakṣaṇas*, which the Sarvāstivādins assign to the group of the *rūpacittaviprayuktasaṃskāras,* and thus confines to *rūpa* the characteristics of origination, of maintenance, of growing old, and impermanence (*rūpassa upacayo, rūpassa santati, rūpassa jaratā, rūpassa aniccatā*). There can be no doubt of the fairness of the deduction hence made by Professor Schayer[2] that in pre-canonical Buddhism the elements of *rūpa* alone were considered impermanent. This view is confirmed by the fact that the Mahāsāṅghika, Ekavya-vahārika, Lokottaravādin and Kaukuṭika (Kukkuṭika) schools place in the category of eternal non-contingent elements the four realms belonging to the *ārūpyadhātu* together with the two forms of extinction recognised by them. As opposed to *rūpadhātu,* therefore, we have the *dharmadhātu* as the eternal supersensual reality, which like the absolute of the Upaniṣads[3] can be discerned by mind alone, while from another aspect it is the absolute truth, which beyond the knowledge of the average man,

1. *Origin of Mahāyāna Buddhism*, pp. 96 ff.
2. *Archiv Orientální,* VII, 128.
3. *BAU.*, IV, 4. 19.

may yet be realised by the *dharmacakṣus* of the omniscient Buddha.[1] It seems that along these lines must be traced the originof the use of *dharmadhātu* in the Mahāyāna to express the absolute. The same idea explains the Mahāyāna doctrine of the *dharmakāya* as one of the forms of the Buddha, the other, in the older version before the development of the Trikāya doctrine of the Yogācārins, beings the *rūpakāya*, the unreal body with which he descended to earth as Śākyamuni. These two bodies correspond to the *paramārtha* and the *saṃvṛti* forms of knowledge. In the Trikāya doctrine we have the *dharmakāya* corresponding to the *pariniṣpanna* aspect of réality, the *sambhogakāya* corresponding to the *paratantra* aspect, and the *rūpakāya* to the *parikalpita*. Here the further refinement of the Yogācāra over the Mahāyāna is clear.

We have therefore clear evidence of a distinction between *rūpa* and *dharma,* but such a distinction is not given in the scholasticism of either Buddhaghosa or Vasubandhu, in which *dharma* is the generic term for elements, while *rūpa* is a category among *dharmas*. But, as Professor Schayer[2] points out, there is a trace of the old antithesis in the fact that in the enumeration of the twelve *āyatanas* and the eighteen *dhātus* the *dharmāyatana* and the *dharmadhātu* contain only non-*rūpa* elements: *vedanā, saṃjñā, saṃskāras, avijñapati,* and *asaṃskṛtas* in vasubandhu's version, while the *Dhammasaṅgaṇi* omits the last two items. It is certainly legitimate here to suppose that the distinction of *dharma* and *rūpa* was originally clearly drawn.

What that distinction was is less easy to say. Professor Schayer insists on the error of contrasting *dharma* and *rūpa* as immaterial spiritual reality and material reality, on the ground that this version introduces into Indian thought a conception familiar since Descartes' contrast between *res ertensae* and *res cogitantes,* but foreign to India, a 'European anomaly', for the idea of a non-extensional being is neither universal nor necessary. From the Āraṇyakas to the Vijñānavāda and the Vedānta Indian philosophy has never conceived the soul, consciousness, psychical phenomena, otherwise than spatially. The true view is afforded by examination of the Buddhist doctrine of the three spheres of the cosmos. The first two, the *kāmadhātu* and the *rūpadhātu* are closely connected, the former being merely a lower and less perfect form of the latter. But the *ārūpyadhātu* is very different; it is composed of four *āyatanas*:

1. Geiger, *Pāli Dhamma,* p. 69.
2. *Archiv Orientálnî,* VII, 126 f.

ākāśānantya, vijñānānantya, ākiṃcānya, and *naivasaṃjñānāsaṃjñā*, whose common characteristic is infinity; in contrast with the elements of earth etc., the *ārūpya* elements are all-pervading and omnipresent. Hence inthe *ārūpya* world there are no storeys one above another; hence too the *ārūpyadhātu* is without place (*adeśastha, asthāna*) that is without localisation in space, but not without extension. Spirituality and extension are not to be regarded as separated inHindu thought. In the same way, we should not regard *rūpa* as material, because it covers in the Abhidhamma lists things which cannot by any means be brought under the western notion of matter. The Vaibhāṣikas, though they have a simpler conception of *rūpa* than the Pāli Abhidhamma classification, yet include under it not only the sense-faculties but also the sense-data which from the western point of view belong rather to psychic than to physical phenomena. This argument, it must be pointed out, is not wholly convincing, for that sense-data should be regarded as physical rather than psychic seems perfectly natural from the Buddhist standpoint and the Abhidhamma view that *kāyaviññatti* etc., are *rūpa* is an easy enough extension. It is easy also to understand how *rūpa* came to be used in *rūpakāya* to denote that that is impermanent, whether we call it psychical or physical. But we certainly may admit that the Buddhist view of matter and spirit was not that of Descartes. Yet we need not reject the belief of Deussen that in the higher flights of the thought of the Upaniṣads those thinkers who negated all possible predicates of the absolute were groping to express the idea that theabsolute was not in space or time.[1]

That early Buddhism recognised the impermanence of things, both physical and psychical, comprehended within the term *rūpa* is clear. But the idea of purely momentary existence was obviously not the first view. The theory of the four general functions (*sāmānyalakṣ aṇa* or *saṃskṛtalakṣaṇa*) which are manifestations of elements always present in every moment of the stream of life process, *jāti, sthiti, jarā*, and *anityatā*, held by the Sarvāstivādins is manifestly inconsistent with true momentary existence.[2] It was left to the Sautrāntikas to drop the element of endurance *sthiti*, and thus to evolve the doctrine of momentariness in its mature and least intelligible form. Here we have a clear example of the manner in which a simple fact, the impermanence of physical and psychical things, which presumably was insisted on in the first instance as a means of inviting the attention of the hearers to the importance of

1. Keith, *Religion and Philosophy of the Veda,* II, 521, 522
2. Schayer, *Ausgewählte Kapitel aus der Prasannapadā*, pp. 83 ff.

that which is permanent, is developed by scholasticism into a metaphysical theory of pronounced difficulty.

In the same way we must expect to find that the *dharmas* of Buddhist speculation have arisen from some much less elaborate idea. In the developed scholasticism it is explained by *svabhāvadhāraṇāt*, a thing which supports its own essence. They are ultimate entities which have their own characteristics as their essence, and therefore are quite different from phenomena referred to ultimate substrata. They are not to be understood as things in themselves, whose attributes alone are revealed. Clearly to say that a *dharma* is a quality, not a substance, but the negation of a substance is a misleading use of words. A quality implies in our speech some substance of which it is a quality, and the *dharmas* are themselves the substances while the substances are the qualities. They are essentially simply things, pure reality. The difficulties of this conception are obvious, and the various efforts of the schools to present lists of *dharmas* afford little satisfaction. We have the *asaṃskṛta dharmas* which are transcendental, uncaused, underived; the Theravādins are contented with one, Nirvāṇa, the Sarvāstivādins have three, the Yogācārins, six. Between them and the *saṃskṛta dharmas* there is a gulf fixed, which it is impossible logically to cross. The *saṃskṛta dharmas* themselves present great divergences of view. The earlier and later lists contain elements which are for us neither material nor mental, though the Theravādins classify them under *rūpaskandha*, while the Sarvāstivādins assign them to a group not connected with matter or mind. Thus homogeneity, decay, vitality and birth figure as distinct *dharmas*.[1] Each dharma is ultimate; the sense-organs are composed of atoms, but every *cakṣurindriyaparamāṇu* is homogeneous, so that all together they constitute but one factor. The *dharma* therefore is quite different from a composite thing like the human body, which contains the four *mahā-bhūtas,* and the sense-organ-atoms and the sense-object-atoms, for the doctrine treats sense-objects as material in the same measure as the sense-organs. The lists of *dharmas* therefore come to be efforts, confused and unsatisfactory, to define ultimate entities which however are admittedly very deep and mysterious. Nothing in reality, it seems, was gained in clearness of understanding by denying that *dharmas* were substances; regarded as qualities which were the only reality they remained wholly unintelligible just as much as substances.

---

1. McGovern, *Buddhist Philosophy,* pp. 104 ff.

The purely arbitrary character of the whole construction became aggravated when the doctrine of atoms was taken over, presumably from the Vaiśeṣika school. The adaptation was late, for the early Sarvāstivādin Abhidharma does not accept it, and it appears only in the *Mahāvibhāṣā* and in works later than that. Evidently it gained popularity rapidly, for the *Abhidharmahṛdaya*, translated into Chinese in the 3rd century, contains the theory in a developed form, and it is prominent in Vasubandhu and accepted by the earlier Yogācārins, though it was rejected by Dignāga as inconsistent with idealism. The Sarvāstivādins admit fourteen kinds of atoms, five for the sense-organs, five for the sense-objects, and four for the *mahābhūtas*. But in a sense the *mahābhūta* atoms are primary, for each of the atoms of the sense-organs and objects originates owing to atoms of the *mahābhūtas* and is sustained by them, each atom having with it one atom of each of the *mahābhūtas*. The atoms of the latter, however, are not permanent; like all else, they pass through the cycle of origination, continuance, decay, and destruction on which follows a like process. It is however only by grouping of the atoms that are formed the molecules of which the material universe consists.[1] All this speculation is without scientific basis and is naturally unedifying, leading merely to verbal ingenuity.

What lies at the basis of these doctrines? If we are to accept the view of Professor Przyluski[2] we are to suppose that the first disciples of Śākyamuni had little taste for pure speculation. The existence of the Questions of Milinda suggests that the spirit of the sons of the Śākyas was sharpened by contact with Greek rhetoricians. But the Buddhist philosophy was essentially original. They seem to have started from a system analogous to Pythagorean arithmology. At first they believed in the reality of numbers, a belief which led them to deny all substances. Everything is in an incessant flux; only the number of elements is constant. In this way appearances go on existing; in this way the illusion of a personal ego endures. There is no essential difference between spirit and matter. The mind and the objects of the senses are formed of elements joined by the law of numbers, a fixed number of which is necessary to form a material of a psychic molecule.. A group of these aggregates gives the illusion of an ego and of a sensible thing; but nothing is permanent. All the component parts are dissolved and recomposed again incessantly. There is neither an immortal soul, nor a personality, nor a mind. The very Buddhas are not excepted; their being is illusive, temporal, and unreal.

---

1. McGovera, *Buddhist Philosophy,* pp. 125 ff.
2. *Journal of Theological Studies,* XXXV, 346 ff.

The sketch of Buddhist views is most interesting, but the prominence given to the idea of number seems not to be borne out by our texts. No doubt there are various indications of the importance attached to numbers, and the numerical enumerations of the Pāli texts attest the fascination, numbers exerted on early thought. But that the philosophy was really based on anything like the Pythagorean arithmology must remain a speculation which, on the whole, seems to have little to commend it.

Another view[1] presents itself in the claim that the *dharmas* are infra-atomic dynamic unities of forces or elements whose interdependence according to casual laws constitutes the illusive objects of our phenomenal life. It is suggested that we may seek for their proto-types in the Sāṃkhya system, which before Buddhism held the idea of *anātman*. It is true that the Hindus regard Sāṃkhya and Buddhism as sharply contrasted. But this is because in the Sāṃkhya all is eternal, since it represents the permutations of unchanging matter; though the manifestations are constantly changing (*nityapariṇāmin*), they remain one in their material cause (*kāraṇāvasthāyām*). In Buddhism, on the other hand, there is no eternal matter, but momentary *dharmas* appearing in functional interdependence (*pratītyasamutpāda*). The antithesis is explained, because here as always the history of philosophy evolves by contrasts. Every new departure starts in opposition to reigning ideas, but it creates the new on the basis of the old. The Buddhist produces the new doctrine of *pratītyasamutpāda*, which negatives the *pariṇāma-vāda* of the Sāṃkhya, but it builds up the doctrine of *dharmas* on the basis of the Sāṃkhya *guṇas*. The aim of the *guṇa*-theory, whatever its origin, is to bridge the gulf between mind and matter. A physical phenomenon and a mental one are equally composed out of minutest infra-atomic quanta of three different stuffs or forces, the Intelligence (or nervous stuff), Energy-stuff and Inertia-stuff. The first is predominant in a mental phenomenon, the last in a material one. Energy is being constantly liberated and absorbed; there is therefore no stability, all is instantaneous. But, though being momentary flashes of instantaneous infra-atomic quanta charged with some energy, the *guṇas* and the phenomena composed of them are said to be ubiquitous and eternal (*vibhu, nitya*), for they are eternal in their causal or potential condition as absorbed in an eternal primordial matter. When in this early period of Indian philosophy the *guṇa*-theory was being philosophically founded, it is more than probable that the atomic

1. *IHQ.*, X, 756 ff.

structure of matter was being discussed. It is probable that at that early period there was a division of opinion. The Jain and some pre-Vaiśeṣika system joined the materialists, and began to assume indivisible atoms, whereas the Sāṃkhyas and some pre-Buddhistic philosophers decided for infinite divisibility. Although later on the Buddhists assume the existence of atoms, they deny their indivisibility. Their atoms, therefore, are not atoms at all, they are *dharmas*, qualities without any stuff. The character of the atoms follows from the nature of the *mahābhūtas*, which though called earth, water, fire, and air, are really the four forces of repulsion, attraction, heat, and motion. The Buddhists indeed defined matter as merely the phenomenon of resistance. All realisable ideas the Hīnayāna and Sarvāstivādins at this early date held, were either concrete data of sense (*bāhyāyatana*) or concrete data of invalid consciousness (*abhyantarāyatana*). Both categories, the outward and the inward data, were called *dharmas*, non-substances, absolute qualities. This designation aimed at bridging over the gulf between matter and mind, not by assumign an equal composition, but by assuming their parallelism, their equal status. This psycho-physical parallelism was natural, because according to the Buddhist theory of causality there is a general parallelism between all elements of existence.

The theory that the *dharmas* are borrowed from the *guṇas* does not appear to rest on anything more solid than this general comparison, which seems sadly lacking in cogency. The assertions regarding the nature of the Sāṃkhya *guṇas* seem to lack any foundation whatever as regards any possible early form of Sāṃkhya, and only an early Sāṃkhya is in point. The names of the *guṇas* are sufficient warning that they do not represent in their early stage anything of the kind stated, and the hypothesis that their purpose is to bridge the gulf between matter and mind seems to be wholly without foundation. To reconstruct Sāṃkhya in a form which the early Sāṃkhya texts wholly ignore[1] and to claim that as the source of Buddhism is not a very convincing argument. The point regarding atoms is an interesting note of the new methods of argumentation. We are told that it is more than probable that the atomic structure of matter must have been discussed at the period when the *guṇa*-theory was being philosophically founded. But Professor Jacobi, whose evidence as a convinced adherent of the influence of Sāṃkhya on Buddhism,[2] is above suspicion of bias, was convinced that the

1. Cf. Keith, *Religion and Philosophy of the Veda*, II, 548.
2. Cf. Keith, *Sāṃkhya System* (2nd ed.). pp. 23 ff.; *Buddhist Philosophy*, pp. 140 ff.

Sāṃkhya was not atomistic in its early days, and calls attention to the silence of the Pāli Suttas and the denial of atomism by the Vedānta, the Mahāyānists and the Sāṃkhya. This denial, it is said, is aime at the eternal atoms of the Vaiśeṣika and does not refer to those systems which have a dynamic or semi-dynamic theory of matter. The *tanmātras* are evidently also some kind of atoms, or infra-atoms. Neither of these assertions is supported by any evidence whatever. Atomism is a perfectly definite conception which is quite different from the *tanmātras*. The effort to find in the *guṇas* a real predecessor of the *dharmas* seems to be wholly unsound, except in the generic sense that every earlier philosophical idea has some effect in moulding the concepts of later philosophy.

The concept of *dharma,* it has been justly remarked,[1] bears obvious traces of reduction from something more concrete; it is not without anthropomorphic traits such as those which affect the structure of the picture of the *ātman* itself. It has symptoms of an individual being whose concrete character has as far as possible bee reduced. But, like mere man, *dharma* has origination, duration, death, and in serving the function of conditioning other *dharmas* it performs its business (*kāritva*). The idea of *dharmas* as purely sepaate beings is quite irreconcilable with their conditioned character and with the fact that they serve to condition other *dharmas*. The fact that any *dharma* conditions another is a direct negation of separation; conditioning is manifestly impossible save in a structure. It is impossible to form any intelligible conception of the *dharmas*, as in his own way Vasubandhu admitted. It seems probable enough that those authorities are right who hold that the Buddhists did not distinguish physical and psychical. The *dharmas* may in their ultimate origin have traits of souls deprived of all concrete character; any real assurance[2] as to their character seems impossible, and their philosophical importance is historical only.

The view that the *satkāryavāda* belongs to the early Sāṃkhya has recently been assailed.[3] The idea of causality in the Sāṃkhya is asserted to have develped in a different manner. The oldest idea of cause is that of the hidden being, *prakṛti*, and the oldest theory of a dynamic is the conception of a change in a lasting substance, *vikāra*, seen in the conception of *tattvavikāra*, the twenty five principles. The further development of this theory lay not in the Sāṃkhya school itself but in a philosophical debate which has its roots in the *Ṛgveda*

---

1. Liebenthal, *Satkārya in der Darstellung seiner buddhistischen Gegner,* p. 11.

2. Cf. Geiger, *Pāli Dhamma,* pp. 8, 9 with Schayer, *Archiv Orientální,* VII, 129-130.

3. Liebenthal, *Satkārya,* pp. 150, 151, and 42 ff. There are difficulties but the view deserves consideration.

itself. While in the beginning it turned on the beging or non-being of the cause, it appears that Vārṣagaṇya provided an answer to the question of the mode of being of the product. His opponents were Hīnayāna Buddhists. Since the formulation of Sāṃkhya doctrines in the *Nyāyabhāṣya* agrees with Vārṣagaṇya's opinions, it is to be conjectured that Vārṣagaṇya counted at that period as the typical Sāṃkhya teacher. A new development of the discussion of origins is found in the Śālistambasūtra and in Nāgārjuna. Here the issue is the likeness or unlikeness of the product with its source. The Sāṃkhya is credited with the belief in the origin of like from like. This points to the source of the *satkārya* doctrine, which perhaps is first formulated in the *Sāṃkhyakaumudī*, and which asserts that the product exists in substance (*svabhāvataḥ*), though unseen (*śaktitaḥ*) in the source. The *pariṇāma-vāda*, it is suggested, was not originally part of the Sāṃkhya docrine. Apart from the *tattvapari-ṇāma,* it plays in the *Sāṃkhyakaumudī* only a minor rôle in the *guṇa-pariṇāma* and the *guṇapariṇāmaviśeṣa*. It is clear that if this view is correct, and *satkārya* was not a doctrine of the older Sāṃkhya, it is impossible to accept as correct the doctrine that the Sarvāstivādins adopted their doctrine from the original Sāṃkhya, and the suggestion that the doctrine of momentary universal change originated in the Sāṃkhya system loses any little possibility it had.

It remains to add that the attribution[1] to early Buddhism of an extraordinarily important classification of mental phenomena in four groups: feeling, ideas, will, and pure sensation, is misleading. The first obvious criticism is that these four groups are placed side by side with *rūpa*, instead of being opposed as one whole group with four subdivisions to *rūpa*; if they had been clearly felt as mental as distinguished from physical, such a distinction would necesarily have been made, for it is far more fundamental than the distinctions between the four other categories. Secondly, to hold that the early Buddhists distinguished in the modern style between feeling, ideas, will, and pure sensation is to read into what is said modern conceptions, just as the *guṇas* and the *dharmas* are reinterpreted in terms of modern scientific conceptions, which were not and couldnot be present to the minds of those who used them *Vedanā* doubtless is feeling, but how little its character was clearly understood is shown by the doctrine of neutral feeling which, it is said, has knowledge as pleasant, not knowing as painful.[2] *Saññā* again includes in the Pāli

1. *IHQ.*, X, 744.
2. *Majjhima Nikāya,* I, 303.

texts cognitive assimilation on occasion of sense and cognitive assimilation by way of naming, or awareness with recognition expressed in naming. In the view of the Sarvāstivādins and the Yogācārins, on the other hand, the conceptual aspect is more marked. *Saṅkhārā* is not merely volitional cognition (*cetanā*) but includes 51 other factors which are rather co-efficients in any conscious state than pre-eminently active or constructive functionings.[1] The nature of Vasubandhu's interest in pure psychology can be judged from his rejection of the effort seem in the *Saṃyuktāgama* to restrict the category to volitional aspects. The other factors must not be excluded, because, if this were done, the *caitasikas* and the *citta-ciprayukta dharmas* would not fall under any of the *skandhus*, and would be independent of suffering and the cause of suffering, and hence could not be cut off and could not be known. Complete analysis alone allows of suffering being brought to an end; hence the other factors must be included in the *skandha*.[2] *Viññāṇa* again is defined early as that which is aware of difference of sensations e.g., tastes, thus according precisely with *saññā* which in the same text figures as discriminating colours. In the *Majjhima Nikāya* we find *viññāṇa* as consciousness of what is pleasant, painful and neither; *vedanā* figures in the same functioning and *saññā* with colour sensations, and the dialogue declines to assert any essential difference between the three, despite the fact that they figure as distinct *khandhas*. More generally, *viññāṇa* appears as awareness, and a friendly critic admits that it is very difficult to understand how the generic term was left to stand as on a footing of equality with the preceding three *skandhas*.[3] The suggestion is made that we may explain this lack of proper classification by the absence of a Buddhist logic of division, and by the intensely practical aim of the psychology to negate the danger of the belief in a substantial consciousness. Later Buddhism recognised the illogical form of the division, and accepted *vijñāna* as consciousness and ranked the other three as *caitasika*, mental properties, bound up with *vijñāna* or *citta*. The mere order of the *skandhas* shows how unscientific early Buddhism was; Buddhaghosa and Nāgārjuna had to explain *rijñāna* immediately after *rūpa* to make any intelligible scheme, and a glance at the quaint reasons given in the *Abhidharmakośa*[4] for the traditional order dispels any belief in real anticipation of Bertrand Russell or Bergson, whatever be the value of their systems. The palpable fact is that Buddhism

1. Mrs. Rhys Davids, *Buddhist Psychology*, pp. 51, 52.
2. McGovern, *Buddhist Philosophy*, p. 87.
3. Mrs. Rhys Davids, *op. cit.*, p. 54.
4. McGovern, *op. cit.*, pp. 93, 94.

was essentially a *mārga*, and purely scientific psychology is not to be expected therein nor is it to be found. We may use modern philosophy to illustrate ideas which we think we should find in the Baddhist texts, but it must be remembered that modern views are the product of definitely modern scientific advances, and, while they can be superimposed on Buddhist doctrines, they do not express what the Buddhists thought. It does no harm no doubt to reinterpret Buddhism in modern guise, but it should be recognised that historically that is not what Buddhists held.

Nor can it be said that the new interpretation makes the Buddhist standpoint any clearer. It may be difficult to understand the Buddhist doctrine of the world, but it is not fair to ascribe to the Buddha the concept of evanescent entities in beginningless commotion, steering to quiescence and annihilation, because that may be a modern interpretation of the universe. The early Buddhist doctrine of the chain of causality[1] need not be ascribed tothe Buddha, but it certainly was early current, and it has no relation whatever to the philosophical doctrine suggested as his. What is essential is that it reveals among the early Buddhists thoughts of a type completely different from the theory now ascribed to the Buddha, but thoughts which, unlike that theory, are easily intelligible in their relation to Indian thought both before and after. Nothing is more unhistorical than to read the minds of early Indian thinkers as if they were products of the twentieth century.

In the case of the *guṇas* it is well to remember the actual facts as attested by the actual philosophical literature, and to compare it with the description given of them as "infra-atomic quanta of three different energies whose interplay produces the phenomenal world, both physical and mental."[2] The facts, of course, with regard to the *guṇas* are summed up with his usual accuracy by Professor S.N. Dasgupta in his *History of Indian Philosophy*;[3] "an important change in the Sāṃkhya doctrine seems to have been introduced by Vijñāna Bhikṣu (16th century A.D.) by his treatment of *guṇas* as types of reals. I have myself accepted this interpretation of Sāṃkhya as the most rational and philosophical one, and have therefore followed it in giving a connected system of the accepted Kapila and the Pātañjala school of Sāṃkhya. But it must be pointed out that originally the notion of *guṇas* was applied to different types of good

1. McGovern, *op. cit.*, pp. 169 ff., La Vallée Poussin, *Théorie des douze causes* (1913); Keith, *Buddhist Philosophy*, pp.97 ff.
2. *IHQ.*, X, 749.
3. i. 221, 222.

and bad mental states, and then they were supposed in some mysterious way by mutual increase and decrease to form the objective world on the one hand and the totality of human psychosis on the other." This is undoubtedly a perfectly fair account of the original nature of the *guṇas*, and it completely destroys the attempt to make them into infra-atomic quanta of energies.

Between the Sāṃkhya and Buddhism there are many essential distinctions. Dr. Nalinaksha Dutt[1] has justly pointed out that the result of attaching too much importance to the influence of Sāṃkhya on Buddhism has been the misinterpretation of Nirvāṇa as an eternal state of death, a lifeless reality corresponding to the undifferentiated matter (*prakṛti*) of Sāṃkhya. Nirvāṇa then is the same as the five *skandhas* in their original undifferentiated state. Dr. Dutt justly points out that this is unsupported by the canonical as well as the non-canonical texts. Both the Theravādins and the Sarvāstivādins are emphatic in their statement that a being once constituted out of the seventy-two elements or five *khandhas* passes through innumerable existences until, by the removal of Avidyā, he enters into the Asaṃskṛtadhātu or Nirvāṇa, which is an element existing by itself. But in the Sāṃkhya the emancipation of any being consists in the realisation of the fact that Puruṣa and Prakṛti remain apart, and not by his passing from the constituted to the unconstituted state. In Sṃkhya the emancipated being is one of the innumerable Puruṣas while in Buddhism he is after death indistinguishable from Nirvāṇa. The agreement between Sāṃkhya and early Buddhism lies in the fact that the undifferentiated matter of Sāṃkhya corresponds in its differentiated form to the five *khandhas* and not to Nirvāṇa as inferred by Prof. Stcherbatsky. If an analogue for Nirvāṇa be sought for in Sāṃkhya, we may say that it could have been found in Puruṣa if the innumerable Puruṣas were one Asaṃskṛtadhātu.

1. *Aspects of Mahāyāna Buddhism*, pp. 163, 164.

Chapter - 10

The Relations between Early Buddhism and Brahmanism*

C.A.F. Rhys Davids

We have an old literature of India handed down by a great class, later called caste, in her sodality calle Brahmans, or as some still prefer to say, Brahmins—a literature which has remained peculiarly that of India herself. If we speak of Indian religious literature, we do not mean the Jain Aṅgas, we do not mean the Buddhist Tripiṭaka, nor any other literature; we mean the Vedas, the Brāhmaṇas, the Upaniṣads and what may be grouped as the Vedānta literature. The Jain scriptures have survived in, and remained of, India; the Buddhist Tripiṭaka has long been lost out of India; but no one would call either the typical literature of India. Hence it is very interesting to consider how-either literature came to rise in India at all. Are these other literatures the result of movements in open opposition to that Indian type-literature? Did these movements arise as ignoring it (in so far as it was then in fixed, if oral form)? Or were those movements, from which these other literatures sprang, in sympathy and agreement with the dominant, the older, the still prevailing teaching, and did they only gradually break away from the mother-teaching?

Here is a very interesting historical problem, and not an easy one. Chiefly why? Because, to leave aside the question of Jainism, neither the older, the type scriptures, nor the Buddhist scriptures (the oldest we yet have) help us out in the least with any record of any rupture whatever, as following on an earlier state of agreement.

---

*This is a lecture deliverd before the Society for Promoting the Study of Religions at its headquarters, 17, Bedford Square, London on January 17th, 1934. By the courtesy of Mr. Loftus Hare, Hon. Editor of the Society's Transactions, I am permitted to publish it here before its appearance in those Transactions. The Lecture opened a series by different exponents on Great Religious Schisms.

As to that, the very word for rupture or schism (*bheda*), I do not so far find in the type-scriptures reckoned as preceding, or as contemporary with early Buddhism. It does occur in the *Maitrī Upaniṣad*, which may more or less overlap the birth of Buddhism, but only in the meaning of parts of a whole, not religiously meant. Yet in just this *Upaniṣad* (vii, 9) we come across one passage, possibly a later accretion, which looks like a smouldering restiveness such as may precede open rupture. It runs: "men are saying that there should be attention to *dharma*, which is destructive of the Vedas and of other teachings (śāstras); hence one should not attend to this."

This is all, and we cannot say whether we have here any allusion to the prominence given in the risen Buddhist movement to the notion of Dharma as mainly replacing the Brahman term for God as working in man as an ever-moving monition—now by us termed 'conscience'. Deussen held that there was here a reference to Buddhism.

Anyway we do not find that this discontent emerged in any open rupture in such relations as there may have been between the nascent Buddhism and Brahmanism. And nowhere do we find reference, in Brahman literature of that date, to a body of teachers identified with this Dharma-teaching by name.

In the Buddhist scriptures there is plenty about *bheda* in the meaning of religious ruptures, reminding us of the anxieties on this score of St. Paul. But one and all such divisions were internecine; there is no reference in the Tripiṭaka about any rupture with the Brahmans. Four 'Councils' held to secure *saṅgīti* or a standardized scriptural reciting, are named in Pāli and Tibetan scriptures, but in all these the unity aimed at is one that has a Buddhist Saṅgha as its centre and not a Brahman priesthood. Nowhere is there any record known to me of a Council convened either by Brahman orthodoxy or Buddhist non-conformity to have it out between them. Neither are meetings on a smaller scale recorded, where convened Brahmans are found censuring Śākyan heterodoxy between themselves, or where convened Śākyans are found denouncing the main tenets of the religion as taught by Brahmans as such.

And so the question may arise: Did not Buddhism start outside Brahmanism from the very first? And thence the further question:—Did it start as neutrally disposed towards the established religion of the Brahmans? Or as open opponents of it? And if the latter, is it possible its votaries could have escaped open and persistent censure and counter-opposition from the Brahmans?

Here we need to avoid making untrue parallels between this matter and the history of the central Church of Christendom and reforming bodies. There was nothing in Brahmanism resembling the ecclesiastical autocracy of the Holy Roman Church of the Middle Ages. We cannot truly say, that there could be neither secession from the orthodox church, nor independent start without the upstarts encountering the open hostility of that church. Brahmanism was concerned with two main things: the ancient ritual, partaking in which was not enforced on the laity, and the education of gentlemen's sons. We also come across Brahmans as official advisers of kings. A new body of missioners, such as were the first Śākyans (i.e. Buddhists) could steer clear of both these activities unscathed. There were many Brahman clans of celebrants, many houses receiving sons of Brahmans and of Kṣatriyas as resident pupils; there was room for all of them to work mainly independently, as there is with us in parallel matters. There was also no social feeling adverse to the free discussion of cultural topics, in which religion was not a specialized subject.

But in the early Buddhist or Pāli scriptures there is not a little which we can lay hold of as fairly good contributory evidence about the relations between Brahmans and early Buddhists—evidence which points, I hold, to something very vital for the first Buddhist teachings. It points to both agreement and disagreement. There is agreement with what was the internal religious teaching of the Brahmans; there is disagreement with what was the external observances among Brahmans. It is of the utmost importance that we keep this double relation in view. I take the former first.

It is unquestioned, that when the first Śākyan mission began, the religion of the Ganges valley was, both as a taught cult and as a system of observances, predominantly Brahman. It is difficult for us of Europe to compare the status of these teacher-celebrants with anything similar in other cults. It was a sort of magnified tribe of Levi in Judaism. It attached value to hereditary descent comparable to what may be found in an exclusive aristocracy. It claimed monopoly in the right of teaching and repeating the (orally) fixed hymns and *mantras* of authoritative religious doctrine. It claimed the right of training in such teaching the sons of nobles and its own children. It claimed a monopoly of conducting such ritual as was in accord with its body of oral sayings on the subject.

As to the inner teaching of matters spiritual, Brahmanism was itself still throbbing with a great religious reform, with a form of what we now call Immanence, of God as not externally conceived, as is for example, relatively true of Judaism and early Christianity, but as identical in nature with the very centre of human individuality. That is, of course, not with man's limited body, nor with any inner functioning that we might call mind or sense, but with the user of all these, with that who experienced by these, valued by these. In other wors, the Brahman teacher had come to believe in God as identical with the self, soul, spirit of man, or with, as India more wiely said, "the man". This was a great change from the older Vedic way, which sought Deity, without, above, around, in rites and soma-juice. *This* said: 'seek God in your very self, your best self. You are That; seek That; know That; thus can you become safe, free from fear, bound for the Immortal.'

Here some may say: In that teaching Buddhism in a way is more like the older Vedism, for in the Pāli Suttas we find a personal Deity, not the impersonal 'Brahman' of the type-literature, but Brahmā, a masculine personage, as the one Creator and Disposer of things. Here is no reference to an immanent Deity.

Yes, and such a personification we also find in the very teachings of that immanence, in the older Upaniṣads. There also (if hardly ever) do we find Brahman as Brahmā, sitting on a throne in a heavenly hall and speaking to a human visitor. But with this difference from the Buddhist references:—In the Upaniṣad the personified Brahman is *identified with the human self.* "What Thou art," says the visitor, "That am I." So we see that it is a picturesque way, for youthful hearers, of making it possible to speak of the ineffable. Just as in the Old Testament prophets, the ineffable Deity, named with the groping utterance "I am That I am," is personified as revealing Itself as "The Lord" an autocratic monarch. The Upaniṣ ads called this way of speaking 'the two Brahmans': the phenomenal and the superphenomenal, the latter only to be described negatively as *akṣara, amṛta.*

But in the Buddhist reference we have the Brahmā picture left uncorrected; we have the phenomenal Brahmā only, with the identity with man left out. The immanent Brahman is there, in the Suttas right enough, but surviving only in compounds: *brahmacariya, brahmacakka, brahmabhūta* and *brahmavihāra*. And the lively presentations of a Brahmā, who is, not Alpha and Omega, but just the titular name for the governor of the Brahma-world, is due to the renascence of Deity as personal that was going on in India *when the Piṭakas were taking shape as literary compositions*, perhaps some 300 years after the birth of Buddhism. With Brahmā as personal were coming up a masculine, not a neuter Śiva, and the Vedic Viṣṇu was reborn. (And it is not impossible that it was also in a later editing, that the old Upaniṣad came in for that more childish, if poetically more impressive vision of a regal Deity). And the later Buddhism was only conforming to the diction of its day, when it referred to this regal Brahmā in terms befitting a universal monarch, such as existed in the ancient tradition of the Cakravarti, and for that matter had, in the Mauryan dynasty, materialized as a political fact.

But let us go back those three centuries or more to the birthday of Buddhism, and find out, if we can, what were the relations between the first Śākyan missioners and Brahmans. There are many Suttas, roughly one hundred, telling of meetings between them. In almost every case the meeting is, in these Suttas, marked by courtesy on both sides. In some cases, where the Brahman visiting or visited is a magnate in property or learning or both, the Śākyan Founder is treated with honour and his views are accepted. Where one young Brahman has shown marked rudeness, his teacher, of high fame, calls to apologize for him. There is shown a wish to obtain Gotama's view on several subjects, and this, not as in certain Jain interviews, for purposes of heckling and dispute, but in order to learn what a teacher of high standing thought. Even before Gotama begins his mission, we find him consulted by an earnest-minded Brahman as to what makes the (true) Brahman. I do not wish to over-estimate the respect here alleged as shown. The Suttas are the work of prejudiced compilers, and we have no Brahman counterparts of these interviews. But it is evident that the Buddhist editors had retained no tradition of any chronic ill-feeling as existing between their founders and Brahmans.

Next, in all these talks, the central tenet of the Brahman teaching of that day, immanence, is never attacked by the Śākyans nor brought up for debate by Brahmans. Let this never be overlooked, for over-looked it strangely is. Contradict me if I have overlooked anything to the contrary. For me, it is not merely contributory evidence; it is crucial. Never do we find Gotama (or his men) attacking Brahmans for seeing Deity in manhood, nor do we find him attacked by Brahmans for holding any contrary and therefore damnable view hereon. Never do Brahmans charge him, in these interviews, with denying either Deity (i.e. Brahman, Source and End of all), or the aspect of Brahman as man's very self in essence, as man's ideal Self. Consider, had the opposite been the case, how much the later Buddhist editors, in their detraction of the self, would have made of such debates. How would they not have shown their Founder triumphant over his opponents! Compared with the heat we can imagine in such non-existent attacks, the few occasions when Brahmans do come with a grievance are as very milk-and-water.[1] Consider how much those editors did make of such debates, when the issue did lie between the man as a real entity and as only to be 'got at' as so many *dhammas*, constituents of body and mind—I refer of course to the Patna Debates in Aśoka's day. There, the debaters maintaining man's reality were the surviving up-holders of the old, the original tradition. It was its own house, which, in the opposite side, turned and rent Buddhism; it ws not Brahmans.

A third point is, that in the older Anthologies of the Canon, the Tri-Piṭaka, the truly worthy, good man is over and over again called 'Brāhmaṇa'. To quote one of many in *Dhammapada* and *Sutta-Nipāta*:

"Whoso has come to know in every way decease of beings and their going to be, without attachment, wellfarer! awake! that man I call a Bahman!"

Do you not agree that it is putting a great strain on probability to judge, that the Śākyans would have so termed the saint as revered by them—and that linked with the very words 'sugata, buddha' (wellfarer, awake) had the word 'Brahman' meant for them a man holding views they detested?

There is one more point hinting at a closer relationship between Brahman tenets and those of the Śākyans, which is all I have time to add. This is, that of the ten or eleven chief disciples cited as often surrounding the Founder, eight were Brahmans, and only three or four of his own class.[2] I do not think this is taken up into our picture of the first missioners as it should be. Do you say: But maynot those Brahmans have been rebels, seceders from the tenets of their class? And may they not have come into the little band, because they thought it was out and up to oppose those tenets, that ritual?

Well, what is the record about the coming in of any of them? In the Canon we have only that of the two reckoned ever after as the 'chief pair': Sāriputta and Moggallāna. These are said to have been earnest seekers after *amata*, which we should call immortality. They

1. E.g. on behaviour towards the aged.

2. Brahmans: Sāriputta, Moggaliāna, Koṭṭhita, Kaccāna, Kassapa, and Sāriputta's brothers: Cunda. Revata. Kṣatrivas. Anuruddha. Kappina, Ānanda, Rāhula.

were disgruntled with their teacher Sañjaya, but he was a noted sceptic or sophist, a man unlikely to have been teaching the sublime faith of the Upaniṣadic Immanence. But the quest of these two *was* Upaniṣ adic, and was the then accepted Brahman creed. And yet it was in Gotama that they appear to have found their good guide, with no recorded abjuration of what they had taken as their ideal. They may have thought their Brahman teachers were not helping them in an adequate way. They were perhaps like Nicodemus the Pharisee, coming to Jesus by night, to get a better Way in religion, than he as a 'teacher in Israel' had found. There is no hint that Nicodemus objected to the teaching of Jewish religious tenets.

These three points are, I contend, strongly suggestive, that the first Śākyans were as far from denying the Immanence accepted and taught in their day as were, say, John and Charles Wesley from denying the central teaching of Christianity. So much for the start of Buddhism in its relation to the inner religious teaching of the Brahman teaching of the young. Let us glance at evidence pointing to a much worsened relation, and finally to what amounts, on the Buddhist side to absence of relations.

If any person have read in the Pāli Suttas he may round on me and say: But look at what we find the Founder saying to young Brahmans about their teachers, say, in the Tevijja Sutta of the *Dīgha-Nikāya*. Is it not a very contemptuous sneering attitude, condemning them as men of faith merely, and not knowledge, and as no better than blind teachers of the blind.

This is quite true. And if we would save Gotama from being revealed as a man who said very inconsistent things, we must perforce choose one of two conclusions: Either this sneering attitude is earlier and the pleasant courtesies later, or the mutually respectful conversations are earlier and the sneering belongs to the editing of a later date. Holding the latter attitude he could not possibly have been welcomed and consulted as those scores of Suttas allege that he was. Nor could the respectful attitude have come later, when, as we can see, the Brahman teaching of Immanence was being ever more rejected by the Buddhist Saṅgha for an altogether worsened teaching about the man or self. The *Tevijja* has for me a core of very old teaching, for it shows both Śākyan and Brahman seeking salvation under the figure of a Way or Path (*mārga*), and it shows us in a most precious way, what that Way meant for the Śākyans, namely, works and not faith only, conduct not ritual. But to sneer at teachers for holding that the End of the Way was, is, always a matter of faith is impossible in the true teacher of religion. And no one held faith (*saddhā*) higher than did the Śākyans. It is the queerest error to hold, as I have seen Buddhist 'verṭs hold, that in Buddhism there is only knowledge, not faith. Let such read the Suttas more thoroughly.

It is fairly obvious that those Dīgha Suttas are very carefully compiled compositions made up from a number of oral sayings, and that into them comes much that is earlier, much that is later. It is not a thing I say lightly, nor with any charge of forgery. We have just to try to imagine the historyof the changing, changed conditions under which the compiling and the much amending of scripture (to which Buddhist chronicles bear witness) were made. And I say, that the lowered esteem of Brahmans as teachers is a later feature.

But to come to the new teaching itself: Was there anything in it to show agreement with, or disagreement from, the cultured religious teaching of the day?

This is a most important point, but it is one I have elsewhere discussed ("The Man", no. I *e.g. Transactions of the Society for Promoting the Study of Religions*). To sum up: (1) We find (if we read closely, and get behind the formulas) the Pāli Scriptures in agreement with the Brahman Immanence, namely, that what is there called 'self' bore the dual meaning of spirit and Holy Spirit; that man was as it were a dual self, the one, the ideal Self, being One who was to be sought after by the other, the actual self, as being the 'Goal', the 'Witness', the 'Guide', the 'Protector', the Judge of the actual self. (2) We find that his tenet is nowhere attacked as being a Brahman tenet, but that there is evidence of a tendency to substitute, for *attā* (self), *dharma* or sense of the 'ought-to-be' in man.

What then must there have been to cause a man to come forward as, not an opponent, but a reformer of things that Brahmans were teaching? This: I find the early Buddhists soon taking up a standpoint involving certain disagreements with Brahmanism as to ritual observances, the paying deference because of birth or caste, and the weight attached, and to be attached in religion to conduct or morals. It is this external system that was weighed and found wanting, not the internal system of spiritual values. It is in those external matters that we find the Suttas critical of the established religious cult.

And here remember, that Buddhism was born in the Eastern half of the so-called Middle Country, or watershed of the Ganges and Indus, not in the Western. There issilence in the Buddhist scriptures about the country west of the junction of the Ganges and

Jumna, save only in a rare sporadic way, such as reference to Ujjeni. I have it on scholars' authority, that eastern Middle Country Brahmanism was in a more morally lax, less organized state than was western Middle Country Brahmanism; hence, may be, the birth and growth of new reform movements in cult in the eastern half, such as Jainism and Buddhism. The Suttas do not hesitate to hint that Brahman morals were lax, where the first Buddhists taught,[1] albeit the class-respect claimed by Brahmans was none the weaker for that. Now, when we reflect, that the very central drive in the new mission work of the first Buddhists lay in this, that the one and only test for a religion lay in thelife, the conduct of its votaries, and that this was not at all stressed in the Brahman teaching—all the moral injunctions in the Upaniṣads could go into a single page—we see here a wedge that was bound to force the new popular teaching apart from the established teaching. The Upaniṣad teaching would seem to have accepted the moral code as making just for social amenity; as what it was proper to do. It is true that we do find one or two isolated passages about man shaping his future life's welfare by his morals. But the teachings as a whole do not rub this in as do the Buddhist Suttas. And it is even possible, that in these few passages we may have glosses, inserted later, due to the grown influence, not of Buddhism only, but of more morally earnest Brahman editors.

I think, that if we look on these two new emphases as wedges; the negative emphasis of dissatisfaction with the importance attaching to rite and sacrifice, and the positive one emphasizing the cardinal importance of conduct in religion (that is, in man as a spiritual being not of earth only), we have the main and first cause of the young Buddhist cult beginning to diverge from the established Brahman cult. Had that first cause been dissatisfaction with the central Brahman teaching of the day, the teaching of Immanence, we should find this included in those other Sutta criticisms of Brahmanism: its externals in observances, its external moral ethical teaching. *But we do not.*

In fact, the shoe is on the other foot. There is one never-quoted Sutta in the Fourth Collection,[2] showing the Founder censuring a Brahman for ruling out the reality of the self as agent in myself, in yourself. The Brahman gives it as his opinion that there

---

1. In the *Brāhmaṇadhammika-Sutta* of the *Sutta-Nipāta*, Gotama is described as (a) consulted at Sāvatthi by Brahmans as to his opinion of how Brahmans compared with their predecessors, (b) comparing them unfavourably with these, (c) not uttering a word of dissent with their religious beliefs, but only disparaging their moral standards.

2. *Anguttard,* iii. p. 337, P.T.S. ed.

is no such agent. The Founder is recorded as saying: "Never have I have even heard of such an opinion; when you move leg or arm, don't you use initiative? If so, how can you say it is not you, the self, who take the initiative?" This may not be a true memory; or the disputer may have been a young Brahman sceptic of the Academy; or the word 'Brahman' may have been interpolated because, at the time of revising the scripture, the Brahman had become the typical dissentient, or holder of wrong view. But the Sutta deserves to come out from oblivion (*Anguttara-Nikāya*, iii, 238).

But there was, following these two wedges, another. Or to shift the metaphor: With those first leakages of disaffection towards the established religion the fission widened, and there flowed out disaffection with the central tenet of Immanence itself. Namely, the lofty uplifted idea of the man gradually gave way, and that in, I think, three stages of decline. *Firstly,* the man was shorn of the Ideal Man, deity as Self, the God-in-Man. *Secondly,* the man could not be identified as real save in this or that state of body or mind. This word 'state' (or thing) was the word *dhamma* used only and always in the plural, as we have in our collective plural: 'things', or 'ills', or 'interests'. When you seek the man you "can't get at him," (*na upalabbhati*); you 'stumble' upon these dhammas, to use the word David Hume used, in a parallel grouping, many centuries later. *Lastly*, it was denied that there was any real man: there were *only* these things or states; they alone were real. Man was but a word for the complex of them.

Now all this growth in the third leakage may be found in the Sutta-Piṭaka, but with great variety in frequency and emphasis. Whenever you see the stock bit of catechism about man cannot be *ātmā* because he is transient and suffers, you should read Man cannot be Deity; manhood is not Godhead. Here it is the Brahman Ātmā view that is denied. It is not atheism; there is plenty to show that man can become the Highest, the Uttermost, the Best, the Perfect, the very Goal if he follow the way of becoming, and if he become all that, he is Deity actually, not potentially only. But the term *Brahman* for that Highest was falling out of favour *together with* the dissent from moral and external Brahmanism. Next, whenever you see, the man cannot be got at save through the mental items of *dhammas*, you have the working of the new psychology called Sāṅkhya or Analysis: the Humian phase in Buddhism. Finally, whenever you see a positive denial that there is any self whatever, not merely of a permanent self, an unchanging self, *but of any self,* you are in the later days of the mediæval scholastics a thousand years later, such as Buddhadatta and Buddhaghosa. These even denied there was a Wayfarer in the Way or Path, or a man saved in salvation, or a doer in doing:—Yes, in just so many words. Utter nihilism! Only ideas! I have found them anticipated, as yet, once in the Suttas, and once at an intermediate period, in the Questions of King Milinda. From the contexts I judge that both are later insertions, so different are they from their contexts, so badly do they fit. It were impossible to give details here and now. I can refer anyone to both and what I have said about them.[1]

This third leakage, in this threefold way, took time; it was more genuinely a leakage than were those first two ways of dissent, namely, with observances and with the importance of conduct. But it came gradually to make the resumption of the friendly relations of past centuries impossible, even when moral reform on the Brahman side might otherwise have gone far to knit, bring them once more into being.

It is curiously hard to elicit anything informative about the relations between Brahman and Buddhist in the centuries between Asoka and the dying out of Buddhism in India. We cannot gather from Asoka's injunctions to tolerance between religions whether he had these two in view at all. A century and a half after his day, in the Questions of Milinda, we find no bitterness about Brahmans, nor anything amounting to interest either. Their duties as a class are recited as just a matter of social tradition. Later again, in the *Jātaka Commentary*, in the "Ten Sorts of Brahman" Jātaka, the criticism of Brahmans in nine of the ten is put into the mouth not of a Buddhist, but of a rājā, rivalry between whose class and the Brahmans was old and social, not religious. And when finally we see the Bauddhas or Saugatas discussed in a Hindu Manual of a late mediæval date, the writer's concern is merely academic.

As to the waning out of Buddhism from practically the whole of India, and how far it may have been a result of its estrangement from the mother stem of Indian religion, this would need a separate treatment. There mayonce have been, to adapt Shakespeare "room enough in India for" both religions. But that day passed. Brahmanism (i.e. Hinduism) and Buddhism had to fight for life with the incoming Muhammadanism. Especially Buddhism, since in it the worship of the Highest, the Most, the Perfect was not nominally kept ever to the front.

---

1. Buddhaghosa, in his *Visuddhi-magga*, gives no heed to Brahmans whatever. save to make passing comment on the immoderate eating to be seen in 'some' of them.

Where, as in the case of decadent Buddhism, that Highest had become dimmed by concentration on, not the MOst, but the More.........I mean, where *arahan* and *Buddha* had replaced Deity.........ejection was easier and quicker. Decadent Buddhism could not stand, and petered out through inherent decay in its religious ideals, and through India's insistence, in her own way, itself decadent, but not so decadent, on man's need of keeping the Most, the Highest, as his main quest.

To sum up: I have tried to show, that if we speak of Buddhism as arising within Brahmanism, we mean, not Brahman externals, either in attention to ritual, or relative want of attention to the religious importance of conduct. We mean, Buddhism started in agreement with the central religious tenets or principles of the Immanence in Brahmanism of that day. Next, that in drifting apart from Brahmanism, Buddhism, in not attaching importance to ritual and on attaching importance to the religious sanction of conduct, did so without any crisis arising such as we look for in schisms or ruptures. Next, that while drifting apart in this twofold way (ritual and conduct) it was inevitable that there should be dragged in 'a drifting apart' also in the central teaching of Immanence. In this way the lofty meaning of 'self' or spirit suffered in Buddhism the same worsening, though in a different way, which it has suffered in our days in Europe. For us, self means usually our worse self; for India self meant, means our best self; for Buddhism it came to mean something that was non-existent. This, the third and gratest phase in the breach in relations, was aided in two ways from non-Brahmanical movements: (i) the study of mind-ways as apart from the man; (ii) the growth of monasticism, in which the standard of manhood was lowered to mean, not something capable of becoming Godhead, but something it was better to end. Finally I hold, that the exile from its parent stem should come more into account than it does when the causes of the decay of Buddhism in its native land are sought.

Chapter - 11

The Buddhist View regarding Eternity of the Vedas

Heramba Chatterjee

Śāntarakṣita in his *Tattvasaṁgraha* has refuted the 'nityatva' (permanence) of the *Vedas*, which are regarded as eternal by the Mīmāṁsakas, according to whom words, meanings and their relationship are all eternal. The Vedas are without any condition before their existence nor have they any conditions after them—they are authorless and eternal. The Mīmāṁsakas urge that the Vedas have unquestionable authority[1] as they are not human creations. As the five kinds of proof fail to establish the author of the Vedas, it is by the sixth proof i.e. proof of absence, the contention is established. Further, the Vedas being eternal are neither produced nor destroyed.[2]

Śāntarakṣita argues that the authority of the Vedas cannot be recognised in view of the fact that as the Vedas have got no author whose excellent qualifications would make him say the truth, knowledge derived from them is bound to be invalid. Again if the eternity of the Vedas is established on the ground of the absence of proof then the sky-flower should also be held as eternal.[3]

The Mīmāṁsakas argue that knowledge derived from the Vedas cannot be proved as invalid by inference, because inference is much inferior in authority to the proof of the revealed literature.[4] The Buddhist

---

1 सा हि प्रमाणं सर्वेषां नराकृततया स्थिता।
वैतथ्यं प्रतिपद्यन्ते पोरुषेय्यो गिरो यतः॥ *Tattvasaṃgraha*, sl. 2086

2 अकृतत्वाविनाशाभ्यां नित्यत्वं हि विवक्षितम्।
तौ चाभावात्मकत्वेन नापेक्षेते स्वसाधनम्॥ Ibid., sl. 2105

3 Vide *Tattvasaṃgraha* sl. 2432: अतो गगनराजीव नित्यता ऽस्ति न वास्तवी।

4 प्रत्यक्षपक्षनिक्षिप्तं शास्त्रमेव यतः स्थितम्।
बलवत्तरमित्ये तदनुमानस्य बाधकम्॥ Ibid., sl. 2108

reply that inference is certainly of a superior authority to the Vedas which are nothing but sounds. If the sounds however are taken as proved by perception, then there is no justification as to why the words uttered by human beings should not be regarded so.

Again when Mīmāṁsakas argue that sound is eternal and omnipresent, because it is always and everywhere known like the Sun, the Buddhists reply that sound should not be accepted as omnipresent for the reason that sounds are produced in different places and at different times. The Sun on the other hand is seen at all places by all persons. Experience (*pratyabhijñā*) not being a valid proof like perception cannot establish the eternity of sounds. Experience expresses—'same as that' and hence cannot represent perception which is free from reflection (*kalpanāpoḍham*).[1]

The words, according to the Mīmāṁsakas, are treated as eternal in as much as they express their meanings. In the *Śabdārthaparī- kṣ ā* it has been shown that there is no relation between the word and its meaning.[2]

Again it has been contended that words and letters being eternal, the sentences should also be accepted as eternal. Though some sentences and words like *guṇa*, *vṛddhi* etc. may be used to express the wishes of their author, yet that does not go against the eternity of the Vedas for they have got no authors and again for the reason that things described in the Vedas are beyond the power of human beings to witness.[3] The Buddhists in this connection argue that eternity of sentences need not be proved in the light of the fact that there is no connection between the objects and the sentences. If the sentences are merely combination of words, then the letters so combined have no meanings to express. If the letters arranged one after another are to be considered as a sentence then how can eternal letters have arrangement as they are for ever existent and omnipresent?

Thus the Buddhists conclude by stating that the Vedas cannot be regarded as eternal and divine for the reason that they contain many unpleasant things as *kāma, mithyā, prāṇihiṁsā* etc.[4] In as much as the theory of momentariness is established by Śugata the question of eternity of the Vedas should be dropped by all means.[5] Therefore as the vedas

---

1 प्रत्यक्षप्रत्यभिज्ञा तु प्रागेव विनिवारिता ।
भ्रान्तेः सकल्पनत्वाच्च नातो नित्यत्वनिश्चयः ॥ Ibid., sl. 2448

2 वस्तुतस्तु न सम्बन्धः शब्दस्यार्थेन विद्यते । Ibid., sl. 2470

3 न ह्येवं वैदिके शब्दे स स्वयम्प्रत्ययो यतः । Ibid., sl. 2775

4 सम्भाव्यते च वेदस्य विस्पष्टं पौरुषेयता ।
काममिथ्या क्रियाप्राणिहिंसाऽसत्याभिधा तथा ॥ Ibid., sl. 2787

5 ततश्चापौरुषेयेषु सत्याशा त्यज्यतामियम् । Ibid., sl. 2795

have no authority on points of Dharma,[1] one should try to learn it from a person who is pure and who possesses pure knowledge of the universe in order to obtain truth and emancipation.[2]

1 धर्म्मं प्रति न सिद्धाऽतश्चोदनानां प्रमाणता । Ibid., sl. 2809

2 ज्ञानालोकव्यपास्तान्तस्तमोराशिः पुमानतः ।
श्रुत्यर्थानां विविक्तानामुपदेशकृदिष्यताम् ॥ Ibid., sl. 2810

Chapter - 12

Sāṅkhya and Original Buddhism

C.A.F Rhys Davids

(A comment on Kalipada Bhyattachrya's recent article)

I have read with mixed feelings the article on 'Some Problems of Sāṅkhya Philosophy and Literature' in the September issue, 1932, of this Journal. I cannot claim to speak as an old student of Sāṅkhya, else I might be questioning the imputing to the shadowy if doubtlessly historical figure of Kapila anything amounting to a 'system' and a 'philosophy', which emerged much later. It is where the Founder of the *Śākyan* new teaching, which very long after came to take shape as what is now called Buddhism, is held up as teaching a philosophy, and a philosophy of four fundamental principles, in accordance with similar principles of Sāṅkhya philosophy, that I find the writer wrong.

I am not saying, the monastic scholastic Buddhism did not frame those so-called four truths, or that later scholastic Sāṅkhya, with a category of four points about *heya* and *hāna*, may not have suggested the late Buddhist four about *dukkha*. I would only contend that, as a feature in the First Utterance of Benares, the four are a pretty obvious gloss (as Deussen saw), and that, as fundamentals in what was not a philosophy, but the mandate of a great world-religion, they are impossible and entirely out of place. That mandate showed forth the man, the *puruṣa*, as the creator of his own salvation by the right choice of his will, in his quest for the Highest, the *paramārtha*. Here we have a revelation to man of a More in him:—in his nature, his life, his destiny. In the four truths, we are mainly concerned with a Less in the man:—with ill as his nature and life, unless he makes his nature will by cutting out desire, or will, the very source of the hope in what lies before him.

Throughout the Pāli Suttas we can see creeping up the influence of the early Sāṅkhyan teaching; not of any 'system', but of a teaching which saw in the composite human being not just *nāma-rūpa*: the man with a shape or body, but the man as having both body *and* a set of mind-ways, distinguishable from the very man. The man is not denied in that teaching; far from it:—*'puruṣo' 'sti'*, it maintains, and for very excellent and unanswerable reasons, given, as Mr. Bhattacharya will know very well, in the Sūtras. But he had an inner procedure as systematic as was that of the body. And it was this procedure that captivated the early Śākyan Saṅgha, probably even during the day of the first Śākyan teachers. Is it not clear enough in the Second Utterance, warning men not to confuse the very *puruṣa* or self with body or mind? This more-in-analysis of the man we see recognised in early Suttas of Pāli as one of two strengths (*balāni*) in the man: *paṭsaṅkhānaṃ*, or discriminating thought, and *bhāvanā*, or 'making-become', which was for the Śākyan world what Yoga became for the Brahman world.

But in all this there is no philosophy, as we understand the word. There never was philosophic system of Buddhism till a thousand years after the day of the Founder. Nor for that matter was there any philosophic system in the Upaniṣads. These were religious utterances, *mantras*, aspirations. It is only *we* who try to read any system into them. Why can we not let them stand in their true value for what they really were? When will Europe cease to talk in this way, and Indian writers no less? When is the Śākyamuni to be made no more to pose as a philosopher, as a pundit, full of wise and wordy discourse, of categories and ideas about men? There is no hope for India having a vision of him as he really was, till we banish from our eyes any imagining of him as prosing on about *skandhas* and the ills of life. A man was he in close touch with the unseen, with men in the unseen worthy to 'inspire' him, as we say—to will and word him with a message to this man and that woman, a message of a new amplitude in life, a new vista, a new joy in the mighty Becoming, the making-become that lay before him, before her. Verily are you That, but That you must make-become in you. There is here no actual Being, else is the religion of India absurd, irrational; there is only potential Being. There is becoming; a long 'Way'. Therein walk, 'attaining to happiness by happiness'.

And we shall not begin to understand him and his message as long as we take the many scriptures about him and his work at their face-value—at the value the compilers and then the revisers, the editors, have come to hold these in, in their later day. Hardly any writer on Buddhism as yet is historically critical in dealing with Pāli literature. Many will assign one whole work as later than another work, but who yet digs into any one work to find what a palimpsest that one work is:—a history in itself? Mr. Bhattacharya, who shows some historical discernment in feeling after a gradual growth in Śāṅkhya, has nothing of the kind when referring to Pāli works. He sees Śāṅkhya, for instance, as pre-Buddhistic, because "Śāṅkhya as a system of philosophy occurs in the Lalitavistara". This is as much as to say, that because a certain teaching (a 'system') is known to the poet of a late Buddhist work, it therefore was known to the first Buddhist teaching of at least 1000 years earlier? I am not saying this is the only evidence adduced; I say it is no evidence and should not have been mentioned, so worthless is it.

We live so remote from the day of the birth of a world-religion, that we, the after-men, have tended to mess up its original nature in wrappings and superstructures of ideas, in 'scriptures', in exegesis. I do no lost sight of the piety and devotion ever at work on these, but I do see the original plant all but buried, of the Man bringing a message to Man to come up higher and behold a broader, brighter view about himself. And that will not have been said in list, formula or category, much less in a system of philosophical fundamentals.

Chapter - 13

The "Dharmas" of the Buddhists and the "Guṇas" of the Sāṃkhyas

Th. Stcherbatsky

Professon Vidhushekhara Bhattacharya has recently devoted a series of lectures to the subject of the Basic Conception of Buddhism.[1] The opinions, expressed by him have elicited the following remarks:

Buddhism stirkes the historian of religion by two quite extraordinary features. First of all, it places man above god. Man can reach the highest position, far above the position of a god, by his own effort without the intervention of a divine power. The gods abide in heaven, they constitute a dive world (*deva-loka*), but the Super-man, the Buddha, stands far above all worlds, he is *lokottara*. At the same time this man, who by his own exertion can attain so high a position, is, deprived of a Soul. For it is most emphatically and repeatedly stated, that the Soul does not exist, neither the Soul, not the Self (*ātman*), nor the Ego (*ahaṃkāra*), nor the personality, the individual (*pudgala*), nor the living being (*jīva*), nor even man (*manuṣya*). All these are mere names, names of unreality, imagined phantoms. Man does not exist! Buddhism is *anātma-vāda, pudgala-nairātmya*. Atheism, the denial of God, should not so much strike the Indian scholars as it stikes the European, for the most orthodox system of Indian philosophy, the Mīmāṃsā, is also atheistic (*anīśvara-vāda*). But the denial of the reality of man and at the same time the worship of Buddhas and Bodhisattvas who are men, not gods, is a puzzle to the Indian historian just as it is to the European.

Mr. Vidhushekhara Bhattacharya proposes a very simple solution of the puzzle. According to him Buddha, like all his predecessors, the sages of the Upaniṣads, was willing "to extinguish desire." He does not tell us what desires Buddha strived to extinguish, he says

---

1. Bhattacharya, Vidhushekhara, *The Basic Conception of Buddhism*, 1934 (Calcutta University), 105 pages.

desire in general, all desires, whatsoever they should be (p. 64). Now, what is the object most desired, asks our author and answers, it is evidently one's own life, the Self (p. 65). "Offer the kingdom of heaven and tell a man that he may accept it, but only on condition, that he shall give up his life. Certainly he would not accept the offer" (*ibid*).

It is also evident, thinks our author, that by extinguishing the Self all desires will *co ipso* completely extinguished. For neither will there be any persons who could desire, nor will there be any objects which could be desired. This the author states in an unambiguous manner, he says, "thus there being neither the subject nor the object there is no room for desire to come forth" (p. 74). A more radical extinction of desire can hardly be imagined!

Such a drastic solution of the puzzle has the merit of simplicity, but I do not think it will find many believers. The author will probably be quite astonished to know that even if his *experimentum crucis* be realized and no subject at all be in existence, this does not at all mean that there will be no objects and no desires. For although there is in Buddhism no subject, there is plenty of objects desired. The objects, like every where, are divided in Buddhism in those that are desired (*upādeya*) and those that are not desired (*heya*). There is a whole class of objects termed "*anāsrava-dharma*" which are never *heya*. Nirvāṇa is not *heya*, the Path (*mārga*) and its various divisions is not *heya*, but *upādeya*. Notwithstanding the circumstance, that there are seemingly no persons who could desire them, the desired objects exist nevertheless. The desires which Buddha wished to extinguish are *klesas* i.e., "oppressors," bad desires. Buddhsim is a doctrine "of defilement and purification" (*sāṃklesa-vyavadāniko dharmaḥ*), a doctrine of defilement by bad desires, and of purification by good desries. In the early histor of Buddhism there are some instances, in which the aim of Buddhsim has been misunderstood just as Mr. Bhattacharya misunderstands it. There have been some religious men who committed suicide. They thought thus to "pull down the very foundation of desire" (p. 70). But they were condemned by the church, and suicide was declared to be a crime equal to assassination. The author says (p. 74),—"desire, the cessation of which is sought for *naturally* requires for its very being both a subject and an object. Therefore while by *pudgalanairātmya* its subject is denied, it is *dharma-nairātmya* that removes its object."

To this we must object first of all that *pudgalanairātmya* is Hīnayāna and *dharma-nairātmya* is Mahāyāna. Buddhism existed seven centuries without *dharma-nairātmya* at all and continues to exist till now without it in Ceylon and other countries.

The argument of the author gives an eloquent demonstration of the fact that it is impossible to treat such problems as the basic conception of Buddhism in ignoring all reasults of modern research[1] and in forgetting the existence of history.

Moreover the argument which to our author seems so strong and so self-evident,—the argument namely that if there is neither subject nor object there can be no desires—is strong only in common life and in realistic systems, it has no strength in an idealistic system.

Thridly, the argument that "desire naturally requires for its very being both subject and object" is contradictorily opposed to what Buddhism has always preached. It is a "natural" argument only in everyday life, but not in philosophy, still less in Buddhism. The basic conception of Buddhism is perhaps exactly the contrary of what Mr. Bhattacharya thinks it to be. For it is most clearly stated and repeated almost in evey Buddhist work "*asti karma, astiphalam kārakas tu nopalabhyate.*" "Action exists, and their results" (i.e. attaining the desirable and avoiding the undesirable) "exist also, but the man who perpetrates these action d o e s n o t e x i s t." That does not mean that he does not exist for the man in the street, but he does not exist in Buddhist philosophy, as well as in all those great European systems of philosophy, which doubted or denied personal identity.

What then exists if man does not exist?

The same text answers "*kārakas tu nopalabhyate........anyatra dharma-saṅketāh.*" The *dharma*-theory exists. And what is the *dharma*-theory? It is causality "*tatrāyam dharma-saṅketo yad uta asmin sati idam bhavatīti.*" The two central conceptions of Buddhism are *dharma* and *pratītya-samutpāda* is the causality inherent in these Elements. The one implies the other, and Element is a c a u s a l l y c o n n e c -t e d Element. There are in Buddhism at least three different conceptions of *dharma* as well as of *pratītya-samutpāda* (Cf. my Buddhist Logic, I, p. 134.)

It is exceedingly important to realize the full compass and all the implications of the principle that the *dharmas* alone exist, but not the *dharmin* and consequently not the man. The overwhelming

---

1. The latest production of European research in the field of *mārga* are, a master-work of Prof. L. d e L a V a l l é e P o u s s i n, La Morale Bouddhique (Paris, 1927) concerned mainly with Hīnayāna, and D. E. O b e r m i l l e r's Doctrine of Prajñāpāramitā (Acta Orientalia, XI) concemed exclusively with Mahāyān. Although the author treats Buddhsim mainly as *mārga*, these two very rich sources of information have apparently completely escaped his attention. Dr. E. Obermiller is at present issuing a further work on the same subject, vis. Analysis of the Abhisamayālaṃkāra (Calcutta Oriental Series)

importance of this principles has escaped the attention of our author. Therefore his work, notwithstanding all its other merits, must be considered as a failure to solve the puzzle of Buddhism. It is clear that we must look for a solution of that puzzle in another direction. We must fully realize the fact that Buddhism always has been not only a religion, but also a system of philosophy. It is *jñānamārga*.

We thus come to the problem of the basic conception of Buddhism as a problem of philosophy. We will look for it not in the emotional or religious field, but in the field of ontology. This philosophic basis of Buddhism however has several time changed. It is Pluralism in Hīnayāna, Monism in Mahāyāna, Relativism in the Mādhyamika and Idealism in the Yogācāra school.

We thus must turn our attention not only to philosophy, but also to history.

When the author posits the problem of a "basic" conception of Buddhism, he apparently seeks after a conception which is never changed and is to be found as the basis of every historical or even modern form of Buddhsim.

He therefore indiscriminately wanders through all sources accessible to him which go under the general stamp of some kind of Buddhism, and seeks to extract the general conception lying at their bottom. Historical treatment is quite foreign to him, unless we hold for such treatment the views expressed on pp. 1-10, where we find very interesting considerations on the store of ideas of the Vedic age out of which Buddhism arose. This want of historical treatment inside Buddhism, this treatment of all Buddhist literature *en bloc,* is a great defect of the otherwise very interesting work.

The want of an historical point of view makes the author recoil in astonishment before three quite contradicting statements. Being glibe assertions regarding all existing things, those statements bear the unmistakable stamp of being intended as basic (p.33). The one says "everything exists" (*sarvam asti*), the other maintains "nothing exists" (*sarvam śūnyam*), the third asserts, "mind only exists" (*vijñāna-mātram asti*). The author tries to find some solution in patching together these quite contradictory assertions. But he fails. By themselves these views are exclusive of one another, and cannot be reconciled unless treated historically. There is absolutely no hope to develop them out of the principle of desire-extinction. But historically we find that there are three kinds of Buddhism, the one maintaining that "everything exists," the other that "nothing exists" and the third that "all things are mind only."

These are the celebrated "three swingings of the law" as stated by the Tibetan historian, the first, the middle and the last we would tell, the three periods in the development of Buddhist philosophy, the first which arose in ancient Magdha in the sixth century B.C., and still exists in Ceylon and in Burma, the second which arose in the last centuries B.C in the Andhra country and was given a definte formulations by Nāgārjuna in the second century A.C., and the third which seems to have arisen in the North-west of the same time as the second and was given a definite formulation by Asaṅga of Peshwar in the fourth century A.D.

But how is it that these three quite different basic conceptions are all included in the general pale of Buddhism? Is there or is there not a conception still more basic which could serve as a starting point for all them?

Yes, there is such a conception. The author rightly points to the connection of *anātman* as the basic of all the forms of Buddhism. This is a conception which by itself needs not to be exclusively Buddhistic[1] but it is the basic in the sence of a starting point from which the historical development began and which has produced many modifications. Buddhism at the beginning is *anātma-vāda*, the theory of no-Soul or no-Self as the author translates the term. This is the conception from which all the later variety of theories developed and which till now is at the basis of that form of Buddhism which prevails in Ceylon and Burma, but which, according to the method of our author, must be the constant basis of all the forms of Buddhism.

Now what really means "no-soul" (*anātma*)? And how does it come that "no-soul" is the common basis of the three conflicting statements, "all exists," "nothing exists," "mind only exists"? It seems very difficult, even quite imposssible, "to develop them out of "no-Soul" and still more difficult to identify them with it. Moreover it is not at all true that all Buddhists believe in no-Soul. For it would be very strange if "no-Soul" had become the creed of almost all Asia. If it is not the creed of its mother country India, it is the creed of Tibet, Mongolia, China, Corea and Japan. They have borrowed it from India and if Vedānta be regarded as the fundamental creed of India at present, we have the testimony of Śrīharṣa that Vedānta does not differ in principle from Mādhyamika.[2] That means that it is also allied to Buddhism. The puzzle is great! The simple solution proposed by Mr. Bhattacharya will not help us.

---

1. Cf. below.
2. Cf. Khaṇḍana-khaṇḍa-khādya, pp. 19 and 29 (Chowkh.)— *Mādhyamikādi-vāgvyacahārāṇām svarūpāpalāpo na śakyate.*

We must distinguish between Buddhism as a religion and Buddhism as a philosophy.

Tradition, which we have no reason to disbelieve, maintains that Buddha himself had recourse to a double language. To the simple man he preached morality, to the educated men he taught philosophy. Buddhism has conquered the people of India and of almost all Asia by its noble and lofty moral ideals, and not by its no-Soul philosophy.

The religious masses in all Buddhist countries hardly have any idea of professing a no-Soul religion. They probably would be very much astonished if they were told that their religion is a no-Soul religion, just as some amature lady-scholars in Europe are astonished and unwilling to admit that Buddha preached no-Soul.

I therefore think that our author is on the wrong way, if he wished to solve the puzzle of no-Soul without either making a difference between religion and philosophy or between the different periods of Buddhist philosophy. The principle of no-Soul has an altogether different meaning. Grammatically and logically it can mean either no-Soul or non-Soul.[1] In the first case the term represents a simple negation (*prasajya-pratiṣedha*), in the second it is a qualified negation (*paryudāsa=apoha*) i.e. a negation which contains not alone its negative part, but also its positive counterpart. This positive counterpart is a positive assertion of those things which are the non-Soul.

Our author evidently conceives no-Soul as a simple negation (*prasajya-pratiṣedha*) whose aim it is to "pull down the very foundation of desire" and to create a condition where there is neither subject nor object.

However on the other view, the *paryudāsa* view, the term *anātman* means the real existence of all this except the Soul. We now understand the meaning of the first of the three dictums on which the basic conception of Buddhism has been expressed, "all exists". It means that all elements even the past and the future, the subtle and the visible, all exist, except the Soul.[2]

How are these all really existing things called? They are called *dharmas*. What does the term *dharma* mean? It means "quality". The qualities exists, but not the substances (*dharmin*), not the possessors of these qualities, not the *kāraka*. The Soul is supposed to be a thinking substance. This substance, according to Buddhism, does not exist, but

---

1. Cf. Aristotle's distinction between "non est homo justus" and "est homo non-justus."
2. Cf. my Central Conception of Buddhism, p. 25.

its supposed qualities, the mental phenomena all really exist. Which are they? They are first of all consciousness, pure consciousness (*vijñāna*). Nobody can deny its reality. Next to consciousness nobody can deny will (*cetanā*[1] =*saṃskārā*). Presentations (*saṃjñā*) or separate ideas are *dharmas,* nobody can deny their existence. There are finally feelings, (*vedanā*), the fellings of pleasure and pain, no one will deny their reality. We thus have a classification of all mental phenomena in four groups (*skandhas*), but there is no-Soul, no thinking substance among them. The author quotes (pp. 63-10) the very eloquent and precise statement of this theory in the Benares sermon by Buddha himself. Buddha goes through all the Elements of body and mind and finds in them only these Elements, but no possessor of the Elements, no Ego, no Soul. This sermon and this quotation should have suggested to the author the right meaning of the term no-Soul, but he seems to have kept past its real import and discovered here the mere repudiation of desire.[2]

---

1. The author is very gravely mistaken when he on p. 48 assumes that citta in Buddhism can be a synonym of *cetanā*. Synonyms are in Buddhism the three terms *cittam-mano-vijñāna* corresponding to *buddhir, upalabdhir, jñānam,* of N.S.I. 1, 15. Both triads are contrasted as synonyms (*anarthāntaram*), the one in Buddhism, the other in Nyāya. In Buddhism they are *vijñāna-skandha*. But *cetanā* is the foremost among *saṃskāras*. It belongs to *saṃkāra-skandha*. Every *dharma* (element can be envisaged as a *saṃskāra* (force) when it is considered as a cause, but *cetanā* is *saṃskāra* in the narrow sense, it is synonymous with *karma*, the driving force of the Universe. The author is also mistaken when he translates on p. 68 *saṃskāra* as "coefficient of consciousness." for such are only the *saṃskāras* of the *samprayukta* class, but by no means those of the *viprayukta* class. *Saṃskāra* is *sambhūya-kārin* i.e. coöperating force or force simply, since all forces in Buddhism are coöperating. The force Soxnv is cetanā "will". Cf. my Central Conception of Buddhism, pp. 20, 32, 100.

2. By the bye, this classification of all mental phenomena in four groups—feeling,, ideas, will and pure sensation—is an extraordinary important feature of all Buddhism. It does the highest credit to the philosophers who established it, it is in the full sense of the term "psychology without a Soul". It corresponds to a quite modern achievement of European Science. It compares most favouably with some modern and old European attempts to arrive at a correct classification of mental phenomena. Such a correct classification is a very important part of psychology and if we take the development of German psycholgy up to the classification of Brentano, the English ones up to that of B. Russel and French philosophy up to M.M. Bergson, we will be astonished to see that India possessed some centuries B.C. that classification which European philosophy arrives at only at a very recent date.

The main difference is this that the Indian classification distinguishes between pure sensation (*vijñāna-skandha*=*nirrikalpa-pratyakṣa*) and a presentation or concept (*saṃjñā-skandha*=*sarikalpa-pratyakṣa*). European science (W. James, B. Russel, etc., doubts whether sensation (*nirrikalpaka*) can be considered as really existing, as a separate element. The Abhidharma also maintains that it is *samprayukta*, i.e.. never appearing alone. But it plays an enormous part in all the history of Indian philosphy appearing there under different names, cf. my Buddhist Logic, I. p. 171.

These are the mental phenomena (*dharma*) as only realities accoring to the no-Soul theory. What about the physical world? Taking *ātmā* to mean substance,[1] is there any substance in the physical world? Under the physical world we must understand our body and the external physical objects. Does Matter exist as a substances? No! Matter exists only as sensible qualities (*dharmas*), sense-data, not as a substance possessing these qualities. The substance (*pradhāna*) does not exist, but the fundamental tactile qualities—repulsion, attraction, heat and motion (the four *mahābhūtas*) are the only fundamental physical facts which are cognizable. They are all classified as varieties of tactile "qualities" (*spraṣṭarya-dharma*). Besides these fundamental Elements of Matter (*mahābhūta*) there are other tactile Element, and there are the sense-data, e.g., the visible, auditory, olfactory and gustatory Element; colour, sound, odour and taste, but no substance, no Matter. Matter is *pradhāna*, this sterile, mute, indefinite enduring, omnipresent "something" which is supposed to be Matter (*vastu*); it does not exist. On the other hand the *dharmas* (mental and physical) exist, they are realities, they are the Elements of the existing world. Existing in the world are only its Elements, mental and physical, sensations and sense-data, but no enduring substances, neither Souls, nor Matter. The terms *dharma* (Element), *sat* (existent), *anitya* (unenduring), *kṣaṇa* (point-instant), *saṃskṛta* (causally produced), *pratītyasamutpanna* (dependently appearing) are synonyms. It is particularly remarkable that their meaning extends equally to mental as well as physical entities. They all refer to the ultimate, simplest, minutest, subtlest Elements of existence (*dharma*).

Now what is according to our author the meaning of the term *"dharma"?* It is very important to have to clear answer on this point since as we have seen, *anātma* (*as paryudāsa*) simply means the *dharma*-theory (*dharma-saṅketa*).

Since the author does not attach due importance to this term, he does not dwell upon its definition, but it is clear from his occasional statements on pp. 75-76 that he accepts the interpretations of *dharma* as "thing", as even "thing round us". It is time that this utterly wrong interpretation should be once for all dismissed and forgotten. *Dharma* is exactly the contrary of a thing, a thing is *dharmin*, a *dharma* is the contrary, it is a non-thing, it is a quality, not a substance, it is the negation of a substance.[2] Substance is *dharmin*, but not *dharma*.

---

1. Cp. Mādh. Vṛtti. 137—*āyms-śalala yaṁ svbhāva-śabda-paryāyaḥ.*

2. It is true that a quality being detached from every substance becomes a thing (*vidyamānam dravyam*), *sui generis*, or, more precisely, "something" and this would perhaps be an adequate translation of the term, it is *vastu-mātra*, an indefinite but pure reality, the ultimate, subtlest Element of reality, implying the negation of *samavāya*, of the relation of substance to quality altogether. But that is a very special standpoint—*yo hi padārtho vidyamānaḥ sa sasvabhāvaḥ*, cf. Mādh. Vṛtt. p. 760, cf. also my Central Conception etc., p. 26, n. 1.

A thing and a thing "round us" first of all means such things as jars and cloths etc. (*ghaṭa-paṭādi*), perhaps also such as cows and horses (*aśva-gavādi*). But is consciousness (*vijñāna*) a thing? Is it a thing round us? The will (*cetanā*), an idea (*saṃjñā*), feeling (*vedanā*)—are they things? But they are all *dharmas*. Admitting the jars and cloths, horses and cows can be called thing, is a horse a *dharma*, is the jar a *dharma*? Let it once for all be known that the jar is not a *dharma*, but an assemblage of *dharmas*.

An assemblage of what *dharmas*? First of all, it consists of a patch of colour (*varṇa*), the lines of its figure (*saṃsthāna*), of matter, i.e. the four phenomena of repulsion, cohesion, a certain temperature and nobility. They are all *dharmas* i.e. elements of the imagined complex called a jar. These *dharmas* together constitute the jar, but the jar is not a *dharma*, because it is an assemblage of *dharmas*. The principle that all things are assemblages of *dharmas*, that they themselves are non-*dharmas*, spurious *dharmas*, that only the ultimate Elements of the empirical things possess full reality, but not all these things themselves, is at the root of all Buddhism. It is a fundamental mistake to admit that the jar is a *dharma*. The jar as *dharmin* is an illusion. A man to whom this basic theory of Buddhism is not clear cannot undertake it to solve the fundamental puzzle of Buddhist philosophy. For not working what a *dharma* means, one never will arrive at a right comprehension of two other very important Buddhist terms, viz., the terms *pratītya-samutpāda*, "dependent origination" and *saṃskāra* (=*sambhūya-kāritva*), "co-operative production". *Dharmas* are infra-atomic minutest, very subtle, separate momentary unities of energy,[1] which are held together not by inherence in a substance, but by causal laws, laws of dependent origination. "Dependent origination" means origination of *dharmas*. Since every *dharma* (except the three eternal ones) is produced by a combination of several *dharma* in the preceding moment, it is called *saṃskṛta* as a product and *saṃskāra* as a cause. Without knowing what *dharma* is, it is quite impossible to have a correct and adequate idea of what *pratītya-samutpāda* and *saṃskāra* are in early Buddhism.

In the later periods the meaning of these three fundamental terms has shifted, but shifted simultaneously in a parallel change.

---

1. Since the four *mahā-bhūtas* are not substances but forces (repulsion, attraction, heat and motion) it is clear that the Buddhist atoms cannot be like the atoms of the Vaiśeṣikas absolutely hard and indivisible particles of matter. The *saṃghāta-paramāṇu* although consisting of 8 parts is not larger or heavier than the simple one. just as a neddle will not become heavier if it becomes hot. i.e. if 'atoms' of the element heat are added to it or get intensified in it.

When the meaning of *dharma* in the Mādhyamika school has changed, the meaning of *pratītya-samutpāda* and of *saṃskāra* has also changed. The same happened in the Yogācāra school.

Thus the basic conception of Buddhist philosophy is *anātma*, but *anātma* in the sense of *reality* of all *dharmas* among which no *ātman* is to be found. Buddhism is a system of philosophic Pluralism, *anātmavāda* means at the beginning the same as *sarvāstivāda*, the reality of all Elements (*dharmas* among which no-Soul and no substance, no things are to be found, it is a pluralistic and realistic psychology without a Soul; *anātma-vāda, sarvāsti-vāda, dharma-vāda* or *dharma-saṅketa* means the same. It is also synonymous with *pratītya-samutpāda* or *saṃskāravāda*, because every *dharma* can be a *saṃskāra* and is *pratītya-samutpanna*.

We thus can consider the following expressions as synonymous and referring to the basic conception of Buddhism: *anātma-vāda=dharma-vāda=dharmatā=dharma-saṅketa=pratītya-samutpāda-vāda=saṃskāra-vāda=saṅghāta-vāda=bauddha-matam*.

Whosoeven wishes to translate *dharma* in whatsoever a language must choose a phrase which would imply (i) plurality (*saṅghāta*) and (ii) denial of substance. The term "thing" misses the point because it implies rather the assertion by no means the denial of *dharmin*. Moreover, and this is the main point, it must be applicable to the physical as well as to the mental domain. The term "element" seems to me preferable, although of course it is also not quite free from defects.[1]

Basic ideas of Sāṃkhya and Buddhism compared

We will perhaps better understand the basic ideas of Buddhism if we compare them with the basic ideas of the Sāṃkhya system. The difference between them is great, but there is unquestionably a family likeness. Just as every empirical thing or every living being, according to Sāṃkhya, is an assemblage of minutest infra-atomic Elements, more forces than substances, which are called "qualities" (guṇa), just so in Buddhism the empirical things and living beings are assemblages of momentary infra-atomic, very subtle unities or forces, which are also called "qualities" (*dharmas*).

1. Prof. H. Jacobi has rallied to the translation of the term *dharma* as an "element of existence," "Seins element," cf. his triṃsikā-vijñapti "uberstzt von Hermann Jacobi (Stuttgart, 1932). Prof. Sylvain Lévi's rendering of *dharma* as "essence" (cf. Matériaux Vijñaptimātra, Paris 1932) is not very much different, it hits the right point, namely that it is *dharma* as opposed to *dharmin*. Remains it for Frenchmen to decide whether such expressions as "les essences de la cruche" or "les essence de la personalité" would be found equally conveninet phrasing. We want a term that would be equally applicable to the mental as well as to the physical domain and would express plurality.

It is a fundamental feature of the Indian mind in general and a firm tradition of all Indian science to be always on the search after invisible, subtlest, infra-atomic, dynamical elements or forces, whose operation produces the visible phenomena of our experience.

What are the so-called "oppressors" or *kleśas*. Are they really oldest Indian science? Are they really "wind, bile and phlegm" as *vāta-pitta-kapha* are often translated? These are only conventional names for very subtle infra-atomic three forces whose equipoise produces health.

What are the four "Great Elements" of Matter? Are they really what their names imply: earth, water, fire and air? They are the forces of repulsion, attraction, heat and nobility, each of them some subtlest energy manifested in tactile phenomena.

What are the elements of grammer? There are invisible suffixes, the so-called *kvipś*, which are active forces forming words.

What are the *dharmā-dharmān* or *karma* which is even called *adṛṣṭa?* It is an invisible force of our former deeds.

What are the so-called "oppressors" or *kleśas*. Are they really "love, hatred and infatuation," as they usually are translated or are they something quite different? One must consider that the extinction of *kleśas* not only makes a man dispassionate, but converts him into a Buddha, hence it converts phenomenal life into the absolute. The *saṃkleśas* are the 12 *nidānas*[1] or phenomenal life as contrasted with the absolute and produced by transcendental illusion (*avidyā=mukhyā bhrāntiḥ*). The *kleśas* are therfore transcendental forces creating and controlling phenomenal life (*saṃsāra*).

What are the *guṇas* of the Sāṃkhya system? Are they really 'goodness,' 'passion' and 'darkness' as *sattva, rajas* and *tamas* are somtimes translated? They are infra-atomic quanta of three different energies whose interplay produces the phenomenal world, both physical and mental.

Now what are the *dharmas* of the Buddhist? As already stated *dharma* means the same as *guṇa* i.e. quality.[2] What is hidden under this designation? There is no mystery, the whole catalogue containing 75 items is presented to you. They first of all are 5 sense-organs, 5 corresponding categories of sense-data and that is all for the physical world. No mysterious Matter! For the mental world there is consciousness as pure consciousness and corresponding to it mental

---

1. Cf. Madhyāntav. p. 29 ff. (ed. Tucci).
2. This meaning has been established by Dr.B.Seal in his *Positive Science of the Hindus.*

phenomena, ideas, feeling, will and different kinds of emotions or mental forces (*saṃprayukta-saṃkāra*), their list contains 46 items.

There are other forces which are general, neither physical nor mental (*rūpa-citta-viprayukta-saṃskāra*), e.g. the forces of production and destruction applicable to both spheres. They are therefore neither specially mental nor specially physical, but general. Their list contains 14 items. Space (*ākāsa*) is a *dharma*. Time, however, is not a *dharma*. What does it mean that it is not a *dharma*? It means that it does not exist. Duration does not exist. Time is past, present and future. The past does not exist, because it is past. The future does not exist, because it is future. Remains the present moment which alone exists, but it also does not exist separately from the thing existing at that moment. A *dharma* is a separate (*pṛthag*) thing, a Thing-in-itself (*svalakṣ-aṇa)*. Thus space, as empty space, is a *dharma*, but time is not. The full catalogue of *dharmas* contains 75 items in the Sarvāstivāda school.

They are alone the *dharmas*; there is apparently no mystery, there ought to be no mystery. The mystery comes from the fact that the *dharmas* are physical and mental at the same time just as the *guṇas* of the Sāṃkhyas, they are the ultimately real. Their synonym is the real (*sat*). The real lying at the bottom of every phenomenon, whether physical or mental, is a *dharma* and this is a mystery! Sthirmati says that in Hīnayāna a *dharma* is the ulimate reality (*pariniṣpanna*).[1] Vasu bandhu recording the controversies which raged in the schools on the problem of the essence of *dharmas,* says that they are something very deep or subtle.[2] They are also infra-atomic, dynamic unities of forces of Elements, whose inter-dependence according to casual laws (*pratītya-samutpāda*) constitutes the illusive objects of our phenomenal life.[3] Sāṃkhya admits besides the moving *guṇas* a motionless (*niṣkriya*) Soul. This Soul is degraded in Buddhism, it is converted into simple consciousness (*vijñāna*) which is also a *dharma*, an Element having the same sense as all other Elements. In Buddhism as well as in Sāṃkhya the human personality consists of an infinite number of point-instants of *guṇas* of *dharmas* which are held together in Sāṃkhya by a pervading Matter (*pradhāna*) and an eternal Soul in Buddhism exclusively by casual laws (*pratītya-samutpāda*).

The individual, according to Sāṃkhya, consists of a Soul enveloped for the time of *saṃsāra* in Matter, which consists of eternally moving minutest elements (*guṇas*) of three different kinds. The process

---

1. Madhyāntav, p. 27. (ed. Tucci).
2. Ab. Kośa, V. 27.
3. Cf. below, p. 27 (*a*) n. 3.

of the Deliverance of the Soul from the embracement of Matter consists in the gradual purification and pacification of the *guṇas* through knowledge. When absolute knowledge is attained, the Soul alone remains in the genuine purity and freedom.

The Buddhist conception of an individual can be imagined as a large circle filled with point-instants of different kinds. Inside the large circle of point-instants united by causality, there is no Soul, but a small island filled with *ānāsrava-dharma*, or Elements which are eternally tranquilised, motionless and pure. They never will be sullied by passion and turmoil.

As long as the process of purification from desire goes on, the turmoil of moving Elements gradually subsides and gets pacified. Finally all will become *anāsrava*. Nirvāṇa will be attained.

In both systems, as we have seen, phenomenal life is represented as a bondage and as a beginningless commotion of minutest infra-atomic particles charged with some energy. In both systems the theory of salvation offers many points of similarity. In both systems there is at the bottom of every personal life an element of purity which is concealed and eneveloped by the commotion of the impurity of phenomenal life. In both systems this life is regarded as burden (*duḥkha*) and liberation from it is the aim of the doctrine. In both systems this is expressed in the formula of the "four principles of the saint" (*catvāriāryasatyāni*). Remaining faithful to its pluralistic principles, Buddhism has replaced the pure Soul of the Sāṃkhya by a plurality of pure elements (*anāsrava-dharma*) and by a complete extinction (*nirodha*) of all life in Nirvāṇa. The annexed chart can to a certain degree represent the comparative outlook of both systems very far from being "things," still less the things "round us," as jars, cows and horses etc., and the *dharmas* are something "very deep", some thing "inexplicable,"[1] something transcendental, the ultimate reality that can be ascertained by philosophic analysis. They can be characterized just as the *guṇas* of the Sāṃkhyas are characterized in an old document,[2] "their ultimate reality trancends the domain of the

1. *drañ-bar-mi-nus-so=bśad-par-mi-nus-so,* op. Ab. Kośa, I. 27, M.de La Vallée Poussin's not in his translation and my Central Conception etc., p. 91..

2. Vyāsa-bhāṣya quotes this couplet from Ṣaṣṭitantra,—

गुणानां परमं रुपं न दृष्टिपथमृच्छति ।
यतु दृष्टिपथं प्राप्तं तन्मायेव सुतुच्छकम् ॥

sensible the objects which are contained in the domain of the sensible are Illusion,[1] they are quite in one."

In Mahāyāna "the ultimate reality which transcends the domain of the sensible" is qute different. Mahāyāna is monistic, the ultimate reality is there called "*parinispanna*," the ultimate or perfect reality. "How is a unity (i.e. Monism) converted into a plurality?" asks Sthiramati[2] and answers "plurality is mere illusion."[3] Only for those philosophers "who assume that the *dharmas* are ultimate realities, only for them, would it be a contradiction to maintain unity and plurality at the same time. But for those who do not assume the ultimate relaity of *dharma*,[3] scripture must not be interpreted in that sense." It is clear from this passage the Sthiramati opposes Hīnayāna and Mahāyāna as Pluralism and Monism. It is also clear that the Hīnayāna the *dharmas* were considered as a plurality of ultimate realities, as a plurality of *parinispanna* Elements while in Mahāyana all this plurality is merged into one single monistic ultimate reality which alone is designated by the term *parinispanna* and its synonyms *tathahā, bhūtakoṭi, animittaḥ, paramārthaḥ, dharmadhātuḥ, śūnyatā* ect.

A long time since, when comparatively little was known of Buddhism, Professor Hermann Jacobi made an attempt to deduce some basic Buddhist ideas out of the Sāṃkhya system.[4] He compared the *tattras* of the Sāṃkhyas with the 12 *nidānas* of Buddhism and noticing some points of similarity he thought it possible to deduce the latter out of the former. This attempt, in the form in which it was initially proposed has been dropped, but it became the starting point of a long

---

1. Prof. R. Garbe writing in 1892 thought it a great merit on the part of Prof. H. Oldenberg to have established that early Buddhism is realistic. He says "the world of the objects is as real for Buddha as it is real for Kapila" (cp. Introd. to his trans. of Sāṃkhya-tattva-kaumudī, p. 10). This would imply, if taken literally, the reality of objects or things, of jar and cows etc. However these objects are illusions (*śūnya*). Oldenberg had the right impression of the realism of Hīnayāna as compared with the illusinism of Mahāyāna, but the *dharma*-theory was quite unknown to him, he confounded the reality of *dharmas*, i.e. of mere Sense-data with the reality of things (*dharmins*). He did not realize the import of the principle *sarvam asti*, he did not know that it refers to the reality of the 12 *āyatanas* alone, (cp. my Central Conception etc., p. 90) and the 12 *āyatanas* are a classification of Elements alone, not of things. He did not know the difference between *dharma-nairātmya* and *pudgala-nairātmya*.

2. कथमेकं विचित्रं cp. Madhyāntav., p. 26.

3. Ibid.— योहि (i.e. the Mahāyānist) धर्मविशावम परितिष्पन्नमिच्छति ......

4. Der Ursprung des Buddhismus aus dem Sāṃkhya-Yoga, gött, Nachrichten. 1896. pp. 1 ff., continued in a further article " Ueber das Verhältniss der Buddhistischen Philosophie zum Sāṃkhya-Yogaud die Bedantung der Nidāna. ZDMG., 52. 1 ff.

discussion in which a number of the leading scholars of Europe participated. It is now more or less generally admitted that the Sāṃkhya system preceded Buddhism in time and constitutes its philosophic basis. It is impossible to speak about the basic ideas of Buddhism without comparing it with Sāṃkhya ideas. According to Prof. R. Pischel[1] "theoretical Buddhism reposes entirely on Sāṃkhya Yoga," "it has borrowed from Sāṃkhya-Yoga almost everything." "Budda has converted into a religion what his teachers had taught before as a philosophy." Prof. H. Oldenberg who at first was unwilling to admit so powerful an influence, accepted later on this opinion in a more moderate form. The thought that "we have ample right to call Sāṃkhya that doctrine which appears as the remote, if not the nearest, background of the fundamental ideas of Buddhism."[2] Prof. R. Garbe[3] fully rallies to this opinion and lays stress upon the fact that Sāṃkhya preceded Buddhism not in the shape of detached ideas, but as a complete, closed system. He enumerates[4] seven points of detail where the similarity seems to him quite convincing. Under point No. 5 we meet here the *anātman* which thus proves to be, in its origin, a Sāṃkhya and not a Buddhist idea. Oldenberg also makes the following remarks:— "When Buddhism repeatedly and constantly laid great stress on the changing and fleeting character of the world process,—the constant change also of feelings, ideas etc. in which no self (*ātmam, attā*) is contained,—this was a Sāṃkhya doctrine." M. E. Senart[5] assumed a still greater in fluence of Sāṃkhya on Buddhism. He however limited it to the practical teaching of the path to Salavation and made Buddhism more dependent on the Yoga than on Sāṃkhya. He maintains that the Yoga shared indeed the speculative doctrines of the Sāṃkhya, but Buddhism could stand very near to Yoga without sharing its philosophy (*tout en divergeont sur les philosophimes purs*). Senart thought that early Buddhism was not philosophic (*incapable d' im effort de logiqne suivie et consciente*), but he could not think otherwise since at that time the *dharma*-theory was quite unknown to him and consequently the meaning of *pratītya-samutpāda* and its contrast with the *pariṇāmavāda* of Sāṃkhya could not be understood. Indeed he assumed the identity of these thories. We thus have the authority of Professors

---

1. Lebeen, u. Lehre des Buddha, seconded by Lüders. pp. 22, 62, 65, 67, 69, 75.
2. Die Lehre der upanishaden u. die Aufänge des Buddhismus (1915), p. 318.
3. Die Sāṃkhya Philosophie, 2 (nd) ed. p. 10.
4. Der Mondshein der Sāṃkhya Wahrheit (München, 1892) pp. 9-10.
5. Bouddhisme et Yoga. in Revne de l' histoire des religions, v. 42, 1900, pp. 345 ff.

Jacobi, Oldenberg, Pischel, and Garbe in favour of the opinion that the doctrine of *anātman* was initially a Sāṃkhya idea.[1] Later on in the run of centuries it had lost its unorthodox character. Of course the *anātma* doctrine is for them not much than the fleeting and constantly changing character of feelings, ideas and notions. The *dharma*-theory, in its full extent, was also completely unknown to them and the meaning of *dharma* as a technical term appeared as a riddle.[2] Nor was the *guṇas* theory of Sāṃkhya sufficiently understood, nay even the translation of the terms *sattva, rajas* and *tamas* remained fluctuating and a series of hypotheses on their meaning and their origin, mythological and foreign, were proposed.[3] It seemed also a contradiction that the Hindus themselves should Sāṃkhya for an eternalist doctrine (*śāśvata-vāda*). Indeed the Hindus assume that Sāṃkhya is diametrically opposed to Buddhism. They admit the existence of two "radical doctrines" (*ekāntā-darśana*) in principle opposed to one another, the one maintianing that "everything is eternal" (*sarvam nityam*),[4] the other, on the contrary, asserting that "everything is non-eternal (*sarvam anityam*"),[5] the first is Sāṃkhya, the second is Buddhism. This contradiction disappears when one realizes that the difference refers to the theories of causations adopted by each system. In Sāṃkhya everything is eternal since it represents the manifestation of one eternal Matter; although these manifestation are eternally-changing (*nitya-pariṇāmin*), they are eternally the same in their material cause (*kāraṇa-avasthāyām*).[6] In Buddhism there is no eternal Matter, the manifestations are detached (*pṛthag*) momentary *dharmas*,

---

1. It means in Sāṃkhya just as it means in Buddhism exactly the same, namely "everything except the Soul," it is a *paryudāsa-negation,* an affirmation of the reality of the non-soul; whatsover exists, i.e. changes and lives, belongs to the domain of the non-Soul, "das alles jenas Pliessen ganz und gar im Bereich des Nicht-Selbest varläuft" (Oldenberg, Buddha,[2] pp. 331-332). Of course the Sāṃkhya System assumed a separate lifeless Soul, this Soul, this Soul being *niskriya* was rejected by the Buddhists just as they rejected *ākāśa, pradhāna,* time, space and other imagined entities.

2. The fist systematic attempt to understand this term was made by Mrs. Magdalene and Wilhem Geiger, in *Pāli Dharma* (Munich, 1921).

3. The *guṇa* theory as the main or central Sāṃkhya doctrine has been fully disclosed by Dr. B. N Seal in his "Positive Sciences of the Hindus" and by Prof. S. N. Dasgupta in his "Study of Patañjali" (Calcutta, 1920) and other works.

4. Nyāya-sūtra, IV, 1. 29.

5. Ibid., IV. 1. 25.

6. In Sāṃkhya virtually there is no intrinsic difference among things, *sarvcam sarvātmakam,* the change of the collocation of atoms only changes potentiality into actuality. Just as in Leibnitzens's system every monad is the mirror of the universe, just so in Sāṃkhya every point instant is "identical" with the eternal and ubiquitous whole. Cp. Dasgupta, The Study of Patañjali, p. 79.

appearing in functional interdependence upon one another (*pratītya-samutpāda*).[1] Thus it is that notwithstanding the unmistakable affinity between the *guṇa*-theory and the *dharma*-theory the two systems to which they belong and in which they play the leading part are diametrically opposed to one another, the one being called Evolution (*pariṇāma-vāda*), the other Functional Interdependence (*pratītya-samutpāda-vāda*). Here as always the history of philosophy evolves by contrasts. It is a general rule in the history of philosophy that every new departure starts in opposition to reigning ideas, but at the same time it creates the new on the basis of the old. Causation as Functional Dependence (*pratītya-samutpāda-vāda*) is unquestionably the new departure of Buddhism. It implies the negation of *pariṇāma-vāda*, which is the Sāṃkhya theory of Causation, asserting "identity" (*tādātmya*) between cause and effect. The first is *a-sat-kārya-vāda*, the second is *sat-kārya-vāda*. But the *dharma* theory of the Buddhists seems only to be a far going modification of the *guṇa*-theory of the Sāṃkhya, a modification made necessary by the change in the theory of Causation. The *guṇas* are Elements or qualities which are "identical" with Matter; the *dharma* are separate Elements.[2] Whatsoever the indirect antecedents of the *guṇa*-theory may have been in the Upaniṣads or in mythology, its definite aim in the Sāṃkhya system is to bridge over the gulf between Mind and Matter. According to this theory a physical phenomenon and a mental one are equally composed out of minutest infra-atomic quanta of three different stuffs, or forces, the Intelligence (or nervous) stuff, Energy-stuff and Inertia-stuff. The first is predominant in a mental phenomenon, the last in physical one. In an idea or a feeling, e.g., the nervous stuff is more active, matter ro inertia is in abeyance. In a plant or in a stone the last is predominant, the first is in abeyance. Energy is constantly being liberated and absorbed. There is therefore no stability at all, everything is moving and instantaneous (*kṣaṇika)*. But although being momentary flashes of instantaneous infra-atomic quanta charged with some energy, the *guṇas* and the phenomena composed by them are said to be ubiquitous and eternal (*vibhu, nitya*). As already stated they are eternal in their causal or potential condition (*kāraṇāvasthāyām*) as absorbed

---

1. These two opposite and contrasting theories, implying the one as the negation of the other have nevertheless often been identified as long as the *dharma*-theory was not understood. In the Yogācāra system *prtitya-samutpāda* is retained only by name, it has become *pariṇāma-vāda* as is quite clear from the initial passage of the *Triṃśikā*. The Chinese tradition is conscious of the difference and calls it *ālaya-pratītya-samutpāda*, cp. Demieville, in *Materiaux Vijñaptimātra*, p. 34, but virtually it is *pariṇāma-vāda*.

2. *Sarvam pṛthag, sarvam, nānā, na kaścit eko bhāvo vidyate*, cp. N. Sūtra, IV, 1, 34.

in an eternal, primordial Matter. At that early period of Indian philosophy when the *guṇa*-theory was being philosophically founded, it is more than probable that the atomic structure of Matter must have been discussed.[1] It is probable that at that early epoch there was a division of opinion. The Jains and some pre-Vaiśeṣika system joined the Materialists and began to assume indivisible atoms whereas the Sāṃkhyas and some pre-Buddhists philosophers decided for infinite divisibility. Although later on the Buddhists assume the existence of atoms, they deny their indivisibility. Their atoms are therefore no atoms at all, they are *dharma* i.e. "qualities" absolute qualities, qualities without any stuff. That the Buddhist atoms cannot by any stuff is a direct consequence from the character of their four fundamental Elements of Matter (*mahā-bhūta*). Although called earth, water, five and air, it is clearly stated that these are only conventional designations and that he four forces of repulsion, attraction, heat and motion are meant by these terms. Vasubandhu states that only the last of these names is adequate, because the Sanskrit term *samīraṇa* means both air and motion. Just as Berkley thought that space is presented to us in our sensuous experience of "resistanc" to organic movement, just so the Buddhists at an early date defined matter as mainly the phenomenon (resistance of *saprati ghatra*). At the early date Buddhism contained already the germs of that Idealism into which it later on developed. At that date Hīnayāna or Sarvāstivāda maintained in general that all realisable ideas must be either concrete data of sense (*bāhya-āyatana*) or concrete data of invalid consciousness (*abhyantara-āyatana*). Substance, whether Spirit or Matter, was denied every separate reality. Both categories, the inward as well as the outward data, were called *dharmas* i.e. non-substances, absolute qualities. This designation evidently also aimed at bridging over the gulf between Matter and Mind, not however by assuming an equal composition, but by assuming their parallelism, their equal status.[2] This psycho-physical parallelism was indeed quite natural, because according to the Buddhist theory of Causality (*pratītya-samutpāda*) there is a general parallelism between all elements of existence (*asmin sati idam bhavati*). Moreover, in marked opposition to the Sāṃkhya tenet that everything is eternal, because Matter is eternal, the Buddhists maintained that nothing is eternal (*sarvam anityam*), because substance does not exist. Existent are only "qualities," i.e., realisable data of sensuous

---

1. Prof. H. Jacobi (art. Atomism in ERE) attaches much importance to the silence of Pāli Suttas and to the denial of atomism by the Vedāntins, Mahāyānists and Sāṃkhyas. But this denial refers to the Vaiśeṣika. eternal atoms and does not refer to those systems who had a dynamic or semi-dynamic theory of Matter. The *tanmātras* are evidently also some kind of atoms or infra-atoms.

2. This psycho-physical parallelism is called by Vasubandhu. Ab. Kośa. I. 45 Sanskrit word.

experience and of inward consciousness (*dharmas*). Therefore the terms Element (*dharma*) and the term "existent" (*sat*) have become synonyms. Thus although *dharma* is a general term embracing both categories of data, assumes a separation between Mind and Body, but only because it assumes a separation between all Elements in general (*sarvam pṛthag*), there is no identity between them at all, and no inherence (*samavāga*) is whatsoever a substance. The idea which the Buddhists made of an Element as an exteral *dharma* is most clearly seen from the manner in which they explain the phenomenon of acceleration in a falling body.[1] Every body is composed of "atoms" ot infra-atomic quanta of four kinds of energy" resistance, attraction, heat and motion. They all are present in every body, in the same propotion, but their intensity (*utkarṣa*) can be different. When a body falls, its quanta of motor energy are intensified. At every moment the falling body is otherwise composed. It is clear from this that the *dharmas* are not "things," but "elements" of things.

Dharma, the basic conception of Buddhism

That the conception of *dharmạ* is the basic conception of Buddhism is most clearly and pregnantly expressed by the Buddhists themselves in their old *credo—Ye dharmā hetuppabhavā*........This formula which professedly contains the shortest statement of the essence and spirit of Buddhism, declares that Buddha discovered the Elements (*dharmā*) of existence, their causal connection (*hetu=pratītya-samutpāda*) and a method to suppress their efficiency for ever (*nirodha*). We have seen that *dharma*, *pratītya-samutpāda* and *anātma* are only different expressions of one and the same idea of philosophic pluralism which is also called *skandha-vāda*. This Buddhist *credo* embraces all the three varieties of Buddhism with some difference of implication. Generally the phrase means—Buddha established the Elements (*Ye dharmā*) which are causally produced (*ketu-ppabhavā=pratītya-samutpannā*) and which are extinguished (*nirodha*) in Nirvāṇa. In Hīnayāna it implies that all Elements are inter-related and real. That is the genuine *pratītya-samutpāda*, Pluralism. In the Mādhyamika system it implies that all Element, being interdependent, can not be intrinsically real by themselves (*svabhāvena*), they are relatively real (*svabhāvena śūnya*). This is the *śūnyatā-pratītya-samutpāda* or *advaya-vāda,* Monism. In the Yogācāra-system a further implication is added, viz., "all Elements are relative, except one, viz. Pure consciousness (*vijñaptimātratā*) which is Absolute. This is the *ālaya-pratityasamutpāda*, Idealism.

1. Cf A.b. Kośa, II. 46 and my Buddhist Logic, I. 101.

As to the intrinsic philosophic value of early Buddhsim, in that form in which it was shaped in the school of the Sarvāstivādins, Professor Stanislav Schayer delivers himself in the following words:—

"This system is by itself a very important subject of scientific. investigation and can be placed on the same level as the great speculative systems of Greece, of the Christian middle ages and of modern Europe."[1]

This textimony from an authoritative pen which has the right to speak in the name of European philosophy can be supplemented by the opinion of a man who without being a professional philospher had nevertheless a life long intimacy with Buddhist ideas to the study of which he devoted his life. He thus summarizes the basic idea of Buddhism which, we have seen, is the *anātma*-theory, as the pluralistic *dharma*-theory but not *anātma* as extinguishing of desire.

"Buddhism,' says he, "stands alone among the religions of India in ignoring the Soul. The vigour and originality of this new departure are evident from the complete isolation in which Buddhism stands in this respect, from all other religious systems then existing in the world. And the very great difficulty which those European writers who are still steeped in animistic preconceptions find in appreciating or even understanding the doctrine, may help us to realize how difficult it must have been for the origination of it to take so decisive and so far-reaching a step in philosophy and religion at so early a period in the history of human thought...........The doctrine of impermanence of each and every condition, physical or mental; the absence of any abiding principle, any entity, any *sub*-stance, any "Soul" is treated from the numerous points of view from which it can be approached, in as many different Suttas."[2]

We do not at all intend to minimize the importance of Buddhist ethics, of *mārga*, of "extinguishing of desire." But this ethical doctrine, it deprived from its philosophic or ontological foundation, is more or less similar in many systems. The author himself lays tress upon the fact that its aim is the same as the aim of the sages of the Upaniṣads. The originality of Buddhism consists in its *anātma-vāda,* and *anātma-vāda* is the same as *dharma-vāda*. The other name of *dharma-vāda* theory is *pratītya-samutpāda-vāda,* and that of *pratītya-samutpāda-vāda,* is *saṃskāra-vāda*. The terms *dharma, pratītya-samutpāda* and *saṃskāra*, if rightly interpreted, bear witnesss to that powerful effort of the human mind which was produced early in the history of India and has received the name of Buddhism.

1. Stanislav Schayer, Ausgewählte Kapitel aus der Prasannopadā (Krakow, 1931), p. XII.
2. T. W. Rhys Davids, Dialogue v. II, p. 212.

Chapter - 14

Buddhism and Vedānta

Bratindra Kumar Sengupta

It has been seen in the history of human thought that man's resolve to avoid philosophical dialecticism has ended in the development of new dialectics in subsequent periods. The reason for this is to be found in the human nature which is a rational bed-rock of speculations and, therefore, does not stop short in all-too-credulous and dogmatic philosophy. The silence and the unsaid of previous philosophers are re-oriented in their subsequent eras and even their sayings are put to severe dialecical tests thus giving birth to a new philosophy. Exactly such has been the position of the teachings of Gautama, the Buddha of India, who flourished in the sixth century B.C., and propagated his ennobling and sanctifying rays of wisdom which in the course of centuries illumined millions of souls all over the world. But Buddha's repeated insistence on non-indulgence in abstruse and recondite paths of dialecticism to prove or disprove that which is beyond experiences and therefore non-describable (*anirvacanīya*) fell flat on the ears of his later followers and preachers. They plunged themselves into endless dialectic through the course of centuries and began to discover hidden meanings in Buddha's tacit philosophy. Thus they gave birth to various schools, which were later carried on to extremities of theologico-ethical speculations, but were mainly divided on one or the other of the inttinsic metaphysical theories gradually evolved. These metaphysical theories can be divided into four broad classes: viz., (1) the Mādhyamikas (Negationalists[1]), (2) the Yogācāras (Subjective Idealists), (3) the Sautrāntikas (Representationists or Critical Realists) and (4) the Vaibhāṣikas (Direct Realists). These schools have developed their own

1. We purposely use this expression and not the common expression Nihilists', for, as will be shown, nihilism is not the Mādhyamika metaphysic.

metaphysico-epistemological theories in the course of ages and thus made Buddhism a recondite system of philosophy. Their religio-moral predilections were also later synthesised and adopted in special languages and countries and thus grew up localised schools which, however, come under the two great religio-moral ones known by the name of Mahāyāna and Hīnayāna. The former is the Buddhism of the North—of China, Tibet, Japan, and the Buddhism of Sanskrit works with their local translations. The latter is the Buddhism of the South—of Ceylon, Burma, Siam, and the Buddhism of Pali language with its expositions in the local texts. These two broad divisions developed numerous sub-schools mainly on religio-moral customs and traditions. Metaphysically speaking, Mahāyāna Buddhism accepts the tenets of Mādhyamika and Yogācāra Schools and Hīnayāna Buddhism those of Sautrāntika and Vaibhāṣika Schools. This in a nutshell is the origin, development and principles of the schools of Buddhism.

The Vedānta philosophy is the most profound, sublime and cogent tradition in the orthodox Indian systems. It is, as its name implies, the culmination ('anta') of the Vedas, the culmination not only in literary strata but in metaphysical consummation. The Upaniṣ ads of the different schools of the Vedas along with their Āraṇyakas became the fitting *denonement* to the high-strung philosophical tradition of the Vedic literature from its earliest periods. Hence this system of the Upaniṣads bears the significant name of Vedānta. The Upaniṣadic doctrines were systematized by Bādarāyaṇa in his *Brahma-sūtra* or *Vedānta-sūtra* or *Śarīrakamīmāṁsā-sūtra* which gradually became the *forte* of Vedānta. In course of ages this cryptic systematization of Bādarāyaṇa came to be interpreted in different lights by philosophers of different shades of opinion and thus grew up an enormous ramification of the schools of Vedānta. As in Buddhism the original teachings of the Master were interpreted in later ages differently in different schools thus giving rise to cobwebs of meta-physical and dialectical subtleties so much so that entirely new philosophies of speculation grew up though not severed from the original doctrines of moral and spiritual progress, so also the Vedānta philosophy in course of ages became divrsified into many schools having entirely new speculations even if it had its firm roots in the doctrines of the Upaniṣads and the system of Bādarāyaṇa. Thus we have the absolute monistic interpretations of Śaṅkara, of qualified monistic interpretations of Rāmānuja and even dualistic interpretations of Madhva, Vallabha and Nimbārka with sub-schools developing within these schools according to further elaborations of the absolute monistic standpoint of complete identity ('abheda') between the individual self (Jīva) and the Ultimate Self (Brahman), between the empirical and the transcendental nature of the soul, or of the qualified monistic standpoint of identity-in-difference ('bhedābheda') or of complete difference ('bheda') between them. In this paper we, however, propose to undertake a study of Buddhism particularly in its Mahāyāna aspects and of Vedānta mainly in its Śaṅkarite interpretations, thus discovering where the great masters showed a communion of minds with regard to the transcendental Reality which they named differently and wherein also lay the points of departure, and how far their philosophies grappled with the problem of final liberation in their peculiar metaphysical conceptions of it.

The Mādhyamika school of Buddhism advocates the doctrine of *śūnya* or *mahāśūnya* and their entire metaphysic is based on the exposition of *śūnyatā*. This doctrine has, however, been subject to much misrepresentation and misinterpretation at the hands of later Indian and Western writers. *Śūnyavāda* had been held to be a kind of nihilism where the ultimate Reality has been equated with a great void and has been bereft of any reality at all. But if we look into the Mādhyamika interpretations of *śūnyatā* we find that such a theory is farthest from the intentions of this school. *Śūnyatā* does not mean anything void as the ultimate Reality. It means only the indescribable nature of the ultimate Reality which is not dependent on any causal series. All the phenomena of the universe are dependent in origin and existence upon others, but the real nature of these phenomena is beyond all *dharmas* (characters) and therefore independent. The very fact of its being independent, of lying beyond the causal series, of being outside the ken of discursive intellect, constitutes the very nature of *Śūnya*, and this fact has been accepted as the ultimate metaphysic in the Mādhyamika school. This *śūnyatā* is nevertheless he real nature of things (*tathatā*) which is indeterminate and indescribable by causal categories. The series of causal categories determines the existence of the phenomenal world, all the objects which are dependent on others in their origin. This theory of origination (*pratītya-samutpāda*) is one of the bedrocks of Buddhistic golden mean. It declares that every event is within the causal series and there are no leaps in nature. Nature presupposes a causal series to explain the origin and existence of her phenomena. Any event (effect) is preceded by another (cause) and in itself is the cause of another. Thus the eternal cycle of causes and effects is going on in the world and everything terrestrial is necessarily transitory. This theory avoids, on the one hand, the extreme of absolute reality and, on the other, that of absolute unreality of the phenomenal world. The world is not an eternal reality independent of any conditional existence, nor is it a great void without anything left behind in the causal series. The phenomenal nature is in a state of eternal flux no doubt, but is not on that account a great void. It is before our eyes, but on that account not the alpha and omega. So long we think of it, it is to be spoken of in terms of dependent origination. But when we think of the *real* nature of it, it is beyond all dependence, an indescribable, indeterminate and transcendental existence where the *pratītyasamutpāda* series plays out its rôle. This is the true meaning in which the Mādhyamikas expound their conception of *śūnyatā* and this real, metaphysical entity is the highest conception in their philosophy.[1] This position of the Mādhyamikas is further clarified by their admission of two grades of truth—the one being empirical, the other being transcendental. The empirical truth (*saṁvṛti-satya*) is what is known of phenomenal objects in their causal determinations; the other truth is absolute (*paramārtha-satya*) which is beyond such dependence of cause and effect. The former cannot be denied so long as we do not have the realization of the true nature of objects which is, as has been explained above, *śūnyatā*. This is absolutely true of the objects while their empirical truth is relative and dependent.[2]

---

1. ''यः प्रतीत्यसमुत्पादः शून्यतां तां प्रचक्ष्महे।
सा प्रज्ञप्तिरुपादाय प्रतिपत् सैव मध्यमा॥''

(*Mādhyamikakārikā* of Nāgārjuna 24/18 : Poussin's Edn. p. 503)

''यस्य हि स्वभावेनानुत्पत्तिस्तस्यास्तित्वाभावः। स्वभावेन चानुत्पन्नस्य विगमाभावान्ना- स्तित्वाभाव इति। अतो भावाभावान्तद्वयरहितत्वात् सर्वस्वभावानुत्पत्तिलक्षणा शून्यता मध्यमा प्रतिपन्मध्यमो मार्ग इत्युच्यते।''

(*Prasannapadā* of Candrakīrti on above, *Ibid*. p. 304)

''अप्रतीत्य समुत्पन्नो धर्मः कश्चिन्न विद्यते।
यस्मात्तस्मादशून्यो हि धर्मः कश्चिन्न विद्यते॥''

(M.K. 24-12 : *Ibid*. p. 505)

''प्रतीत्यसमुत्पन्नश्च शून्यस्तस्मादशून्यो धर्मो नास्ति। यत एतदेवमतोऽस्माकं सर्व-धर्माश्च शून्या न च परोक्तदोषप्रसङ्गः।'' (*Prasannapadā* on above, *Ibid*, p. 505)

2 ''द्वे सत्ये समुपाश्रित्य बुद्धानां धर्मदेशना।
लोकसंवृत्तिसत्यश्च सत्यश्च परमार्थतः॥''
''येऽनयोर्न विजानन्ति विभागं सत्ययोर्द्वयोः।
ते तत्त्वं न विजानन्ति गम्भीरं बुद्धशासने॥''

(M.K. 24/8-9 : *Ibid*. p. 492 & p. 494)

Now if we tryto understand the doctrines of the Yogācāras, we shall see that they have admitted *Vijñāna* as the ultimate metaphysical reality. They argue that we cannot deny the *real* existence of *Vijñāna* which must be accepted as the fundamental truth of metaphysical speculations. This *Vijñāna* is consciousness of the subject who cannot logically deny its *real* existence, for to do so will be to commit logical suicide. How can the Mādhyamikas explain the truth of their own argument if there is no conscious agency as the upholder of that truth? Things and objects have their empirical truth no doubt, but their absolute truth is not veiled in a mysterious world of mere indeterminateness and sheer indescribability (*śūnyatā*). Their *real* truth is to be found in the subjective consciousness which alone is *real*. Now this consciousness, the Yogācāras declare, is two-fold; the one is the *ālayavijñāna* and the other is the *pravṛttivijñāna*. The consciousness (*vijñāna*) which determines the existence of things is no doubt grounded in the subject who is the knower of them (this is called the *ālayavijñāna*), but that same subjective consciousness is tinged with the objective hue when the external objects are known as definite objects of consciousness (this is known as the *pravṛtti-vijñāna*). But things do not *really* exist out and there in the world on their own merit, but as the external presentation of the ideas in the mind in which they are grounded. The logical argument of the Yogācāras consists in the explanation of the immediacy in perception of an object, the consciousness of which cannot arise either before the object has come into existence, or after its existence, which is of one moment only (*kṣaṇikavāda* of the Buddhists). Hence the object, to be immediately perceived, should be thought of as not external to consciousness but grounded in it. Another logical justification of the *vijñānavādī* (Yogācāra) position is to be found in the difficulty in explaining the perception of an externally present object from the fact that neither can its atomic character be perceived nor can its composite whole be perceived simultaneously; even when we conceive of *piece-meal perception* the same difficulties arise. Hence the Yogācāras conclude that only one reality is to be admitted and that is consciousness of the subject (*ālayavijñāna*) getting objectified (*pravṛttivijñāna*). The objection of the absolute creation by the mind (subject) at any time of any object is met by the Yogācāras by the admission of impressions (*vāsanā*) of past experiences which lie buried in consciousness. These *vāsanās* being roused up (*paripāka*) under particular circumstances give rise to particular objects revealed in knowledge and not all. This subjective idealism of the Yogācāras has, however, admitted a distinct nature of *Vijñāna* (consciousness) which is rooted in the subject and known by the name of *ālayavijñāna*. It speaks in the highest idealistic strain when it declares that the object being simultaneously present or co-eval with consciousness is not distinguishable from it; to see it as a separate *real* entity is due to false knowledge like the illusory perception of two moons in place of one.[1] But this reality of consciousness is not one which is changeless, but is of the very nature of eternal change. It is a stream of the constantly changing states of consciousness. The *kṣaṇikavādī* Buddhist cannot give a permanently realised existence to any single entity which is the very soul of perpetual changes. Hence *Vijñāna*, too, is of the nature of such a constant flux and flow, and is like a flowing stream, not a placid pool, of such changing states. The metaphysical reality of consciousness is to be regarded as the ground of the phenomenal world, but in its eternally changeful aspect. Bergsonian Idealism of the present century has admitted such a Reality (*élan vital*) whose very life is *Time* or *Duration*.

Now the conception of *Nirvāṇa* which is the *summum bonum* of Buddhistic culture is very much misrepresented in the writings of many writers and the common notion that it is not a state of existence but of annihilation finds a favoured place in them. *Nirvāṇa* is explained bythese thinkers as a state of self-annihilation and pure empirical transcendence where the *Arbat* or the liberated saint loses all meaning of life and becomes an extinct soul, so that a liberated *Arbat* attains to some kind of a negative *esse* which is tantamount to non-entity. Such being the grossly misrepresented nature of *Nirvāṇa*, Buddhism is sought to be divested of the living, vibrating philosophy of perfect wisdom-cum-existence which is realised in the ideal of *Buddhatva*. This state is the *alpha* and *omega* of all spiritual gymnastics in the Mahāyāna philosophy and it is the ideal of true knowledge, perfect wisdom and pure existence for which all sentient beings should strive. This is not merely an ethico-religious bluff, but the very soul of the highest norm of development for all human beings. This is the highest form of Enlightenment for which Buddha himself lived and died. This engenders in the liberated a pure life, full of

---

1. "सहोपलम्भनियमोदभेदो नीलतद्धियोः ।
भेदश्च भ्रान्तिविज्ञानैर्दृश्यतेन्दा विवाद्वये ॥"
(Dharmakirti; quoted in *Sarvadarśanasamgraha*—J. Vidyāsāgara's Edn. p. 15)

compassion and love for all creatures and perfect wisdom born out of freedom from sins and attachments.[1] If we read this conception of highest perfection along with that of *Nirvāṇa*, we can definitely say one thing for certain, and that is, *Nirvāṇa* in the tenets of the founder of Buddhism is farthest from a self-denying and self-annihilating philosophy. The Enlightened Soul lives in the state of *Buddhatva* even after *Nirvāṇa* has been achieved and no proof will be greater than the life of the Master himself. He lived in this world with perfect peace and wisdom, with a heart full of love and compassion for a long stretch of 45 years even after Enlightenment (*Nirvāṇa*). On the point of the state of the liberated soul after death Buddha himself was perfectly silent and this is one of the ten great questions on which the Master gave no reply whatsoever. Buddha's reticence, therefore, means that such questions are of the most indescribable character and hence outside the ken of ordinary ratiocinative experiences. The upshot of the discussions on the nature of *Nirvāṇa* comes to this that it is the *summum bonum* of life which has a negative aspect, no doubt, but which is, therefore, not a self-denying state on that score; its positive aspect is as potent as the other. Ultimately the ideal of *Nirvāṇa* is to be found in the annihilation of the endless cycle of births and deaths in the progressive realization of the unity of all selves with the transcendental Reality (*śūnyatā* of the Mādhyamikas, *vijñānamātra* of the Yogācāras) which has its partial manifestations in the individual entities (selves) dancing on its bosom to the fiddle of the empirico-rational processes (the *pañcaskandhas*, viz., *rūpa, vedanā, vijñāna, saṁjñā* and *saṁskāra*), but positively it is a life full of perfect wisdom, perfect purity and perfect existence by which it helps the Arhat to pull the oars of his raft of crossing the high seas of births and deaths for the liberation of other souls as well.

A study of Śaṅkara's interpretations of the Vedānta metaphysic is a very interesting and well-thinking-of one in the perspective of the Mahāyāna Buddhistic metaphysic. The Mādhyamika conception of *śūnyatā*, the Yogācāra conception of *vijñānamātra* and the general Buddhistic ideal of *Nirvāṇa*, as have been explained above, come very close to the highest idealistic conception of Advaita Vedānta of Śaṅkara. But we must be very much on our guards to draw over-

1. Cf. "Thus the essential nature of all Bodhisattvas is a great loving heart (*mahākarunācitta*) and all sentient beings constitute the object of its love." (Translation form Nāgārjuna's *Bodhicitta* quoted in *Outlines of Mahāyāna Buddhism* by D.T. Suzuki, p. 292). "Therefore all Bodhisattvas in order to emancipate sentient beings from misery, are inspired with great spiritual energy and mingle themselves in the filth of birth and death" (*Ibid.* p. 293).

hasty conclusions from similarities in the metaphysical conceptions of the two systems. It is better and wiser to draw no lines of sim litude at all than to present misjudged and misinterpreted conclusions. As a matter of fact, every metaphysic, be it realistic or idealistic, has a peculiar history of its own development of thought, and no sane student of philosophy should stoop to under-estimate the theories of one at the expense of rough and rady generalisations with other systems; still a clear outlook, an unprejudiced mind may carry one long along the path of a cautious comparison and true vision of the truths of different systems. In this light and with this approach we venture to have something of a 'comparative' study of the two of the most developed forms of idealistic philosophy in India.

Now let us examine how Śaṅkara conceives of the ultimate Reality, its relation with the world and its true nature. Advaita Vedānta of Śaṅkara is the absolute monistic theory of Idealism and is the most systematized study to that end. It conceives of only one Reality which is the Highest Truth that can be thought of. This one Reality which is nown in the Upaniṣads as *Brahman* or *Ātman* is the pure transcendental Entity and all the forms of phenomenal existence from the lowest to the highest grades are but grounded in that Reality and are never different from it. It is the consummation of all Existence where the highest form of unity exists. It is not the sum-total of all existents which have an existence, however dubious they may be, nor the highest form of Existence not precluding the lower and lower forms of Existence, but is the *only* Existent Being (*Sat*) conceivable. There is no difference, but complete identity and unity of all Existence. Such being the highest conception of Reality, Śaṅkara cannot explain the origin and existence of the world and the finite selves but by a truly idealistic theory which receives the greatest enunciation in his system. What is this world and all the finite selves in it with their "eating, drinking and being merry" due to? Śaṅkara comes here as the expounder of a clear path and that is the only path consistent with his absolute monistic idealism. He says that *Brahman,* the Highest Reality, is the creator, preserver and destroyer of the world with all its phenomenal existents ("जन्माद्यस्य यतः" *Brahmasūtra,* 1/1/2). How can the one Reality which has no shade of difference conceivable either within itself or with others be said to shred into the endless differences of the phenomenal world with its finite objects and souls? Hence to explain the differentiation of the one Reality into endless forms we cannot with logical impunity take the forms in the same ultimate truth as the Absolute Reality has.

The endless forms are therefore nothing but *apparently real* existents which are tossed up in the beginningless cycle of manifestations of the Absolute Reality. This is the theory of *māyā* and *avidyā* which has been the cornerstone of Śaṅkara's interpretations. Māyā universalised is the potential nature of *Brahman* to make an endless number of finitudes *appear* as real when their true nature of absolute identity and infinitude is veiled; *avidyā* individualised is the normal pitfall of individual souls (jīvas) to fall into, in their vision of the world as through 'coloured glasses.' *Avidyā* is the natural tendency of individual souls to lose themselves in the great turmoil and 'fitful fever' of life. The essential unity in transcendence, the absolute identity with the Absolute, are hidden by the veil of ignorance—ignorance individual and Nescience universal. Hence all the stages of life through which the *Soul is supposed to pass* are all appearance—appearance of duality and plurality in the reality of unity and identity.

This is the cardinal doctrine of the Upaniṣads and the *Brahma-sūtras* and Śaṅkara interprets the universe in this light. Hence Śaṅkara conceives of the Absolute Reality as the transcendental unity and identity of all Existence which under subjective ignorance (*avidyā*) and trans-subjective Nescience (*Māyā*) *appears* to be of endless diversified positive realities. But Reality being one and that being Absolute Consciousness (*Brahman* or *Ātman*), all the finite *reals* lose all their meaning and significance in its light. They become meaningless because of their diversity and significant on account of their unity. So Śaṅkara has given only *apparent reality* which, though sounding as paradoxical, is *empirically* unquestioned. The world with all the manifestations of finitude—objects and selves—is given by Śaṅkara the *empirical* reality (*vyavahārika-satya*) it has; so long as the play of 'a blind led by another blind' will continue in empirical divisions and distinctions of subject and object, of means and target, the reality, however apparent, of this empirico-rational process is not denied by Śaṅkara. It is denied by him only when the vision of Absolute Reality (*paramārtha-satya*) is realised and complete unity and identity in its transcendence over subject and object, means and target, are revealed. To Śaṅkara, therefore, two categories or grades of truth are an empirical necessity, not a metaphysical reality. Out of purely empirical necessity, Śaṅkara is prepared to grant even *prātibhāsika-satya* or truth of much lower empirical value in that it is empirical appearance as real for the moment only of a falsely cognised object (as a serpent on a piece of rope—*rajjusarpabhrama*).

These *relative* criteria of truth have validity in their own empirico-rational or empirical spheres, but truth as truth is one and indivisible and that is the Highest Truth consummated in the conception of the Highest Being (*Brahman*) which is the ground of explanation of all Existence.

The standpoint of Śaṅkara's metaphysics is far removed from that of the Mahāyāna Buddhism which has also a very good idealistic basis and a well-nigh monistic approach. Śaṅkara's conception of the Absolute (*Brahman*) is a distinct one from the Mādhyamika conception of *Śūnyatā* or the Yogācāra conception of *Vijñāna*, a conception at once a sound positivity and a solid Reality. *Brahman* is no doubt the transcendental Reality beyond all phenomena but does not hover around a completely mysterious, indescribable and unstable Existence which we meet with in the other two conceptions. Vedāntic *Brahman* is the positive Reality of transcendental spirit which is the very consummation of Existence, Knowledge and Bliss (*Saccidānandasvarūpa*). The Upaniṣadic dicta "Satyaṁ Jñānam Anantaṃ Brahma" (*Taitt. Up*. 2/1/1, "Ānandaṃ Brahmeti vyajānāt" (*Taitt. Up.*) "Vijñānam Ānandaṃ Brahma" (*Bṛhad. Up*. 3/9/28), "Sadeva Somyedamagra āsīt" (*Ch. Up*. 6/2/3) point to the fact that *Brahman* is the Pure Spirit which is the very consummation of Existence—Knowledge—Bliss immanent in every phenomenal entity, conscious or unconscious (*jīva* or *jaḍa*). All these entities have these three characteristics—it has existence (*asti*), it has revelation (*bhāti*) and it has pleasurability (*priya*) but have all the variations in their name (*nāma*) and form (*rūpa*). So existence, revelation and pleasurability are the common marks of all phenomenal entities but they have not these on their own merit. These are the immanental expression of the transcendental Reality of Existence—Knowledge—Bliss which is Brahman. So the realization of this transcendental Reality is one of a positive Entity—an Entity which is without any characterization, the mark of finitude—but the One, Unqualified, Undifferentiated Entity which is Existence, Knowledge and Bliss all combined in their consummation. If that be so, how is it that *Brahman* has been spoken of in all forms of *negativity* in the Upaniṣads, (e.g., एतद्वै तदक्षरं गार्गि ब्राह्मणा अभिवदत्यस्थूलमनणवह्रस्वमदीर्घ भमलोहितमस्नेहमच्छायम तमोऽवाय्वनाकाशमसङ्गमरसमगन्धमचक्षुष्कमश्रोत्रमवागमनोऽतेजस्कमप्राणममात्र मनन्तरमब्राह्मम्—*Bṛhad. Up*. 3/8/8)? Śaṅkara's reply is that *Brahman* is indeed to be spoken of in negativity when the real, transcendental nature of *Brahman* is to be thought of. *Brahman* is the positive background, or rather ground, of the world, but *Brahman* as the transcendental Reality is the very *negation of all finitude* expressed in being thought of. The Upaniṣadic process of 'neti', 'neti' ('not this', 'not that') is te application of the *negative process of futility* in conceiving of *Brahman* with the coloured glasses of all finitude. So Brahman as the real transcendental spirit is not a *negative Entity* but a *negating Infinitude*. The *śūnyatā* of the Mādhyamikas is no doubt a conception of a transcendental Reality behind and beyond all phenomenal existence which is the cyclic order of dependent origination in the eternal cause-and-effect series, but, nevertheless, is indescribable indeterminate, even mysterious, something *Other* which is willy-nilly to be recognised to explain this cyclic order; the *vijñāna* of the Yogācāras is likewise the only Reality and every phenomenon is but the external manifestation of it and is dependent on the same cause-and-effect series but resolved in the unitary Reality of *vijñāna*.

Now the very conception of the cyclic order of cause-and-effect cannot itself be sufficient reason for phenomenal existence as supposed in Buddhism. The twelvefold chain (*dvādaśa nidāna*) of dependent origination (*pratītyasamutpāda*) necessarily pre-supposes a positive Entity which is Sufficient Reason for such an order. Buddhism in its conception of eternal flux and flow (*kṣaṇikavāda*) fails in its twofold conception of *śūnyatā* (Mādhyamika) and *vijñānamātra* (Yogācāra) of such a dubiously existing transcendence to provide the conception of such an Entity.[1] The Yogācāra conception of *ālayavijñāna* is open to the serious objection that this stream of *momentary* bits of consciousness cannot sufficiently explain recollective knowledge (*anusmṛti*) which pre-supposes a stable positive Being.[2] The Yogācāra argument of an Entity acting unitarily on the ground of similitude is untenable, for the unitary actions of the same Self pre-supposes an identity and not similitude.[3]

---

1. ''भवेदुपपन्नः सङ्घातो यदि सङ्घातस्य किंञ्चिन्निमित्तामवगम्यते, न त्ववगम्यते। यत इतरेतरप्रत्ययत्वेऽप्यविद्यादीनां पूर्वपूर्वमुत्तरोत्तरस्योत्पत्तिमात्रनिमित्तं भवद्भवेत्, न तु सङ्घातोत्पत्तेः किञ्चिन्निमित्तं सम्भवति। नन्वविद्यादिभिरर्थादाक्षिप्यते सङ्घात इत्युक्तम्, अत्रोच्यते। यदि तावदयमभिप्रायः अविद्यादयः सङ्घातमन्तरेणात्मानमलभमाना अपेक्षन्ते सङ्घातमिति, ततस्तस्य संघातस्य किञ्चिन्निमित्तं वक्तव्यम्, तत्व नित्येष्वप्यणुष्वभ्यु- पगम्यमानेष्वाश्रयाश्रयिभूतेषु भोकृषु सतसु न सम्भवतीत्युक्तं वैशेषिकपरीक्षायां, किमङ्ग पुनः क्षणिकेष्वप्यणुषु भोक्तरहिते- ष्वाश्रयाश्रयिशून्येषु चाम्युपगम्यमानेषु सम्भवेत्।''

(*Śārīrakamīmāṁsābhāṣya* of Śaṅkara, 2/219)

2. ''अनुभवमुपलब्धिमनूत्पद्यमानं स्मरणमेवानुस्मृतिः सा चोपलब्ध्येककर्तृकासती सम्भवति, पुरुषान्तरोपलब्धि विषये पुरुषान्तरस्य स्मृत्यदर्शनात्।'' (*Ibid.* 2/2/25)

3. ''न चायं सादृश्यात् संव्यवहारो युक्तः तद्भावावगमात् तत्सदृशभावानवगमाश्च, भवे-दपि कदाचित् ब्राह्यवस्तुनि विप्रलम्भसम्भवात् तदेवेदं स्यात् तत्सदृशं वेति सन्देहः, उपलब्धरि त सन्देहोऽपि न कदाचिद्भवति, स एवाहं स्यां तत्सदृशो वेति।'' (*Ibid.* 2/2/25)

Their exposition of the external manifestation of the internal *vijñāna* is likewise unsatisfactory, for the external manifestation cannot be regarded a non-entity inasmuch as it would have been impossible to say that *vijñāna* appears *as* external where we presume the entity of the external. A complete non-entity like 'the son of a barren woman' cannot be conceived of as a ground of appearance of somebody (as 'That man appears *as* the son of a barren woman').[1] Hence the external world cannot be sufficiently explained as the mere projection of the internal subjective consciousness (*ālayavijñāna*), for there is a duality between consciousness and its object. The *ālayavijñāna* of the Yogācāra Buddhists is not the sufficient explanation for the *appearance* of the external objects; it cannot have self-revelation, for then it will have action engendered on itself.[2] The Vedāntic conception of Pure Transcendental Self which is of the nature of Consciousness (*Sākṣicaitanya*) is not liable to these objections; for this Absolute Consciousness is the real background behind all phenomenal existence which *appears* to be out and there not as its projections but as the creation of individualised ignorance and universalised Nescience which rake it up in the bosom of the Absolute Reality (Brahman) that is itself self-revealed. Hence Vedāntic Absolute Consciousness (*Sākṣicaitanya*) and Yogācāra conception of the stream of momentary conscious states (*ālayavijñāna*) are at poles asunder; the latter is the lower category which is under the all-comprehensive conception of the former.[3] Subjective conscious states, however linked up in a stream, are as much finite as the finite objects and hence is never the Infinite Consciousness which is the Vedāntic *Sākṣin*. It is equated with Brahman as being beyond all qualifications and differentiations, as the only ultimate Reality which needs no other

---

1. "तेऽपि हि सर्वलोकप्रसिद्धां बहिरवभासां सम्विदं प्रतिलभमानाः प्रत्याख्यातुकामाश्च बाह्यमर्थं बर्हिवदिति वत्कारं कुर्वन्ति। इतरथा हि कस्माद्बहिर्वदिति ब्रुयुः। न हि विष्णमित्रो बन्ध्यापुत्रवदवभासत इति कश्चिदाचक्षीत।" (*Ibid.* 2/2/28)

2. "न चार्थव्यतिरिक्तमपि विज्ञानं स्वयमेवानुभूयते स्वात्मनि क्रियाविरोधादेव।" (*Śārīrakamīmāṁsābhāṣya* of Śaṅkara, 2/2/28)

3. "साक्षिप्रत्यययोश्च स्वभाववैषम्यादुपलब्ध्युपलभ्यभावोपपत्तेः, स्वयंसिद्धस्य च साक्षिणोऽप्रत्याख्येयत्वात्। * * * * * * * अतो विज्ञानस्याप्यवभास्यत्वाविशेषात् सत्येवान्यस्मिन्नवगन्तरि प्रथमं प्रदीपवदवगम्यते। साक्षिणोऽगन्तुः स्वयंसिद्धतामुपक्षिपता स्वयं प्रथते विज्ञानमित्येष एव मम पक्षस्त्वया वाचो-युक्त्यन्तरेणाश्रित इति चेत्, न विज्ञानस्योत्पत्तिप्रध्वंसानेकत्वादि विशेषवत्त्वाभ्युपगमात्। अतः प्रदीपवद्विज्ञानस्यापि व्यतिरिक्तावगम्यत्वमस्माभिः प्रसाधितम्।" (*Ibid.* 2/2/28)

aid to its revelation but is self-revealed, at the same time revealing all the finite objects only *appearing* to be existent.[1]

The conception of *Nirvāṇa* as the highest form of liberation from the body-mind causal complex is the last word in Buddhistic metaphysics. We have discussed above at some length this conception and tried to show that it is not only a negative super-normal experience of unity with the Transcendental Reality (*Śunyatā* of the Mādhyamikas or *Vijñānamātra* of the Yogācāras), but is always accompanied with the solid, positive conception of *Buddhatva* in which state a heart over-flowing with the milk of human kindness and a mind pure with extreme placidity are the key-notes of the Enlightened Soul. This state of *Nirvāṇa* is therefore not incompatible with active, bodily existence, only that the existence is transmuted under the fire of Supreme Knowledge. The *Buddha* tries for the uplift of other souls with an extremely compassionate heart (*mahākaruṇācitta*) even after perfect Enlightenment (*Nirvāṇa*). At least the life of the Master himself is an eloquent testimony to this fact. The concept of *Mokṣa* or ultimate liberation in Advaita Vedānta is very much at home with its metaphysical stand and hence is something different from that of Buddhism (*Nirvāṇa*). Liberation does not mean anything external to be attained by external processes, but is the very nature of the Soul (*svabhāva*) which is only veiled under the omnipotent Nescience. The dispelling of ignorance (*avidyānāśa*) is not a *means* to the end of liberation (*mokṣa*) but is equivalent to it. The veil of ignorance being dispelled by the eternal light of true knowledge only means that the soul has come to its *own* which therefore is not an external end. This concept of *Mokṣa* is one of distinct realization of what is true and eternal as they very embodiment of the Soul and therefore the most positive Existence which is supra-ratio-cinative-process. All empirical knowledge which is necessarily of the finite is false in regard to this Supreme Knowledge which is the Highest Truth of all the finite. So Śaṅkara does not think of anything outside of the Soul as the object of *Mokṣa* but the very nature of the Soul which is realised by constant endeavour towards discriminatory knowledge between the self and the not-self. This is

---

1. ''न तत्र सूर्यो भाति न चन्द्रतारकं ।
नेमा विद्युतो भान्ति कुतोऽयमग्निः ॥
तमेव भान्तमनुभाति सर्वं ।
तस्य भासा सर्वमिदं विभाति ॥'' (*Kaṭhopaniṣad*)

what is meant by Self-realisation which is spoken of in the Upaniṣads as 'Ātmānaṁ viddhi' (Know Thyself), and 'Tattvamasi' (Thou art That). What then is the nature of the liberated Soul? Advaita Vedānta is not reluctant to recognise the life of action of the liberated Soul (*jīvanmukta*) as the Buddhists think of the *Buddhatva* state. But all the actions flowing from the liberated Soul become mechanical as the revolving movements of the wheel even when external force has ceased to be applied thereto. The actions of the *jīvanmukta* will no doubt exist as long as he lives, but those actions will all have been merged into the fire of Pure Knowledge. All finitude, all discrimination, all limitation will cease in the liberated Soul; this will be the life of the Infinite, the Unlimited, the Supreme Unity of all Existence. Hence the *jīvanmukta* will be free from all the sordid touches of wilful limitation but will have the only spark of True Knowledge. This is what the *Śrīmadbhagavadgītā* teaches when it says: "*Jñānāgniḥ sarvakarmāṇi bhasmasātkurute tathā*" (4/38). The *Buddhatva* conception is one of transmuted Existence where the *Buddha* lives *for* the world. But Śaṅkara's *Mukta Puruṣa* lives only in the light of Pure Knowledge where the world coming and going is the least affective object to his Pure Existence. The actions in and for the world come out in an automatic succession, which, however are far from the nature of the liberated Soul. This is Śaṅkara's conception of *Mokṣa* and *Mukta* and unless we keep in view this metaphysical outlook, we shall fail to evaluate him dispassionately.

Mahāyāna Buddhism and Advaita Vedānta are great systems of Idealistic metaphysics; both advocate ultimate monism, both go a long way together in their metaphysical outlook, but both part ways after a certain point. Śaṅkara takes a parting way from the Mahāyānist in more respects than one. This is a system which is something unique in Indian Idealistic Monism and he unreservedly advocates it in all his writings. Mādhyamika and Yogācāra go to a great length to propound their idealistic monism, but the one lapses into irrevocable mysticism while the other into irreconcilable solipsism. Śaṅkara with firm determination does not falter in his steps which stair by stair rise up to the highest peak of Idealistic Monism where there is no contradiction within or without itself.

Chapter - 15

Was there any Conflict between the Brahmins and the Buddhists ?

Y. Krishan

It is common for the historians to trace the origin of Buddhism as a protest against (i) the ceremonialism and ritualism enjoined by the Vedas, and (ii) the caste system based on denial of human equality and the supremacy of Brāhmins—the priestly class. Caste and rituals were sources of power and wealth of the Brāhmins and since Buddhism tried to undermine popular faith in them, it is said to have incurred the bitter and undying hostility of the vested interests—the Brāhmins.

At the outset, it may be pointed out that evidence of Buddhist-Brāhminical conflict is extremely tenuous in Sanskrit literature. In such a vast literature extending over 1500 years, only a few such references can be traced. On the contrary, absence of any particularly anti-Buddhist or anti-Brāhminical feeling in the literature is significant.

The premise that Buddhism attacked Brāhminical supremacy is itself erroneous. In fact, the caste system in the form in which we know it had not come into existence at the time of the Buddha.[1] There are numerous references to castes in the Buddhist literature but hardly anyone is deprecatory.

There are five important sutas of the Buddha dealing with theinstitution of caste—Vāseṭṭha sutta of the *Sutta Nipāta*, Soṇadaṇḍa sutta and Aggañña sutta of the *Dīgha Nikāya* and Madhura sutta and Assalāyana sutta of the *Majjhima Nikāya.* The first thing to be

1. "The key-stone of the arch of the peculiarly Indian Caste Organisation—the absolute supremacy of the Brāhmin had not yet ben put in position, had not, in fact, been yet made ready. The caste system in any proper or exact use of the term did not exist." Rhys Davids: *Sacred Books of the Buddhists*; vol. II, p. 101.

noticed in these sayings is that it is the Kṣatriyas who were ranked the foremost in the caste hierarchy and not the Brāhmins; the latter appear to be trying to assert their superiority over the former. In the Ambaṭṭha sutta, the Buddha establishes that "the Kṣatriyas are higher and the Brāhmans inferior."[1] Invariably and significantly the Kṣatriyas are mentioned first in the caste hierarchy.

Secondly, the Buddha did not challenge the caste sytem as such. All that he urged was that this social classification should be based on karma (action) and not on birth.[2] In the Soṇadaṇḍa sutta again a person is a Brāhmin if he possesses virtues and wisdom, and not because of colour, birth or knowledge of sacred verses.[3] The Madhura sutta[4] states that *karma* (deeds) and not caste determines the consequences a man has to undergo for his acts, good or evil. In the Assalāyana sutta the claim that Brāhmins form the best caste, as of right, is repudiated. According to the Buddha, the superiority of caste depends upon character, upon *karma*. A Brāhmin given to evil doing "would arise in the Waste, the Bad Bourn, the Downfall Hell" notwithstanding his caste. A person of lower caste who refrains from evil ways, on the other hand, "would arise in a Good Bourn, a Heaven World."[5]

Thirdly, it was not the Buddha alone who assailed social classification based on birth. The Brāhmins were themselves divided over this question.[6] In the Ambaṭṭha sutta, the Buddha quotes the example of Kaṇha, the son of a slave woman who became a great seer and founded a Brāhmin family.[7] Did not certain Brāhmins say:

---

1. *Dīgha Nikāya*, ii, 26-27. *Dialogues of the Buddha*, S.B.B., vol. II, pp. 120-121. In the Kaṇṇakatthala sutta of the *Majjhima Nikāya* (ii, 128 Pali Text Society Translation series, vol. XV, p. 67) in the Buddha's enumeration of the four castes, Kṣatriyas are mentioned before Brāhmin. The Aggañña sutta (*Dīgha Nikāya*, iii), in tracing the evolution of the world, states that the Kṣatriyas arose first to curb the evil doers by punitive action and then the Brāhmins to restrain evil disposition which led to evil doing.
2. *Vāseṭṭha Sutta*, 57; *Sutta Nipāta, Mahāvagga*, 9; *Sacred Books of the East*, vol. X, p. 116. In the *Vasalasutta*, we read: "Not by birth does one become an outcast, not by birth does one become a Brāhmaṇa; by deeds one becomes an outcast, by deeds one becomes a Brāhmaṇa." *Sutta Nipāta*, 135.
3. *Dīgha Nikāya*, IV 14-16. S.B.B. II, p. 153-54.
4. Translated by Chalmers in *JRAS*. 1894.
5. Coomaraswamy and Horner: *Living Thoughts of Gotama the Buddha*, pp. 125-28.
6. In the *Vāseṭṭha Sutta*, two Brāhmins Bhāradvāja and Vāseṭṭha, well versed in the Vedas approach the Buddha for settlement of their dispute. "We have a controversy regarding (the distinctions of) birth, O Gotama! Bhāradvāja says, one is a Brāhmaṇa by birth, and I say, by deeds........" (*Vāseṭṭha Sutta*, 3).
7. *Dīgha Nikāya*, iii, S.B.B., vol. II.

'*Janmanā jāyate śūdra, karmaṇā jāyate dvijaḥ*' (A man is a śūdra by birth and brāhmin by karma)?

The views of the Buddha about caste were in keeping with the teaching of the Upaniṣads.[1] The two Buddhist treat *Vajrasūci* and *Sūtrālaṃkāra,* attack the caste system based on birth. The *Vajrasūci*[2] does not repudiate caste distinction or superiority of Brāhmins but merely asserts that it should be based on conduct and not lineage. It quotes the Vedas, the Mahābhārata and even Manu to support its thesis which again shows that the Brāhmins themselves were not unanimous in upholding a caste system based on birth. In *Kalpanāmaṇḍitikā*[3] (Sūtrālaṃkāra), Kumāralata in the same way attacks caste system by quotations from Manu.

In spite of its repudiation of a hereditary caste system, the Brāhmins occupy a high position in Buddhism. In the Nikāyas, the Brāhmins are considered superior to and distinct from ordinary men.[4] In the Jātakas, the brāhmins are almost invariably referred to respectfully. As a Bodhisattva, the Buddha in his previous births, is frequently stated to have taken birth as a brāhmin.[5] One of the four things in which the Buddhas, according to *Milindapañha*, differ is that some are born as Brāhmins and others as Kṣatriyas.[6]

---

1. Satyakāma, the illegitimate son of a servant, Jābāla, was considered a true Brāhmin fit to be initiated as a brahmacāri because he spoke the truth. Chāndogya, iv, 4.
2. Translated by Hodgson in *The Languages, Literature and Religion of Nepal and Tibet*, pp. 126-33.
3. Winternitz: *History of Indian Literature,* vol. II, p. 265 f. n. 2.
4. "He (Buddha) by himself thoroughly knows and sees the worlds of gods, māras, recluses, brāhmins and men..." (Ambaṭṭha sutta 2, *Dīgha Nikāya*). In the Pāsādika sutta 29, Dīgha, it is stated that whatever is seen, known and accomplished by men, recluses or brāhmins is all understood by the Tathāgata. See also Mahāsīhanāda Sutta, Majjhima, 1. 69 (*Early Buddhist Scriptures,* Ed. Thomas, p. 141) and *Mahāvastu* 330; translated by J.J. Jones, Part I, S.B.B., vol. XVI. "When the Buddhists" wrote T.W. Rhys Davids" in selecting a title of honour for those they valued so highly, for the best of men, for the Arahats, selected the name of Brāhman, it is clear that the word, in the opinion of the early Buddhists, conveyed to the minds of the people an exalted meaning, a connotation of real veneration and respect. And it is not likely that this would have been the case unless the Brāhmans had, at least as a general rule, deserved it—and on other grounds than the mere prerogative of birth." S.B.B. Vol. II: Introduction to *Soṇadaṇḍasutta* IV, p. 140-41. "Even the fact that the true, genuine Brāhman is not seldom represented as the noblest of creatures, in contradistinction to those who are merely Brāhmans by birth.........would have been impossible if the type had wholly failed in common life." Kern: *Manual of Buddhism*, p. 67.
5. "Bodhisattvas are born in one of two classes of families either noble or brāhman." *Mahāvastu* 197, Translated by J.J. Jones: S.B.B. vol. XVI, part I, p. 156.
6. Hardy: *A Manual of Buddhism,* p. 87.

The relationship between the Brāhmin and Buddhist monks is thus described in *Itivuttaka*, 107: "Exceedingly helpful to you, O monks, are Brāhman householders who present you with garments, medicines and utensils. And you verily, O monks, are exceedingly helpful to the Brāhman householders for ye point out to them the law of their first, middle and last good actions and ye do proclaim unto them the life of chastity, with its meaning and its characteristics absolutely complete and perfect."[1] In the edicts of Aśoka, respect and liberality towards Brāhmins and Śramaṇas is enjoined upon the people. *Mahāvastu* (3rd century B.C.), *Avadāna Śataka* (2nd century A.D.), *Jātaka mālā* (6th century A.D.) and *Śikṣā Samuccaya* (7th century A.D.) all required a bodhisattva to bestow gifts on Brāhmins and Śramaṇas. Harṣa, the Buddhist monarch, patronized Hinduism. In his quinquinnial assemblies, Āditya Deva and Īśvara Deva[2] were worshipped after the Buddha, and the Brāhmins, after Buddhist monks, enjoyed his fabulous charities. The Chinese travellers make no mention whatsoever of antagonism between the Brāhmins and the Buddhists. Their accounts testify to the manner in which the peoples of Inia professing different faiths lived amicably. According to Fa Hien,[3] Brāhmins gave gifts to Buddhist monks. According to Sung Yung,[4] the people of Gandhāra belonged entirely to the Brāhmin caste who "had a great respect for the law of Buddha and loved to read the sacred books........." Hiuen Tsiang tells us that there were 100 Buddhist saṅghārāmas and 200 Deva (Hindu) temples in Kanauj.[5] According to this Chinese traveller, Śilāditya (Śri Harṣa), the Buddhist King, convened a general council of Śramaṇas and Brāhmins.[6] He also mentions that the Buddhist monks at Nālandā studied "even ordinary works as the Vedas."[7] The episode mentioned by that traveller of the attempted assassination of Harṣa by heretics cannot be attributed to Brāhmins in general with certainty and is extremely doubtful as the version in the life of Hiuen Tsiang is that the dissatisfied Hīnayānist monks plotted against the life of the pilgrim.[8] In any case, it is an isolated instance from which even the narrator does not draw an inference of general hostility between the two groups. Bāṇa, in *Harṣacarita* in his description of the hermitage

1. Quoted from Proceedings of the Fifth Indian Oriental Conference. vol. II (1930), p. 923.
2. Beal: *Life of Hiuen Tsing*, p. 186.
3. Beal: *Buddhist Records of the Western World*, vol. I, XXXIX.
4. *Ibid.*
5. *Ibid.*, vol. I, p. 207.
6. *Ibid.*, p. 218. Beal: *Life of Hiuen Tsiang*, p. 176.
7. Beal: *Life of Hiuen Tsiang*, p. 112.
8. *Ibid.*, p. 179.

of Divākaramitra tells us that the adherents of various faiths including the Buddhists and Brāhmins were "all diligently following their own tenets, pondering, urging objections, raising doubts and resolving them."[1]

Nor was there any reason for Brāhmins to consider Buddhism a hostile faith. Buddhism, when it arose, was not a religion. It was merely the fourth Āśrama of the Hindus—the Sannyāsa Āśrama writ large. In that stage of life, there are no caste distinctions;[2] the Sannyāsi is not to observe the Vedic Karmakāṇḍa—performance of prayers, sacrifices and rituals. He is, in fact, above social rules of morality. He is to cultivate *vairāgya*, complete detachment from the world, and concentrate himself on Mokṣa. Verily the code of the Buddhist Bhikṣus was little different from that of the Sannyāsin. Buddhism was not antagonistic to Brāhminism; it was merely an aspect of it magnified and Brāhmins paid to the Buddhist monks the respect that was their due.[3]

In *Majjhima Nikāya* Bhāradvājagotra, Brāhmin sacrificer, asks the paribbājaka Māgandiya not to speak ill of the Buddha as he was much respected by the learned Brāhmins, Khattiyas, householders and monks.[4] The Brāhmins of Veṭhadīpa had a share in the relics of

---

1. Bāṇa: *Harṣacarita*: Translated by Cowell and Thomas, p. 236.

2. "Just as, O monks, the great rivers such as the Gaṅgā, the Yamunā, Aciravati, Sarabhū and Māhi when they fall into the ocean lose their former names and clans and are known as the ocean, even so do the four castes of Kṣatriyas, Brāhmins, Vaiśyas and Śūdras, when they have gone forth in the Doctrine and Discipline taught by the Tathāgata, from a home to a homeless life lose their former names and clans (nāmagotra) and are known as ascetics." Udāna V. 5. As pointed out by Rhys Davids (S.B.B. vol. II, p. 103), the Sāmaññaphala sutta (35-36) indicates that a slave could join any order and in the Aggañña sutta of the Dīgha and the Madhura sutta V. of the Majjhima there is express mention that a śūdra could become a Samana (not necessarily a Buddhist śramaṇa) who was entitled to and was given uniform respect. Speaking of the moral obligation of the śramaṇas i.e. those who have renounced the world, Kern says that "No one, unless unacquainted with Brāhmanic literature, will fail to perceive that this superior morality is nothing else but the rule of life of the Dvija in the fourth Āśrama, when he is a Yati or Mukta." (*Manual of Indian Buddhism*, p. 70).

3. Not long after the death of the Buddha, Ajātaśatru was having the fortifications of Rājagṛha strengthened as he was distrustful of King Pajjota. At this time Ānanda was at Rājagṛha. One day, when it was too early to go for alms, he went to see the work of construction by Brāhmin Gopaka—Moggallāna. The latter spoke to Ānanda thus: "Let the respected Ānanda come; welcome to the respected Ānanda; it is long since the venerable Ānanda has passed this way, that is so as to come here—"Then the venerable Ānanda sat down in the seat pointed out and at one side Vassakara, the Brāhman Chief Minister of Magadha, who was visiting the work at Rājagṛha also came and sat down at one side." Gopaka Moggallāna sutta in *Majjhima Nikāya*, iii, 7.

4. *Majjhima Nikāya*, vol. I, pp. 501-13. Quoted in *Buddhistic Studies*: Ed by B.C. Law, p. 97.

the Master and the Brāhmin Droṇa mediated between the kings who were preparing for a battle for having a share in the relics "as it would have been a dishonour to the Buddha.[1]

In fact, "it was precisely the Brāhmins themselves who often took the most earnest interest in his (Buddha's) speculations."[2] The Buddhist literature specifically mentions the conversions of Brāhmins and it was from their ranks that the greatest exponents of the philosophy of the Buddha were recruited. The Buddha's two chief disciples Sāriputta and Moggallāna came of Brāhmin families and so also Mahā-kassapa and other distinguished disciples of the Buddha. Nāgasena, who converted king Milinda was the son of a Brāhmin. Nāgārjuna, the greatest Buddhist philosopher, and the founder of the Mādhyamika school of philosophy, was a Brāhmin. Aśvaghoṣa, the greatest Buddhist literateur and spiritual adviser of the Buddhist king Kaniṣka, was a Brāhmin by birth. Asaṅga, the founder of the Yogācāra School of Buddhist philosophy, was a Brāhmin convert from N.W. India. His brother Vasu-bandhu was another great Buddhist luminary and author of the *Abhi-dharmakośa*. Buddhaghoṣa, author of the *Visuddhimagga* and a great commentator of the Pali literature, came of a Brāhmin family of Bodhi Gayā (5th century A.D.). Dignāga, the founder of the Buddhist School of Logic in 6th century A.D., was the son of a Brāhmin of Conjeevaram. Some scholars identify Gauḍapāda, the teacher of Saṅkara's tacher Govinda, as a Buddhist. On the other hand, the greatest champion of orthodox Hinduism and enemy of Buddhism—Kumārila Bhaṭṭa, was a Hindu convert from Buddhism. Similarly, Bhatṛhari, the famous logician and grammarian, became a Buddhist monk several times and again returned to the Hindu fold. In such an atmosphere of intellectual freedom—easy transfer of allegiance from one faith to another and with the greatest champions of the heretical faith having been provided by that section of the Hindu community whose vested interests it sought to attack,—religious antagonism is inconceivable.

On the contrary, there is evidence of Brāhmins patronizing Buddhism. According to Hiuen Tsiang, the Vihāra at Buddha Gayā was reconstructed on a large scale by a Brāhmin[3] about the 1st century B.C.[4] The first monastery at Nālandā is also said to have been built by two Brāhmin brothers.[5] The coins[6] of Yaudheya Chief, Brāhmaṇa

1. Hardy: A *Manual of Buddhism*, p. 351.
2. Rhys Davids: *History of Buddhist Literature*, p. 115.
3. Beal: *Buddhist Records of the Western World*, vol. II, p. 119.
4. *Archaeological Survey Report*, III, p. 93.
5. *Ibid.*, pp. 93-95.
6. Cunningham: *Archaeological Survey of India Report*, vol. XIV, p. 143.

Deva, a worshipper of Bhāgavata, carry images of Bodhi tree, Caitya, Buddhist railing and Dharma Cakra. Brāhminical revival, which started under the Śuṅgas, reached its high water mark under the Guptas, the greatest champions of orthodoxy. The Gupta rulers gave numerous grants for the maintenance of Buddhist monasteries and Vasubandhu the Buddhist, already mentioned, was the teacher of Samudragupta when he was a prince. In the Purāṇas, the Buddha became the ninth avatāra of Viṣṇu.

Śaṅkara is credited with having driven Buddhism out of India.[1] But it may besaid without exaggeration that Śaṅkara's philosophy is Nāgārjuna's in a new bottle. He undoubtedly represents the most complete synthesis of Brāhmanical and Buddhist streams of thought, but his most important contribution, the concept of Brahman, is neo-Śūnyavāda. In his *Dasāvatāra-stotram*, Śaṅkara described the Buddhá as the prince among Yogis who dwelt in the centre of his heart. Not without reason he was dubbed as a Pracchanna Bauddha or Crypto Buddhist[2] by his critics. As such, the story of his bitter hostility towards Buddhism appears to be puzzling.[3] It was perhaps a tactical move to silence his critics viz. the Mīmāṁsaka, without compromising his principles. It would be observed that Śaṅkara was chided by Maṇḍana Miśra, a stauch Mīmāṁsaka, for considering Jñāna (knowledge of the absolute) as superior to Karma Kāṇḍa of the Vedas.

Naturally, the question arises as to how do we explain the few anti-Buddhistic instances in history and references in literature.

Of all the schools of Indian philosophy, Pūrva Mīmāṁsā of Jaimini alone considers the Vedas as the source of the highest knowledge. It regards the Vedas as eternal and self-existent and not the work of God. In their anxiety to uphold the supremacy of the Vedas, the Mīmāṁsakas even ignored God. At the same time, they emphasized Karma Kāṇḍa—the performance of sacrifices and rituals as enjoined by the law makers for the various castes was considered

---

1. There is hardly anything specially Buddhistic in Śaṅkara-Vijaya's Chapter on Buddha-mata nirākaraṇa: Nariman: *Literary History of Sanskrit Buddhism*, p. 287.

2. *Padma-Purāṇa* says. "The great doctrine of Māyā (that is Śaṅkara's philosophy) appears to be an interpretation of the Vedas but really is anti-Vedic. It has been proclaimed to the world to hasten its destruction. This doctrine of Māyā is a false philosophy; verily it is Buddhism in disguise. It has been preached by the Destructive Power in the form of a Brāhman of the Kali Age (namely Śaṅkarācārya)." (*Padma Purāṇa* quoted by Vijñāna Bhikṣu in his commentary on the Sāṅkhya philosophy—See p. 56 of *Buddha Mīmāṁsā* by Yogiraja Disciple Maitreya).

3. I guess that in Mādhavācārya's *Śaṅkara-Digvijaya* and Anandagiri's *Śaṅkaravijaya*, emphasis on Śaṅkara's hostility towards Buddhism may have been due to rivalry between Śaivism and Vaiṣṇavism Śaṅkara is supposed to be an incarnation of Śiva, while the Buddha is that of Viṣṇu.

a religious duty. While other philosophical schools regarded the Vedas as one of the valid sources of knowledge and testimony, the heretical schools like the Buddhists, Jainas and Lokāyatakas even repudiated that. They emphasised the futility of sacrificial rites. As the Bodhisattva observes in the Bhūridatta Jātaka:

"The Vedas have no hidden power to save
The Traitor or the Coward or the Knave,
The fire though tended well for long years past,
Leaves his base master without hope at last."[1]

The Nāstikas (those who do not believe in the Vedas) therefore came in direct conflict with the Mīmāṁsakas. Subandhu, the author of *Vāsavadattā* tells us that the followers of Jaimini, i.e. Pūrva Mīmāṁsakas attacked Buddhism.[2] Kumārila, who denounced Buddhism with the zeal of a convert, was a Mīmāṁsaka. According to him the Buddha, who wa a Kṣatriya who "transgressed the duties of his own class in taking upon himself the works of teaching and receiving presents; and hence how can we believe that true Dharma or Duty would be taught by one who has transgressed his own Dharma?" "For the sake of the well-being of humanity. He (the Buddha) transgressed his own duties of the Kṣatriya, and having taken up the duties of the Brāhmaṇa, he taught, even to the people outside the pali of Vedic religion, such truths relating to the Dharma, as were not taught by the Brāhmaṇas who were unable to transgress the prohibition (of such teaching being imparted to outsiders); and thus prompted by his mercy to others, he even went to the length of transgressing his own Dharma."[3] Hindu Law has been largely influenced by Pūrva-Mīmāṁsā. Hence Manu's injunction that those who deny the authority of the Vedas would lose their caste.[4]

Conflict of economic interest perhaps reinforced the hostility of Mīmāṁsaka brāhmins towards the Buddhist monks. The latter, along with other followers of the *jñāna mārga*, discounted the utility

---

1. The *Jātaka* XXII. 200 Trans: *Cowell and Rouse,* vol. VI.
2. Subandhu: *Vāsavadattā,* 144 Translated by Gray p. 88. According to Pandit R.V. Krishnamachariar, Subandhu was a Vaiṣṇavite and an adherent of the Mīmāṁsā philosophy. Gray: *ibid.*, p. 13 footnote 2.
3. *Tantra-vārttika*, Adhyāya I, Pada III, Adhi III, Trans. by G.N. Jha, pp. 167-68.
4. Nīlakaṇṭha, a jurist, in his *Prāyaścitta Mayūkha* quotes a verse from Manu to this effect: "If a person touches a Buddhist or a follower of Paśupata, Lokāyataka, Nāstika and Mahāpātaki, he shall purify himself by a bath." The development of rules regarding expiatory ceremonies has been greatly influenced by Pūrva-Mīmāṁsā. Besides, Nīlakaṇṭha an his family were leading Mīmāṁsakas. See the *Introduction to Vyavahāra Mayūkha* by P.V. Kane: *Bombay Sanskrit and Prākrit Series* No. LXXX.

of performance of rites and ceremonies enjoined by the followers of Karma-mārga viz. the Mīmāṁsakas. These practices had no value at all for persons who had renounced the world. This naturally affected adversely the interests of Brāhmins inasmuch as the performance of rites and ceremonies was a source of income to them. That is how we can explain the hostility of the Mīmāṁsakas towards monks. In the story of Mālinī, narrated in the *Mahāvastu*, the brahmins were to put Mālinī to death. "For", said they, "she is a thorn in the side of the brāhmaṇs in the King's Court. King Kṛki was devoted to the brāhmaṇs and twenty thousand of them ate daily at his court—. But she, disdaining the Brāhmaṇs has introduced recluses into the King's Court and has treated them with all this veneration and honour. She has served and honoured the recluses with the means of subsistence which was due to the brāhmaṇs at the King's Court."[1] Again, referring to sacrificial Brāhmins, the Bodhisattva in *Bhūridatta Jātaka* says:

"These Brāhmins all *a livelihood require*

And so they tell us Brahma worships fire."[2]

The *Brāhmadhammika sutta* of the Sutta Nipāta states that the Brāhmins became degraded by accumulating wealth through sacrifices performed by kings as per instructions of the Brāhmins. The charge levelled against the Buddha in the *Tantravārttika* in having violated his Dharma by not only undertaking the task of teaching but also by receiving presents obliquely points to the underlying economic conflict. But it is to be noted that there is a recognition, however reluctant, that the Buddha preached the truth even to the outcastes.

According to Hiuen Tsiang,[3] the heretics including 500 Brāhmins had plotted to assassinate Śilāditya (Harṣa) because they were "jealous of the Śramaṇas, whom the King had reverenced and exceedingly honoured.......[4]

---

1. The *Mahāvastu*, 309, Translated by Jones S.B.B. vol. XVI p. 258.
2. *The Jātaka*, XXII, 199 Trans. Cowell and Rouse, vol VI, p. 207.
3. Beal: *Buddhist Records of the Western World*, vol. I, p. 221.
4. In this connection, we may quote an episode narrated by Ānandagiri in his Śaṅkaravijaya showing the contempt with which the Mīmāṁsakas treated all Sannyāsins. "At that time, while Maṇḍana Miśra, having invited all the gods by the invocation of Śālagrāma, was washing his hand of the darbha grass, he saw the feet of Śaṅkarācārya inside the sanctified circle. On inspection of his person, he knew him to be a Sannyāsin and was in a moment ruffled with clamorous wrath and cried out, "Whence comes this shaven headed man?" It is significant that the fire worshipper Brāhmin Aggikabhāradvāja of the Vasalasutta seeing the Buddha coming at a distance cried out: "Stay there O' shaveling; (stay) there O Samanaka (wretched samana); (stay) there O Vasalaka (i.e, outcast)." Likewise Brāhmin Sundarikabhāradvāja, a fire worshipper, seeing the Buddha, thought: "This man is shaved. this man is a shaveling." *Sutta Nipāta*.

Puśyamitra Śuṅga is the only important Indian ruler who is charged with anti-Buddhistic activities. evidently, he was a Mīmāṁsaka as he was a Sāmavedī Brāhmin[1] who revived sacrifices and re-established the supremacy of Brāhmins. Perhaps, he was influenced by political motives; he had wrested power from the Mauryas whose greatest ruler was also the greatest patron of Buddhism. In Brāhmins, he could find a valuable ally. Religious bigotry, however, seems to have been a personal trait of Puśyamitra for the gateways of the Bharhut and Sāñci stūpas were built during the Śuṅga period, those of the former by Dhanabhūti, an ally or feudatory of the Śuṅgas. The references to Buddhist persecution by Mihirgula and Śaśāṅka[2] are too vague, and highly exaggerated in the case of the obscure prince Sudhanvan. The latter was under the influence of Mīmāṁsakas. The evidence on the other hand, proving absence of any antagonism or conflict except to a very limited extent, is weighty and conclusive. In fact the Purāṇas appropriated the Buddha as an Avatāra (an incarnation) of Viṣṇu. The Buddhists, on the other hand, identified Bodhisattva Avalokiteśvara with the Hindu gods, Brahma, Indra, Īśvara and Maheśvara (Śiva).[3]

---

1. The Jaiminīyas are an important branch of the Sāmavedins.
2. Beal: *Life of Hiuen Tsiang*, p. 171.
3. In the *Saddhamapuṇḍarīka* (S.B.E. vol. XX, chap. XIV, p. 411). Avalokiteśvara preaches the law in the form of Brahmā, Indra, Iśvara and Maheśvara according to the needs of beings. In *Kāraṇḍa Vyūha*, it is related that in the time of Vipasvyin Buddha when Avalokiteśvara created the world, Maheśvara sprang from the forehead, Brahmā from the shoulders, Nārāyaṇa (Viṣṇu) from the heart and Sarasvatī from his mouth. (Quoted in Winter-nitz: *A History of Indian Literature*, vol. II, p. 308). In the *Dasabhūmika-sūtra*, again, a bodhisattva is born as Indra, Mahābrahmā and Maheśvara (Śiva) in various stages. (Dr. Har Dayal: *The Bodhisattva Doctrine*, p. 284).

Chapter - 16
Buddha and Asceticism

U. Dhammaratana

In his first sermon delivered at Banaras Bhagavān Buddha expounded the doctrine of Majjhimā paṭipadā or the Middle Path. It is so called because it avoids the true extremes of Kāmasukhallikānuyoga or self-indulgence on the one hand and Attakilamathānuyoga or self-mortification on the other hand. The Buddha has characterised them as *anariyo* or unworthy and *anatthasaṁhito* or unprofitable.

The position of the first extreme is clear. There was a great tradition in India that the seeker after truth must be a person of renunciation. Thus renunciation was the first and foremost condition of the life of the seeker after truth.

The Buddha was born a prince. He was brought up in the lap of luxury. His was a life full of pleasures. But when the call came to him to be a seeker after truth he made the great renunciation and in doing so he followed the tradition of the country. Through conviction gained by experience he also upheld that tradition. So when the Buddha advised his disciples to abstain from a life of indulgence he was one with that great tradition.

As for asceticism, there was again a long tradition behind it, i.e. that the seeker after truth must lead a life of asceticism. Here too, true to the tradition, he followed the path of asceticism. But through experience he found extreme asceticism not only unhelpful but definitely harmful. So he rejected it as unworthy and unprofitable.

There are references in the Nikāyas scattered in different discourses of the Buddha which give an account of the ascetic practices prevalent at the time, how and to what extent the Buddha underwent them and why he rejected them in toto. Here some of these references have been collected and arranged so as to give some idea of it.

Asceticism is as old as the religious history of mankind. This is equally true of both the east and the west. The most obvious reason for this universal practice must have been the subjugation of the lower impulses through the mortification of the flesh. The pampering up of the body tends to intensify the lower impulses. As such, mortification of the same, at first sight, would seem to be the most natural way of getting rid of them. So we can attribute the origin of asceticism to this motive.

While these practices have vanished from other parts of the world, here in India they still have got the living tradition. Some practices which had been prevalent some two and a half thousand years ago are still to be found in this land. The following account, recorded in the *Udumbarikasīhanāda Sutta*, refers to the ascetic practices prevalent at the time of the Buddha.

"There are ascetics given to these practices; they go about naked. They accept nothing expressly brought or prepared for them. They do not accept invitations. They accept nothing taken from the cooking pot in their presence, nor placed within the threshold, nor within a mortar, nor among sticks, nor anything from two eating together, nor from a pregnant woman, nor from a nursing mother. They do not accept food collected at the time of a famine, nor from where a dog is, nor from where flies are swarming... They visit one house and take one mouthful, visit two houses and take two mouthfuls...visit seven houses and take seven mouthfuls...They take food once a day, once every two days...or once every seven days. Thus they take food according to rule, at regular intervals, up to even once a fortnight... They feed themselves on herbs, on Nivara seeds, leather parings, powder of rice husks, rice scum, flower of oil seeds, grass, cow-dung...on fruits and roots from the woods and windfalls.

"They wear coarse hempen cloth, discarded corpse-cloth, rags, barks of trees, antelope-hides, kusá-grass, human-hair blanket, horse-hair blanket, a garment made of owl-feathers... They pluck their hair and beard.

"They keep on standing or crouching on heels and walk on all fours. They sleep on beds of thorns or iron spikes. They sleep on ground and on one side. They besmear their body with dust and dirt and live in the open air...They never drink cold water and take bath thrice a day in order to wash away their sins." (*Dīghanikāya*, sutta 25).

In this long list there are some twenty two observances in the matter of food, thirteen in clothing and twenty in physical torture.

Now these practices do not refer to some old-world tradition that has nothing to do with the present. As already mentioned, they refer to a living tradition that is still prevalent in this ancient land. For instance in Banaras, Haridwar and such other places, even to-day we can see ascetics undergoing these practices with all sincerity and earnestness.

Now to come to the Buddha, he renonunced the world in order to find out a panacea for the suffering humanity. First he went to the well-known teachers of the day, studied their systems and practised their disciplines. In the scriptures special mention has been made of the two sages- Ālārakālāma and Uddakarāmaputta. He soon mastered their systems in both theory and practice. But he was not satisfied with them. So he left them for making further investigations. When he failed in all these efforts, as a last resort, he took to the life of asceticism at Uruvelā.

Referring to this event the Buddha says: "Seeking for the supreme state of peace I gradually made my way to Magadha and went to Senānigama or the army township at Uruvelā. There I saw a delightful spot with a pleasant grove, a river flowing delightfully, with clear water and good fords, and round about a place for seeking alms. Then I thoughts: "This is truly a delightful spot for one who is given to the struggle for attaining the supreme state." (*Jātakanidānakathā*).

Thus at Uruvelā, near Buddhagaya, on the banks of the river Nerañjarā, he started his life of penances and carried it on for six long years.

There are several discourses in the Nikāyas which give graphic descriptions of his ascetic practices. The most graphic among them all is that given in *Mahāsīhanāda Sutta* where the Buddha relates his experience in the matter to Sāriputta, his chief disciple.

Addressing Sāriputta the Master says: "Sāriputta I have lived the four-fold higher life. I have been an ascetic of ascetics, lothly have I been; scrupulous have I been, foremost in scrupulosity; solitary have I been, foremost in solitary life.

"To such a pitch of asceticism have I gone that naked was I, flouting life's decencies...never heeding invitations extended to me, never accepting food brought to me or cooked expressly for me...I did not accept food from two people messing together, from a pregnant woman or a nursing mother, never from collections made in the time of famine, nor from where a dog was ready at hand, or where hungry flies congregate... I have visited only one house a day and there taken only one morsel... ...I have visited seven houses a day and taken only seven morsels there. I have lived on a single saucer of food a day... I have had but one meal a day, or once every two days...or every seven days...or a fortnight on a rigid scale of rationing...My sole diet has been herbs gathered green, or the grain of wild millet or paddy, snippings of hide or water plants, or the powder of the rice husks or the discarded scum of boiled rice, flour of oil-seeds, or grams...I have lived on wild roots and fruits and wind-falls only.

"My raiment has been of hemp...of rags from the dust heaps, of bark, antelope hide...or blankets made of hair of men or animals, or the wings of owls.

"In fulfilment of my vows I plucked out the hair of my head and beard. I kept on standing or crouching up for days together and moved on all fours...I slept on a bed of thorns and iron spikes...... Thus I tortured my body and to such a length, Sāriputta, have I gone in asceticism.

"To such a length have I gone in lothliness that on my body I have accumulated the dirt and filth of years till it dropped off of itself, even as the rank growths of years fall away from the stump of a Tinduka tree. But never once came the thought to me to clean it off with my own hands or to get others to clean it off for me. So firm was I in the fulfilment of the vows.

"To such a length in scrupulosity have I gone that my footsteps, out and in, were always attended by a mindfulness so vigilant as to awake compassion within me over even a drop of water lest I might harm tiny creatures in crevices. So scrupulous was I in keeping my vows.

"To such a length have I gone in leading a solitary life that when my abode was in the depths of the forest, the mere glimpse of a cowherd, a grass-cutter, or a man gathering fire-woods or edible roots in the forest, was enough to make me dart from dale to dale, and from hill to hill in order that they might not see me or I them. As a deer at the sight of a man darts away at the mere glimpse of a cowherd or a grass-cutter, over hill and dale, even so did I dart away......To such a length have I gone in leading a solitary life.

"When the cow-herds had driven their herds from the pastures, up I came on all fours to find a subsistence on the droppings of the young milch-cow...So foul a filth eater was I.

"I took up my abode in the awesome depths of the forests, depths so awesome that it was reputed that none but the passionless could venture in, without hair standing on end. When the cold season brought chilly wintry nights, then it was that, in the dark half of the month when snow was falling, I dwelt by night in the open air and in the dark thicket by day. But when there came the last broiling month of the summer before the rains, I made my dwelling under the baking sun by day and in the stifling thicket by night......In a cemetery I lay down with human bones for a pillow.

"Sāriputta! there are some recluses who hold and say that purity comes by way of food, and accordingly proclaim that they live exclusively on āmlaki fruits, which, in one form or the other, constitute their sole diet. Now I can claim to have lived on a single āmlaki fruit a day. If this leads for Sāriputta to think that this fruit was larger in those days, you are mistaken, for it was precisely the same as it is today. When I was living on a single fruit a day, my body grew emaciated in the extreme, because I ate so little; my limbs grew like the knotted joints of a withered creeper...like a buffalo's hoof were my sunken buttocks; like the twists in a rope were my spinal vertebrae; like the rafters of a tumbled down roof were my ribs; like the stars gleaming deep down in the depths of a well, gleamed my eyes deep down in the depths of their sockets. As the rind of a cut-gourd shrinks and shrivels in the heat, so shrank and shrivelled the scalp of my head, and that because I ate so little. If I sought to feel my belly I found myself grasping my backbone. So closely did my belly cleave to backbone, and that because I ate so little. When I wanted to retire for the calls of nature, I fell down on my face, and all that because I ate so little. If for ease of body I chafed my limbs, the hairs of my body fell away under my hand, rotten at the roots, and all that because I ate so little." (*Majjhimanikāya* sutta, 12).

All these paragraphs refer to his observances in the matter of food, clothing and physical torture.

Mahāsaccaka Sutta records an account of the breathing practices he underwent. In course of a discussion with Saccaka, a follower of Nigaṇṭha Nāṭaputta or Mahāvīra, the Buddha says:-

"With teeth clenched and with tongue pressed against my palate, by sheer force of mind......I started the breathing practices. I stopped breathing in or out, through mouth and nose, and then great was the noise of the air as it passed through my ear-holes, like the blast from a smith's bellow. I stopped breathing in or out, through mouth and nose and ears and then violent winds wrecked my head as though a strong man were boring into my skull with the point of a sword...Violent pains attacked my head as though a strong man had twisted a leather thong round my head...violent winds pierced my inside through and through as though an expert butcher were hacking my inside with cleavers...there was a violent burning within me as though two strong men, taking a weaker man by both arms, were roasting him and burning him up in a fiery furnace.

"Thus I underwent all forms of sever and acute penances. Of such penances that have been undergone through the ages past, or will be undergone through the ages to come, or are now being undergone by recluses, mine are pre-eminent. There was nothing worse beyond. Nothing more left in this direction to be experimented with. Yet with all these severe austerities I failed to transcend ordinary human limits, attain enlightenment and the supreme state of peace." (*Majjhimanikāya* sutta, 36).

So Siddhārtha gave up the path of asceticism, and the five companions, who had been attending on him all the time, lost all faith in him. They deserted him and went to Banaras. Siddhārtha did not mind it at all. He had made that great renunciation not to please anybody or to uphold a certain system or a tradition. He had been out to find out a panacea for the suffering humanity. Since the day of his renunciation he had been experimenting with truth. He was determined not to be satisfied with anything less than truth. So he gave up asceticism and took to a new path.

Here it has to be borne in mind that when Siddhārtha realised the futility of asceticism he got a suggestion from his past experience to proceed in the right direction for light. There are the words of the Buddha on the point:

"A memory came to me of how once, seated in the cool shade of a Rose-apple tree in the garden of my father, King Suddhodana, I, divested of pleasures of sense and of wrong states of mind, entered upon an abode in the first Jhāna with all its bliss—a state bred of inward aloofness, but not divorced from observation and reflection. Could this be the path to Enlightenment? In prompt response to this memory, my consciousness told me that here lay the true path to Enlightenment." (*Jātakanidānakatha*).

With this suggestion from his past experience Siddhārtha started his quest in a new direction. How the Buddha took to the Middle Path, what supreme effort he made and how he attained Sammāsambodhi—the full Enlightenment under the Bodhi tree at Buddhagaya is a long story which is not concerned with the present topic.

The above account gives a picture of the background of experience against which the Buddha rejected the path of asceticism in his first sermon.

Here we have to remember that when the Buddha rejected asceticism he also rejected a long tradition and naturally there was opposition from the side of the followers of that tradition. *Kassapasīhanāda Sutta* is a case in point.

According to this Sutta the naked ascetic Kassapa goes to the Buddha and asks him: "Gotama! is it true that you disparage all penances, find faults with all ascetics and with every one who leads a hard life."

The Buddha replied, "Kassapa! my words have been misreported. The Tathāgata does not indulge in such generalisations nor does he make such sweeping statements. The Tathāgata appreciates all the good points in ascetics.[1] Then he proceeds to explain the futile nature of the ascetic practices above referred to in the life of his own experience. He further points out to him that higher life consists in the purity of character and the cultivation of inner virtues. Thus one must get rid of the mental defilements and cultivate such noble virtues as love, compassion and so on. It is this kind of self-culture that leads to a higher and nobler life and not those practices. The opponent, of course, was unarmed and won over by the Buddha.

Then again *Udumbarikasīhanāda Sutta*, already referred to, records a discussion between the ascetic Nigrodhakappa and the Buddha. Here the Buddha points out to Nigrodhakappa that those practices were alright for catching the popular imagination, as done by certain ascetics, for name, fame and gain. But then they were far away from anything like a higher life.

In *Kassapasīhanāda Sutta* another ascetic defending the life of asceticism says that these practices mean a harder life and such a life, in turn, means a higher life. The Buddha disagrees with him. He points our that these practices are not so hard as they appear to be. Moreover they can be practised by people without any virtue in them. So the Buddha asks him not to make fuss about them. He further points out to him that cultivation of mind is the most difficult thing and the thing that matters most, and as such real asceticism lies in this kind of life and discipline and not in physical tortures and low habits.

Another point to be taken into consideration, in this connection, is that all kinds of indecencies were practised and paraded in the name of asceticism. *Kukkuravatika Sutta*[2] bears ample testimony to the same. According to it, there were two ascetics—Puṇṇa and Seṇiya.

---

1. *Digha Nikāya*, Sutta 8.
2. *Majjhima-nikāya*, Sutta 57.

One observed kukkuravata and as such behaved like a dog and the other sūkaravata and behaved like a pig. When the Buddha was asked about their fate he plainly said that those who behaved like animals and developed animal characters must be born as such.

There are some of the references which give us an idea of the ascetic practices, their nature and the Buddha's opinion of the same. It is clear from all this that the Buddha did not advocate their practice in any form. On the contrary, he declared them as obstacles to a higher life and made a total rejection of asceticism as such.

When we say that the Buddha rejected asceticism it does not mean that he encouraged the other extreme. As mentioned in the first sermon, he rejects it with the same deprecation.

What the Buddha wanted was that the people should lead a decent life and not a shabby one, a healthy life of simple habits and not a life of luxury, and cultivate the noble virtues. He believed in a healthy mind in a healthy body and vice versa.

While the Buddha rejected asceticism, he believed in strict moral discipline. This is amply borne out by the nature of the rules and regulations laid down for the guidance of the members of his monastic order. In this connection we have to take into consideration that Lord Buddha recognised the existence of what may be called the ascetic temperament. The *dhutaṅgas* have been recommended for their benefit. But then they are voluntary practices not binding on the members of the order. Moreover it has been strictly laid down that their practice should not be advertised. They are to be observed by a member even without the knowledge of his fellow brethren. The Buddha did not want to attach undue importance to them. He put the right emphasis on the right place so that people may not be taken up with forms and formalities at the cost of the spirit.

According to *Mahāsakuladāyi Sutta*[1] when Udāyī, an ascetic, told the Buddha that the latter was venerated by people for his life of holiness, purity and simplicity, the Buddha remarked that in the matter of simplicity there were his disciples who surpassed him. For instance, there was Mahākassapa who observed all the thirteen *Dhutaṅgas*. He lived all his life on alms begged from door to door and spent all his days in the forest, whereas the Buddha used to live occasionally in palatial buildings and accept royal invitations. Further he says to Udāyī that wise men pay homage to the Tathāgata for his attainments and achievements in *sīla* (moral culture), *samādhi* (mental culture), *paññā*

1. *Ibid.*, Sutta 77.

(spiritual vision) and above all *akuppā cetovimutti* or that liberation of mind which can never be perturbed and disturbed again.

The following two stanzas provide a fitting conclusion to this topic:

na naggacariyā na jaṭā na paṅkā
nānāsakā thaṇḍilasāyikā vā
rajo ca jallaṁ ukkuṭikappadhānaṁ
sodhernti maccaṁ avitiṇṇakaṅkhaṁ

[Nakedness, matted hair, fasting, lying on the ground, rubbing the body with ashes and sitting motionless do not purify man.]

alaṅkato cepi samaṁ careyya
sánto danto niyato brahmacāri
sabbesu bhūtesu nidhāya daṇdaṁ
so brāhmaṇo sa samaṇo sa bhikkhu

[He who, though adorned with fine clothes, fosters the serene mind, is calm, controlled, is established in the noble way of life and has ceased to injure all other beings, he indeed is a noble one (brāhmaṇa), a recluse (samaṇa), a mendicant (bhikkhu).]

These two stanzas sum up the whole attitude of the Buddha on the matter.

Chapter - 17

An account of the Buddha's Nirvāṇa And the first Councils According to the Vinayaṣudraka

E. Obermiller

Vol. VIII, part 2 of the *IHQ.*, contains a most interesting article of Professor L. Finot "*Mahāparinibbāna-sutta and Cullavagga*". The author expresses his opinion to the effect that these two important texts of the Pāli Canon originally represented one work which was subsequently dismembered, the motive for this dismembering being the desire of the compliers to include the part containing the utterances of the Buddha himself in the *Sutta-piṭaka*, whereas the other part, relating to the events after the Buddha's death and especially the rules of monastic discipline were regarded as having their proper place in the *Vinaya-piṭaka.*[1]

The arguments advanced by Professor Finot in support of his opinion are the following: "The events contained in the *Cullavagga* XI follow chronologically those which form the subject-matter of the *Mahāparrinibbāna-sutta.*" "Beside the unbroken sequence of the events which they relate the two sections share a peculiar character suggestive of a common origin, that is their historical, annalistic garb."[2] Moreover, Prof. Finot mentions the *Saṃyuktavastu* (Nanjio N. 1121.) containing an account of both Parinirvāṇa and Councils. This analogy, says Prof. Finot, makes it possible to suppose that the Theravādins (just as the Sarvāstivādins to whom the *Saṃyuktavastu belongs) "could have had among their sacred books an historical record of the same description."*[3]

1. *Op.cit.*, p. 243
2. *Ibid.*, p. 242
3. *Ibid.*

Now, as regard analogies, the Tibetan tradition puts us in the possession of materials according to which it becomes possible to affirm that Prof. Finot must be unquestionably right in his opinion, as will be illustrated by the following:

In the History of Buddhism of the celebrated Tibetan scholar Bu-ston, Rin-chebn-ḍub (grub), the historical part proper,[1] begins with an account of the twelve principal events in the Buddha's life.[2] The first eleven, ending with the "First Rolling of the Wheel of the Doctrine"[3] are rendered in accordance with the *Lalitavistara*. The twelfth and last event, viz. the *Buddha's departure into Nirvāṇa* is borrowed from the text called *Vinayakṣudraka*.[4] This text, as preserved in the Tibetan translation in the Kangyur, consists of three bulky volumes[5] and is in its greater part devoted to the minutæ of monastic discipline.[6] The narrative of the Buddha's Nirvāṇa which is incorporated by Bu-ston in his History is contained *in the first of these volumes.*[7] We have the description of the following events thus,-

1. *The Buddha stops that Biotic Force which keeps the continuity of his life on earth going on.*[8]

2. *The Buddha's departure to Kuśanagara and the precepts delivered by him on the way there.*[9]

3. *The Buddha's instructions concerning the funeral rites to be performed after his death.*[10]

4. *The conversion of Sunanda*[11] *and of the Parivrājaka Subhadra*[12]

5. *The last words of the Buddha and his departure into Nirvāṇa.*[13]

6. *The message of the Buddha's Nirvāṇa brought to Ajātaśatru.*[14]

---

1. Vol. II of my translation, Heidelberg, 1932.
2. Tib. *mdzad-pa bcu gñis.*
3. *prathama-dharma-cakra-pravartana,* i.e. the first Benares sermon.
4. Tib., *Hdul-ba phran-tshegs. Bu-ston, Xyl. 88 a. 3. - mya-ṅan-las-ḥdas-paḥi tshul (Ḥdul-ba) phran-tshegs bzin bśad-do.* Transl., p.72
5. *Kg. ḤDUL. (Vinaya), vols.XI (da), XII (na), and XIII (pa).*
6. Just as in the *Cullavagga.*
7. Fol. 247 a.—301 a. of the Derge edition.
8. *āyuḥ-saṃskāra=tsheḥi ḥdu-byed. Vin-kṣudr. (Kg. ḤDUL., XI), 247 a. 6—249 a.5* Bu-ston, Transl., *p. 57.*
9. *Vin.-kṣudr., 250 b. 6 sqq.*—Bu-ston. Transl., *57.*
10. *Vin.-kṣudr., 275 b. 5.—276 a. 3.*—Bu-ston, Transl., *59.*
11. Rab-dgaḥ.
12. Rab-bzaṅ. *Vin.-kṣudr., 279 a. 6—280 a. 5*—Bu-ston, Transl., pp. 59, 60.
13. *Vin.-kṣudr., 287 b. 2.—290 a. 6.*—Bu-ston. Transl., p. 61.
14. *Vin.-kṣudr., 290 a. 6 sqq.* —Bu-ston. Transl., p. 62.

7. *The funeral rites.* [1]

8. *The quarrel about the relics of the Buddha and pacification by Droṇa*[2] Conclusion in verse.

A comparison of Bu-ston's text with the version of the *Vinayakṣudraka* shows a very close correspondence. All the verses are quoted by Bu-ston at full length; the passages in prose are only slightly abridged.

Thereafter, having dialated on the meaning of Nirvāṇa and its interpretation according to Hīnayāna and Mahāyāna, etc.,[3] Bu-ston passes over to the narrative of the first and second Councils. He does not indicate his source, but even at the first glance it becomes quite clear that this source is no other than the *Vinayakṣudraka*. As before, the version of the latter appears in a slightly condensed form, all the verses being quoted at full length. We have here:-

1. *The intention of Mahākāśyapa to assemble a Council of the Clergy for the sake of rehearsing the Scriptures.*[4]

2. *The invitation of Gavāmpati by Pūrṇa. The refusal of Gavāmpati to take part in the Council and his death.*[5]

3. *The arrival of the Clergy at Rājagṛha. The expulsion of Ānanda by Mahākāśyapa.*[6]

4. *Ānanda's attainment of Arhatship, his return to the Council and the accomplishment of the First Rehearsal.* (Ānanda rehearses the *Sūtras,* Upāli the *Vinaya* and Mahākāśyapa the *Abhidharma).*[7]

5. *Mahākāśyapa's and Ānanda's departure into Nirvāṇa.*[8]

6. *The arrival of Madhyāntika in Kashmir.*[9]

7. *The Second Rehearsal.* —The ten indulgences admitted by the monks of Vaiśālī, the arrival of the Arhat Yaśas and the excommunication of the monks of Vaiśālī. The place and the date of the second Rehearsal.[10]

---

1. *Vin.-kṣudr., 291 b. sqq.*—Bu-ston, Transl., p. 63.
2. *Vin.-kṣudr., 297 a. 3.—301 a. 3.*—Bu-ston, Transl., pp. 65-67.
3. Transl., pp. 67-72.
4. *Vin.-kṣudr., 301 a. 3—b. 3.*—Bu-ston, Transl., pp. 73.
5. *Vin.-kṣudr., 301 b. 7—303 b. 2.*—Bu-ston, Transl., pp. 73-76.
6. *Vin.-kṣudr., 305 a. 6—309 b. 2.*—Bu-ston, Transl., pp. 77-81.
7. *Vin.-kṣudr., 309 b. 2—316 b. 3.*—Bu-ston, Transl., pp. 81-85.
8. *Vin.-kṣudr., 316 b. 7—322 a. 4.*—Bu-ston, Transl., pp. 85-90.
9. *Vin.-kṣudr., 322 a. 4—323 a. 7.*—Bu-ston, Transl., p. 90.
10. *Vin.-kṣudr., 323 b. 4—332 a. 2.*—Bu-ston, Transl., pp. 91-96.

So we have the narrative of the Buddha's attainment of Nirvāṇa and that of the first and the second Councils *actually contained in one text*. And even more: —The story of the Councils begins *just on the same line in which the narrative of the burial of the Buddha finishes,*[1] without any indication whatsoever.

Prof. Finot says that "we have reason to suppose that the account of the Councils of Rājagṛha and Vaiśālī once formed the latter part of a larger historical work."[2] —We may now affirm that such a work actually exists; it is contained in the first volume of the *Vinayakṣudraka*. The two parts which were severed from each other in the Pāli Canon appear in the Northern Vinaya text as one whole.[3]

Thus it is that Prof. Finot's very illuminating suggestions find a striking confirmation by the perusal of the *Vinayakṣudraka* and Buston's reference to it.

Chapter - 18

The Buddha and Language

Franklin Edgerton

Language is one of the most fundamental features of human culture; some would say *the* most fundamentally important. The use of language distinguishes man, as a biological genus, from other animals. No other animals have yet been shown to possess articulate speech as we know it in men; no doubt many animals succeed in communicating with each other in limited ways by the use of vocal sounds, but in spite of the efforts of many able biologists, no one has yet proved that such communication approaches the elaborate conventionalized systems which characterize all known human speech. And conversely, no human group has ever been found which lacked a language in this sense.

In one way, then, language may be said to be a unitary feature characterizing all men. But in another sense, which is socially much more important, language divides man from man. For no two languages, no two dialects of the same language even, are exactly alike. And language differences are very noticeable. The most naive human being quickly becomes aware of them, though it usually does not occur to him to formulate them, and if pressed, he would often find it hard to do so. If he hears speech in a language so remote from his experience that he cannot understand it, his first reaction may be that the alien speaker cannot really talk at all. The Russian word for Germans means literally "dumb; people who can't talk"- that is, can't talk Russian. There are many similar instances. If the alien speaker uses a dialect closely related to the hearer's own, then, while the hearer may understand perfectly or nearly so, he may be more or less surprised, and his surprise may be tinged with amusement or scorn; the speaker may seem to him to be strangely ignorant of the "proper" way of talking.

There are countries where only one language is spoken, but where in the course of time strikingly different dialects of that language have developed. It often happens then that one such dialect acquires superior social prestige, most commonly for political reasons; it is often the language of the capital. This becomes the "standard" language of the country, like standard Southern British, or standard French (originally local to Paris), and all members of the politically or culturally dominant class speak it; but often many of them can also speak the dialects of their original homes.

A peculiar variant of this situation occurs when the "upper" classes adopt a language of culture which is not the same as any dialect actually spoken (by the uneducated) in the country. It may be a language quite unrelated to any of the country's living dialects; Latin occupied this position in Hungary for centuries; until 1825 Latin was the only language allowed to be spoken in the Hungarian parliament. In the Roman Catholic Church, wherever it flourishes, Latin even now has a certain vogue, in writing and speech. It is thus used especially when Roman Catholic priests need to communicate with each other but cannot speak or understand each other's vernaculars; for example, when a German and a Spanish priest have occasion to write or speak to one another. A very similar situation exists in India. Most Indians know that when a South India paṇḍit, whose native language is Dravidian, communicates with a North Indian paṇḍit, both will naturally write or speak in Sanskrit, which is ordinarily the only language known to both.

With this we draw near to the main topic of this paper. The general historic position in India of Sanskrit as a literary and religious language is so well known to Indian readers, and to most others who are likely to see this article, that I shall not discuss it. What interests me here is its relation, and the relation of linguistic usage in general, to Buddhism, and to the Buddha himself.

I begin with a somewhat abbreviated translation of a passage from the Pali canon (*Cullavagga 5. 33; Vinaya Piṭaka,* PTS. *ed., ii. 139. lff.*)

> Two monks, brothers, of fine (cultivated) language and fine (eloquent) speech, came to the Buddha and said: Lord, here monks of miscellaneous origin (literally, of various names, clan-names, races or castes, and families) are corrupting the Buddha's words by (repeating them in) their own dialects; let us put them into Vedic (*cbandaso āropema*). The Lord Buddha rebuked them: Deluded men, how can you say this? This will

> ot lead to the conversion of the unconverted......And he delivered a sermon and commanded (all) the monks: You are not to put the Buddha's words into Vedic. Who does so would commit a sin. I authorize you, monks, to learn the Buddha's words each in his own dialect.

This incident is certainly a part of the oldest Buddhist tradition, for very similar accounts are found in a number of Chinese translations of the Buddhist canonical works. They are fully presented in French translations by Lin Li-kouang, *L'aide-memoire de la vraie loi* (Paris, 1949), 218 ff. I have given excerpts from the most important parts in English (based on Lin's French) in my Buddhist Hybrid Sanskrit Grammar (New Haven, 1953) I. 10-12 (see also the adjoining sections). These will not be repeated here, but should be consulted by any one who wishes fully to understand the reasons for the inferences I am about to draw.

Several facts of considerable interest emerge from a study of the various forms of this ancient passage.

First: dialect differences were clearly and easily preceptible in the speech of the monks who attended the Buddha. It is said, in a Chinese translation, that "their pronunciations are not the same."

Second: many, doubtless most of these monks spoke Middle Indic dialects. There were some, particularly born brahmans, who knew and could use the sacred language of brahmanism; but it may perhaps be assumed that even they, when not speaking to one another, made use of Middle Indic. In one of the Chinese translations the two originally brahman monks complain that their fellow-monks "do not know masculine and feminine gender, nor singular and plural, nor present, past and future, nor long and short vowels, nor metrically light and heavy syllables." Such traits of language, which seemed errors to the brahmans, characterize some Middle Indic dialects as they would appear from the standpoint of Sanskrit, when compared with it'.

Third: when proposing to codify the Buddha's teachings in their own "cultured" language, the two brahman monks say *chandaso āropema*, which certainly means "let us put (them) into Vedic." Some have understood, "into verse". But this makes no sense in the context; it is clearly not verse as contrasted with prose, but a different *language*, which they wish to use. The word *chandas* is regularly used by Pāṇini when he notes a Vedic usage that differs from his own Sanskrit; he always says *chandasi*, "in the Veda" (such and such a form is used).

This use of *chandas* is also familiar in epic and classical Sanskrit literature (Boehtlingk and Roth, Sanskrit-Wörterbuch, II. 1080, s.v. *chandas* 3; V. S. Apte, The Student's Sanskrit-English Dictionary, Bombay, 1922,, p. 212, s.v. *chandas* 5.) Here *chandas* need not refer to the poetic parts of the Veda alone, and it is not at all likely that it was so intended. The Brāhmaṇas and Upaniṣads, which are mainly prose, are classed as parts of the Veda, that is *chandas*. The language of the Upaniṣads, even the oldest of them like *Bṛhadāraṇyaka* and *Chāndogya*, is fairly close to classical Sanskrit, but it could still be called linguistically *chandas* "Vedic". It was probably something like this language that the brahman monks wanted to use. It may, of course, have been even closer to Pāṇinean Sanskrit. We have no way of telling. But no such term as "Sanskrit" is used in the Pali text, nor even in the commentaries on it; indeed, the Pali equivalent (Saṃkhata) of the word Saṃskṛta seems never to be used in a linguistic sense. Nor do the Chinese translators use any word which proves that their Indic originals used that word. Pāṇini's date is still uncertain, and it is at least possible that he was later than the Buddha. In any event, the use of the word Saṃskṛta of the Sanskrit language seems to be relatively late. The high, cultivated language of brahmans, into which the two monks wanted to translate the Buddha's teachings was known to them as "Vedic" (*chandas*), in contrast with the Middle Indic dialects which were used by most of their brother-monks; some Middle Indic dialect was doubtless used by the Buddha himself.

Fourth: the Buddha emphatically rejected the proposal of the brahman monks, and gave orders that all monks should learn and repeat his teachings in their own several dialects. This clearly implies that when the Buddhist gospel was carried by missionaries into new regions, the converts were to exercize the same privilege. They were to learn and recite the teachings in their own local dialects. This is very definitely stated in several of the Chinese translations, which command use of "the popular language" of the various regions or countries. And all versions of this passage, northern and southern, make very clear the Buddha's reason for this injunction. He was preaching a gospel for all men, not for a select elite. He wanted to be sure that every human being could understand his message. He felt that his aim would be defeated if his words were codified in a learned, literary language (Vedic) which only the upper classes could understand.

At first, it seems clear that Buddhist monks and missionaries obeyed this injunction. Early Buddhist inscriptions, like those of Bharhut, give evidence of this. Wherever Buddhist communities were established, versions of the sacred texts, or some of them, were recited in the local vernaculars. In one or two cases, extensive local canons of this sort, or parts of them, in Middle Indic vernaculars, have survived to this day. The best known is the Pali canon; it originated somewhere in west-central India. We may be certain that there were many others, but most of them have been lost.

As long as Buddhism spread only in the northern parts of India the use of local vernaculars can hardly have involved anything like what we should call "translation". In the Buddha's time, the popular dialects of those regions were almost exclusively Indo-Aryan, and chiefly in the Middle Indic stage. They must also at that time have been so close to each other as to be mutually intelligible. (Even some centuries later, the edicts of Aśoka suggest that this may still have been true). A Buddhist missionary could recite the texts in his own vernacular, and his hearers would repeat them in their, perhaps without even clearly apprehending the linguistic differences. (But it is quite possible, also, that the dialect of the missionary may at times have been imitated, to some extent, by the local converts, consciously or unconsciously.) Translation cannot have become a serious problem until Buddhism spread to Dravidian-speaking regions in the south, and to extra-Indian countries like Chinese Turkestan, Tibet and China.

However, after a few centuries the Buddha's followers in India, and in some adjoining countries, began to ignore his injunction to clothe his teachings only in genuine, popular vernaculars. Instead they began to make use of canons composed in learned languages, which were not, or no longer, the native dialect of any people. Pali itself was originally based on a north Indian vernacular; but after Buddhist monks carried the Pali canon to Ceylon, Burma, Siam, and Cambodia, it came to be church language, like Latin in Europe. It had to be learned in school, and is still so learned in southern Buddhist countries. In short, it came to have a position in those regions similar to Sanskrit in brahmanical India.

In India itself, or in some parts of it, what happened was different. The great social prestige of Sanskrit, as a language of literature and culture among brahmanical Hindus, began to influence their Buddhist neighbours and associates. Like the two learned monks in the old Vinaya story, later Buddhists felt that it would be more dignified if they imitated the brahmans and Sanskritized their compositions. Some of them—the poet Aśvaghoṣa is an example—frankly abandoned the use of vernaculars in literary works, and used standard Sanskrit as a vehicle. Aśvaghoṣa is believed to have been a brahman himself originally, and to have undergone the usual brahmanical Sanskrit education in his youth.

A different and a very curious course was adopted by one group of Buddhists. Instead of completely giving up the literary use of vernaculars, they took an old Middle Indic dialect (its original locale is unknown to us) in which Buddhist texts existed, and partially Sanskritized it, but so imperfectly that the underlying Middle Indic still showed through the half-veneer of Sanskrit. Thus arose what I have called Buddhist Hybrid Sanskrit (it could have been called, perhaps, Hybrid Middle Indic), a strange language in which for centuries most North Indian Buddhist texts (so far as we know them) were composed. It has often been described as a corrupt or bad Sanskrit, but this distorts the truth. It is a blend of Middle Indic with Sanskrit, but its basis, or substratum, is Middle Indic; the Sanskrit features are secondarily and superficially laid on.

To be sure, as time went on, this Sanskritizing process was carried further and further. In the oldest texts preserved to us, notably the *Mahāvastu*, Middle Indic or hybridized phonology and grammatical forms are still very abundant, though genuine Sanskrit forms are perhaps equally so. In later times, more and more regular Sanskrit forms appear. Often these replace original Middle Indic or hybrid forms in later versions of the same passages, so that we can see the process of Sanskritization going on before our eyes. The latest works of this tradition came to look superficially like almost standard Sanskrit, though careful study will always reveal some Middle Indic forms. But even the latest Buddhist Hybrid Sanskrit texts still retain numerous *words*, lexical items, which show their vernacular origin. Though they may be made to look like Sanskrit, though their phonetic shape and grammatical formation may be perfectly standard Sanskrit, these items of vocabulary never occur in Sanskrit, or never in the same meanings, whereas they do occur (for the most part) in Middle Indic dialects, especially Pali. They thus prove that they belong to the Hybrid tradition, going back ultimately to Middle Indic, in spite of their seeming Sanskrit guise.

Thus the Buddha's desire that his teachings be couched in the native dialects of all peoples was frustrated, at least in his native land. It would not have consoled him to know it, but there ensued one result of interest to linguists—the development of a strange, artificial, literary language, perhaps unique in its nature—Buddhist Hybrid Sanskrit.

Chapter - 19

Buddha as an Architect

P. K. Acharyya

"In Buddha's time and in that portion or northern India where the Buddhist influence was most early felt—that is to say, in the districts including and adjoining those now called the United Provinces and Behar"—the arrangements of villages were practically similar. "We nowhere hear of isolated houses. The houses were all together, in a group, separated only by narrow lanes. Immediately adjoining was the sacred grove of trees of the cultivated field, usually rice-field. Villagers are described as uniting of their own accord to build mote-halls and rest-houses and reservoirs, to mend the roads between their own and adjacent villages, and even to lay out parks."[1]

The exact details of town-planning are not available. But "we are told of lofty walls, ramparts with buttresses and watch-towers and great gates; the whole surrounded by a moat or even a double moat, one of water and one of mud. But we are nowhere told of the length of the fortifications of the extent of the space they enclosed. It would seem that we have to think not so much of a large walled city as of a fort surrounded by a number of surburbs......From the frequent mention of the windows of the great houses opening directly on to the streets or squares it would appear that it was not the custom to have them surrounded by any private grounds. There were, however, no doubt, enclosed spaces behind the fronts of the houses, which latter abutted on the streets."[2]

---

1. Buddhist India, Rhys Davids, pp.42, 45, 49.

2. R.D., pp. 64, 65. Cf. The hill fortress, Girivraja, four and half miles in circumference, is said to have been built by Mahāgovinda, the architect. Bimbisāra is stated to have built Rājagaha, king's house, which was three miles in circumference. "The stone walls of Girivraja are the oldest extant stone buildings in India". Mention is also made of Ayojjhā, Bārānasi, Kampilla, Kosambī, Madhurā, Mithilā, Sāgala, Sāketa, Sāvatthī, Ujjenī, Vesālī and other cities, of which however the architectural details are not enough. (Vimānavatthu commentary, p. 82), compare Dīgn. xix, 86:

Unlike villages and towns, the details of buildings are found in abundance in the canonical text as well as the Jātakas. At places it appears as if Buddha were delivering discourses on architecture. As a matter of fact, he enjoined upon his devotees the supervision of building construction as one of the duties of the order[1]. It is stated in one of the early texts that the bhikkhus were told on a certain occasion by the Blessed One after the delivery of a religious discourse with respect to dwellings: I allow you, O Bhikkhus, abodes of five kinds— *Vihāra, Ardhayoga, Prāsāda, Harmya, and Guhā*[2]. Buildings are thus divided into five classes. The details of the distinctions are not methodically given in the texts inasmuch as these are not architectural treatises[3].

Vihāras are the well-known monasteries or temples of the Buddhists, originally implying halls, where the monks met. *Ardhayogas* seem to be a special kind of Bengal buildings, partly for religious and partly for residential purposes. *Prāsādas* are wholly residential storeyed buildings; *harmyas* are a larger and more pompous type of storeyed buildings. *Guhās* seem to be less dignified buildings, originally built underground for middle class people. The extensiveness of these buildings

---

Dantapuraṃ Kāliṅgānaṃ Assakānañca Potanaṃ
Māhissatī Avantīnaṃ Sovīrānañca Rorukam
Mithilā ca Videhānaṃ Campā Aṅgesu māpitā,
Bārānasi ca Kāsīnaṃ ete Govinda-māpitā ti.

1. Cullavagga, VI, 17, 1 (transl., pp. 212-216).
2. Vinaya texts, Mahāvagga, I, 30, 4 (pp. 73-4): Cullavagga, VI, 1, 2 (p. 158).
3. The commentator Buddhaghosa has, however, submitted an explanatory note. 'Vihāra' is the well-known Buddhist monastery. 'Ardhayoga,' which literally means 'half-joining' is stated by this commentator to imply 'Suvarṇa-vaṅga-gṛha' or "gold-coloured Bengal house". as rendered by Oldenberg and Rhys Davids. There seems. however. no such class of houses in Bengal. Nor has this class of buildings been mentioned in the śilpa-śāstras. It is clear, however, that these are meant to imply some sort of luxurious buildings of the then Bengal. Regarding prāsāda' Buddhaghosa simply says that it is a long prāsāda. Rhys Davids has made these conjectures,—"a long storied mansion, or the whole of an upper storey, or the storied buildings". Sir M.M. Williams seems to explain this by "the monks' hall for assembly and confession". 'Harmya' is stated to be a prāsāda with an upper chamber placed on the top-most storey. The references to the uses of 'prāsāda' and 'harmya' as found in the śilpa-śāstras, general Sanskrit literatures, and the archœological records will be found in the writer's Dictionary under those terms. 'Guhā' literally means cave and would seem to refer to underground buildings. One of the Jātakas (Ummagga, p. 430) actually contains an elaborate description of an underground palace, and such have been the rock cut temples, as in the famous Ajanta caves. According to Buddhaghosa these 'guhā' buildings are of four kinds, namely, as they are built of bricks, stone, wood, or earth. Rhys Davids has rendered 'śilāguhā' by 'hut made in a rock' and left out the translation of 'paṃsu-(Sanskrit 'pāṃśu' meaning sand, dust, or crumbling soil) guhā.' Buddhaghosa has thus explained the pañca-lenāni under Mahāvagga 1.30.4—

can be imagined from the length of time devoted to getting a house completely built. Thus it is stated that "with reference to the work of a small *Vihāra*, it may be given in charge (to an overseer) as a *navakamma* (new work) for a period of five or six years, that on an *Aḍḍhayoga* for a period of seven or eight years, that on a large *Vihāra*, or a *Pāsāda* for ten or twelve years[1]." That the long periods were not idled away will be clear from the detail of houses gathered mainly from the Vinaya texts.[2]

The selection of building sites shows a highly developed good taste. The *Ārāma*, well fitted for quiet-loving people is stated to be built "not too far from the town and not too near, convenient for going and for coming, easily accessible for all who wish to visit him, by day not too crowded, by night not exposed to too much noise and alarm......"[3] The whole compound is enclosed with ramparts (*prākāra*) of three kinds, namely, brick walls, stone walls, and wooden fences which are again surrounded with bamboo fences, thorn fences, and ditches.[4]

Houses were built comprising "dwelling-rooms and retiring rooms, and store-rooms, and service-halls and halls with fire-places in them, and store-house, and closets, and cloisters, and halls for exercise, and wells, and sheds for the well, and bath-rooms, and halls attached to the bath-rooms, and ponds and open-roofed sheds (*maṇḍapas*)[5]. These buildings are meant to be dwelling houses; so it is stated that "an *upāsaka* (devotee) has built for his own use a residence, a sleeping room, a stable, a tower, an one-peaked building, a shop, a boutique, a storeyed house, an attic, a cave, a cell, a store-room, a refectory, a fire-room, a kitchen, a privy, a place to walk in, a well, a well-house, a *yantragṛha* (which is supposed by Bühler 'to be a bathing place for hot sitting baths'), a *yantragṛha* room, a lotus pond and a pavilion"[6].

"Aḍḍhayoga ti suvaṇṇavaṅgagehaṃ. Pāsādo ti dīghapāsādo. Hammiyān ti upari ākāsatale patiṭṭhitakūṭāgāro pāsādo yeva. Guhā ti iṭṭhakaguhā silāguhā dāruguhā paṃsuguhā.

Compare also Oldenberg and Rhys David's Vinaya texts, translation. Mahāvagga, p. 173 note, also Cullavagga, p. 151 note 2.

1. Cullavagga. VI, 17, 1.
2. Cullavagga, VI, 5.
3. *Ibid.*, VI, 4, 8.
4. *Ibid.*, VI, 3, 7, 10.
5. *Ibid.*, VI, 4, 10.
6. Mahavagga III, 5, 9; also III, 5, 6.

The inner chambers are divided into three classes, called *Śivikā-garbha* or square balls, Nālikā-garbha or rectangular halls, and *Harmya-garbha*, which seems to be a large dining hall[1]. The verandahs (*alinda*) seem to have been a special characteristic of these buildings. The Blessed One (Buddha) says "I allow you, O Bhikkhus, covered terraces, inner verandahs, and over-hanging caves"[2]. The storeyed buildings (*prāsāda*) are stated to be furnished with "a verandah to it supported on pillars with capitals of elephant head"[3].

Details of gates, doors and windows are also elaborate. Gateways are built with rooms, and ornamental screen-work over them[4]. And gates are made of stakes interlaced with thorny brakes[5].

Doors are furnished with "door posts and lintel, with hollows like a mortar for the door to revolve in, with projections to revolve in those hollows, with rings on the door for the bolt to work along in, with a block of wood fixed in to the edge of the door-post, and containing a cavity for the bolt to go into (called the monkey's head), with a pin to secure the bolt by, with a connecting bolt, with a key-hole, with a hole for a string with which the door may be closed, and with a string for that purpose[6]". The windows are stated to be of three kinds according as they are made with railings, lattices, or slips of wood[7]. The shutters are adjustable

---

1. About this last Buddhaghosa seems to be doubtful and says hammiya gabbho ti kūṭāgāra gabbho mudaṇuchādana gabbho vā; but about the other two terms he is clear; sivikā gabbho ti caturasya gabbho; nālika gabbho ti vitthārato dviguṇatiguṇāyāmo dīgho gabbho (Cullavagga, VI, 3,3). But Oldenberg and. Rhys Davids seem to have been wholly misled when they translate these last two by "palankeen shaped and quart measure shaped," about the last of which the Indians of even to-day are quite unfamiliar.

2. Cullavaga, VI, 3, 5. commented by Buddhaghosa: Alindo nāma pamukhaṃ vuccati. (Compare Abhidhānappadīpikā, verse 218). Paghanaṃ nāma yaṃnikhamantā ca pavisantā ca pādehi hananti, tassa vihāra-dvāra ubhato kuṭṭaṃ niharitvā katapadesassa etam adhivacanaṃ, paghānam ti pi vuccati. Pakuṭṭana ti majjhe gabbhassa samanta pariyāgāro vuccati pakuṭan ti pāṭho. Osarako ti anālindake vaṃsaṃ datvā tato daṇḍake osāretvā kataṃ chādanapamukhaṃ.

3. *Ibid.*, VI, 14, 1 hatthinakhakaṃ supported on the frontal globes (*kumbhe*) of elephants, says Buddhaghosa.

4. Cullavagga, VI, 4, 10; 3, 1; 'tosaṇa' of which excellent examples in stone have been found at the Sāñchi and Bharhut Topes.

5. *Ibid.*, VI, 3, 10.

6. *Ibid.*, Vi, 3, 8 also 2, 1 and 17, 1. Compare the distinction between 'kavāṭa' door proper and 'dvāra' door-way or gate-way. The keys are stated to be of three kinds—as they are made of bronze, hard wood, or horn (VI, 2, 1).

7. Cullavaga, VI, 2, 3.—'Vedikā vātapānaṃ' which according to Buddhaghosa means 'cetiye vedikāsadisaṃ' of which 'vedikā' has been explained by Rhys Davids in his note on Mahā-Sudassana Sutta 1; 60 (see R. D's Buddhist Suttas, p. 262) 'jāla vātāpanaṃ nāma jalakevadghaṃ' of which 'jāla' literally means 'net' but corresponds to lattice. R. D. advise to compare Anglo Indian jalousic (p. 162). 'Sālaka vātapānaṃ nāma thambhaka vātapānam' which "possibly means with slips of wood arranged horizontally as in our venetian blinds" (p. 163). In spite of all

and can be closed or opened whenever required[1]. Five kinds of roofing are mentioned,—brick roofing, stone roofing, cement roofing, straw roofing, and roofing of leaves[2]. The roof is first covered over with skins and plastered within and without; then follow white wash, blocking, red-colouring, wreath work and creeper work[3]. "The floors were of earth, not of wood, and were restored from time to time by fresh clay or dry cowdung being laid down, and then covered with a white wash, in which sometimes black or red was mixed. From the parallel passage in Mahāvagga (1. 25. 15) and Cullavagga (VIII. 3. 1), it would seem that the red colouring was used rather for walls, and the black one for floors". It appears, however, that with a view to removing the dampness[4] gravel was spread over the floor[5].

There were stairs of three kinds, namely, brick stairs, stone stairs, and wooden stairs. And they were furnished with *ālambana-bāhā* or balustrades[6]. A more detailed description of flights of stairs (*sopāna*) is given in the Mahā Sudassana Sutta. "Each of these had a thambhā, evidently posts or banisters; *sūciyo*, apparently cross-bars let into these banister; and *uṇhisam*, either a head-line running along the top of the banisters, or a figure-head at the lower end of such a head-line[7]".

Thus it is clear that very minute details also were mentioned in this literature. The subject, therefore, seems to have been treated more than in a casual manner.

"The entrance to the great houses was through a large gateway. To the right and left of the entrance passage were the treasure and grain stores. The gateway led into an inner courtyard round which were chambers on the ground-floor. And above these chambers was a flat roof called the *uparipāsāda-tala*, the upper flat surface of the house, where the owner sat, usually under a pavilion, which answered the purpose at once of a drawing-room, and office, and a dining hall."

---

these the learned orientalists Rhys Davids and Oldenberg would say that "There were, of course, no windows in our modern sense, but only spaces left in the wall to admit light and air, and covered by lattices of three kinds" (note on Ibid, VIII, 2, 2, translation p. 279).

1. Mahāvagga, I, 25, 18; Cullavagga VIII, 2, 2.

2. Cullavagga, VI, 3, 10. Compare also VI, 3, 8; 3, 3 etc.

3. *Ibid.*, V, 11, 6; the rendering of the term 'ogumpheti', which also occurs in Mahāvagga V, 11, by 'skins' seems doubtful and unsuitable. Buddhaghosa in his note at the latter place says 'aguṃ phiyantīti bhitti daṇḍakādisu veṭhetvā bandhāti.'

4. Rhys Davids and Oldenberg, note on Cullavagga, VI, 20, 2.

5. Compare Cullavagga, V, 14, 5.

6. Cullavagga, V, 11, 6.

7. Mahā-Sudassana Sutta 1, 59. See also R. Davids' Buddhist Suttas, p. 262, and compare Cullavagga, VI, 3, 3.

"In the king's palace there was accommodation also for all the business of the state, and for the numerous retinue and the extensive harem.............The supplementary buildings included three institutions which are strange to us, and of considerable historical interest."

"We are told several times of a building of seven storeys in height[1]." Rhys Davids seems to be of opinion that these buildings must have some connection with the seven-storeyed Ziggarats of Chaldœa. "But in India the use to which such seven-storeyed palaces were put was entirely private, and had nothing to do with any worship of the stars." Still the learned Professor would add that "in this case also the Indians were borrowers of an idea.

"Another sort of building historically interesting were the hot-air baths, described in full in the Vinaya texts[2]. They were built on an elevated basement faced with brick or stone with stone stairs up to it, and a railing round the verandah. The roof and walls were of wood, covered first with skins, and then with plaster; the lower part only of the wall being faced with bricks. There was an ante-chamber, and a hot-room, and a pool to bathe in. Seats were arranged round a fire-place in the middle of the hot room; and to induce perspiration hot water was poured over the bathers..........."

In the Dīgha Nikāya[3] there is a description of another sort of bath, an open-air bathing tank, with flights of steps leading to it faced entirely of stone, and ornamented both with flowers and carvings."

The Dāgobas or topes were another class of monuments erected in the cemeteries[4]. They were pre-Buddhistic in origin[5] but became very prominent after Buddha. The priestly records, however, ignore these topes, because they were erected "more especially by those who had thrown off their allegiance to the priests, and were desirous to honour the memory of their teachers, who were leaders of thought, or reformers, or philosophers."

---

1. Satta-bhūmaka-pāsāda, Jātaka, 1, pp. 227, 346; v, pp. 52, 426; VI, p. 577. R. Davids refers to a building "still standing at Pulasti-pura in Ceylon and the thousand stone pillars on which another was erected at Anurādhapura". *Buddhist India*, p. 70.

2. III, pp. 110. 297. "After the bath there was shampooing, and then a plunge into the pool." "It is very curious to find" observes Rhys Davids "at this very early date in the Ganges valley a sort of bathing so closely resembling our modern so-called 'Turkish bath". "Did the Turks" he asks "derive this custom from India?" p.74.

3. Buddhist Suttas, pp. 262 foll. translated by R. Davids, who refers to "several ancient baths still to be seen at Anurādhapura in a fair state of preservation in spite of the more than two thousand years that have elapsed since they were first constructed", p. 76.

4. Vinaya texts, IV, p. 308.

5. Cf. White Yajurveda, chap. 35 and Writer's Dictionary.

"The first step was probably merely to build the cairn more carefully then usual with stones and to cover the outside with fine *cunnam* plaster to give a marble-like surface. The next step was to build the cairn of concentric layers of the huge bricks in use at the time, and to surround the whole with a wooden railing."

"Even in Buddha's time the size of the monuments had already reached very considerable dimensions. The solid dome erected by the Sākiyas over their share of the ashes from Buddha's funeral pyre must have been about the same height as the dome of the St. Paul measured from the roof"[1].

In the books referring to the earlier Buddhist period stone seems to have been used only for pillars, walls, and stair-cases. A Palace of stone is once mentioned in a fairy land[2]. According to Rhys Davids, "the superstructure, at least, of all dwellings was either of woodwork or brickwork. In either case it was often covered, both internally and externally, with fine *cunnam* plaster-works, and brilliantly painted in fresco, with figures or patterns", four of which have been preserved, namely, wreath-work, creeper-work, fine-ribbon-work, and dragon's tooth-work[3]. When the figures predominated the result is often called a picture-gallery (*cittāgāra*)[4].

The articles of furniture which form an important part of the architectural treatises are also elaborately described in the Buddhist literature. "Benches were made long enough to accommodate three persons"[5]. The bedstead (*pallaṅka*) or divan was a separate piece of furniture[6]. Large couches (*āsandi*) or chairs seem to have been some important articles of furniture[7]. Couches covered with canopies are also mentioned[8]. Mention is made of a large variety of chairs— rectangular chair (*āsandaka*), arm-chair, sofa (*sattaṅgo*), sofa with arms

---

1. R Davids, pp. 83-4. The reference to the large number of topes will be found in the Writer's Dictionary under stūpa. Buddhaghosa's enumeration of the parts of a palace also shows the popularity of the subject of architecture in Buddhist literature. "Ayaṃ phasso nāma yathā pāsādaṃ patvā thambho nāma, sesadabbasambhārānaṃ balavapaccayo tulāsaṃghāṭabhittipādaidkuṭagopānasipakkhapāsamukhavaṭṭiyo thambhe baddhā thambhe patiṭṭhitā evam eva sahajātasampayuttadhamānaṃ balavapaccayo hoti". Atthasālinī, p. 107.
2. Jāt., VI, p. 269.
3. Vinaya texts, II, p. 67; IV p. 47.
4. R. Davids, p. 68.
5. Cullavagga, VI. 13, 2.
6. Cullavagga, VI, 141; VI, 8, 1. etc Mahāvagga, V, 10, 3.
7. *Ibid.*, VI, 14, 1; VI, 8, 1 etc. Mahāvagga, V, 10, 3. Rhys Davids and Oldenberg render āsandi twice by cushions and once by couches and Childeren by chairs in his Dictionary. It seems to imply Sanskrit 'āsana' which means 'seat'.
8. Mahāvagga, V, 10, 3.

to it, state chair (*bhadda-pīṭham*), cushioned chair, (*vīthikā)*, chair raised on a pedestal (*elaka-padaka-pīṭham*), chair with many legs (*āmalaka-vaṇṭika-pīṭham)*, leaning board (*phalakam*), cane-bottomed chair (*koccham*) and straw-bottomed chair[1]. Mention is also made of the litter or sedan-chair[2].

Valuable carpets, rugs, pillows, curtains, and such other luxurious decorations also are elaborately described. Thus mention is made of "coverlets with long fleece, counterpanes of many colours, wollen coverlets white or marked with thick flowers, mattresses, cotton coverlets dyed with figures of animals, rugs with long hair on one or both side, carpet in wrought with gold or with silk, large wollen carpets such as the nautch (dancing) girls dance upon, rich elephant housings, horse rugs or carriage rugs, panther or antelope skins, large cushions and crimson cushions[3]." Pillows are of various kinds. Pillows are stated to be of both "the size of a man's head" and half " the size of a man's body." The Buddha allows the bhikkhus "to comb out the cotton, and make the cotton up into pillows if it be of any of these three kinds— cotton produced on trees, cotton produced on creepers, and cotton produced from potaki-grass[4]." The bolsters made for the use of high officials were of five kinds as they were stuffed with wool, cotton cloth, bark, grass or leaves. There were also coverlets for them[5]. The smaller articles like the floor cloth, mosquito curtain, handkerchief and spittoon did not escape the notice of the then house-decorators[6].

---

1. Cullavagga. VI, 2, 4. Rendering are mostly those made by Rhys Davids and Oldenberg depending on Buddhaghosa's note. Compare aslo Cullavagga, VI, 20. 2 and VIII, 1, 3. Apassena-phalakam as a "board to lean aganist" is also mentioned in the Mahāvagga 1, 25, 15, 16. For arm-chair and sofa there seems to be another expression *apasayam*; see Buddhaghosa's note Cullavagga, VI, 2, 4.
2. Mahāvagga, V, 10, 2.
3. Mahāvagga, V, 10, 3.
4. Cullavagga, VI, 2. 6; see also IV, 44 and VIII, 1, 3.
5. *Ibid.*, VI, 27, 1.
6. *Ibid.*, VI, 20, 1; V, 14, 1; Mahāvagga, VII, 18 for colaka or handkerchief; see also Cullavagga, VI, 19; V, 9, 4

Chapter - 20

The Buddhist Meditation

Nalinaksha Dutt

Sīlavisuddhi (ethical purity) and *cittavisuddhi* (mental purity) are the two vital conditions to be fulfilled by the bhikkhus for the realisation of Nibbāna, and the major portion of the Buddhist texts is devoted to the exposition of these two *visuddhis*. Many modern writers have dealt comprehensively with *sīla-visuddhis* teachings of Buddhism but few have taken up for detailed study the teachings dealing with *cittavisuddhi*. The principal reason for such one-sided study is that the purification of mind is attained through meditational practices, and the lessons on such practices can be best, and are actually, imparted orally, and perhaps secretly, by the ācārya to his *antevāsika*. An exposition however detailed of these practices cannot make itself sufficiently explicit. The only comprehensive attempt to give an exposition of the practices has been made by Buddhaghosa in his *Visuddhimagga*. The object of this paper is to present to the inquisitive a connected intelligible account of what Buddhaghosa has said. It will serve as a guide to those who feel interested in the Nikāya passages dealing with *satipaṭṭhānas*, *jhānas*, *brahmavihāras*, *abhiññās*, etc. Dr. Rhys Davids has edited a late Sinhalese work on the subject, entitle the *Yogāvacara's Manual of Indian Mysticisms practised by the Buddhists* with an Introduction. This work, however, does not help us much. Very recently Mr. G. Constant Lounsbery has complied a treatise entitled *La Meditation Bouddhique* (Paris 1935), in which he has put together most of the available materials scattered in the Buddhist texts with the aid of personal instructions of the well-known Sinhalese monks Ñāṇatiloka, Nārada, Parawahera Vajirañāṇa and Samana Mahinda. This is a useful work and its value would have been much enhanced if he had utilised the *Visuddhimagga* exhaustively. The present paper, we hope, will facilitate to a certain extent the study of the Buddhist meditational practices.

A series of spiritual exercises has been prescribed for a monk for attaining complete control over the mind (*citta*). In verse after verse in the Dhammapada and in passages after passages in te Nikāyas the difficulty of controlling the fickle *citta* has been dilated upon, and at the same time it has been emphasised that the only means of attaining *Nibbāna* is by curbing the citta, i.e. withdrawing it from all that is attractive in the world and directing it to the highest goal. There are endless *upakkilesas* like rāga, dosa, moha which never permit *citta* to rest at peace, and the various meditational practices prescribed in the Buddhist texts have for their first object the steadying of the mind so as not to be affected by the weal and woes of the world. It is only with a steady mind that one is capable of comprehending the essential oneness or sameness and vastness of the beings of the universe—the Nibbāna of the different schools of Buddhist philosophy.

It is almost an axiomatic truth that control over mind is attained through meditational exercises. Buddhaghosa has often used the two words *citta* and *samādhi* synonymously. He gives the etymological meaning of samādhi thus:

"Samādhānatthena samādhi, ekārammaṇe citta-cetasikānaṃ samaṃ sammā ca ādhāraṃ ṭhapanan ti vuttaṃ hoti." (*Vism.*, p. 84).

[Samādhi means firmly placing; on one object the act of putting or placing the mind and mental functions equally and properly is so called.]

There is a graduated course in these meditational exercises, and this course ranges from the most elementary form of samādhi, i.e. simple fixation of mind on a black or white circular spot to the most subtle when the meditator loses wholly his consciousness and sensation and reaches a state which is almost akin to the state of death (*saññāredayitanirodha*). (See Dutt, *Aspects of Mahāyāna Buddhism*, pp. 158-61).

Buddhaghosa, in order to bring out the various characteristic features of a *samādhi*, has adopted the usual Buddhist (*aṅguttara*) method of numerical classification which is as follows:—

(A) Samādhis of two kinds:

1. upacāra-samādhi and appanā-samādhi. While attempting concentration of mind, *upacāra* is said to be that mental state which immediately precedes the fixation of the mind on a certain point; the fixation is *appaṇā* (Sans. *arpaṇā*). It may be described also as the preparatory attempts for developing thorough concentration of mind, i.e. *appanā*;

2. (a) lokiya (i.e. with Kuṣalacitta) and lokuttara (i.e with ariya-magga);

(b) sappītika (with joy) and nippītika (without joy);

(c) sukhasahagata (associated with a happy state of mind and upekkhāsahagata (associated with equable state of mind).

(B) Samādhis of three kinds:

3. (a) hīna (lower), majjhima (middle), and paṇīta (higher);

(b) savitakka-savicāra (with discursive and discriminatory thoughts), avitakka-vicāramatta (without discursive thoughts but with discrimination), and avitakka-avicāra (without discursive and discriminatory thoughts);

(c) pīti-sahagata (with joy), sukha-sahagata (with happy state of mind), and upekkhā-sahagata (with equanimity of mind):

(d) paritia (small) (while in upacāra-bhūmi), mahaggata (large) (while in rūpāvacara-kusala and arūpāvacara-kusala bhūmis) and appamāṇa (measureless) (while ariyamagga-sampayutta).

(C) Samādhis of four kinds:

4. (a) dukkhāpaṭipado dandhābhiñño, dukkhāpaṭipado khippābhiñño, sukhāpaṭipado, dandhābhiñño, and sukhāpaṭipado khippābhiñño.

[*Paṭipada* is that part of mental excercise which is necessary for collecting one's thoughts and reaching the upacāra stage, and *abhiññā* refers to the next course of exercises which lead to appanā (i.e. fixing mind upon one point).

Dukkhā here means 'with difficulty' as opposed to *sukhā* 'with ease': similarly *dandhā* means 'slow' as opposed to *khippā* 'quick'.]

(b) paritto parittārammaṇo (not of a high order with limited basis of meditation), paritto appamāṇārammaṇo (not of a high order but with unlimited basis of meditation), appamāṇo parittārammaṇo (unlimited but with a limited basis of meditation), appamāṇo appamāṇārammaṇo (unlimited with unlimited basis of meditation).

(c) vitakka (discursive thoughts), vicāra (discriminatory thoughts), pīti (joy), and sukha (happy state of mind)—four combinations of any two or more of these.

(d) hānabhāgiya (belonging to a lower category), ṭhitibhāgiyo, (belonging to steadying category), visesabhāgiyo (belonging to a higher category), and nibbedhabhāgiyo (belonging to the highest);

(e) kāmāvacaro (belonging to the sensus sphere), rūpāvacaro (belonging to the sphere of forms), arūpāvacaro (belonging to the sphere of formless), and apariyāpanno (belonging to the highest);

(f) chanda-samādhi (concentration by means of strong will), viriya-samādhi (by means of energy), citta-samādhi (by means of mind-control) and vīmaṃsā-samādhi (by means of examination); see also *Majjhima*, II, p. 11.

The above classification helps us only to comprehend the various mental states accompanying the different kinds of meditation but it does not tell us anything about the graduated course to be followed by an adept for passing from the lowest to the highest samādhi. Buddhaghosa, however, has gone into minute details of the processes which induce samādhi and it will now be our object to go into them. We shall consider the following in due order:

(i) the *Palibodhas* or hindrances to the practice of samādhis,

(ii) forty kammaṭṭhānas or the objects of meditation,

(iii) kalyāṇamitta hammaṭṭhānadāyaka or the spiritual preceptor;

(iv) the candidate, and

(v) the successive steps in meditation.

(i) Palibodhas

The observations to one practising meditation may be of a varied nature as described in the *Milindapañha* (pp. 365-399). Buddhaghosa puts them in a more practical form and enumerates them as follows:

Āvāso ca kulaṃ lābho gaṇo kammañ ca pañcamam

addhānaṃ ñāti ābādho gantho iddhī ti te dasâ ti.

These ten, Buddhaghosa explains, act as hindrances not to all but only to those who has got mental weaknesses as detailed below:

(i) *Āvāsa* or dwelling places of monks. This affects those monks who take interest in the construction of monastries, stūpas, and so forth.

(ii) *Kula* or family. It affects those who care more for the welfare of his relatives or families of his lay-devotees than that of his own self.

(iii) *Lābha* or gain of food and clothes. It sometimes becomes a source of distraction to the monks of repute, for greater demand is made upon their time by people for the privilege of giving them food and clothes, and not unoften these demands are created by his fellow-brethern who take advantage of his company and receive gifts alongwith him.

(iv) *Gaṇa* or members of the congregations. There are some monks whose time is taken up in teaching the texts of the Sutta or Abhidhammapiṭaka and hardly find time to be alone and practice meditations.

(v) *Kammam* or works. Buddhaghosa takes it to mean navakammaṃ (construction or repair of buildings). He says that much of a monk's time who supervises the building works is taken up in calculating wages of labourers or the works done or to be done.

(vi) *Addhānam* or wayfaring. There are occassions when a monk has got to go to a place to give ordination to a person or to procure any requisite. By leaving it undone, he tries to gain concentration of mind but fails to do so.

(vii) *Ñāti* or relatives including in this case the teachers, disciples or fellow-brethern of the church. Sickness of any of the *ñātis* is a source of distraction to some monks.

(viii) *Ābādha* or one's own sickness which requires medicine to be cured.

(ix) *Gantha* or scriptures. Some are so absorbed in studying the scriptures that they do not find time or feel inclined to practise meditation.

(x) *Iddhi* or miraculous powers. These are attained as one advances in meditation but their use causes hindrance to the development of insight (*vipassanā*) and so these also are treated as one of the palibodhas.[1]

There are some other palibodhas enumerated by Buddhaghosa (*Vism.*, p. 122), e.g., long hairs and nails which should be trimmed off; old robes which should be repaired; discoloured robes which should be dyed; unclean bowls which should be cleansed and weak beds which should be strengthened.[2]

(ii) The Forty Khmmaṭṭhānas

The subjects of meditation are hardly possible of enumeration though traditionally they are set to be forty in number. The selection of the subject, as has been shown above, was left to the Kalyāṇamitta who was free to choose any subject which, he thought, would be the most suitable for his disciple, no matter whether it was included in the traditional list or not. As, for instance, one of the very common subjects

---

1. Cf. Pātañjala, I, 30: व्याधिस्त्यानसंशयप्रमादालस्याविरतिभ्रान्तिदर्शनालब्धभूमिकत्वानवस्थितत्वानि चित्तविक्षेपास्तेऽन्तरायाः ।
2. *Vism.*, p. 122.

of meditation found in the Nikāya is *aniccasaññā* to destroy the sense of I-ness (*asmimāna*), but it is not included in our traditional list.[1]

The forty subjects are:-

1. Ten Kasiṇas
2. Ten Asubhas
3. Ten Anussatis
4. Four Brahmavihāras
5. Four Āruppas
6. One saññā, and
7. One Vavatthāna.

Ten Kasiṇas

The word 'Kasiṇa' is very probably a Prākṛt form of the Sanskrit word 'Kṛtsna' meaning 'entire'. In the Buddhist meditational practices the terms is applied to those subjects of meditation, which occupy the 'entire' mind, and as such does not give scope to the rising of any other thought.[2]

I. The first of the Kasiṇas in the list is *Paṭhavīkasiṇa*, i.e. when earth is taken as an object of meditation. To induce concentration of mind, a beginner is generally asked to fix his attention on a piece of earth which may or may not be specially prepared for him (*kata* or *akata*), i.e. he may choose a circular-shaped or square-shaped piece of earth when it is called *kata* (prepared) or he may choose, say a ploughed field when it is called *akata* (unprepared). In the former case particular attention should be given to the fact that the earth must be without any colour as it is likely to divert attention from the earth to its *lakkhaṇas*, e.g. colour: It is, however, recommended that the earth should be of reddish-brown colour like that of dawn; and taken, if possible, from the bed of the Ganges.[3] In a secluded place the adept is to take his seat and try to concentrate his mind on the paṭhavīkasiṇa, cogitating all the while the evils of *kāma*, the solace in overcoming it and the fact that great saints had obtained emancipation by means of such dhyānas, and repeating constantly the term *paṭhavī* or any of its synonymns, *mahī*, *medinī*, *bhumī*, *vasudhā*, or *vasundharā*. The adept is to try to see with his eyes shut the image of the *paṭhavī* inwardly

---

1. Udāna, iv. 1.
2. Cf. Childers, sv. Kasiṇo. Rhys Davids translates it by the words 'Predominant Ideas' (see *Yogāvacāra's Manual*, p. viii) and Maung Tin by 'Devise' (see *Path of Purity*, II, p. 138).
3. *Vism.*, p. 123-4. There are many other directions about its location, the position of the meditator and so forth.

with as vividness and distinctness as he was doing with his eyes open. As soon as this is accomplished, the *uggahanimittaṃ* is said to have come to stay (*jātam*).[1] He can now go back to his usual place of residence, and cogitate on the *nimitta* acquired by him.[2] By doing so, he gradually gets rid of the five *nīvaraṇas* (or hindrances to religious life),[3] and the impurities (*kilesas*).[4] By this first attempt at concentration (*upacārasamādhī*), his mind becomes concentrated, and there appears in the mind the *paṭ-ibhāganimitta*, i.e. the image of the object of meditation (*uggahanimitta*) but that it is much clearer and brighter than the *uggahanimitta* and without the *kasiṇadosa* which remains in *uggahanimitta*. Now commences really the course of meditational practices from upacāra and appanāto catukka or pañcaka-jhāna.[5]

II. The second is *Āpo-kasiṇa*, i.e. when the object of meditation is water. It may be any natural or existing expanse of water as that of a tank or a lake, or even of the sea, or clean rain water collected in a vessel before it has reached the earth. The vessel must be full and placed in a quiet secluded corner of the monastery. As in the case of *paṭhavī*, the colour-question must be avoided, i.e. the lakkhaṇa of water must not divert the attention of the adept, and the concentration should be induced in the same way as has been explained in the case of *paṭhavī*, uttering in this case the word 'āpo' or its synonyms *ambu*, *udakaṃ*, *vāri*, *salilaṃ*, etc.[6] Gradually the uggahanimitta and paṭ-ibhāganimitta appear and the adept proceeds along the course of meditation.

III. The third is *Tejokasiṇo*, i.e. when the object of meditation is fire. It may be the flame of a lamp, fire in an oven, or a jungle-fire. The fire may also be specially prepared; in that case, some faggots are to be collected and a pile made of them near a tree and then it should be set on fire. A suitable screen with a hole about four fingers wide is to be placed between the fire and the adept. The adept now is to look at the fire without minding the faggots or the smoke or its colour, even its heat. He should utter the word 'tejo' or any of its synonyms and acquire the uggaha and paṭibhāganimittas as detailed above in connection with Paṭhavīkasiṇa.

---

1. *Vism.*, p. 125.
2. He is now advised to use shoes to avoid wasting time in washing his feet and a walking stick. *Vism.*, p. 125.
3. *Viz.*, *kāmacchanda* (strong desire), *vyāpāda* (hatred), *thīnamiddha* (idleness) *uddhaccakukkucea* (arrogance) and *vicikicchā* (doubts).
4. The Kilesas are ten in number, viz., lobha, dosa, moha, māna, diṭṭhi, vicilicchā, thīnaṃ, uddhaccam, ahirikā, anottapaṃ. The first four and uddhaccaṃ are enumerated when the kilesas are calculated to be five in number.
5. See *infra* for details; also *Comp. of Phil.*, pp. 54-5.
6. *Vism.*, p. 170.

IV. The fourth is *Vāyokasiṇa*, i.e. when the object of meditation is wind. It may be seen or felt. In the former case, the adept observes the swaying or shaking of the sugarcane tops or bamboo tops or hair-tips, and in the latter he feels by his body the rush of wind through a hole in a wall or through a window. He realises that it is wind which is moving the tops of sugarcane, etc. or striking his body, and then as described above he is to utter the word 'vāyu' or its synonyms and gradually develop the two nimittas and induce the jhānas.

V. The fifth is *Nīlakasiṇa*, i.e., when the object of meditation is blue colour. It may be of flowers, a piece of cloth or a blue gem. It may be specially prepared by filling a basked up to the brim with blue flowers in such a way so that the pollens or stalk may be seen. The basked should be covered by a piece of blue cloth in such a way that the mouth of the basked is to appear like the surface of a drum. I should be surrounded by a band of a different colour. Then he is to concentrate his mind on the blue colour avoiding the other lakkhaṇas of the flowers and develop the uggaha and paṭibhāga nimittas.

VI-VIII. The sixth, seventh and eighth are *Pītakasiṇa*, *Lohitakasiṇa* and *Odāṭakasiṇa*, i.e., when the objects of meditation are yellow, red and white respectively. The kasiṇas are to be prepared as detailed above like the *Nīlakasiṇa* and the process is the same for developing the nimittas and jhānas.

IX. The ninth is *Āloka-kasiṇa*, i.e., when the object of meditation is a spot of light. The sun's or the moon's rays, if received through a chink in the walls, or windows or through an opening in a thick foliage, form a circular spot of light on the earth. The adept fixes his attention on it and utters 'obhāso obhāso', 'āloko āloko'. The spot of light may also be obtained artificially by putting a lamp within a jar having a hole in its side. As said before, the adept by concentrating his mind on the spot of light develops the nimittas and jhānas.[1]

X. The tenth is *Paricchinnākāsa-kasiṇa*, i.e. when the object of meditation is limited space. The openings in a wall or a window may well be utilised as paricchinna-ākāsa, or an opening may be made, say, four fingers wide in a well-covered pavilion or in a sheet of leather. The adept is to fix his attention on the opening and utter 'ākāso ākāso' and develop gradually the nimittas and jhānas.[2]

In conclusion, Buddhaghosa speaks of the various miraculous powers acquired by successfully practising the above ten kasiṇas.[3]

---

1. *Vism.*, pp. 174-5.
2. *Vism.*, p. 175
3. *Ibid.*, pp. 175-7.

Ten Asubhas

The ten *asubha* (unpleasant) objects of meditation refer to the ten states through which an uncared for corpse passes before it is completely destroyed. They are,—

(i) *uddumātakam* or swollen corpse;

(ii) *vinīlakam*, i.e. when the colour of the corpse has become blue;

(iii) *vipubbakam* or the corpse full of pus;

(iv) *vicchiddakam* or the corpse with limbs torn asunder (e.g. dead bodies of thieves);

(v) *vikkhāyitam*, i.e. when the corpse has been mangled by dogs and jackals;

(vi) *vikkhittam* or the corpse with dismembered limbs;

(vii) *hatavikkhittam* or the corpse with its limbs partly destroyed and partly scattered;

(viii) *lohitakam* or the corpse covered here and there with blood (e.g. of soldier in a battle field);

(ix) *puluvakam* or the corpse full of worms;

(x) *aṭṭhikam* or the skeleton.

After enumerating these ten unpleasant objects of meditation, Buddhaghosa deals with the following:

(i) safety of the place where a corpse is found;

(ii) how he should behave or what he should ponder over while going to or coming from the place of meditation;

(iii) sex of the corpse and its suitability;

(iv) advantages of leaving instructions with the teacher and fellow-brethren about the place selected by him for meditation;

(v) the path and direction to be chosen;

(vi) the nature of the noticeable objects around the place where the corpse is found;

(vii) the six characteristics of the corpse to be observed by him, viz., colour, sex, position, direction and limits of the corpse, as also joints, apertures, depth of eye sockets etc., thickness, and a general view of the corpse.

The meditator, as in the case of *paṭharī*, tries to convert the corpse into a concept (*paṭibhāga*), and then as usual gets rid of the five nīvaraṇas, and induce the ecstacies by gradually doing away with vitakka and vicāra, pīti and sukha.[1]

1. See *Vism.*, p. 189.

The Six Anussatis

The two previous lists of Kammaṭṭhānas speak of actual object upon which the adept concentrates his mind, gradually converting them into concepts. The present list speaks of pure cogitation of the merits (*guṇas*) of (i) Buddha, (ii) Dhamma and (iii) Saṅgha, as also of (iv) *sīlas* (observance of precepts), (v) *cāga* (making gifts) and (vi) *devatās*[1] (ways and means by which one is reborn in the realm of the gods). Such cogitation leads to quietude of the mind (*cittaṃ pasidata*) and destroys the five nīvaraṇas, produces great joy and ultimately induces vipassanā (insight) leading to arhathood.

Other Anussatis

Besides the six anussatis mentioned above, there are three other *anussatis* called (i) maraṇa-sati, and (ii) ānāpāna-sati, and (iii) upasamānussati. Unlike the first twenty *kammaṭṭhānas*, these are matters of cognition and not external objects to be converted into concepts.

The practice of *maraṇa-sati* implies that the adept after having seen a corpse is to ponder over the fact that he is also subject to that inevitable death and by doing so he rouses his mindfulness of death, mental agitation and also knowledge relating to it. This leads to the destruction of the nīvaraṇas and induction of the jhānas. Buddhaghosa gives detailed direction about the suitable death, instances to be selected by the meditator.[2]

---

1. In the *Visuddhimagga*, the merits (*guṇas*) of each of these have been culled out from the Piṭaka and explained in detail. They are as follows:

(i) Buddhānussati—Iti pi so Bhagavā arahaṃ sammāsambuddho vijjācaraṇasampanno sugato lokavidū anuttaro purisadammasārathi satthā devamanussānaṃ Buddho Bhagavā ti.

(ii) Dhammānussati—svākkhāto Bhagavatā dhammo sandiṭṭhiko akāliko ehipassiko opanaviko paceattaṃ veditabbo viññūhī ti.

(iii) Saṅghānussati—supaṭipanno Bhagavato sāvakasaṅgho ujup. b. s., ñāyap. bi. s., sāmicip. b. s., yad-idam eattāri purisa-yugānī aṭṭhapurisapuggalā esa bhagavato sāvakasaṅgho āhuneyyo pāhuneyyo dakkhiṇeyyo. añjalīkaraṇīyo anuttaraṃ puññakhettaṃ lokassā ti.

(iv) Sīlānussati—aho vata me sīlāni akhaṇḍāni acchiddāni asabalāni akammāsāni bhujissāni viññūpasatthāni aparāmaṭṭhāni samādhisaṃvattanikānī ti.

(v) Cāgānussati—Lābhā vata me, suladdhaṃ vata me, yo'ham maccheramalapariyuṭ ṭhitāya paiāya vigatamalamaccherena cetasā viharāmi, muttacāgo payatapāṇi vossaggarato yāca-yoga dānasaṃvibhāgarato ti.

(vi) Devatānussati—Santi devā Cātuṃmahārājikā, santi deva Tāvatiṃsā, Yāmā. Tusitā. Nimmānaratino. Paranimitta-vasvattino, santi devā Brahmakāyikā. santi devā tat'uttarim: yathārūpāya saddhāya samannāgatā tā devatā ito eutā tattha uppannā. 'Mayham pī tathāūpena saddhā saṃvikkali yathārūpena sīlena.........yathā-rūpena sutena.........vathārūpena eāgena.........yathārūpāya anññāya samannāgatā tā devatā ito eutā tattha uppannā. Mayhaṃ pi tathārūpā paññā saṃvijjatī ti.

2. See *Vism.*, pp. 230 ff.

The practice of *kāyagatā-sati* means that the adept is to ponder over the fact that this body from head to foot is full of many impure things and that are in it hair, nails, spleen, intestines, etc. The most popular way of taking up this kammaṭṭhāna is to repeat the list of things contained in the body hundreds or thousands of times either loudly or mentally and thereby induce, concentration of mind. Buddhaghosa then gives many other directions about the best way of practising kāyagatāsati,[1] and treats in detail the various contents of the body,[2]—a treatment which may well bear comparison to a modern anatomical study.

The second is *Ānāpānasati*. The induction of meditation by the process of controlling breath is very widely known and is, in fact, adopted by all religions which advocates concentration of mind. It corresponds partly to the Prāṇāyāma as described in the Brāhmaṇic Tantras and Purāṇas and Pātañjala, I, 34, in which *pūraka* (inhailing), *Kumbhaka* (stoppage of breath) and *recaka* (exhailing) form the three essential factors.[3] In the Buddhist meditational practices it is given an important place and forms one of the chief subject-matters of discourse under the heading *Satipaṭṭhāna*. In the *Yogāracara's Manual*, it is given the first place among the various meditational exercises.

Those, who choose breath-control as their Kammaṭṭhāna, are required to go to a forest or enter into a secluded spot, cut off his memories of the outside world and direct his attention to his own inhalation and exhalation and thus gradually develop *upacāra* and *appanā*.[4] He should sit cross-legged, keeping his body erect. Then he is to exhale (*assāso*) and inhale (*passāso*), observing the time it takes for full inhalation and full exhalation, watching also when exhalation or inhalation starts (*ādi*), reaches the middle (*majjha*) and the end (*pariyosāna*). In exhalation the breath starts from navel (*nābhi*), passes through heart (*hṛdaya*) and reaches the nosetip (*nāsikaggaṃ*),[5] and in inhalation the process is just in the reverse direction. The mind follows the course of the breath consciously. It is only by long practice that an

---

1. *Vism.*, pp. 243 ff.
2. *Ibid.*, pp. 250 ff.
3. Cf. Majjhima, I, p. 243-4, Pātañjala, I, 49.
4. *Vism.*, p. 269.
5. Not *nābhikaggaṃ*. See *Vism.*, p. 280. In the *Sandhyā-upāsanā* of the Brāhmaṇas, the three points are nābhi, hṛdaya and lalāṭa, the first being the seat of Brahmā, the second of Keśava and the third of Sambhu.

Cf. Pātañjalabhāṣya, I, 34: कौष्ठ्यस्य वायोर्नासिकापुटाभ्यां प्रयत्नविशेषात् वमन प्रच्छर्दनम्, विधारणं प्राणायाय:, ताम्यां वा मनस: स्थिति सम्पादयेत्।

adept is able to keep himself aware of all the three stages of in-breathing and out-breathing. Such observation and control of the breath lead to stoppage of all bodily movement (*passambhayaṃ kāyasaṅkhāraṃ*).[1]

The artificial aids[2] taken by an adept for ānāpānasati are mainly (i) gaṇaṇā, i.e. counting, which is not to exceed ten; (ii) anubandhanā, i.e. following the course in its three stages, viz., beginning middle and end; and (iii) phusanā i.e. watching the points of contact, nābhi, hṛdaya and nāsikaggaṃ.[3] By these aids the adept soon acquires the *paṭ ibhāga-nimitta* (concept) and develops *appanā* (or ṭhapanā, fixation of the mind) and in some cases the body of the adept becomes so light as to rise up in the air.[4] At this stage the external inhalation and exhalation cease but there are internal inhalation and exhalation, to which then the adept's mind is directed. The subject of meditation may be either assāsa or passāsa, or nimitta (after-image) of either.[5]

By meditating upon the *nimitta* without vaṇṇa and lakkhaṇa (characteristics) one destroys the five nīvaraṇas and develops the jhānas.[6] The last of the anussatis is *Uapasmānussati* or cogitation of Nibbāna. The adept as usual is to retire to a lonely place and think of the fact that the absence of attachment (*virāga*) is the best of all dhammas constituted and unconstituted. He thereby develops concentration of mind and the jhānas.

The Four Bhamavihāras

The four Bhamavihāras are *mettā*, *karuṇā*, *mudita* and *upekkha*.[7] These are so called because they make the minds of the adepts pure like those of Brahma-kāyikā gods and after death they obtain the highest place among living beings.[8]

i. The adept desirous of practising *mettā-bhāvanā* should take his seat in a secluded place after he has finished his meal and realise the evils of dosa-citta (mind full of hatred) and merits of khanti (forbearance), for my mettā-bhāvanā, dosa is removed and khanti developed.

---

1. *Vism.*, pp. 274-7.
2. Cf. Pātañjala-bhāṣya, I, 50.
3. See *Vism.*, p. 278.
4. *Ibid.*, pp. 292-3. Cf. *Pātañjala-bhāṣya*, I. 34.
5. *Vism.*, p. 285.
6. *Vism.*, p. 286.
7. Cf. Pātañjala, III, 23. and Bhāṣya, I, 33: तत्र सर्वप्राणिषु सुखसम्भोगापन्नेष्ठ मैत्री भावयेत्, दुःखितेषु करुणां, पुणयात्मकेसु मुदितां, अपुणयात्ममेषु उपेक्षाम्। एवमस्य भावयतः शुल्को धर्म उपजायते। ततश्च चित्तं प्रसीदति, प्रसन्नमेकाग्रं स्थितिपदं लभते॥
8. *Vism.*, p. 320.

The first step in mettā-bhāvanā is to select the person upon whom the adept is to look upon with a friendly eye but at the same time be free from *rāga* and such other feelings. After pointing out the various difficulties in selecting the person, it is suggested that mettā-feeling should be first exercised in connection with one's own self, i.e. wish for one's own good and then in connection with his spiritual preceptor and so forth wishing him all happiness. In this way he is first to develop *appanā* and then gradually extend his range, including ultimately his enemies, after having completely destroyed his *paṭigha*, if any. He is to extend his range from the inmates of his own āvāsa to those of another and so on, to nine or ten āvāsas, and then to the inhabitants of a village, town and so forth up to a cakkavāla.[1] The next step for him is to break down the line of demarcation (*sīmāsambheda*) between any two persons, i.e. his feeling of love towards himself, his friends, his enemies or neutrals should be absolutely without any distinction. As for instance, if a man wants to kill his enemy, he must not say that the life of his enemy be spared and his be taken instead; it will not then be *sīmāsambheda*. To him there should be no distinction between himself and his enemy and it is this state of mind that mettā-bhāvanā is expected to create. As soon as *sīmā-asambheda* is developed, he has the necessary nimitta, upacāra and appanā and soon acquires the four jhānas.[2]

In the Nikāyas, the usual statement is that the adept exercises the mettā-fellings towards all beings in all the directions one after another. This is possible only after the adept has gone through the procedure described above.

ii. In *karuṇā-bhāvanā* also the adept is to choose a suitable object of compassion, e.g., an indigent person begging for alms or a criminal when being taken to the place of punishment and so forth. In this way be is to extend his range for compassion, including ultimately his enemies, after removing *paṭigha*, if any. Like mettā-bhāvanā, he is to practise *sīmā-asambheda* and gradually develop nimitta, upacāra, appanā and the jhānas.

iii. In *muditā-bhāranā* the adept is to have a feeling of joy at another's happiness (*muditā*). The best to start with is a close friend (*atippiyasahāyako*) of the adept and then other persons may be selected and ultimately his enemy. The remaining process is the same as that of mettā-bhāvanā.

---

1. *Vism.*, p. 320.
2. *Vism.*, p. 307.

iv. *Upekkhā-bhāranā* is generally taken up by an adept who has practised the previous three bhāvanās and acquired the jhānas. In the jhānas too, there are the feelings of pīti and virāga, which, being akin to *anunaya* (fondness) and *paṭigha* (hatred), have to be eschewed in upekkhā-bhāvanā.

In practising upekkhā-bhāvanā it is suggested that the person to be selected for the exercise of the feeling of equanimity should be a neutral one and then a friend and then an enemy. Like mettā-bhāvanā, in upekkhā too, the *sīmā-asambheda* is to be practised, developing ultimately the jhānas.

The Four Āruppas

The Kammaṭṭhānas that we have so far dealt with were meant to induce the jhānas up to the fourth, which keep the mind of the adept within the limits of *Rūpaloka*. The subjects of meditation that we propose to treat now induce the higher jhānas from the fifth to the eighth and carry the mind of the adept to the region of *Arūpaloka*.

1. The first subject of meditation of the Āruppas is *ākāsānañcāyatana* (=ananta-ākāsāyatana). It starts with ākāsa-kasiṇa as dealt with above with the difference that *ākāsa* in this case is unlimited extending over the whole *cakkavāḷa*. So long the conception of ākāsa is associated with cakkavāḷa; though it is unlimited, the adept does not go beyond Rūpaloka. The adept is to think constantly of ananta-ākāsa, but without any kasiṇa, i.e. without any reference to the ākāsa as extending over a cakkavāḷa or so forth. In short, his mind is to be severed from rūpa-saññā[1] (*sabbaso rūpasaññānaṃ samakikkamā)*, and hence without the possibility of *nānatta-sañña* (sense of distinction). By constantly meditating over this nimitta, he destroys the nīvaraṇas, develops mindfulness (*sati*) and concentrates his mind through upacāra,[2] and attains the fifth jhāna.

2. The second subject of meditation of the Āruppas is *viññāṇañcāyatanā* (=ananta-viññāṇaāyatana). This is closely connected with the previous subject of meditation and at the same time a further step ahead of it. In the ākāsānañcāyatana meditation, the adept's mind is not without some notion of sphere (*desa*). This is considered as faulty and the adept seeks to withdraw his mind from the sense of sphere and confines his attention to the 'consciousness'[3] only of ananta-ākāsa and cogitates of *ananta-viññāṇa* only and develops as usual the jhānas, reaching the sixth.

---

1. Rūpasaññā=Paṭigha-saññā, because by the *paṭighāta* (contact) of form and eye the rūpasaññā arises. See *Vism.*, p. 329.
2. *Vism.*, p. 328.
3. The *pavatta-viññāṇa*, i.e. the consciousness that has arisen in the adept's mind by concentrating his mind on ananta-ākāsa.

3. The third subject of meditation of the Āruppas is *ākiñcaññāyatana* (=n'atthi kiñci and āyatana). In this case the adept withdraws his mind from the consciousness (*viññāṇa*), of ananta-ākāsa, and cogitates on voidness or absence of viññāṇa or anything else (n'atthi n'atthī' ti vā suññaṃ suññan ti vā vivittaṃ vivittan ti vā). By such cogitation, his mind realises the non-existence of *viññāṇa* and thus gradually develops the seventh jhāna, the jhāna of nothingness.

4. The fourth subject of meditation of the Āruppas is said to be *n'evasaññā-nāsaññāyatana*, but in fact, the mental state of n'evasaññānāsaññā is derived by cogitation of *ākiñcaññāyatana*, i.e. *abhāra* of *viññāṇa* as explained above. While in the seventh jhāna, the meditator gradually gets rid of the *saññā* (*perception*) of the four khandhas (rūpa, vedanā, saṅkhārā and viññāṅa), but retains perception of extreme subtlety. He cannot perceive ordinary things but he is not without perception of the subtlest form—the residuum of saṅkhārā. Hence the mental state of the meditation in the eighth jhāna (or samāpatti as it is usually called) is without perception of ordinary things (n'evasaññā) but not without the subtlest perception (na+asaññā).

The last two Kammaṭṭhānas

The last two Kammaṭṭhānas are (i) āhāre paṭikūlasaññā-bhāvanā and (iii) eatudhātu-vavatthānassa bhāvanā.

1. *Āhāre paṭikūla-saññā* or disgust for food. The adept is to ponder over the evils connected with the food. The evils may be of many kinds, e.g., the botheration of going out for alms and seeking for it: performing the preliminaries when taking food; the unclean stomach which receives the food, the undigestibility of food and so forth. By meditating over these evils, he gets rid of desire for food and gradually of all desires (*taṇhā*). He feels no attachment for his body, and thus attains the summum bonum in this life (*Vism.*, pp. 341-7).

2. *Catudhāta-vavatthāna*, or determination of the four elements of the body. The adept, taking up this Kammaṭṭhāna, examines the contents of his body under the four heads: paṭhayī, āpo, tejo and vāyu. He takes into consideration one by one his skin, flesh, sinews, marrow, kidneys, bones etc.,[1] and examines their functions and then looks upon them as nothing but one of the four elements, and as such they are mere material objects (*acctana*), indeterminable (*aryākata*), substanceless (*suñña*), non-sentient (*nissatto*) and so forth. Such examination and cogitation make the adept realise the voidness

1. For details, see *Vism.*, pp. 358-67.

(*suññalaṃ*) of his self and so of the world and can no longer perceive the existence of different beings. As soon as he develops this mental state, he in fact attains the highest knowledge (*Vism.*, p. 347-70).

(iii) Kalyāṇamitta

A monk, anxious to take up a subject for meditation, must, at the first place, choose a competent spiritual preceptor (*kalyāṇamitta*). He should first try to find out one who has practised the fourth and fifth *jhānas* and by means of them has developed insight (*vipassanā*) into the truths of the universe, and has, in fact, become an Arhat, by destroying all the impurities (*āsaras*). Failing to get hold of such persons, he should seek for the next best in the descending scale, thus (*vism.*, pp. 98 ff.):

(i) an anāgāmi;

(ii) a sakadāgāmi;

(iii) a sotāpanna;

(iv) a puthujjana who practises the jhānas;

(v-vii) a master of three or two or one piṭaka;

(viii) a master of one nikāya with its aṭṭhakathā, and lastly,

(ix) a lajjī (a man of self-restraint).

If the candidate finds a suitable preceptor in the monastery where he lives, so far so good; if not, he should proceed to the place where he may find his preceptor. On his way to, as also on his arrival at, his destination he must not be failing in the duties prescribed in the *Vinaya* (ii. 231, 223) for an antevāsika, and he should reverentially and discreetly approach his preceptor, and apprise him of his intention of taking up a subject of meditation.

(iv) The Candidate

He should then offer himself to his kalyāṇamitta (spiritual preceptor) saying that he is resolved to carry out his commands and even, if necessary, he would not hesitate to throw himself down a cliff or suffocafe himself to death if his kalyāṇamitta wanted him to do so. A candidate with such resolution is not afraid of fearful lonely forest resorts and readily listens to the admonitions of his preceptor.[1]

He must possess the requisite *ajjhāsaya* (intention), *viz.*, aversion to *lobha*, *dosa*, and *moha* as well as to *gharāvāsa* (household life), *saṅganikā* (society) and *sabbabhavagati* (all forms of existence in the world).[2] He should have *adhimutti* i.e. strong desire for samādhi and ultimately for Nibbāna.

---

1. *Vism.*, pp. 115-6.
2. The opposites of these respectively are alobha, adosa, amoha, nekkhamma. paviveka, and nissaraṇa. See *Vism.*, p. 116.

When he approaches his preceptor for a Kammaṭṭhāna, he is to answer the questions, which will be put by his preceptor to find out the Kammaṭṭhāna that would suit him best. He is to receive his instructions and ponder over them carefully.[1]

Anurūpa-Vihāra

The suitability of the place of meditation should also be taken into consideration. The candidate preferably should dwell with his preceptor in the same monastery. Failing same, he should find out a suitable place not far from the abode of his preceptor, for he is to see him occasionally in order to correct himself about the practice of Kammaṭṭhāna. Buddhaghosa enumerates eighteen kinds of places[2] unsuited to meditational purposes. The suitable place for meditation must fulfil the following conditions:

(a) not far nor too close,

(b) easy of access,[3]

(c) not crowded by day,

(d) not exposed to mosquitoes, or serpents, wind or sun

About the suitability of the time for meditation, it is recommended that it should be after the monk has returned from his begging round and taken his mid-day meal.[4]

Candidate's Mental States

The first and foremost duty of the Katyāṇmitta (spiritual preceptor) is to study the mental leanings of the candidate before he can prescribe his subject of meditation. It may be incidentally remarked that unless the Kalyāṇamitta is a Khīṇāsava or at least an Anāgāmi or Sakadāgāmi, he cannot be expected to have acquired the higher powers (*abhiññā*) of knowing others' minds (*paracittañāṇa*) or one's previous births (*pubbenivāsānussatiñāṇa*) which are indispensable for ascertaining properly the mental leanings of the candidate. For practical purposes, it is suggested that the spiritual preceptor should ascertain the leanings of the candidate by asking him about his likes and dislikes.[5] A person's leanings should be ascertained by observing closely his movements (*iriyāpatha*), actions (*kiccā*), food (*bhojana*), ways of looking at things (*dassanādi*)[6] and lastly the qualities peculiar to him.

---

1. *Vism.*, p. 117.
2. *Vism.*, pp. 118-122. The eighteen places are: Mahāvāsaṃ navāvāsaṃ jarāvāsañ ca panthaniṃ, soṇḍiṃ paññañ ca, phalaṃ patthitaṃ eva ca nagaraṃ dāruṇā khettaṃ, visabhāgena paṭṭanaṃ paccantasīmāsappāyam, yattha mitto na labhati.
3. *Vism.*, p. 122.
4. *Vism.*, p. 123.
5. *Vism.*, p. 107.
6. For those interested in details. I would refer to the *Vism.*, pp. 104 ff.

Buddhaghosa in his *Visuddhimagga* (pp. 101 ff.) has made six divisions of such mental leanings of individuals towards viz., (i) *rāga* (attachment), (ii) *dosa* (hatred), (iii) *moha* (delusion), (iv) *saddhā* (faith), (v) *buddhi* (intelligence) and (vi) *ritakka* (argumentation). Class (i) has for characteristics more of deceitfulness, pride, evil desires, ambition, discontentedness, lascivousness, fickleness, etc.: class (ii) has more of anger, hypocrisy, envy, and miserliness etc.: class (iii) has more of idleness, doubts, obstinacy, etc.: class (iv) i.e. those with *saddhā* have the characteristics of being given more to charity, desire of seeing holy persons and hearing religious discourses, joy, solitude, credulousness etc.: class (v) has amiability, friendship, moderation in food, mindfulness, watchfulness, emotion and exertion etc.: and class (vi) has propensity for argumentation, love for frequenting societies lack of keenness in application for good objects, unsteadiness, fondness of moving about etc.

The above is only a very general classification, for Buddhaghosa points out the possibility of further analysis of mental leanings, e.g., those with *rāga* love evil deeds as those with saddhā love moral precepts and so forth: hence there is commonness between these two classes, i.e. both have a strong feeling or earnestness for evil in one case and for good in the other.

In this way, all the six classes admit of further analysis and a closer discrimination about the prescription of the subjects of meditation.

Another interesting explanation is offered by Buddhaghosa regarding the first three classes. He says that a person's nature may be ascertained by knowing his previous lives, e.g., those who performed good deeds through *rāga* and were as a result born in *sagga* have in their present life proneness to *rāga,* while those who in their previous lives injured others in various ways and were as a result born in the hells or nāga worlds develop in this existence a leaning towards *dosa*; similarly those, who were in their previous lives given to drinking and did not care for learning, have more of *moha* (delusion). Buddhaghosa gives another interesting explanation of these three classes of persons.[1] He says that those with moha have in their body more of the two elements, earth and water, while those with *dosa* have more of fire and air, and those with *rāga* have all the four elements in due proportion.

Further information has been furnished by him about the kind of spot to be chosen for a candidate with a particular leaning, what

1. *Vism.*, p. 103.

should be the nature of his dress, bowl, begging places, food offerers, food, etc., postures (*iriyāpathas*), the colour of his subjects of meditation.[1]

A selection has been made from among the forty Kammaṭṭhānas (subjects of meditation) according to the different mental leanings thus:[2]

Mental Leanings	Kammaṭṭhānas
For *rāgacarita*,	the ten asubhas (unpleasant objects) and kāyagatā sati (mindfulness about body:
For *dosacarita*,	the four brahmavihāras and four colours (vaṇṇakasiṇāni);
For *mohacarita* and *vitakkacarita*,	only ānāpāna-sati (inhaling and exhaling mindfulness);
For *saddhāsarita*,	the six kinds of anussati (mindfulness about six different objects);
For *buddhicarita*,	maraṇasati, upasamānussati, catudhātuvavatthāna and āhūre paṭikūlasaññā.

It is never possible to deal comprehensively with all the mental states in any treatise, but the above exposition makes it clear that the choice of the subjects of meditation was given a very important place in the code of Buddhist meditational practices. Buddhaghosa, however, admits that there is neither any original treatise (Pāli) nor any commentary (aṭṭhakathā) which deals with the mental leanings of a candidate and what has been said above is gleaned by him from the oral instructions of teachers.[3]

The Preliminaries

In the *Visuddhimagga*, a few details are lacking about the preliminaries that a candidate has to go through it before he commences his meditational exercises. These are to be found in the *Yogāvacāra's Manual* (edited by Dr. Rhys Davids in P.T.S. Series).

---

1. See for details *Vism.*, pp. 108 ff.
2. *Vism.*, p. 114; *Abhidhammattha-saṅgaha*, pp. 41-2. Cf. *Udāna*, iv. 1:

asubha	bhāvetabha rāgassa pahānāya
mettā	bhāvetabha vyāpādassa pahānāya
ānāpānasati	bhāvetabha vitakka-upacchedāya
aniccasaññā	bhāvetabha asmimānassa samugghātāya.

3. *Vism.*, p. 107.

The candidate first salutes the Buddha, Dhamma and Saṅgha by uttering the usual formulæ with the belief that this not only makes him meritorious but also removes many of the hindrances to meditation.[1]

Then he prays for happiness for all beings including his friends and relatives and at the same time wishes that Māra be kept away from him so that he may succeed in his mission.

He then utters the formulæ of confession, praying that he may be absolved from all wrongs what he may have committed knowingly or unknowingly.

He now promises to abide by the teachings of the omniscient Gotama and prays for *uggahanimitta*, *paṭibhāga-nimitta*, *upacāra-vidhi*, *appanā-samādhi*.[2] To strengthen his mind he brings to his memory the fact that numberless disciples of Buddha has before him followed this path and succeeded in attaining their object and that he will, likewise, with the help of his teacher, be able to reach the goal, Nibbāna.

He now sits cross-legged keeping his body erect and fixes his mind on the subject of meditation (*Kammaṭṭhāna*).[3]

(v) The Successive Steps in Meditation

I. Upacāra

We have spoken of the various objects of meditation on which the adept fixes his attention, trying all the while to convert it into a concept as clear and distinct as the object he sees with open eyes. The first attempts that he makes at fixation of his mind on the *nimitta* (i.e. parikkamma-nimitta) are called *parikkamma-bhāvana*.[4] When the adept has been able to see the object in his own mind as vividly as he has been doing with eyes open, he is said to have acquired the *uggaha-nimita*[5]. The attempts that are now being made by the adept to make the concept not only clearer and brighter than the actual object as seen by his physical eyes but free from the *lakkhaṇas* (characteristics)

---

1. Iccevam accanta namassaneyyam.
   Namassamāno ratanattayaṃ yaṃ
   Puññābhisandaṃ vipulaṃ aladdhaṃ
   Tassaānubhāvena hatantarāyo *Yogāvacāra's Manual*, p. 3.
2. See infra for detailed treatment.
3. The *Yogāvacāra's Manual* does not treat the subject systematically as has been wrongly supposed by Dr. Rhys Davids. It contains just an enumeration, like all other Buddhist texts of the different mental states and objects of meditation, connected with the four jhānas.
4. *Abhidhammattha-saṅgaha*, p. 42.
5. *Vism.*, p. 125.

of colour, form, etc. (vattudhamma-vimuccitaṃ)[1] which are regarded as Kasiṇadosas are known as *Upacārabhāvana.*[2] Even at this stage the mind of the adept cannot be steady in concentration; it is like a child unable to stand though making attempts to stand on his legs. The brighter concept, which he now possesses though intermittently, is called *paṭibhāga-nimitta.*[3] It is exceedingly difficult to make the *paṭibhāga-nimitta* steady and this is not possible for an adept so long he is in the upacāra stage. He will now have to exert to pass from *upacāra* to the *appanā* state. He has got to be very particular about the selection of his *āvāsa* (dwelling place), *gocara* (places from which to collect alms), *bhassaṃ* (improper talks), *puggalo* (associates), *bhojanaṃ* (food), *utu* (seasonal food), and *iriyāpathas* (postures in which he should pass his time).[4]

II. Appanā

The stage next to upacāra is *appanā* in which the adept's power of concentration becomes strong and steady; and the mind is likened to a grown up man able to stand on his legs as long as he likes. In the appanā stage, the adept can fix his attention on the subject of meditation one whole day or one whole night.[5] It is not possible to maintain the paṭibhāga-nimitta for any length of time unless the adept reaches the *appanā* stage. It sometimes happens that the adept becomes over-energetic and thereby gets excited and fails to attain the firmness of *appanā* state. As a reaction to it, sometimes, it so happens that he gets dejected, his energy slackens and his mind drifts to slothfulness. It is therefore advised (see next fn. items 4-6)[6] that the adept should neither be over-energetic nor slack in directing his mind towards the *nimitta.* It is by maintaining the balance of mental energy that an adept easily obtains *appanā.*[7]

---

1. *Abhidhammattha-saṅgaha*, p. 24.
2. *Ibid.*
3. *Vism.*, p. 125.
4. *Ibid.*, pp. 127-8.
5. *Vism.*, p. 126.
6. *Vism.*, p. 137.
7. The ten ways and means for passing from the upacāra to the appanā stage are enumerated as follows:

1. Cleanliness in regard to body and clothing.
2. Equipose (*samabhāva*) of the faculties of faith (*saddhā*), energy (*viriya*), memory (*sati*), concentration (*samādhi*) and intellect (*paññā*).
3. Proficiency in acquiring the nimitta (object of meditation) and in maintaining it.
4. Avoidance of mental slackness. This is to be done not by passaddhi, samādhi and upekkhā sambojjhaṅga, but by dhammavicaya, viriya and pīti-sambojjhaṅgas. The dhammavicaya sambojjaṅga helps the adept to choose those dhammas which put in him more and more of energy (i.e. *ārambha*, *nikkama* and *parakkama*). He develops

For the attainment of *appanā* state the adept stops his *bhavaṅga* thoughts and concentrates his mind on the object of meditation, which then becomes an object of mental reflection (*manodvārāvajjaṃ*). It is followed as usual by the seven thought-moments (*sattakkhattuṃ*) *javanaṃ javati. —Abhi. S.*, p. 17). It is in the fourth or the fifth moment that the *appanā* state of mind develops.[1] It is ekacittakkhaṇika. Immediately after *appanā*, i.e. in the sixth or seventh moment, the usual currents of thought (*bhavaṅga-citta*) reappear. The *appanā* state therefore refers to a certain mental development which the adept acquires in course of meditational practices. One who has developed that state is able to keep up the *paṭibhāga-nimitta* for a certain length of time and becomes fit for practising the *jhānas*. He is a *gotrabhū*.[2] By repeatedly meditating over the *paṭibhāga-nimitta*, he can induce the *paṭhamajjhāna*.[3]

I. The First Trance

The conditions precedent to the attainment of the first trance are:

1. Dissociation form *vatthukāma*[4] and *kilesakāma*,[5] the former referring to attractive things of the world and the latter to mental impurities like chanda, rāga, or the five nīvaraṇas.

---

ririya sambojjhaṅga by remembering the fact that it is by being energetic persons have became great and that he can also be like them if he applies his energy and dismisses his slothfulness. The third is pīti-sambojjhaṅgas which the adept can develop by practising the *anussatis* (see *infra*) and by associating with gentle persons to the exclusion of the vulgar and by reflecting on suttantas which produce serene pleasure (*pasāda*). These three sambojjhaṅgas help the adept to make his mind strong and energetic when necessary and protect his mind from becoming weak. Buddhaghosa enumerates the various ways and means by which these *sambojjhaṅgas* are to be developed.

5. Not allowing the mind to get excited (*uddhata*). This is done not by the dhammavicava, viriya and pīti-sambojjhaṅgas but by passaddhi (tranquility), samādhi (calm) and upekkhā (equanimity) sambojjhaṅgas. Buddhaghosa enumerates the various ways and means, by which these three sambojjhaṅgas are developed (*Vism.*, p. 134.)

6. Toning the mind. Sometimes the adept gets disheartened by failing to acquire the desired object viz., knowledge or quietude. To get over such depression of mind, he is advised to remember things which would agitate his mind (saṃvegavatthūni) for enumeration, see *Vism.*, p. 135)

7. Looking upon the mind with equanimity.

8 & 9. Avoidance of persons not engaged in meditation and association with persons engaged in meditation: and

10. Strong desire for concentration of mind.

1. *Vism.*, pp. 137-8: *Abhi. S.*, p. 18.
2. *Vism.*, pp. 138-139.
3. *Abhi. S.*, pp. 42-43: Tato paraṃ tam eva paṭibhāgamittaṃ upacārasamādhinā samasevantassa rūpāvacara-pathamajjhānam appeti.
4. *vivicc'era kāmchi.*
5. *vivicca akusalchi dhammchi.*

2. Directing (*abhiniropaṇa*) one's mind to the object of meditation.[1] It is compared to the spreading of wings when the bird is about to fly up (*abhiniropaṇa*).

3. Roaming of one's mind on the object of meditation.[2] It is compared to the turning round of the bees on the top of lotus[3] (*anuppabandhana*).

4. Derivation of mental and physical joy (*pīnaṇa*) through the removal of nīvaraṇas[4] and its enjoyment (*anubrāhaṇa*) and lastly.

5. Full concentration of mind (*ekaggatā*).[5]

The first trance, in short, is composed of five aṅgas, viz., vitakka, vicāra, pīti, sukha and cittekaggatā and leads to (i) *paṭipadā-visuddhi*, or purification from the hindrances (*kāma* and *akusala-dhamma*), (ii) *upekkhānubrūhāṇa* or development of equanimity on account of the mind becoming pure, calm and concentrated on the subject, and (iii) *sampáhaṃsanā* or mental thrill obtained by bringing into being the mental states as described above and by making all the facilities (*indriyas*) perform one function.

The adept, who has once obtained the first trance, should repeat it, and for the sake of doing it, he should choose the same food, place of residence, companions, etc., as he had when he first developed it. He should be very careful about the hindrances which may spoil his attained fruit. He should now try to enlarge the *paṭibhāga-nimitta*, i.e. if his *paṭibhāga-nimitta* be that of a small piece of land, it should be increased gradually to that of a village, a town, a province, a kingdom, the world and so on. He should also constantly practise *āvajjana* (adverting to trance), *samāpajjana* (entering into trance), *adhiṭṭhāma* (maintaining the trance), vuṭṭhāna (issuing out of the trance), and *paccavvkkhaṇa* (reflecting).[6]

---

1. *saṿitakko*.
2. *savicāro*.
3. In the *Dukanipātaṭṭhakathā* (see *Vism*., p. 142), the simile given of *vilakka* and *vicāra* is as follows:

The bird's act of flying by resting on its wings in the air is compared to the adept's putting of his mind on the object of meditation (*vitakka*) while its actual flying by moving its wings is compared to the adept's thoughts going deep into the object of meditation (*vicāra*).

Another simile of *vitakka* and *vicāra* is as follows: firm grasping of a dirty bowl by one hand is *vitakka*, while the act of cleansing it by the other hand is *vicāra*.

4. *Vivekajaṃ pītusukhaṃ*: *iṭṭhārammaṇapaṭilābhatuṭṭhi* pīti, paṭiladdharasānubhavanaṃ sukhaṃ. For distinction between *pīti* and *sukha* see *Vism*., p. 145.
5. *Paṭhamaṃ jhānam upasampajja riharati*.
6. *Vism*., p.154.

II. The Second Trance

The psychological conditions relating to the second trance are indicated as follows:

1. Cessation of *vitakka* and *vicāra*,[1] which are matters of the first trance. In the second trance, the object of meditation takes a firm hold of the mind (*aṅgapātubhāra*), and the physical sensations are no longer external (*oḷārika*) but purely internal.

2. Attainment of inward[2] calmness and concentration of thoughts on one object (free from *vitakka* and *vicāra*).[3] The calmness (*sampasādanaṃ*) is attained by the development of faith (*saddhā*). In the first trance, *saddhā* is present, but it does not produce complete calmness on account of the presence of *vitakka* and *vicāra*. In the second trance, *saddhā* becomes stronger, tranquillizes the mind completely, ending in complete concentration of thoughts.

3. Total removal of *vitakka* and *vicāra*.[4] On account of complete concentration of mind, the *indriyas* remain impervious to both inward and outward sensations and as such there is not the remote possibility of the appearance of *vitakka* and *vicāra*.

4. Derivation of joy (*pīti*) through concentration of mind (*samādhija*) and its enjoyment (*sukha*),[5] and

5. Full concentration of mind *(cittekaggatā)*.

Like the first trance, the adept should repeat the second trance. He gradually realises that *pīti* also is a source of disturbance to mental tranquillity and he should now get rid of it in order to reach the third trance.

III. The Third Trance

The conditions for the induction of the third trance are that the adept should be (i) *upekkhakko*, (ii) *satimā*, and (iii) *sukha-vihārī*.

(i) By *upekkhakko,* it is meant that the mind of the adept should be unaffected either by joy (*pīti*), or disgust (*virāga*),[6] i.e., his mind must not be perturbed by thoughts of *anicca*, *dukkha* and *anattā* and at the same time it should be passive (*anābhoga*) and inactive (*avyāpāra*);

---

1. Vitakkavicārānaṃ vūoasamo.
2. In the *Vibhaṅga*, "ajjhattaṃ" is explained as "self-realised" (paccattaṃ skt. pratyātma).
3. ajjhattaṃ sampasādanaṃ eetaso ekodibhāvam.
4. avitakkaṃ avicāraṃ.
5. samādhijaṃ pītisukhaṃ.
6. pītiyā ca virāgā upekkhako. For ten forms of upekkhā, see *Vism.*, p. 160.

(ii) By *satimā*, it is meant that adept should have power of remembrance (*sato*) and be cognizant of the various mental conditions concomitant to the second trance without any delusion (*asammoha*). These two factors *sati* and *samapajāno* are required in *upacāra* and *appanā*; so the reason shown for mentioning it in connection with the third trance is that *sati* and *samapajāno* are necessary in this case also for keeping the mind away from *pīti* and *sukha* acquired by the adept in the preceding trance.

(iii) By *sukhavihārī*, it is meant that though the adept's mind is unaffected by *sukha* while in meditation, his body is pervaded by a feeling of ease which he realises only after he has arisen from the trance.[1]

Constant practice of this meditation makes the adept firm in this trance and he can now proceed to the fourth.

IV. The Fourth Trance

In the fourth trance, no new mental factor are acquired or got rid of by the adept. This trance is more or less the resultant of the first three. The mental states described in connection with this trance are as follows:

(i) free from physical pain or happiness (*sukhassa ca pahanā dukkhassa ca pahanā*);

(ii) free from mental pain or happiness (*somanassadomanassānam atthaṅgamā*);

[These two states are acquired by the adept in the first stage (*upacāra*) of meditation;[2] only *somanassa* is completely eradicated in the upacarā state of the fourth jhāna].

(iii) Adukkhamasukkhaṃ, i.e., being devoid of *rāga* and *dosa*,[3] as the former is the source of *sukha* and the latter of *dukkha*.

(iv) Memory and other mental states reach the purest state through upekkhā (*upekkhā satipārisuddhiṃ*). In this trance when all the obstructing factors to higher meditation have subsided, *sati* and other factors conducive to the fourth trance becomes pure and serene.

It should be noted that all these four trances[4] are induced by meditating on the various Kammaṭṭhānas detailed above. In every

---

1. Sukhañ ca kāyena paṭisaṃvedeti.
2. For details, see *Vism.*, pp. 166-7.
3. See *ante* pp. 730-1 in connection with analysis of mental states of candidates for meditation.
4. By splitting up the second trance into two, four trances are sometimes spoken of as five in number. See *Vism.*, p. 169

trance, the adept has to take up the Kammaṭṭhānas, say, paṭhavī, induce upacāra and appanā, and then if he has previously acquired the first, he easily develops it and passes on to the second. Similarly, in the case of the third and fourth also, the adept has to induce upacāra and appanā with paṭhavī, pass through the first and second and reach the third or fourth.

There are four higher trances called *Samāpattis*.[1] These trances are induced by the cogitation of the four āruppas, (see above pp. 725-6).

1. In another paper these will be dealt with in detail.

Chapter - 21

Dhyāna in Early Buddhism

C.A.F. Rhys Davids

Learned men have told us in a certain Encyclopaedia that there is no mysticism in Buddhism.[1] This is true to some extent because they, with fellow-writers in that work, have certain preconceptions about what we have come to call mysticism. And perhaps it is also because a critical, i.e. a historical, knowledge of the Buddhist texts is as yet, or certainly was a decade and more ago, very immature.

'Mysticism' was unknown to Johnson's Dictionary. But he defined 'mystical' as 'sacredly obscure.' And Dhyāna, in Pali *Jhāna*, had a meaning in early Buddhism that is nearly, if not quite, hidden. It is an 'obscure' subject; Dr. Heiler's admirable study in it, also of a decade ago, shows it clearly as a 'sacredly obscure' subject.[2] For him its obscurity lies more in the history of its appearance, growth and decadence in Buddhism, than in its object. He makes wise and suggestive comments about its history, but about the object of Jhāna he reckons to have found in the texts adequate explanation. He sees in Buddhist, Jaina and Vedāntist Dhyāna a triple expansion, the roots of which run down to obscure pre-Yoga beginnings. But the object of Buddhist Jhāna he claims to have been a gradual but sure way to attainment, cathartic and strenuous, of that Nirvāṇa here and now which is different only in degree from, and is the antechamber of, the final goal, Parinirvāṇa. In other words, he sees in Buddhism "not philosophy nor metaphysic nor ethic, but a mystical religion of deliverance," *the* way to which was the way of rapt musing or absorption known as Dhyāna or Jhāna. With a worthy jealousy for the genius of the Founder—the genius of warding and leading individually the individual—he repudiates the idea, that Gotama himself taught this 'way' in the stereotyped, four-fold Jhāna formula (much less in the

1. *Encyclopædia of Religion and Ethics, art:* Dhyāna.
2. *Die Buddhistische Versenkung,* 1918.

four and five-fold formula of the abstractions called Arūpa-jhāna). With a less worthy rejection of Gotama's significant 'manifesto'[1] of the Way, the Mārga, of life as a wayfaring according to a man's inner guidance through the worlds to the goal—this he calls "an incomplete and inexact popular-poetical conception of the path of salvation"—he makes the Founder turn away from the need and the call of a world he had set out to help, turn away from the warding of Everyman, and hold out a way of salvation to the world lorn, world-forsaking recluse (a strange picture of a world-saviour!).

For me early Buddhism may be worthed as 'mystical' or not. The word of course means now not merely obscure. But the ascription may produce more obscurity than it clears. Mysticism in its broadest, its most real, because its (for us) most practical, meaning is *converse, usually solitary, with the unseen.* Converse is access. It is comm-union; it is not necessarily union. When the earth comes to accept this humbler, more practicable aspect of mysticism, instead of using terms of an as yet inconceivable union with the Highest, we may then come to worth a mysticism that is not attainable only by a saintly aspirant now in this continent, now in that century, but one that is a way for the help of the many: *ye keci sikkhakāmā*; whosoever are willing to learn.[2]

If we take converse, communion, with the unseen as our meaning of 'mystic', we can, as I shall show, claim that there is mysticism, and much of it in early Buddhism. Some years ago I took a different line in making out such a claim. It was in connection with a modern untitled Pali and Sinhalese manuscript, which my husband called the Yogāvacra's Manual, and its English translation by Mr. Woodward, which we called the Manual of a Mystic. There I took penetration (paṭiveḍha) into 'things' as admittedly belonging to at least European mysticism. I have been learning much since then. Later Buddhism dealt far too exclusively with 'things' (*dhammā*). Early Buddhism, like the true gospel as which it started, was far more concerned with men, and in each man with the very man, the *puruṣa* or *ātman*.

But so-called mysticism is of both the old world and the new, both of primitive culture anywhere, and of riper culture in East and West. And the tendency at present is for the new and the riper to read later traditions and concepts into the old and the more primitive. I propose, here as elsewhere, to drop the words 'mysticism' and 'mystic' as more hindersome than helpful, and to try to show whether the Pali books do not betray, when closely scanned, an evolution in the specific form of Indian Samādh called Buddhist 'musing' (Jhāna).

---

1. I refer to the so-called 'first sermon'.
2. *Mahāparinibbāna Suttanta*

I find myself in disagreement with much that has lately been written on Buddhist Jhāna. Whatever Dhyāna may now mean in Japan or elsewhere in the East, in the Pali books it does *not* mean 'meditation'[1]. Meditation requires, if it be worthy, the whole synergy of the thinking man. Early Buddhist Jhāna is a deliberate putting off (*pahāna*) of applying and sustaining thought. What is stated to be left is *sati* (with indifference emotionally). And *sati* in those books is just lucid awareness, the state needed by the listener who is purged of preconceptions and *waiting to learn*.

This final state in what is known as Fourth Jhāna is not kept in view by writers on Dhyāna or musing. Is it because such a state is so little worthed by modern writers, both of East and West?

I agree that Buddhist Jhāna and Yoga Dhyāna may have a common root in India's remote past. But when it comes to calling the former the latter, I would say, they have naught in common save the fact of the solitary muser and the unseen. The values placed in the muser and imputed to the musing are in each cult very different. So different, that between the formularized Jhāna and the Yoga aphorisms some historic link is needed, a link which may not show the one as derived from the other, but which may show them as at one time less widely divergent.

Once more, the object in Buddhist Jhāna is not to me so clear as some writers make out. Dr. Heiler, like other German writers, sees in the object, both of Buddhism and of Jhāna, the very general Indian ideal of 'deliverance' or release (*Erlösug, mokṣa, vimutti*). This is not a Vedic doctrine, and it is not very clear whether its first appearance in Indian literature is pre-Buddhistic. It became a familiar word in the Buddhist tradition, but for me it is not in the mandate of Buddhism,[2] and it is with the early mandate that I am trying to deal. Nor is it by any means given as the constant object of Jhāna. What I find is the Pi-ṭkas (I purposely exclude mediaeval literature) is a double set of formulas, working no 'release' but only a 'practice', and inserted in very different contexts. Taken in themselves, they suggest a ladder placed against a wall, but not reaching to the top.

Dr. Heiler admits that in Buddhism, Jhāna is but a preliminary, a preparing, not an end in itself. But he calls the culminating step in the four-fold formula the immediate threshold (*Vorstufe*) of full deliverance, *i.e.* of 'visible Nirvāṇa' *parama-diṭṭhadhamma-nibbāna*, which is "in essence one and the same saving good and deliverance-ideal" as "Nirvāṇa of the other side". But this is by no means the

---

1. *E.R.E.*, art: Dhyāna.
2. It is only imputed to Gotama in one of the records of the 'Enlightenment'. But it is made the *diploma* of the first missioners.

position clearly and unvaryingly assigned to Fourth Jhāna in the canonical books. In the highly authoritative Brahmajāla Suttanta[1] the four Jhānas are classed in the same category as the healthy enjoyment of sense (which was also a form of Nirvāṇa, as the Māgandiya Sutta testifies[2]), and are stated to be out classed by many other higher and better things left and known by the 'tathāgata'. It is true that these 'things' may refer to Nirvāṇa-experience, the error being to see in Jhāna the *patti* or attainment itself. But it is very improbable that had Fourth Jhāna been held as the very 'threshold' of the highest, it would have been so *classed* as it is there. It is true that we find a baser king of Jhāna contrasted with that of the formulas, when a man brooding over one of the 'hindrances' to right Jhāna 'muses and bemuses, unmuses and de-bemuses[3]. But it is not this but the Jhāna of the formulas which here classified. The Dhammapada declares that it is the combination of Jhāna and wisdom *(pañña)* that makes a man "near to Nirvāṇa"[4]. But the less poetical, academic procedure in Abhidhamma sees in Fourth Jhāna, not only a stage in 'transmundane' (*lokuttara*) study, but a stage no less in access to the conditions called Rūpa, or Rūpaloka, the world, or conditions of Brahmā-devas. Now these were not for Buddhist coincident with Nirvāṇa; they are even referred to on one occasion as "hīna", inferior[5]. *Yasmiṇ samaye rūpûpupattiyā maggaṃ bhâveti* "at what time...he makes a way to become for access to (or rebirth in) the Rūpa (-world)" :- such is the unvarying formula in Jhāna when undertaken *with this object*[6]. In 'supramundane' Jhāna, where object, and that object Nirvāṇa, or anyway arahantship, none is given. We are only told that this Jhāna is a 'going-away-from' (*niyyānikaṃ*), and 'not-making-for-unheaping' (*apacayagāminaṃ*),[7] and we are left with these negatives. And so little is Jhāna here the one threshold, that nineteen other forms of 'making-to-become' are added, beginning with 'the Way.' as equally important with Jhāna. I may add in passing, that the Jhāna placed between these two, that of 'Arūpa', is, like Rūpa-jhāna, said to have the definite object of 'access' to the hypothetical immaterial world.

Let it not however be supposed, that this relatively tidy treatment on Jhāna appears throughout the Abhidhamma-Piṭaka. If we pass from

---

1. *Dīgha-Nikāya*, i, 1; cf. *Majjhima-Nikāya*, ii, 228.
2. *Majjhima-Nikāya*, no. 75.
3. *Majjhima-Nikāya*, no. 108. Lord Chalmers' transl. Ānanda is the speaker.
4. Verse 372.
5. *Majjhima*, no.97. I find one case of a monk making Jhāna his 'base' (*pādaka*), on which he won arahantship, but he was an *exceptional* jhāyin: Kaṅkhā-Revata. *Commentary on Aṅguttara*.
6. *Dhammasaṅgaṇi; Vibhaṅga*.
7. *Dhammasaṅgaṇi*.

the first book just cited, the *Dhamma-saṅgaṇi*, to the second, the *Vibhaṅga*, we seem to light on curious confusions. The Jhāna formulas never vary, here too the aspirant is said to eliminate all desires of sense and of things evil, then all active work of intellect, then all commotion of emotion, remaining in a state of utterly cleansed indifference and mindfulness (or memory). But we read in what immediately follows, that 'at that time' the contents fo the aspirants's thought (*citta*) include many factors of intellect and emotion, even after attainment of Fourth Jhāna, prior to which all such have been eliminated. It is not easy, for instance, to understand how a man in Fourth Jhāna, with both thought and emotion eliminated, can be developing the 'emancipating thought' of pity, or of a fellow-feeling with another's joy (*muditā*), or be understanding the causes of ill. Emergence from Jhāna (*vuṭṭhāna*) may have first been necessary, but there is no recorded indication of it[1]. And Mettājhāna, 'amity-musing', such as Subhūti and Nandā were noted for, contravenes that[2].

Any way, it may be said, the *object* of Jhāna (*Rūpûpapatti Arūpûpapatti*) is here clear enough. That is true. The commentary concedes, from the Suttas, that there are higher things to be got by *samādhi*, or *jhāna*, but that, for this access, the four-fold Jhāna is the only way[3]. And I am not yet aware of any teaching in the Suttas urging a man to practise Jhāna for rebirth's sake. Rebirth was 'becoming', and that led rather to Ill than to the end of Ill.

Is there then more consistency of treatment in the subject of Jhāna in the other two Piṭakas? What do we learn in them about the purpose, end, or object of Jhāna?

The Vinaya almost entirely ignores Jhāna. This is not a little remarkable, seeing how much it was commended in the Suttas, how much it was said to enter into the life of the earnest monk. Yet there appear to be only four distinct references in this bulky work to the Jhānas as a formulated system, and the same number of references to monks as Jhāyins, needing as such the quiet of the cave (*leṇa*) or other separate lodging[4]. It may of course be replied, that the Vinaya rules deal mainly with the bad monk, who would not be Jhāyin. The reply does not satisfy. The more worthy protesting monk, who brings about the making of new rules, is a prominent feature. If we had a corresponding encyclopaedia of Christian discipline, we should never read far without reference to prayer or prayers, a factor to which some writers refer as the equivalent to Jhāna. For me

1. The far later *Visuddhi Magga* has such 'emergences'.
2. Commentary on *Theragāthā*, Ist verse; commentary on *Aṅguttara* (Etad-agga).
3. Commentary on *Dhammasaṅgaṇi*.
4. *Cullavagga*, iv, 4.

there is not doubt that had the Saṅgha, during the centuries when the Vinaya was growing by accretions, held Jhāna in its original worth, it would have produced a disciplinary chronicle glowing with Jhāna atmosphere throughout. It is true that, in the over-elaborated set off, given at the beginning of the Pāti-mokkha-commentary in the Vinaya, the Founder declares himself to have been a muser, but it is a mere passing allusion in stereotyped sequence, and there is no recurrence in the work even of this in connexion with any other saint. So low could the Saṅgha at one time and place fall in piety, both in general and with reference to Jhāna, that during a scarcity at the important town of Vesālī, the monks decided by a majority not to lend a hand and work with their distressed lay-fellowmen, but to advertise each other as holy Jhāna-experts, so as the better to wheedle alms. Public rebuke, ascribed as usual to the Founder himself, albeit probably after his day, was duly given and an older rule enforced, but the occurrence is suggestive[1].

In the Sutta-Piṭaka on the other hand there is never a long silence about Jhāna. In the four principal Nikāyas alone I have noted some 240 references at least, the *average* distribution being as follow:-

Dīgha-Nikāya : once in 39 pages

Majjhima-Nikāya: once in 26 pages

Saṃyutta-Nikāya: once in 19 pages

Anguttara-Nikāya: once in 20 pages

The formulas never vary, but the context does considerably, giving thereby more or less of living actuality to the congealed ritual of the fixed wording. Certain results are said to be obtained consequent upon attainment of Jhāna, albeit uttermost consummation is nowhere, I believe, given as one. In the fifth Nikāya, excluding the Jātaka, as consisting mainly of much later commentary, and three other later works, I have the following rough, approximate quantities:

In the Dhammapada 12 references

In the Sutta-Nipāta, 19 references

In the Khuddaka-Pāṭha, no reference

In the Udāna 1 reference

In the Iti-vuttaka 4 references

In the Peta-vatthu 1 reference

In the Vimāna-vatthu 1 reference

---

1. *Vinaya*, Pāittiya, viii.

In the Theragāthā 5 references
In the Theragāthā 3 references
In the Niddesa (Mahā) 5 references
In the Apadāna 30 references}
In the Buddhavaṃsa 2 references} not included in
In the Cariyā-Piṭaka, no reference} estimate[1]
In the Paṭisambhidāmagga 33 references

This is a very rough estimate[2], but is sufficiently informative to show an average frequency of reference which is about the same taken together, as that in the other four Nikāyas. And the average frequency is sufficient to show Jhāna as a very prominent feature in the doctrinal part of the Canon. The frequency would loom even greater had I included all references to the contexts where 'samādhi' occurs. This is sometimes equated with Jhāna, but it is the genus of which Jhāna is a species, and hence the inclusion would not be justifiable. For instance in the *Udāna*, when Sāriputta is said to be rapt in a certain samādhi, the commentary claims that this was the fourth Brahmavihāra of indifference or equanimity. And the calling these states a kind of Jhāna, as in the case of Subhūti of the Theragāthā, is a commentarial, not a Piṭaka usage.

Taking then *Jhāna* and *jhāyin* only, I ask my readers to consider what conclusion can we infer from their frequent occurrence? For it may be a different conclusion from that which safely be drawn (1) were the Sutta-Piṭaka the whole of the Canon, and (2) were it the work of a group of men compiling and completing the group of sayings at the same time and in the same place. We know that Jhāna and jhāyin anticipated the beginnings of Buddhism, just as we know also that even in the Buddhism of today we find their resultants, to mention only the Zen school of Japan and the Diyan centres of Tibet[3]. We are then, in this matter of Jhāna, up against what would seem to be a chronic need of the Buddhist religious mind, and not only of that, but of the Indian religious mind when Buddhism arose. This is by no means to agree with the opinion of a writer, that 'Buddhism is through and through nothing but Yoga'[4].) Buddhist Jhāna may represent what current Yoga became in Buddhism. But Jhāna is not the whole of Buddhism, save by a gross misrepresentation. What men value much, they word often. But we find the first Piṭaka almost silent

1. Poems in later diction, probably written when competed.
2. Based *mainly* on Index references to *Jhāna and jhāyin*, and therefore erring on the side of omission.
3. See 'Dhyāna and Samāhdi im Mongolischen Lamaismus,' A.M. Pozdnejev, *Zeitsch. f. Buddhismus*, 1926, 3/4.
4. H.Beckh, *Buddhismus*, II 11; quoted and criticized by Dr. Heiler.

on Jhāna, and the third Piṭaka dropping the subject more and more after the first two books, a portion of which treats of it. We come back to the proportion in reference to it in the second Piṭaka, and to the question: what did the recorders and editors of the sayings in prose and verse hold there was of welfare and of interest in Jhāna to warrent the preserving of these references, amounting to a mention in about one out of every twenty of our pages here, or perhaps rather more, in the middle collection of their scriptures?

Our answer is made the less easy by our having to say no! to the second point above. We are coming to admit that the Sutta Piṭaka, as well as the other two, was not the work of one inner group at the same time and place. And when this is conceded, other complications arise. Was it always one and the same good that was valued and sought in Jhāna? It is true, there was a fixed wording, in some detail, to serve—I borrow the Vinaya simile[1] on a more general case—as a string (*sutta*) to bind the bunch of flowers together. But as to that, we have no sound evidence to feel sure, that the formulas now in the books were either the original fixed wordings, or whatever even those, if there were any truly expressed what Jhāna really meant for Gotama and his first fellow-workers, men and women. If Buddhism were indeed imported Yoga, that is, the very spirit of Indian Yoga, we are almost forced to postulate some earlier formulas, showing less sharp severance between the two,—which would show us at least the more gradual, the more usual method of pouring an old wine into new bottles.

Some likeness there is between Jhāna formulas and the Brahmanized Yoga (nothing earlier being, I find, available), but it is in detail only. The antithesis to Sāṅkhya is in both literatures, albeit almost hidden in Buddhism. The Mahābhārata sets it out more than once and clearly; in Buddhism we trace it in such outline as "There are these two strengths: reasoned calculation and making-to-become (*paṭ isaṅkhānabalaṃ, bhāvanā-balaṃ*)[2]" where the latter is explained by the fourfold Jhāna-formula. And there is, in both Yoga and Buddhist procedure, elimination of sense-impressions and mind-work on them. But in the latter, that which in Yoga is the heart, the very object, the very justification, is lacking. "How" asks the Yoga inquirer can a man find deliverance without a God (*īśvara*)?... "Let the Yogin bearing Me within, sit solely devoted to Me."[3] The Buddhist formula not only sees no perfection of concentration resulting from devotion to God", not only sees no "beholding of the Self in the Yogin's self"[4] in Jhāna, but even

1. *Vin.*, III. 9.
2. *Aṅguttara-Nikāya*. i, pp. 52,94.
3. Mokṣadharma, Adh. 302.
4. *Ibid.*

bars out all reference to the jhāyin as such. Gotama, it is true, is shown investing it with emphatic personal touch in his own case:- *So kho ahaṃ...jhānaṃ upasampajja vihāsiṃ.* 'I indeed abode in the attainment etc.'[1], or in the case of other,[2] but no person finds mention in the bare formula, save as understood in the verb, and the pronoun *so*. Even where the Jhāna is connected with a definite personal object,- access to Rūpa or Arūpa-the aspirant is wholly merged in the verb.

This may seem a modern Western captiousness, but no, the Commentator himself takes note of it. "Why", he says, "should the foregoing analysis of mind presuppose things only, and this teaching presuppose a person (*puggala*)? Because we have here a way (or course, *paṭipadā*), which he makes-to-become... And a way has to be accomplished, and this must be accomplished by somebody."[3] O wise little Buddhaghosa, why were you not elsewhere, as here, a 'man who sees'? Let no man call you here pernickety. You are here giving away the whole of that 'anatta' dogma which you for the most part so doughtily defend! You were not afraid to write, that a way required a wayfarer, a *paṭ ipadā* needed *paṭipannaka*. But had you lived six centuries earlier, when even the Master's use of the word *puggala* had to be in a sense explained away, as in the Kathāvatthu, you might not have trotted out 'the man' so airily. You were writing in Ceylon, far away from renascent Brahmanism, and you did not fear to have to eat your words when you thus brought in the *ātman* and the *puruṣa*.

Both in Buddhist Jhāna and in Yoga the process of concentration sets out with the individual, the man, the solitary aspirant. But as soon as we touch on attainment, the values alter. In Buddhist Jhāna the man vanishes; we are left with his mind only, refinded down to a state of 'purity, indifference and mindfulness'. This last word is *sati* (*smṛti*), a term not used in Pali for memory, but for mental clearness. And we hear nothing of any object partly or wholly won beyond the mental state itself. I have in mind here the four-fold Rūpajhāna, but even where, as is often the case, the jhāyin is made to pass on to Arūpajhāna, the serial attainment reached cannot, even from the Buddhist point of view, be called truly a religious or spiritual Better. A certain vantage-point in gripping an abstraction is the utmost that can be claimed, unless this Jhāna was ever seriously held to promote a man's prospects of rebirth in a world believed to be arūpa, or immaterial. But in Yoga the *Yogin*, the *man*, is in full view from first to last, and there is *no doubt* about what is sought. It is the man and not his mind only that is before us, the man breaking his bars and bonds, waxing in strength and fearlessness, winning to absorption in, to vision of, the Ātman in him, who also is that Ātman.

---

1. *Vin.*, III. 4; *Majjhima*. i.21. etc.
2. *Ibid.*, p. 40 *etc.*
3. *Dhammasaṅgaṇi* commentary. p. 163. He is referring to the analysis of *citta's* preceding the Jhāna chapters.

And with the man thus prominent, the Yoga literature leaves us with no shadow of doubt as to the good, the 'well', the *artha*, which comes to him through attainment. It is the vision or conception, as 'within his heart', of Man transcendent, akin to the man himself, but above and beyond the best, the finest he has ever realized. This is declared to bring him release, that is from *prakṛti*, or in brief from body and mind. Nearer perhaps to Western religion is the expression of the good in the associated description of Sāṅkhya-attainment, albeit it fits even better with Yoga-attainment:-"This (Ātman) here is my true Kinsman; I can no other than be with Him; won to evenness and unity with Him, then only become I really he who I am" (Mokṣa: Adh. 309).

What is there in the way of a worded welfare-in-purpose to set over against this when we contemplate Buddhist Jhāna? It may be said that, when such ideas are held to be error and delusion, it is also 'release' to attain to and rest in a state where they are not. To this we might reply, in the first place :-It is true that Buddhist saints are shown, in their own works, as actually deriving an amount of peace and even rapture from a negative form of 'release' coupled with a purely backward view, such as can scarcely be found in any other cult. But man's nature is such, that this attitude cannot very long be maintained in fervour and purity; it will degenerate as such into a complacency which we word sometimes as 'that blessed word Mesopotamia!' In the second place, whereas it is true that the 'Ātmanism' in the last quotation is closely allied to the (possibly older) Brahman-Ātmanism which is attacked in the Buddhist Suttas, it is not correct to hold, that there was nothing of 'divine immanence' in the mandate given by the founder of Buddhism. For the message of the Way words the wayfarer, by implication, as 'self-resorting' (*attasaraṇa*), naturally choosing the way he thinks, right, that is, willing the better. But I find in Buddhist Jhāna, as such, not clear connection made out, as is made out, however all too briefly, in the Way-mandate, a connection between practise and object, as we find in Yoga.

I used to puzzle over this and wonder whether, in what was so evidently a four-fold series in *preparation only*, the benefit (discounting rebirth-prospects) was held to lie in the preparation itself? Coming into Buddhism by way of Abhidhamma, I missed at first the varied contexts of the Sutta-Piṭaka. I was inclined to see in the detached mental lucidity of Fourth Jhāna a possible starting point for concentrated work on concepts, such as the otherwise aimless insertion of Jhāna formula in parts of the Vibhaṅga seemed to suggest[1]. For I found also a shrunken and specialised meaning of the thinking :-*vitakka*, *vicāra*—which is

1. Chapters on Paccayâkāra, Iddhipādā, Magga, Appamañña.

suppressed after First Jhāna, and not the more inclusive, unspecialized meaning of these two words used in older Suttas. The object was not trance; save in an occasional appendix to the Arūpajhānas, that was quite clear. Then was it perhaps keener, sublimated work of intellection? Modern training in the building up of inductions and the applying of deductions tells me, that no good beginning to such work could come in the unworthing of mental application and discursive thinking. Was it that by concentrating without these, fresh insight might come as in a flash, a thrill of new knowledge, new worded thought, not got by conscious reasoning? There is talk now about this that we call intuition, to using the word quite as Bergson does, and it is well that there should be. But is intuition really a beholding from within? The great musician or artist would not always grant that. Why should any other muser be so confident about it? Aristotle was not. *Thurathen*, 'from without', is his conclusion as to our constructive thinking[1]. And is our 'inspiration' a mere fancy? Or did the mental exercise in Jhāna, whatever other advantage it offered, serve as a respite and withdrawal, otiose yet strenuous, from the preoccupations of daily life, much as books now afford us? It is not easy for us here and now to fill out the mental day of the studious meditative man in a bookless world, nay, a manuscriptless world, who had turned away from the life of his fellowmen, nor saw any good in the study of the world of nature.

Then I came to learn a little of the Zen (Jhāna) sect of Buddhism in Japan, mainly through Professor Takakusu's essay (Journal of the Pali Text Society, 1906-7). In that interesting article there are some sayings of Zen adherents that are quaint and even foolish, but this essential point was clear:- in a world where imported Buddhism had found, not a bookless world, but a world of books, the jhāyin flouted books, and professed to find the good sought in musing in the seeker himself. If he would, through his musing, divest himself of everything he considered morally lowering and intellectually hindering, and seek to win to the best self he could conceive, enlightenment would come from within. Jhāna is pictured here as a sort of cure of tonic, purging, restful, stimulating. And the writer considers, that 'this special discipline came to be emphasized...as a saving power, when the Buddhist faith began to wither under the baneful influence of scholasticism'.

It is always interesting to see an idea, or course of action, or attitude, when transplanted to new soil, flourishing there with a new and fresh energy. In Zen, Jhāna regains that central well-spring of 'the man', his nature, his objective, which was in Yoga, but which became blurred and lost in Buddhism. And yet it is not exactly a replica of Yoga. It is

1. *Peri Neotétos.*

more positive, more self'-concentrated, less religious, less superpersonal than Yoga. It is still Buddhist, in that it seeks the divine in man rather than to develop man into, or raise man to the divine. It bids man look within, not beyond himself.

In Indian Buddhism we see both emphases in ātman—manself and divine self—blurred and lost. What do we find in Jhāna replacing them? The emphasis, I would say, is on, not man, but *mind*. It is form first to last the mental process in which we are kept informed:-first the deadening of sensations by way of the self-hypnosis of the 'kasiṇa'. or artifice of concentration on a special object of sense; then the deadening of active work of mind, and so on, in a curious and psychologically interesting procedure. Those who approach Buddhism through the 'legend' or story of its founder, and its early church and rule (Vinaya), do not always realize the absorbing interest that is betrayed in its scriptures in mental phenomena, in the mind. But this interest colours very markedly its Sutta literature, and points, I venture to think, to a very notable feature in the spirit of the time when Gotama was teaching. I have said it already and I say it again,—there seems to be herein, if in nothing else, something akin between that time-spirit and our own; the interest in, not the very man—*we* call him self, soul, spirit—but in his complex of body and mind, the interest in mind-procedure, and with this the blurred, lost vision of 'the man'.

But when Gotama's mission began, the 'man' was not yet dimmed; the dimness was, I believe, nascent only. It was rather to the greater appreciation of the 'man', that the academic lay-(that is, extra-Brahman) movement, founded by Kapila, had been analyzing in a way of new thoroughness all that was of man, yet was not the 'man' (*puru-ṣa*). We owe much to the scholars, Drs. Jacobi and Garbe, for pointing out how this Sāṅkhyan influence affected Buddhism. They may go too far, in the way prevailing still (as we have just seen) in 'deriving' Buddhism (or at least what is called its philosophy) from Sāṅkhya, when what we see appears more like an infiltration into a religious mandate of ideas in vogue at its birth. But the Sāṅkhyan analysis of 'the man' as a wondrous being, working upon matter through a very interesting, complicated procedure (mind), which could be resolved into several factors (*aṅgas*), was, we may assume, known to the thoughtful and earnest little group around the founder of Buddhism, including the founder himself. So that in the Buddhist books we may see how preoccupying, how absorbing was this mind—*citta, mano, viññāṇa*—how it was fed, how it reacted[1], how it kept changing whether it survived death, and how it might be wholly or in part suppressed. That this

1. 'Struck back', *paṭihaññati, Dhs.*

suppressing, this governance implied a suppressed, a governor here it was that Buddhist thought, albeit not in its founder, not in some Dhammapada verses, slipped up. Gotama is shown as saying: "what if I (the explicit, emphasized 'aham') were to repress thought by mind?"[1] And the way of the Dhammapada, e.g.

Attanā coday' attānaṃ paṭimāse attam attanā,

(let him censure self by self, let him restrain self by self)[2], compiled in a land where *attan* meant 'the man', the spirit, both divine and human,—not to mention many other verses,— show the 'governor' not yet blotted out. But blotted out he was, and that, it may be, at an early date. It is Ānanda himself, who, as an exponent of authority, is shown teaching Jhāna as pure and simple mind-practise (*cittaparisuddhiyaṅga*), to be perfected and kept up, as one of four such factors, conducing to an end of highest worth, definitely worded.[3]

But so markedly, in the self-willing process of Jhāna, has the blotting out of the self taken place, and the mental process itself become solely of interest, that we come—if we are thoughtful—to a halt, and ask ourselves: If Buddhism was indeed a daughter of Yoga, how did the she come to value Yoga-samādhi and to word it in a way so different, that it is as if we were to reckon mechanical power with no machine, or to value the music of an instrument leaving out the player? Can a period of transition be shown? Can we show it from the Pāli books, late in date as, in their present form, they are? Can we draw out of them (1) that Gotama was an ardent *jhāyin*, and with him many of his early fellow-workers, (2) that for Gotama, and for these, Jhāna was valued, not for just what the Yogin (of any age) valued it, still less as mere mind-practice, but for something else—for an 'access' felt to be, in their work and their 'wayfaring' through the worlds, as a help and an enlightening?

1. That Gotama was an habitual muser has hardly perhaps till now received the attention it merits. And yet, apart from the frequency of mention in the discourses fathered on him, we find him called muser more than once:-

Muniṃ vanasmiṃ jhāyantaṃ ehi passāma Gotamaṃ

(Come, see we Gotama the seer, the muser, in the wood)[4].

Jhāyiṃ virajam āsīnaṃ[5]......

to the pure the seated the muser (am I come).

---

1. *Majjhima*, i, 242 etc.
2. Verse 379.
3. Aṅguttara, ii. 195. Much play is now made with the sophisticated distinction between philosophic and popular meaning (*paramattha, sammuti*). This is *first* mentioned in the late *Questions of king Milinda*.
4. *Sutta-Nipāta*, 165.
5. *Ibid.*, 1105.

The tempter rallies him:-

Sokāvatiṇṇo nu vanasmiṃ jhāyasi[1]

Art thou sunk in grief that in the wood thou musest?

The muser's posture is said to be peculiarly his[2], and Ānanda's memory of him declared him as "having both practised and engaged in Jhāna, and advocated it[3]". Of his fellow-workers we note musing associated with Sāriputta[4], Anuruddha, Kaṅkhā-Revata[5], and Moggallāna[6], Nandā the nun[7], and Uttarā Nandamātā the lay woman[8],

Now this man and these persons and others were at the well-spring of the movement, and to them the work of spreading and making acceptable among the many a gospel of a self-directed living, such as would bring 'well', welfare, to man here and in the worlds to come, was the all-absorbing thing. Can we believe that they would have often gone aside to cultivate a stereotyped way of musing which was nothing more than a sort of glorified practice in mental, mindworsening scale-plying? Would they not be far more occupied with the question of man's salvation, witness Sāriputta's inquiry about it (*amata*)[9], than about a practice expounded as an elimination of mental phases. So near are we today to analysis of these phases, so far are we from the conditions attending the birth of a world-gospel, that we need a more quickened imagination than such as our psychology is usually content to graze upon. What we actually find Gotama first bidding men seek was *not the mind, but the self*: "Were it not better that you sought the *attan*, the *ātman*?"[10]

2 Did he then bid men seek, in musing, the world-ātmanṭBrahmanṭ and Īśvara? He did not. Much had come to this man that lay between the Highest and the new pre-occupation with man's mind as such, and, as I think we might add, the rising pre-occupation with man's life in this world. He had, at some time in his life, come to acquire clairaudience and clairvoyance. It was owing to this psychic development that he was able to be willed and induced to become a teacher, for he must have

1. *Saṃyutta*, i, 123.
2. *Aṅguttara*, ii, 245.
3. *Majjhima*, iii, 108.
4. *Apadāna*, Sāriputta's poem refers 5 times to Jhāna. Cf. *Buddhavaṃsa*, I: *Sāriputto samādhijhānakovido*.
5. *Aṅguttara*, i, 24.
6. *Saṃyutta*, ii, 213; iv, 262f.
7. *Aṅguttara*, i, 25.
8. *Ibid.*, 26; also iv. 63 where she is shown (in a curiously edited record) to be clairaudient.
9. *Vinaya*, I, 39.
10. *Ibid.*, 23.

himself told of his lonely hesitation, and of the entreaty of a man of another world, whom the books came to call Brahmā Sahampati[1]. And he admitted more than once, that something he knew was due to information from a *deva*, a *devatā*, a man of another world[2]. (It is true that he is made to add, 'I also knew it of myself'; but whereas the worshipping recorders of a teacher, ranked later on as omniscient, would not have invented the informing *deva*, the case is different as to the clause vindicating that omniscience.) Again, there are frequent talks recorded between him and *devas*, notably the governor or the next world, entitled Sakka, and others called *devaputtas*; in that, says the Commentary, their names were known. Among these were sometimes men whom the clairvoyant Gotama recognized as still resembling, in their new bodies, men he had known on earth, notably his wealthy friend Anāthapiṇḍika, his first patron, king Bimbisāra and a Licchavi officer, Ajita. His gifts as a psychic medium were well-known, for we read that he was consulted in all the countries where he taught as to what had befallen this person and that whom death had removed[3]. And that he should have been thus consulted, points as much to a widespread need for light as to interest in his person and powers.

Now is it unreasonable to hold, that Gotama used Jhāna as the best way of obtaining, or at least of facilitating access to, and converse with, worthy men who had been reborn in other worlds? If the word 'reborn' be too Eastern, let us say, 'had survived the death of their earth-body'. Do the books help us further?

We read that, on leaving home to find help for men subject, without light and leading, to old age and death, he resorted to one after another noted teacher of Jhāna; it may be, in order to develop himself psychically. Further we may note a recurrent appreciation of the practice of Jhāna shown by *devas* in the chapters on them in the Saṃyutta[4]. "The monk should be a *jhāyin*," says one, Kassapa. "The man awake (*buddho*) who has understood Jhāna," says another, Pañcālacanda. Another, Candimāsa, commends Jhāna; two others do no less. Further, the Jhānas (the Four) are in many places made to serve as a preparation to certain 'higher knowledges' (*abhiññā*) which are all, with the exception of the last, forms of psychic or 'super-normal' development. These abhiññās are given in two series. The one we usually find is only three of the six:

1. *Ibid.*, 5.
2. *Dīgha*, ii, 10. Cf. 39f.; 241; iii, 17.
3. *Dīgha*, ii, 200 ff., cf. 91f. ; 266; iii, 15; *Saṃyutta*, i, 46, 55; cf. *Therag.*, 1263f.
4. *Saṃyutta*, i, pp. 46-52.

memory of former lives, clairvoyance and awareness of 'cankers' as destroyed, called together '*te-vijjā*'. The other, which gives the six abhiññās, and adds two others, gives, as no. 4, clairaudience and as no. 6, clairvoyance. By a misconception of the word 'dibba,' these have been rendered in translations 'heavenly' or 'celestial' ear and eye. But *dibba* is for Buddhism just 'belonging to *devas*', that is, men happily reborn. A man gifted with nos. 4 and 6 can both see such persons when they are near him, and can hear what they tell him, tell, for instance, of the fate of x, y, and z, who have passed over and have undergone the verdict of Yama, or tell concerning matters in which he may seek guidance. Thus a man in Fourth Jhāna was held to be in the most favourable conditions to profit by such seeing and hearing, if they were either inborn gifts, or had been acquired.

But I have not yet found any writer commenting on why clairvoyance and clairaudience take such an important place in venerable Suttas, not as ultimate objects of Jhāna but as abnormal states to which Jhāna often appears as a preparation. If Jhāna was a condition of deva-converse, then those two states fall, as also essential conditions, into their natural places. If early Buddhism, on the other hand, did not in some at least of its apostles cultivate devas-converse, I fail to account for these abhiññās. Disuse in the Saṅgha gives them the appearance of ruins, but was there not a time when they were 'live wires'? Writers, however, call them just 'mystic' or 'hallucinations' and pass them by. Or they do not even stay to call them that.

Modern writers have their own way— a way of today which may ere long be that of yesterday— of dealing with this very prominent feature in Buddhism. They either push it into a corner as ancient super-naturalism, or they speak of it as so much hallucination which is true subjectively. Both views hinder the earth from getting at much in Buddhism that is historically, and objectively true. Take these two passages— "How does a monk become one who has reached the *devas*?" The answer is the Jhāna-formula[1]. And this is ascribed to Gotama— a very precious context— he is commending the use of Jhāna[2]. He is asked, during a conversation, "when is a purely happy world made present?" He replies: "As long as a man in Fourth Jhāna has attained to converse with those *devas* who are living in a purely happy world, is present (santi*ṭṭhati*) with them, talks with them." Do not these show that, at least at one period in the history of Buddhism, Jhāna was not a mere discipline of sense or of mind, any more than it was a straight short-cut of Nirvāṇa, but was something that lay between the two? That it was *then* not

1. *Aṅguttara Nikāya*, ii, 184.
2. *Majjhima Nikāya*, ii, 37.

merely a training of the earth-body-and-mind, with the Inner-goer, the *antarayāmin*, left out, nor an effort to precipitate a mysterious, inconceivable state of 'going out,' but a seeking to enlarge and enrich earth-welfare, so bedimmed with sorrow and evil, by converse of man to man with those who, not yet by a long way knowing the highest things, *knew more* than the man of the earth.

How does it not enrich and enlarge our little knowledge of Gotama the man, if we picture him, the Muser, musing in this way! Too cramped and prejudiced is our view of him, for either it is of a monk among monks, preaching a forced growth or 'making-to-become' (*bhāvanā*) in this life, which shall do away with all becoming (*bhava*) hereafter, or it is of a teacher of just earthly ethics, or it is of a superman who knew everything. Why do we not take the truer view of him, which we may also find in the books if we look a little more closely and historically the view of the noble man who (*sânukampī anuddayā*)[1] 'moved by compassion and by kindness' for men, sought to help them and himself by 'making present' to himself more worlds than one, and by converse with their inmates learning how this might best be done? Of him it was said:

> And rolling back the (murky) veil,
> And pain gone by and weariness,
> He sees both this world and the next.[2]

By him we are told, it was said, repeatedly, that the man-who could-see, standing between, saw 'the two houses' clairvoyantly with separate doors and men faring from the one to the other.[3]

He is recorded as not overrating the value of psychic gifts in religious ends, but as clearly affirming their reality. "Yes, Mahāli, such deva-sounds (or words or speech) *are*, they are not things of nought. If he (Sunakkhatta) is clairaudient only, not clairvoyant, it is only because he has not concentrated on both, as may be done. But in the matter of joining the religious life, there are higher considerations than these."[4] (I have condensed in translating.) His experiences while exercising these gifts figure in a great number of records, over which modern writers quickly slide. He is listener; he is interlocutor; often he is recorded as relating the experience; often we are left to infer it. One series of such he decided not to tell, for men would not have believed him, and that would have hurt them.[5]

---

1. *Saṃyutta Nikāya*, i, 206.
2. *Dīgha*, iii, 178.
3. *Majjhima*, i, 279; ii, 21; iii, 178.
4. *Dīgha*, i, 152.
5. *Saṃyutta*, ii, 255.

I see this helper of men as neither the atheist concerning the world-ātman, nor the denier of man the ātman as some make him out, nor as one who spoke of himself as a little god on earth, nor as just an ascetic, monastic mystic. I see him as a man with an inspired mandate to the 'man'. There was in his day no worthy conception of the Highest; there *was* a dawning sense that religion was mainly a matter of *living*, and there *was* a very general belief, that living was no mere matter of a brief three score years and ten. His mandate was to show the great significance of life in a figure, and that figure was the Way, the Way in and for each man, the Way which 'went to Nirvāṇa, yet 'went on with it, flowed with it, as Gaṅgā and Yamunā flowed in and with each other'.[1] "He made a Way where Way was none; he traced out a Way till then unrevealed; he knew and saw the Way; master of the Way was he. To-day his disciples follow him in the way which has come down to them from him."[2] His age called him *Sārathī*, 'chariot-driver', Satthavāha, 'leader of the caravan.'[3] And like a good leader, his immediate aim was not to dwell only on the ultimate goal, but like England's most famous journal, to try to judge what lay on the other side of the hill, round the bend of the way;[4] the next step, and the next after that. That was enough for the worthiest, more than enough for most.

And in his habit of 'musing in the wood' he will have found that quiet and concentration which he judged necessary, for which he is often made to show his preference. He found too the '*jhāna-sukha*'[5] — that fine delicate sense of added well-being known to those who claim to have been in converse with the very worthy of the other side. Some of his disciples knew of it; we note it in the verses of both women and men; we can hardly wonder that they call themselves 'lovers of musing' (*jhānaratā*). And the tradition at least of it yet lingers in Burma.[6]

But that the traditional memory of him was closely associated with the Jhāna habit is betrayed by the curious insertion of the Jhāna formulas into the account of the moment of his passing.[7] The Buddhist would say, that the back and forth narrative of the process (knowable by none save a thought-reader) indicated the deliberateness with which the great man put off mental and bodily life. The critic of my theory will say, that at any rate the absence of any allusion to deva-visitants during

---

1. *Dīgha*, ii. 223.
2. *Majjhima*, iii, 15. The Speaker is Ānanda, but the last clause reveals a later hand.
3. *Dīgha*, ii, 39; *Theragāthā*. 1236; cf. *Apadāna*, p. 80.
4. Gleig's *Life of Wellington*.
5. *Dīgha*, iii. 78.
6. *Compendium of Philosophy*, p. 57.
7. *Dīgha*, ii. 157.

that Jhāna disproves its soundness. To both, I would say, that whatever induced the insertion here of the formulas, silence as to presences at the end, when at the beginning at the first 'sermon', there is not silence, may only mean that, when the man passed, Jhāna *for the men about him* no longer meant musing for access to the unseen. Only Ānanda and Anuruddha were left, the latter, though a jhāyin, a very timid aged recluse, the former recorded as willing to 'make inferences' when his cousin Gotama told of his psychic experiences.[1] The newer cult of the positive, the earthly, the things seen, as alone important was prevailing; psychic gifts were held as possible only for the very few; the man of the two houses was suffered to depart with no one listening, let alone seeing, whether in Jhāna or not.

Here then was what I conceive may have been for the co-founders of the Sākkaputta movement, later called Buddhism, the more especial advantage which they sought in musing. In their days there would seem to have been the contrasted cultures of Sāṅkhya (*paṭisankhā*) and Yoga (the *bhāvanā of samādhi or jhāna*). Never do they appear to *call* the latter 'Yoga'. But for them too it meant not a merely negative eliminating of things seen; for them it was a coming to see or at least hear the unseen, and therein not only to taste a joy, but also to come to have a veil shrouding the long way rolled back for a little (vivaṭṭ-*achadda*).

Faith in the old Great Devas was in the melting-pot, but devas, devatās, the men who had passed on, had come with a new significance to man's help; they were seen as intermediaries along the whole upward way to Amata, aiding their fellow earth-wayfarers with such knowledge as he was yet able to bear. Modern books, as is natural, estimate them and their wording variously. But *on the whole* devas appear as worthy and kindly warders of the man they have left behind, who (discounting a Sabbaññu) must, as behind the veil, have known more than those they warded. They held Gotama in high worth, but not the monk as monk; they believed in 'the man' as real; they believed in the good life; they believed in man as willing to seek the Better. We may with most writers on Buddhism minimise all that this converse meant for the founders of the movement; we may with immature pen write it down as rubbish; or as not 'of the essence' of the matter. But we shall only do so by shutting our eyes to very much in the records that we do not wish to see.

But Buddhism blotted out the 'man' from its creed, and that, it may be, little by little, during the Founder's day. Not heeding his warnings, "not body, not mind", men came to see in man just body and mind. Then

---

1. *Saṃyutta*, i. 55 'as far as it is to be got by inference, you have got it.'

they came to see in Jhāna an interesting procedure in bodily and mental training. And then the kindly deva-warders are less and less heard of. Rūpajhāna and Arūpajhāna became associated with after-death prospects only, and to-day not even with that. As worded in the Abhidhamma they would seem to be now dead words in a stereotyped routine.

Chapter - 22

Place of Faith in Buddhism

N. Dutt

Saddhā (=Sans. *Śraddhā*) in Buddhism carries two distinct meanings: one is faith (*pasāda*), producing *pīti* (serene pleasure) and the other is self-confidence, producing *viriya* (energy). *Saddhā*, when it is *pasāda* (faith), is an antidote to *vicikicchā* (doubt about the greatness of Buddha, excellence of his teaching, and uprightness of his disciples) and *moha* (deluded state of mind),[1] its characteristic, according to the *Milindapañha*,[2] *Visuddhimagga*[3] and *Abhidharma-kośa*[4] being serenity of mind (*sampasādana*). *Saddhā*, when it is self-confidence, puts energy (*viriya*) into one's mind to achieve an object which another person like him has achieved. It makes him rely on his capabilities and work out the same to their fullest extent. Siddhārtha was not willing to take Rudraka Rāmaputta at his words and decided to find out the truth himself as he possessed like his teacher *saddhā, viriya, sati, samādhi* and *paññā*. By *saddhā*, he meant confidence in his abilities to develop the powers necessary to achieve his object.[5] It is mostly in the latter sense that *saddhā* is used in the compounds *saddhindriya* and *saddhābala*.

---

1. Anāgārika B. Govinda writes in his work on the *Psychological attitude of Early Buddhist Philosophy* (pp. 166, 234) that "it is a form of inner confidence which arises from an intuitive or intellectual insight into the truth of the *dhamma* and which grows in the course of meditation on account of profound and direct experience into a state of certainty and knowledge in which the last traces of delusion are removed."
2. *Milindapañha*, p. 35.
3. *Visuddhimagga*, p. 156; *Atthasālini*, p. 304.
4. *Kośa*, I, p. 156; *Vyākhyā* (C.O. Series), p. 43: *Śraddhā=cetaso prāsadaḥ* (see *Jñānaprasthāna sūtra*, 1. 19.). It is the dharma, with the association of which, the thoughts disturbed by *kleśa* and *upakleśa* become clear as the disturbed water becomes clear by the presence of alum. The *Vyākhyā* (p. 43) explains *śraddhā* in detail thus:—सत्येषु चतुर्षु रत्नेषु च त्रिषु कर्मषु च शुभाशुभेषु। तत्फलेषु च इष्टानिष्टेषु सन्त्यैवैतानीत्यभिसंप्रत्ययोऽभिसंप्रतिपत्तिः श्रद्धेति।

   Kośa, II. 25: चित्तविशुद्धिः श्रद्धा; II, 32 प्रेम एव श्रद्ध
5. Cf. *Milindapañha*, p. 35: *sampakkhandanalakkhaṇa*.

The object of this paper is to show how far *saddhā* in the former sense (i.e. *pasāda*) came to be regarded as a means for the attainment of Nibbāna.

Three Paths leading to Nibbāna

The first and well-known path leading to Nibbāna is the aṭṭhaṅgikamagga, in other words, all those practices connoted by the words *sīla, citta and paññā.*[1] It is an out and out practical code for physical, mental, and intellectual discipline and hardly offers any scope for faith (*saddhā*). Let us call it '*citta and paññā*' path or process.

The second but not so well-known as the previous one is the path of *satipaṭṭhāna* or the close observation of what is passing within and outside one's mind and body. It gives particular attention to mental discipline, and attaches little importance to physical discipline or to faith (*saddhā*). By *satipaṭṭhāna* alone, it is said, that *nibbāna* is attained, so let us call it '*satipaṭṭhāna*' path or process.[2]

In a few places in the *Nikāyas saddhā* is recognised as the path for the attainment of Nibbāna, inspite of the fact that it does not go well with the rationalistic principles, of which the Buddhists are the avowed champion. But this third path, which we may call '*aveccappasāda*' path or process, is particularly important for the laity whose interest is almost ignored at the early stage of the religion, and so it is not improbable that the third path came to be recognised only at a later date but in any case, before the Pali canon was closed.

Saddhā and the Laity

In early Buddhism, the laity had no place in the scheme of spiritual advancement, for none but a recluse could derive the benefit of the teaching. It is frequently stated in the Nikāyas that it is not easy for a householder to practise the *brahmacarya* which is thoroughly pure and complete in all respects.[3] The utmost that a householder could practise were the five *sikkhāpadas*,[4] or temporarily the eight *sikkhāpadas*,[5] and that also for the purpose of *uposatha*. The teaching to be imparted to a householder was limited to *dānakathaṃ sīlakathaṃ saggakathaṃ kāmānaṃ ādīnavaṃ okāraṃ saṃkilesaṃ nekkhamme*

---

1. Exhaustively treated in the *Visuddhimagga*. See my *Early Buddhism*.
2. Ekāyano ayaṃ maggo sattānaṃ visuddhiyā. *Dīgha*, II, p. 290.
3. Nayidam sukaraṃ agāram ajjhāvasatā ekantaparipuṇṇaṃ ekantaparisuddhaṃ brahmacariyaṃ carituṃ. *Majjhima*, II, p. 55.
4. Pāṇātipātā vermaṇī, adinnādānā v., micchācārā v., musāvādā v., surāmerayamajjapamādaṭṭhānā v.
5. The three additional are vikālabhojanā v., naccagītavāditavisukadassanamālāgandhavilepanadhāraṇamaṇḍanavibhūsaṇaṭṭhānā v., and uccāsana-mahāsayanā v.

ānisaṃsaṃ (talks relating to charity, moral precepts, and heaven, the evils of indulging in worldly desires, and the good effects of renunciation)[1] and a bhikkhu imparting to a householder deeper or subtler teaching was punished according to the rules of the *Pātimokkha*.[2] The highest spiritual teaching that could be imparted to a householder and that also only in special cases was the exposition of the four *ariyasaccas*. The householders were allowed to practise only *dāna* and *sīla*, later on they were advised to develop *saddhā* and *paññā*. By *saddhā* was meant cultivation of faith in Buddha, Dhamma and Saṅgha, and by *paññā* comprehension of the four truths, and in some cases, also *paṭiccasamuppāda*. The programme of duties laid down for the laity is detailed thus:[3] An ariyasāvaka is to develop firm faith in Buddha, Dhamma and Saṅgha, and then he should perfect himself in the five *sīlas* (*sikkhāpadas*), be liberal in gifts,[4] and lastly he should try to comprehend the four truths, and, if possible also the *paṭiccasamuppāda*.[5] A person endowed with these four,[6] which are called *sotāpattiyaṅgas*, becomes a sotāpanna, and may rest assured that he will be reborn as a god, and will never be reborn in the hells, or in the *preta* world and that in the long run he is destined to attain *sambodhi*.[7] The above account shows that saddhā (faith) was primarily meant for the laity and formed one of the vital items of practice for their spiritual uplift. Deep *saddhā*, in some cases, produced *pīti* (serene pleasure) and helped concentration of mind, but in any case, Nibbāna, according to the early Buddhists, was unattainable by a householder.

Saddhā and the Bhikkhus

The expression frequent in the Nikāyas: *saddhāya kulaputtā agārasmā anāgāriyaṃ pabbajanti* (out of faith sons of good families retire from home to homeless life) shows that the bhikkhu-life generally commenced out of *saddhā* (faith). The first duty of a bhikkhu is to become a sotāpanna by removing the *nīvaraṇas*,[8] one of which is *vicikicchā*. The removal of *vicikicchā* can only be effected by developing *saddhā* as stated above (vide p. 639). Again, in the sixteen moments of comprehension of the four aryan truths, *jñāna* is always

1. Cf. *Aṅguttara*, IV, p. 209.
2. Cf. Pācittiya, 3: Yo pana bhikkhu anupasampannaṃ padaso dhammaṃ vāceyya pācittiyaṃ.
3. *Aṅguttara*, II, p. 212; IV. p. 271.
4. *Muttacāgā payatapāṇi vossaggaratā yācayogā dānasaṃvibhāgaratā.*
5. *Aṅguttara*, V, p. 184.
6. *Saddhā, sīla, cāgā, paññā.*
7. *Aṅguttara*, V. p. 182.
8. Sakkāyadiṭṭhi. sīlabbataparāmāsa, vicikicchā.

preceded by *kṣānti* (i.e. faith)[1] and so *saddhā* was not wholly dispensed with by the bhikkhus. But the bhikkhus are warned against growing *saddhā* for the teacher for it is akin to *prema* (affection) and works more as an obstacle than as an aid to spiritual progress.[2] It is said that Ānanda's spiritual progress was hampered on account of his *saddhā* for Buddha.

The two dhūras

It is worth while to refer in this connection to the two *dhūras* mentioned in the Buddhist texts, viz., *Saddhā-dhūra* and *Paññā-dhūra*. *Saddhā*, however, does not play an important part in *Saddhā-dhūras*, for, the distinction made between the two dhūras is not on account of the degree of predominance of *saddhā* or *paññā* but on account of the dullness or sharpness of the faculties of monks. *Saddhā-dhūras* is prescribed for monks with dull faculties while *Paññā-dhūra* for monks with sharp faculties. Though the *saddhānu-sārīs* do not make their main prop, they first grow faith in, and regard for, the Tathāgata,[3] and then acquire the five indriyas[4] including *paññā*. Likewise the *dhammānusārīs* do not dispense with *saddhā* but make *paññā* their first item of acquisition[5] and then develop the other indriyas including *saddhā*.[6]

It will be observed that *saddhā* is explained here as faith or affection but not as self-confidence, which is the usual sense in which *saddhā* is interpreted when it is grouped with *viriya* and other indriyas. It seems that in the Buddhist texts the two meanings of *saddhā* have not always been carefully distinguished. *Saddhā* as an *indriya* (predominating factor) and *bala* (force) should ordinarily mean "self-confidence" and not faith.

Saddhā (faith) as a means to liberation

There are passages in the *Majjhima* and *Aṅguttara Nikāyas* where emphasis is laid on faith (*saddhā*) as a means to liberation. In the *Majjhima* (I, p. 480-1) it is stated that there are bhikkhus who have taken resort to Buddhism out of *faith*. They believe that Bhagavā knows everything while they do not, that his teaching is forceful and attractive, and that they should exert for the goal until their bodies

---

1. E.g., (i) duḥkhe dharmajñāna-kṣānti, (ii) duḥkhe dharmajñānaṃ, (iii) duḥkhe anvayajñāna-kṣānti, (iv) duḥkhe anvayajñānaṃ.

2. *Kośa*, II, 32; cf. *Vyākhyā* (C.O. Series), p. 54: प्रेमैव श्रद्धा न गौरवम्। नतु श्रद्धैव प्रेम।.........दुःखसमुदयसत्ययोः श्रद्धैवभिसंप्रत्ययरूपा। न प्रेम अस्पृहनीयत्वात्। प्रियतारूपा तृष्णा नाभिसंप्रत्ययरूपेति श्रद्धा न भवति। सार्धविहारिणः अन्त्येवासिनः। तेषु पुत्रादिषु प्रेम न गौरवं क्लिष्टमक्लिष्टं वेति संभवतः। गौरवं न प्रेम।

3. Tathāgate c'ssa saddhāmattaṃ hoti pemamattaṃ.

4. Saddhā, viriya, sati, samādhi and paññā.

5. Tathāgatappaveditā c'assa dhammā paññāya mattaso nijjhānaṃ khamanti.

6. Cf. *Majjhima*, I, p. 478 f.; *Kośa*, vi. 31.

are dried up leaving only the bare skin, bones and sinews. These monks, the texts state, acquire the highest knowledge in this life, or at least, the *anāgāmi* stage.

'Aveccappasāda' process

In the *Vatthupama Sutta*, a complete course of training is prescribed for those monks who intend to make *pasāda* (faith) their main prop for the attainment of liberation. The process is as follow:

I. An adept should first get rid of the mental impurities such as *abhijjhā* (strong attachment), *macchariya* (avarice), *makkha* (hypocrisy), *māyā* (cheating others), *sātheyya* (double-dealing), *thambho and sārambho* (pride and haughtiness), *māno and ati māno* (conceit); *mada* (pride or excitement caused by attachment to one's own acquisitions),[1] and *pamāda* (carelessness).[2]

II. After the removal of the above-mentioned impurities, which may well be compared to the *sīla* practices of the 'sīla-citta-paññā' process, the adept is required to develop unflinching faith in Buddha, Dhamma, and Saṅgha. The usual terms in which the faith is to be expressed are as follows:—

(1) *Bhagavā* the enlightened is endowed with knowledge and good conduct, he is the knower of world, the guide in disciplining men, the incomparable, the teacher of men and gods.

(2) The *Dhamma* preached by Bhagavā produces fruit in this life, invites every body, knows no limitation of time, leads one to the goal and is realisable only by the wise within one's own self.

(3) The *Saṅgha* consists of monks who are in one of the eight stages of sanctification, and righteous, who are exerting for knowledge, observing good conduct, who are worthy of gifts and praise and respects, and who are fit recipients of gifts from laymen.

III. The more the mental impurities are removed the stronger becomes his faith in Buddha, Dhamma and Saṅgha. This faith produces in his mind the satisfaction that he has achieved something good. This satisfaction in its turn produces joy and a sense of deep pleasure (*pīti*) which makes the body calm and the mind serene, and ultimately, the mind gets concentrated.[3]

It will be observed that all the processes, be it ;sīla-citta-paññā' or 'satipaṭṭhāna' or 'aveccappasāda,' aim at *samādhi* (concentration of mind). In the sīla-citta-paññā' process, this is achieved by means of the four jhānas. By the first jhānas one acquires 'viveka-jaṃ

1. *Kośa*, II, 33: मदः स्वधर्मरक्तस्य पर्यादानं तु चेतसः ।
2. See *kleśa, upakleśsa, paryatvasthāna* and *anuśaya* in the *Kośa*, ch. V.
3. *Sukhino cittaṃ samādhiyati.*

pītisukhaṃ',[1] by the second 'samādhijaṃ pītisukhaṃ',[2] and then by the third and forth, he dismisses the *pīti-sukha* in order to develop 'upekkhā' (equanimity). In the 'aveccappasāda' process, *pīti-sukha* subsides, giving rise to *samādhi*, i.e., it skips over the processes of the third and forth jhānas.[3]

IV. After developing concentration of mind, the adept is required to practice the four *brahmavihāras*, i.e., he is to extend *mettā* (love), *karuṇā* (compassion), *mudtiā* (feeling of joy at others' success) and upekkhā (feeling of equanimity) to all beings of all the corners of the world.

V. After attaining perfection in the practice of the *brahma-vihāras*, the adept realises the four truths,[4] and destroys the three āsavas, *viz.*, *kāma*, *bhava* and *avijjā*.[5] He is now convinced that he has completed his task and has nothing more to do and that he will have no more birth.

It is remarkable that in this process the practice of *brahma-vihāras* is made an integral part, while no mention is made of the *samāpattis*. As a rule, the *brahmavihāras* are excluded from the list of practises prescribed in the 'sīla-citta-paññā' process. These are not even included in the thirty-seven *bodhipakkhiya dhammas*. In the Nikāyas the *brahmavihāras* are hardly mentioned, and if at all, in such suttas which was Mahāyānic in character.[6] The *brahmavihāras* go best with the pāramis, as is clearly shown in the *Visuddhimagga*.[7]

Another remarkable feature in course of training this is that there is no insistence on the observance of the Pātimjokkha rules, and as such it can be followed by a person who has not embraced the austere life of a Buddhist monk. This latitude is particularly noticeable in the remark that a person following this course of life is free to take luxurious food, as that will not be a hindrance to his spiritual progress.[8]

---

1. "Deep pleasure due to solitude."
2. "Deep pleasure due to concentration of mind."
3. Cf. *Majjhima*, I, p. 37-38 and p. 21-22.
4. Expressed thus:—Atthi idaṃ, atthi hinaṃ, atthi paṇitaṃ, atthi imassa sāññāgatassa uttariṃ nissaraṇaṃ—*Majjhima*, I p. 38.
5. It will be noticed that *diṭṭhi-āsava* is not included, for the question of *diṭṭhi* does not arise in this process.
6. This '*aveccappasāda*' process with the inclusion of the practice of the *brahmavihāras*, it seems, was an outcome of the Mahāyānic influence, and that the Suttas, which speak of the *brahmavihāras*, belong to a date when Hīnayāna was in the state of transition to Mahāyāna. The *Vatthupama* and *Makhādeva suttas* of the *Majjhima Nikāya* should therefore be ascribed to a date when the Mahāsaṅghika school was making its influence felt in the Buddhist circles.
7. *Visuddhimagga*, ch. IX.
8. *Majjhima*, I, p. 38: So kho so bhikkhu evam sīlo evam dhtammo evam pañño

Chapter - 23

Place of Laity in Early Buddhism

N. Dutt

The principles of early Buddhism did not make any special provision for the laity.[1] Its mission was to persuade householders to embrace the life of a recluse,[2] and Buddha was so successful in his mission in Magadha that people of the country raised a hue and cry over it, saying that Samaṇa Gotama was bent upon making the families sonless, women widowed and line of succession discontinued.[3] Many householders retired from the worldly life because of the teaching that the life of a householder was impure and an obstruction to spiritual progress while that of a recluse was pure, open and free, and besides it was not easy for a person living a householder's life to follow the teachings propounded by the teacher and to lead the thoroughly pure life of a *brahmacārī*.[4] Thus, it is evident that the new religion was primarily meant for those who would retire from the householder life. For householders generally some rites or ceremonies are provided, or some form of worship is recommended, by the founder of a religion but there was nothing of the kind in Buddhism. On the other hand the householders were asked to eschew rites and ceremonies (*sīlabbata*),[5] and this was made one of the primary conditions for becoming a devotee of Buddha.

---

1. See "*Early Buddhism and Laity*" in *Studies in Indian History and Culture* by Dr. N.N. Law.
2. *Vinaya*, i, p.37: caratha brahmacariyaṃ sammā dukkhassa antakiriyāyā ti.
3. *Vinaya*, i, p.37: aputtakāya paṭipanno samaṇo Gotamo, vedhavyāya paṭipanno samaṇo Gotamo, kulūpacchedāya paṭipanno samaṇo Gotamo.
4. Cf. *Majjhima*, i. p. 344: Sambādho gharāvāso rajāpatho abbhokāso pabbajjā, nayidaṃ sukaram agāram ajjhāvasatā ekantaparipuṇṇam ekantaparisuddhaṃ saṅkhalikhitaṃ brahmacariyaṃ carituṃ. Cf. *Majjhima*, ii, p. 55: Yathā yathā khvāhaṃ Bhagavatā dhammaṃ desitaṃ ājānami nayidaṃ sukaraṃ gharam ajjhāvasatā etc. as above.
5. Sans. *Śīla* and *Vrata*.

At the same time, it has to be admitted that the Buddhist Saṅgha must have a lay-community for its very existence, some supporting families from which the members could have the bare necessaries of their life. In ancient India, however, the formation of a lay-community need not be a condition precedent to the formation and growth of a body of recluses. Without any distinction of caste and creed, the householders welcomed every ascetic approaching them for food and dress, and hence the Buddhist monks at first did not experience any difficulty to get their requirements from the existing families. As time went on, they picked up some householders who showed them more veneration and who were more prompt in making offerings to them than others. These householders were designated *upāsakas* or *upāsikās* and received special attention of the Buddhist monks. In the early days of Buddhism, these householders looked after the needs of the monks during the rainy-season retreats (*vassā-vāsa*) and got opportunities to come into frequent contact with them and to listen to their discourses. Such closer contacts led to the institution of certain rites and ceremonies which Buddhism wanted so much to avoid at its inception. The rites and ceremonies observed by these householders were as follows:—

(i) To utter the formulae of *Trisaraṇa*,

(ii) To listen to religious discourses on *uposatha* days,

(iii) To observe eight *sīlas* occasionally, and

(iv) To offer robes to the monks on certain occasions, specially at the end of the rainy season retreat.

Later on the faithful persons were advised,

(v) to visit the four places of pilgrimage,[1] and,

(vi) to visit the four *stūpas*, particularly those containing the relics of Buddha.[2]

The six items mentioned above, it should be noted, came into vogue gradually. We are told that Tapussa and Bhallika were the first to become *upāsakas* (*dvevācika*)[3] while Yasa's father became the next upāsaka with Trisarṇa (*tevācika*).[4] Henceforward several Khattiyas, Brāhmaṇs and Gahapatis[5] became upāsakas. After listening to a discourse they usually declared themselves as upāsakas in these words:—

1. *Mahāparinibbanāsutta,* p. 141.
2. *Ibid.* p. 142.
3. *Vinaya*.i, p. 4. i.e. they took refuge in Buddha and Dhamma only, as the Saṅgha had not yet been formed.
4. *Ibid.* p. 17.
5. See infra, p. 165-66.

"Abhikkantaṃ bho Gotama abhikkantaṃ bho Gotama. Seyyathā pi bho Gotama nikujjitaṃ vā ukkujjeyya, paṭicchannaṃ vā vivareyya, mūḷhassa va maggaṃ ācikkheyya, andhakāre va telapajjotaṃ dhāreyya: cakkhumanto rūpāni dakkhintīti; evam evaṃ bhotā Gotamena anekapriyāyena dhammo pakāsito. Ete mayaṃ bhavantaṃ Gotamaṃ saraṇaṃ gacchāma dhammañ ca bhikkhusaṅghañ ca upāsake no bhavaṃ Gotamo dhāretu ajjatagge pāṇupete saraṇagate ti."

(Excellent O Gotama, excellent. Just as one who turns the upturned, opens the covered ones, shows the path to the deluded, holds a lighted lamp in darkness, you have preached the doctrine in such a way that those who possess eyes (of knowledge) can see the actual objects. We seek refuge in you, O Gotama, in your Dhamma and in your Dhamma and in your Saṅgha. Accept us as your life-long lay-devotees).

The extract cited above appears *verbatim* at the end of almost ever discourse addressed to a householder or a group of householders. It should not however be taken as indicative of a person's actually changing his creed and becoming an upāsaka. Several brāhmaṇas and gahapatis expressed their appreciation of the discourses by these set words, and did not care to follow up the declaration by observing the moral precepts and performing the duties specially prescribed for the Upāsakas and Upāsikas.

The Three Parisās

This class of devout listeners to Buddha's discourses is referred to in the Nikāyas as Khattiya-parisā, Brāhmaṇa-parisā and Gahapati-parisā.[1] There are occasional references to the four castes[2] as well but the more common way of referring to this class of people was by the above mentioned three *parisās* (assemblies).[3] In some passages the word 'parisā' is replaced by 'mahāsāla' (nobles or rich men).[4] Not unoften is the word '*paṇḍitā*' (wise men) used instead of '*parisā*.[5] The juxtaposition of the word 'gahapati' to 'khattiya' and 'brāhmaṇa'

---

1. *Majjhima*, i, p. 72: Abhijānāmi kho panāhaṃ Sāriputta, anekasataṃ khattiya-parisaṃ upasaṅkamitā, tatra pi maya sannisinnapubbañ c'eva sallapitapubbañ ca sākacchā ca samapajjitapubbā.
2. *Aṅguttara*, iv, p. 259: Sabbe khattiyā aṭṭhaṅgasamannāgataṃ uposatham upavaseyyuṃ sabbe pi brāhmaṇā...sabbe pi vessā...sabbe pi suddā aṭṭ aṅgasamannāgataṃ uposatham upavaseyyuṃ.
3. The other parisās are Samaṇa-parisā, Cātummahārājika-parisā, Tāvatiṃsu-p., Māra-p., Brahma-p. See *Majjhima*, i, p. 72; *Dīgha*, II, p. 109; *Saṃyutta*, v. p. 51.
4. *Saṃyutta*, i. p. 71: Khattiyamhāsālā and Brāhmaṇa-mahāsālā have ample gold and silver and other treasures. *Aṅguttara*, iv, pp. 104, 130, 239; *Dīgha*, ii, p. 146.
5. Khattiya-paṇḍitā etc., *Saṃyutta*, iii, p. 6; *Majjhima*, i, p. 176; *Aṅguttara*, iv, pp. 104, 130, 239.

suggests that it meant usually the *seṭṭhis* (bankers) or businessmen or men who have taken to some vocations, such as agriculture, carpentry, smithy and so forth.[1]

In the *Aṅguttara-nikāya*[2] the distinctive features of the three *parisās* are pointed out thus: All the three classes of men seek worldly enjoyment (*bhogādhippāya*) and try to acquire knowledge (*paññupavicārā*). The Khattiyas rely on their prowess (*balādhiṭṭhānā*), is bent upon acquiring lands (*paṭhavībhinivesā*) and aim at dominance (*issariyapariyosanā*), the Brāhmaṇas depend on hymns and chants (*mantādhiṭṭhānā*), is attached to sacrifices (*yaññābhinivesā*) and aim at reaching Brahmaloka, while the Gahapatis depend on arts and crafts (*sippādhiṭṭhānā*), remains engaged with their works (*kammantābhinivesā*) and aim at fruition of their works (*niṭṭhita kammantapariyosānā*).

Aims and objects of Gahapatis

Of these three parisās, the largest number of devotees of Buddha came from the Gahapati parisā, few from Brāhmaṇa and a very few from the Khattiya. About the characteristics of the Gahapatis, the Nikāyas say that they were keen about accumulation of gold, crops, buildings, lands, wife, male and female servants.[3] Their happiness consisted in possessing worldly objects, in enjoyment of the same, and in remaining free from debts and faults.[4] In short, the Gahapatis enjoyed all worldly pleasures derivable through the five organs of sense.[5] Dīghjānu Koliyaputta said that the householders sought worldly objects, sons and wife, unguents, garlands and other articles of luxury, gold and silver; he wanted instructions from the Teacher as to the ways and means by which the householders could be happy in this life and the next. The reply was that the householders should be energetic in his vocation (*uṭṭhānasampadā*), take good care of the wealth earned righteously by the sweat of his brow (*ārakkhasampadā*), associate with men having faith, good morals, charitable disposition and wisdom (*kalyāṇomittatā*), and try to acquire their good qualities[6] and be like them (*samajīvitā*). Tapussa gahapati[7] was frank enough to admit that the gahapatis were afraid of retirement, and given to worldly pleasures because they had not realised the evil consequence of attachment to

1. Cf. Kassakagahapati in *Aṅguttara*, i. p. 229.
2. *Aṅguttara*, iii, p. 363.
3. *Majjhima*, i. p. 452.
4. *Aṅguttara*, ii. p. 69: atthisukha, bhogasukha, anaṇa-sukha and anavajja-sukha.
5. *Majjhima*, i, p. 505.
6. *Aṅguttara*, i, p. 281-2; iii, p.45
7. *Aṅguttara*, iv, p. 438.

worldly objects. Potaliya gahapati[1] thought that as he had retired from his works (*kammanta*) and business (*vohāra*), leaving his possessions to his sons, and as he had been living on bare requirement of food and dress, he should no longer be called a *gahapati*, but Buddha would not listen to him as he had not yet fulfilled the elementary conditions of a retired life. Though the householders remained engrossed in their worldly possessions, some of them were religious minded and approached different religious teachers for instructions. The Brāhmaṇas and Gahapatis of the village Sālā[2] said that they had listened to the teachings of different teachers and had not yet made up their mind to accept any of them as their spiritual guide. They approached Buddha and his disciples and listened to their instructions now and then, and some of them avowed themselves as upāsakas of Buddha, but not necessarily complying with all the conditions to be fulfilled by an upāsaka.

Discourses to Gahapatis

In every Nikāya, excepting the *Dīgha*, there is a *Gahapativagga,*[3] in which Buddha administered instructions to a particular *gahapati* or delivered discourses for the benefit of *gahapatis* in general. There are also discourses dealing incidentally with the general rules of morality, effects of *karma*, ideals of a householder and his wife, and the fundamental principles of Buddhism. The Gahapati-vaggas are found to contain discussions on all aspects of Buddhist ethics and philosophy. There were also many learned Brāhmaṇas, Khattiyas and Gahapatis who took part in abstruse discussions with Buddha and his disciples. In the *Gahapativagga* of the *Majjhima Nikāya,*[4] there are ten *suttas*. In the Kandarakasutta, Pessa Hatthārohaputta spoke in appreciation of the four *satipaṭṭhānas* and said that he and other householders occasionally tried these four practices.[5] He was then told about the various ascetic practices prevalent in the country, and the superiority of the practices and acquisitions of Buddhist monks. To Dasama Gahapati was explained how a monk attained the *anāgāmi* and *arahatta* stages, and practised the four *brahmavihāras* and *arūpasamāpattis*.[6] The Sakkas of Kapilavatthu, specially Mahānāma, listened to a discourse on what made a *sekha*

---

1. *Majjhima*, ii, p. 359.
2. *Ibid.*, i, p. 401.
3. *Majjhima*, i. pp. 339-413; *Saṃyutta*, ii, pp. 68-80; iv, pp. 109-124; *Aṅguttara*, iv, pp. 208-235.
4. *Majjhima*, i, pp. 330-413.
5. *Ibid.*, p. 340: Mayam pi hi bhate gihī odātavasanā kālena kālaṃ imesu catusu satipaṭṭhānesu supatiṭṭhitacittā viharāma.
6. *Majjhima*, I. pp. 350-353.

(i.e. a monk progressing towards Nibbāna). Potaliya gahapati felt offended at being called a *gahapati* in his so-called retired life and he was made to understand how one ceased to be a householder according to Buddha's law (*ariyassa vinaye*). Jīvaka could not believe that Buddha was taking meat specially prepared for him and on enquiry he was told how could the Buddha, perfect in the four *brahmavihāras*, do so. In the Upālisutta, one of the longest discourses, the teachings of Nigaṇṭha Nāṭaputta were discussed, and Upāli gahapati, a distinguished disciple of Nigaṇṭha Nāṭaputta, was convinced of the superiority of Buddhist teachings and was won over to the Buddhist faith. Puṇṇa Koliyaputta and Acela Seniya listened to a discourse on the effects of *kamma*,[1] gave up their austerities and joined the Buddhist order. Abhayarājkumāra, a lay disciple of Nigaṇṭha Nāṭaputta, wanted to cross words with Buddha at the instigation of his teacher but ultimately succumbed to Buddha's arguments. Pañcakaṇga thapati would not recognise the *adukkhamasukha-vedanā* as the third *vedanā*, the two other being *sukha* and *dukkha*. Buddha explained that *sukha* was a relative term and then gave an exposition of the stages of *sukha* through which a monk passed in order to reach the highest state of mental concentration. In the last sutta of this *Gahapativagga* is given an exposition of the views of a few heretical teachers as well as the wrong views held about *Arūpa-brahmaloka* and *Nibbāna*; at the end of this discourse all the Brāhmaṇas and Gahapatis of the village Sālā expressed their desire to become devotees of Buddha.[2]

There are two *Gahapativaggas* in the Saṃyutta-nikāya.[3] In the first, the Gahapatis were admonished to observe the five moral precepts, develop faith in the *Triratna*, and comprehend the law of causation including the four truths. Incidentally the question of the identity and difference of soul and *khandhas* is discussed. In the second *Gahapativagga*, there are discourses on hindrances (*saṃyojanas*) which kept one away from *Nibbāna*, on watchfulness over body (*kāya-satipaṭṭhāna*) and its movements, on restraint in act, speech and thought, and on feelings of pain and pleasure derived through the organs of sense. There is a reference to the fall of Brāhmaṇas from their ancient ideal which was similar to the present Buddhist ideal of self-restraint.

As regards the duties of a gahapati it is stated in this Nikāya that a gahapati should (i) maintain his parents; (ii) rever elders of the family; (iii) use gentle words; (iv) avoid malicious talks; (v) discard miserliness: (iv) be open-handed; (vii) be truthful and (viii) never be angry.

1. *Majjhima*, i, p. 389.
2. *Ibid.*, i, p. 413.
3. *Saṃyutta*, ii, pp. 68-80; iv, pp. 109-184.

The *Gahapatvagga* of the time *Aṅguttara Nikāya* (iv. pp. 209-235) deals more with the duties of a gahapati than with the general principles of Buddhism. The eight special virtues of a gahapati are (i) firm faith in Buddha; (ii) appreciation of the Dhamma; and (iii) regard for the Saṅgha; (iv) charitableness even to the extent of giving away one's wife, (v) open-handedness in distributing property among the saints; (vi) keenness to listen to religious discourses; (vii) lack of pride due to spiritual success; and (viii) severance from five impurities (*orambhāgiyas*). The Gahapatis are expected to possess seven other virtues, viz., faith (*saddhū*), moral restraint (*śīla*), modesty (*hiri*), shame (*otappa*),[1] learning (*bahussuta*), charitable disposition (*cāga*) and knowledge (*paññā*). Some of the Gahapatis practise the four *saṃgahavatthus*[2] viz., gift, sweet words, beneficial acts and treat others as his equals, and thereby obtain a large circle of friends.[3] Hatthaka of Alavi was the chief of those who practised the *saṅgaha-vatthus*.[4]

Though there is no *Gahapativagga* in the *Dīgha Nikāya*, there are two suttas (*Lakkhaṇa* and *Sigālovāda*) which deal with the duties of a Gahapati. In the *Lakkhaṇa-sutta*, the virtues or duties of a gahapati are mentioned though not in a systematic form, e.g., a good man should perform good deeds, restrain himself in body, speech and thought, the charitable, observe *uposathas*, take care of parents, Samaṇas and Brāhmaṇas[5] practise the four *saṅgahavatthus*,[6] exert for others' good, both moral and secular,[7] approach Samaṇas and Brāhmaṇas for instructions,[8] never harbour any anger or hatred,[9] try to bring about concord among quarrelsome persons,[10] and help others in increasing their faith, moral virtues, knowledge, charity, religiosity, wisdom, and secular possessions, look upon others with friendly eyes, never utter a lie, malicious, harsh or useless word; or never cheat others, and so forth.

In the *Sigālovādasutta*, the following duties are prescribed for a Gahapati:— (i) Abstinence from killing, speaking falsehood, stealing and adultery; (ii) avoiding commission of offences through strong will

1. See *Saṃyutta*, ii, p. 197.
2. dāna, peyyavāca, atthacariyā and samānattatā.
3. The last four discourses in this Vagga have nothing to do with the duties of Gahapatis and so they are passed over here.
4. *Aṅguttara*, I. p. 26.
5. *Dīgha*, III, p. 145.
6. *Ibid.*, p. 152.
7. *Ibid.*, p. 154.
8. *Ibid.*, p. 157.
9. *Ibid.*, p. 159.
10. *Ibid.*, p. 160.

(*chanda*), hatred (*dosa*), delusion (*moha*) and fear (*bhaya*); (iii) refraining from drinking and merry-making, evening shows; dramatic performance, dice-plays, evil friends and idleness; (iv) avoidance of enemies posing as friends and obtaining sincere friends: (v) looking after parents, teachers, sons and wife, friends and advisers, servants and workers, Samaṇas and Brāhmaṇas.[1]

Gahapatānī

There are not many discourses specially devoted to the duties of the female members of a household. In the *Saṃyutta-nikāya*[2] a woman is enjoined to earn merits by good deeds, so that she may be reborn in a good family, be married in a good family, have no co-wife, be blessed with sons, and possess influence over her husband. Her strength, it is said, consisted in her appearance (*rūpa*), wealth (*bhoga*), relatives (*ñāti*), sons (*putta*) and moral virtues (*sīla*).[3] Like the gahapatis, they should also develop faith (*saddhā*), observe moral precepts (*sīla*), listen to religious discourses (*suta*), be charitable (*cāga*) and acquire knowledge (*paññā*).[4] They should be quiet, gentle and obedient.[5]

Women[6] generally are more miserly (*macchariyā*) envious (*issukī*), more strongly attached to worldly objects[7] than men, and their knowledge also is less than that of men.[8] They must drive away from their minds anger, hatred and disrespect for others,[9] and be chaste, diligent, modest and bashful. They must not be greedy, wish others' evil, indulge in malicious, harsh or useless talks, and discard wrong views.[10]

There are certain special directions given to women, which are as follows:—

They should (i) be well-wisher of their husbands, cater to their comforts and be sweet and attractive to them, (ii) respect the parents of the husband, and rever the Samaṇas and Brāhmaṇas revered by the husband's family, (iii) be efficient in household work, e.g., in spinning, (iv) look after the needs of the servants and workers of the household and feed them properly, (v) protect paddy, gold and other articles

1. Cf. *Saṃyutta*, i, p. 231.
2. *Saṃyutta*, iv, p. 249-240.
3. *Saṃyutta*, iv, p. 246.
4. *Ibid.*, p. 250.
5. *Majjhima*, i, p. 125.
6. *Aṅguttara*, iv, p. 270; *Saṃyutta*, iv, p. 250.
7. *Aṅguttara*, p. 281; *Saṃyutta*, iv, p. 240. It is said that for these deficiencies they were not allowed to sit in the assemblies.
8. *Aṅguttara*, ii, p. 203: *Kopa, dosa* and *appaccaya*. See also *Saṃyutta*, iv. p. 240f.
9. *Aṅguttara*, v, p. 286.
10. *Saṃyutta*, iv, p. 216.

brought by her husband, (vi) become an upāsikā by taking Trisaraṇa, (vii) observe the five precepts, and (viii) be charitable[1] and (ix) acquire knowledge. The first five bring her success in this life and the succeeding four (i.e. *saddhā, sīla, suta* and *paññā*) make her happy in the next.

The conversation that Nakulamātā gahapatānī had with her husband in deathbed shows how spiritually advanced sometimes the gahapatānis were. Nakulamātā said to her husband that (i) death with anxiety is disapproved by Buddha and so he should not die with any anxiety (*sāpekho*) for her as to how she would meet both ends and rear her sons; she knew spinning and shaving hair (*veniṃ olikhituṃ*) and by plying that trade,[2] she would be able to tide over her difficulties. (ii) He need not apprehend that she would go to another family, for both of them knew that they had been living as *brahmacārīs* for the 16 years. (iii) He must not think that she would not care to approach Bhagavān or his monks after his death; on the other hand, she would be more eager to approach them, or (iv) that she would not observe the moral precepts; on the contrary she would be no less energetic than the best of the householder disciples of Buddha. (v) He must not have any doubt that she would not attain mental tranquillity (*cetosamatha*); on the contrary she would be the best of those upāsakas who practised *ceto-samatha.* (vi) He must rest assured that she was deeply interested in this doctrine and was not wanting in deep faith, in Buddha, Dhamma and Saṅgha.[3] There were other upāsikās also like Sujātā, Visākhā, Khujjuttarā, Sāmāvatī, Uttarā, Nandamātā, Suppavāsā Koliyadhītā, Suppiyā, Kātiyānī, and Kālī of Kuraraghara, who were extolled by Buddha as leading female devotees for having some extraordinary virtues.[4] In spiritual attainments, the female lay-devotees vied equally well with the male-devotees.[5]

Upāsakas and Upāsikās

The Gahapatis mentioned above were more or less listeners to the moral or religious discourses delivered by the monks. They offered food, clothing and other necessaries of life to the monks. Occasionally at the end of a discourse, they signified their appreciation by saying that they would take Trisaraṇa and become upāsakas till the end of their lives. A number of Brāhmaṇas, Gahapatis, Gāmaṇis, Paribbājakas

1. *Aṅguttara*, iv, p. 265-266; iii, p. 37.
2. It seems that Nakulapitā was a barber by profession.
3. *Aṅguttara*, II, pp. 295.
4. *Aṅguttara*, i, p. 26.
5. See Infra, p. 21.

nobles and princes[1] are found to say that they would become upāsakas, but there is nothing to show that they actually followed the moral code and performed the duties prescribed for the Upāsakas. These may be taken as lay-supporters of the Buddhist Saṅgha. The fact that there was a large number of such supporters is evidenced by the remark in the *Mahāparinibbānasutta* that Buddha should choose for his *parinibbāna* one of the towns like Campā, Rājagaha, Sāvatthi, Sāketa, Kosambī, and Vārāṇasī where are many Khattiya, Brāhmaṇa and Gahapati Mahāsālas to worship his relics.

Out of this body of lay-supporters appeared a group of persons who were more earnest in their devotion to Buddhism, and naturally tried to follow the principles of Buddhism as far as compatible with their life as a householder. In order to distinguish this body, Mahānāma the Sākyan raised the question as to what should be the marks of an upāsaka.[2] Buddha's answer, however was not very helpful for he simply said that anyone taking the Trisaraṇa was an upāsaka. In another context, however, it is stated that an upāsaka must have not only faith in the Triratna, observe moral precepts, and do good to people in return but also not resort to auspicious rites, and offer gifts to persons outside the Buddhist Saṅgha.[3] There are instances to show that some householders eschewed their old teacher and became an upāsaka of Buddha. Pukkusa Mallaputta, a disciple of Ālāra Kālāma,[4] Upāli Gahapati and Abhaya Rājakumāra, a rich upāsaka of Nigaṇṭha Nāṭ aputta,[5] a gahapati-devotee of an Ājīvaka[6] changed their teachers and became upāsakas of Buddha. There are evidence to show that a number of householders was distinguished as devout upāsakas, and that their number was large in certain localities.[7] The stereotyped remark found in the Nikāyas that Buddhist Upāsakas do not like noisy discussions shows that some householders were distinguished as Buddhist upāsakas. Then passages like "*yavatā kho pana samaṇassa Gotamassa sāvakā gihī odātavasanā Sāvatthiyaṃ paṭivasanti, ayaṃ tesaṃ aññataro Pañcakaṅgo thapati*" (Pañcakaṅgo the architect is one of the

---

1. E.g. Caṅkī brāhamṇa (M. ii. 177); Goṭṭamukha-br. (M. ii. 163); Assalāyana-br. (M. ii. 157); Brahamāyu-br. (M. ii. 145); Citta-Gahapati (S. iv. 301); (for other Gahapatis, see above); Vekhanassa paribbājaka (M. ii.): Susima-paribbājaka (S. ii. 120); Madhuro Avantiputta (M. ii. 90); Bodhirājakumāra (M. ii. 97). For Gāmaṇīs, see Gāmaṇis-Saṃyutta in *Saṃyutta-Nikāya*, iv.
2. *Aṅguttara*, iv; p. 220; *Saṃyutta*, v, p. 395; Kittavatā nu kho bhante upāsako tī ti?
3. *Dīgha*, ii, p. 132-3.
4. *Majjhima*, i, p. 379.
5. *Aṅguttara*, i, p. 219.
6. Cf. *Aṅguttara*, iv, p. 59: Campeyyakā upāsakā approached Sāriputta for requesting Buddha to deliver a discourse to them.
7. *Majjhima*, ii, p. 23.

distinguished white-dressed householder disciples of Gotama residing at Sāvatthī)[1] leave no room for doubt that some persons were marked out as Buddhist upāsakas.

The members of these families received the special attention of the Buddhist monks, who prescribed for them certain moral duties, which were classified under five heads, viz., *Saddhā* (faith), *Sīla* (observance of moral precepts), *Cāga* (chairty); *Suta* (listening to religious discourses) and *Paññā* (comprehending the higher truths)[2].

(i) By *Saddhā* is meant that an upāsaka must have firm faith in the Buddha, Dharma and Saṅgha. There is a set formulae to express that faith, which is, in short, as follows:— Bhagavān the perfectly enlightened endowed with knowledge and good conduct is the highest, the knower of the world, the leader of men and gods. His Dharma is well-preached, produces fruit in this life, knows no limitation of time and is realisable within one's ownself. The Saṅgha of his disciples, who are in one of the eight stages of sanctifications, is well-established in good conduct, is bent upon acquiring knowledge, is worthy of gifts, praise and reverence and is a fit recipient of gifts.

(ii) By *Sīla* is meant that an upāsaka must abstain from killing, stealing, adultery, speaking falsehood and indulging in drinks and merrymakings.[3] He must discard all mental impurities like excessive greed (*abhijjhā*), hatred (*vyāpāda*), slothfulness (*thīnamiddha*), flurry, (*uddhaccakukkucca*), and doubt (*vicikicchā*).

(iii) By *Cāga* is meant that an upāsaka should be charitable, provide the monks with food, robes, beds and medicinal requisites.[4] He should be open-handed, and prone to giving gifts[5] to the needy.

(iv) By *Suta* is meant that an upāsaka should reverentially listen to religious discourses and moral teachings imparted by the monks.

(v) By Paññā is meant that an upāsaka should try to comprehend the origin and decay of worldly objects,[6] in other words, realise the four truths and the law of causation.[7]

---

1. *Majjhima*,
2. *Majjhima*, i, p. 467; iii. p. 99; *Saṃyutta*, p. 231; *Aṅguttara*, i, p. 210; iv, p. 270.
3. *Aṅguttara*, iv, p. 220.
4. Cf. *Aṅguttara*, ii, 65.
5. *Aṅguttara*, ii, p. 65; Muttacāgā payatapānī vosaggaratā yācayogā dānasaṃvibhāgaratā.
6. *Aṅguttara*, iv, p. 271: Udayatthagāminiyā paññāya samannāgato ariyāya nibbedhikāya sammādukkhakkhayagāminiyā.
7. *Aṅguttara*, v, p. 184; *Saṃyutta*, v, p. 61; *Aṅguttara*, ii, p. 67, For Nīvaraṇas, see *Saṃyutta*, v, pp. 60, 146.

The above mentioned five practices are fully described in the *Gahapativagga*[1] and elsewhere. Ugga Gahapati said that his *saddhā* was of such an order that the moment he saw Buddha even from a distance, his mind obtained satisfaction (*pasidi*). He observed the five *sikkhāpadas*, and thereby completed the practice of *sīlas*. He approached bhikkhus and listened to their discourses with due respect (*sakkaccam eva suṇami no asakkaccaṁ*). For the sake of sacrifice (*cāga*) he would give away his young wives and divide his property among the religious people, and while giving gifts to the monks he would not discriminate between one monk and another on account of their spiritual attainments. He would listen to the higher teachings of Buddhism and thereby become *paññavā*.

To Brāhmṇa gahapatis of Veludvāra, Buddha delivered a discourse dilating on the five precepts referred to above. He said that an upāsaka in order to become a sotāpanna should bear in mind the following *dhammas*:—

(i) Realising how painful is one's own death, a person should not cause other's death.

(ii) Remembering how a thief is hated by one whose possessions are stolen, a person must not steal other's property.

(iii) Knowing how much a person is hated by the man with whose wife he commits adultery, one must not commit adultery.

(iv) As a liar is disliked by everybody so one must not speak a lie.

(v) As a man who by malicious words brings about dissension is abhorred by everybody, so one should not utter malicious words.

(vi) As a person is disliked for harsh words, so one must avoid uttering the same.

(vii) As a person is looked down for his frivolous talks, one must not indulge in the same.[2]

A person should not only practice the seven dhammas mentioned above for his own benefit but also persuade others to do the same.[3]

An upāsaka is further prohibited from trading in (i) weapons; (ii) livestock; (iii) meat; (iv) wine and (v) poison.[4]

In the *Milindapañha* (p. 94) there are a few additional instructions given to the upāsakas. These are as follows:—

---

1. *Aṅguttara*, iv, pp. 209 ff.
2. *Saṃyutta*, v, p. 353 f.
3. Cf. *Aṅguttara*, iv, p. 221.
4. *Aṅguttara*, i, p. 208.

An upāsaka should (i) feel happy or sad at the happiness or sorrow of the Saṅgha; (ii) make the *dhamma* the leading factor of his life; (iii) share his gain with others as far as possible (iv) exert his best for the growth of the religion of the teacher whenever its decline is noticed; (v) hold the right view; (iv) avoid performing any auspicious rite or venerating another teacher even for the sake of his life; (vii) observe restraint in acts and words; (viii) be keen in maintaining concord; (ix) discard jealousy and (x) avoid hypocrisy in following the religion. In the *Vinaya*[1] are enumerated the five advantages obtained by a householder by observing the sīlas. He (i) gains immense wealth and property; (ii) acquires fame; (iii) can appear boldly before any social congregation; (iv) dies consciously and (v) goes to heaven.

Lay-devotees and Saṅgha

Apart from the moral precepts to be observed by the upāsakas and upāsikās, they were enjoined to supply the members of the Saṅgha with robe, food, bed and medicinal requisites.[2] As a result of such gifts they were given the hope that in the next world they would have long life, good appearance, happiness and strength.[3] In making these gifts, however they must not have any selfish end in view (*sāpekha*).[4] Some of the upāsakas and upāsikās visited the several ārāmas to find out if any one was sick and needed medicines which they procured to the best of their abilities.[5] The monks on the other hand were warned that with complete self-restraint they should approach householders for food and dress, or for any other purpose. They are not to associate themselves with the joys and sorrows of householders,[6] for there were instances of monks having got entangled with women[7] by such association. They were also advised not to accept alms from those householders who had at any time made attempts to bring about adversity to the monks, or injure them in any way, or oust them from their residence (*āvāsa*), or have abused them or tried to cause dissension between one monk and another, or have spoken ill of Buddha, Dhamma and Saṅgha.[8] The monks were further instructed to avoid those householders who would not welcome them with sweet words, not show respects to them, or not offer them seats kindly, conceal

1. *Vinaya*, I. p. 227-228.
2. *Aṅguttara*, ii, p. 66.
3. *Ibid.*, ii, p. 64.
4. *Ibid.*, ii, p. 59.
5. *Vinaya*, I, p. 216.
6. *Saṃyutta*, iii, p. 11.
7. *Aṅguttara*, iii. p. 259; iv, p. 54.
8. *Aṅguttara*, iv, p. 344.

his possessions, give little and bad things though they have ample and good things, offer gifts irreverentially, do not approach monks for listening to discourses, and do not like instructions.[1] At the end of the rainy season the Saṅgha held a ceremony called Pavāraṇā and Kaṭhina at every *āvāsa*. On these occasions, the upāsakas were advised to offer robes and were told that gifts on such occasions carried special merits.

Uposatha of the Upāsakas

On the uposatha days, the more devout upāsakas were advised to observe eight precepts[2] instead of five. They sometimes spent the day in a monastery in company of the monks. The eight precepts were,—

(i) complete abstention from killing by laying aside all weapons, and developing a kindly and friendly feeling towards all being;

(ii) complete abstention from stealing, and remaining pure and satisfied with what is given;

(iii) total abstention from sexual enjoyments, and living the life of a true *brahmacārī*:

(iv) complete discarding of untruth, and remaining always anxious to be truthful;

(v) refraining from all kinds of drinks and merrymakings;

(vi) taking only one meal a day, and refraining from afternoon meals;

(vii) avoidance of all places of amusement where there is dance and music, also rejection of scents, unguents and garlands, and lastly;

(viii) sleeping on low beds or grass mats and discarding high beds.

Some of the advanced upāsakas were able to attain concentration of mind. This concentration was induced in them by their deep faith in Buddha, Dhamma and Saṅgha. This faith engendered in their minds deep satisfaction that they had achieved something good. Through this satisfaction, their mind became serene and concentrated.[3] They practised the *jhānas* one after another and perfected themselves in all the four *jhānas*. Cittagahapati[4] and Uttarā Nandamātā[5] became highly

---

1. *Aṅguttara*, v, p. 387.
2. *Aṅguttara*, iv, p. 254: Pāṇaṃ na haññe na ca majjapo siyā abrahmacariyā virameyya methunā rattiṃ na bhuñjeyya vikālabhojanaṃ mālaṃ na dhāraye na ca gandham ācare mañce chamāyaṃ vasayetha santhate etaṃ hi aṭṭhaṅgikaṃ ah' uposatham buddhena dukkhantagunā pakāsitam.
3. *Aṅguttara*, v, p. 330.
4. *Saṃyutta*, iv, p. 281.
5. *Aṅguttara*, i, p. 26; iv., p. 66.

proficient in the *jhānas*. Some of the Upāsakas practised the four *brahmavihāras* and four *satipaṭṭhānas*.[1] Sāmāvatī Upāsikā[2] was the chief of those who practised *mettā*.

Khujjuttarā Upāsikā acquired *paṭisambhidā*[3] and abilities in learning Buddha's words.[4] Nandamātā upāsikā was so spiritually advanced that her mind was not moved when she saw her husband reborn as an ogre. Her chastity was unimpeachable and there was no occasion for her to confess (*paṭidesitā*) any transgression of the moral laws. Nandamātā mastered the four *jhānas* and removed all the five orambhāgiya impurities. Sirivaddha and Mānadinna were advised to practise satipaṭṭhāna in order to overcome acute pain due to disease.[5]

Teaching imparted to lay-devotees

In delivering discourses to the householders, Buddha and his disciples uniformly observed an order (*anupubbikathaṃ*). They first expatiated on the merits of giving gifts (*dānakathaṃ*) and observing moral precepts (*sīlakatham*), and the reward obtained thereby, viz., a heavenly existence (*saggakathaṃ*).[6] Then they dilated on the evils of enjoying worldly pleasures (*kāmānaṃ ādīnavaṁ*) and the merit of retirement from the world (*nekkhamme ānisaṁsaṁ*). When they found that this teaching had made a good impression on the mind of a householder, they passed on to the next higher teaching, the exposition of the four truths, *dukkha, samudaya, nirodha and magga*, and made them realise that whatever has origin must have decay (*yaṃ kiñci samudayadhammaṃ sabban taṃ niroghadhamman ti*).[7]

There were householders who took greater and greater interest in Buddhist religion and philosophy, and actually we find that they took interest in the deepest problems of Buddhist philosophy.[8] Cittagahapati was complimented for being able to understand the subtleties of Buddhist philosophy[9] while Anāthapiṇḍika was told that topics not to be explained to a householder were being laid before

---

1. *Majjhima*, i, p. 340: mayam pi gihī odātavasanā kālaṃ imesu eatusus satipaṭṭhānesu supaṭṭhitacittā viharāma.
2. *Aṅguttara*, i, p. 26.
3. *Visuddhimagga*; p. 442.
4. It is said that she reproduced the *Itivuttaka* heard by her from the teacher.
5. *Saṃyutta*, v, pp. 176.
6. The first discourse was delivered by Buddha to the Brāhmaṇa gahapatis of Magadha. see *Vinaya*, p. 37.
7. Cf. *Majjhima*, i, p. 379; ii, p. 145.
8. See above.
9. *Saṃyutta*, iv, pp. 282 f: Suladdhaṃ te gahapati yassa to gambhire buddhavacane paññācakkhu kamatī ti.

him for his edification.[1] There is a rule in the *Pācittiya* (no. 4) that to an uninitiated the *dhamma* is not to be preached syllable by syllable. The upāsakas were advised to avoid reading Suttantas.[2] It is however clear that the householders were as far as possible kept away from the deeper teachings, lest they should be frightened away, from taking interest in the religion.[3] But again, we find that Nandamātā upāsikā recited the *Pārāyaṇa* at dawn and that Sāriputta explained to Hāliddikāni gahapati the verses of Aṭṭhakavagga.[4] When Anāthpiṇḍika was in his deathbed, Sāriputta delivered to him a discourse on Buddhist philosophy so that he might overcome the extreme pain.[5] In the discourse he pointed out that a person must not cling to the six organs of sense or to the perceptions and feelings derived through the organs of sense, or to the *dhātus* like earth, water, fire, air, space (*ākāsa*) and consciousness (*viññaṇa*), or to the five constituents of a being, or to the four Arūpadhātus, or to this world or the next, or to things seen, heard, thought or known.

To Nakulapitā Buddha explained how the unenlightened persons identified soul with one or all of the *khandhas* and thus suffered from the misconception of the existence of a self, while to Hāliddikāni, Mahakaccāna explained the stanza of the *Aṭṭhakavagga* (*Sutta Nipāta*, p. 165):

"Okaṃ pahāya aniketasārī gāme akubbaṃ muni santhavāni

Kāmehi ritto apurekkharāṇo kathaṃ na viggayha janena kayirā"

[A monk should give up clinging to the five constituents, remain unattached to the characteristics of the perceived objects (*aniketasārī*). He must not associate himself with the weal and woe of householders, discard love, desire, attachment and despair, not speculate about his future existence (*apurakkharāṇo*) and quarrel with other monks regarding correctness and incorrectness of a *dhamma* or a rule of discipline.]

In all the discourses delivered to Citta, Nakulapitā and Hāliddikāni, the main topic dealt with was that a person must not take pleasure in the origin of *khandhas*, which were subject to decay; that an unwise person misconceived one or all of the *khandhas* as soul, and developed a notion of I-ness. A true disciple of Buddha should not care for his past *khandhas*, not think of his future *khandhas* and

---

1. *Majjhima*, iii, p. 261; Na kho gahapati gihīnam odātavasanānaṃ evarūpī dhammakathā paṭibhāti.
2. *Saṃyutta*, v, p. 407.
3. *Aṅguttara*, iv, p. 63.
4. See Infra.
5. *Majjhima*, iv, p. 258 f. Cf. *Saṃyutta*, iv, p. 115 f.

must not have any attachment to his present *khandhas*.[1] Ugga gahapati and others were taught that those who were engrossed with the sense-objects would not attain Nibbāna.[2] Soṇa gahapati[3] was taught that the *khandhas* were impermanent and impermanence was grief, and that none of the *khandhas* or all the *khandhas* taken together was soul. In the *Citta-saṃyutta*,[4] we have practically all the abstruse discussions on Buddhist philosophy. These are as follows:—

(i) Neither the organs of sense nor their objects are worldly ties—the tie is thirst that arises out of the contact of the two.

(ii) The distinction that lies between the organ of sense, its object, and the perception caused by the contact of the two.

(iii) The sixty-two non-Buddhistic doctrines are nothing but the outcome of the misapprehensions of one or all of the *khandhas* as soul.

(iv) The exact implications of saṅkhārā in *Kāya-Vacī-* and *Citta-saṅkhārā*.

(v) The method by which a meditator induces and discontinues the meditation in which perception and consciousness become inactive (*saññāvedayitanirodha*), and the distinction between death and *saññāvedayitanirodha*.

(vi) The meaning of mental emancipation (*ceto-vimutti*) through realisation of the absence of desire (*akiñcañña*), of substancelessness (*suññatā*), and characteristiclessness (*animittatā*) of worldly objects.

(vii) Exposition of the four *brahmavihāras* viz., love, compassion, joy at other's success, and equanimity.

(viii) Elucidation of the four meditations: *savitakka-savicāra*, *avitakka-avicāra*, etc.

From the above, it will be observed that the advanced householders tried to comprehend the deepest problems of Buddhist philosophy, and on occasions even entered into discussions with the teachers of other sects.[5] Though still in white robes they were as spiritually advanced as a monk.

Upāsaka's Spiritual Attainments

The goal that was held before the householders was rebirth in one of the heavens[6] or as Sakka, the king of gods. This conception was

1. *Saṃyutta*, iii, pp. 1 f.
2. *Ibid.*, iv. p. 109.
3. *Ibid.*, iii, p. 48.
4. *Ibid.*, iv, pp. 281 f.
5. Citta gahapati crossed words with Nigaṇṭha Nāṭaputta. See *Saṃyutta*, iv, p. 298 f.
6. *Majjhima*. i, p. 505: Householders enjoying worldly pleasures by good conduct goes to *sagga*.

already existing in the pre-Buddhist days, and all religions which accepted the theory of *karma* endorsed it. A householder should be first instructed to make gifts and to observe the precepts, and he is to be convinced that as fruit of this he would be reborn in the heavens (*sagga*). The Nikāyas are full of instances of good householders, who by leading a virtuous life were reborn as gods, and then there is the whole of the *Vimānavatthu* to illustrate this theory of *karma*. Aśoka also upheld this view, and did not like to go beyond. But the principles of Buddhism could not support it fully. Immediately after *saggakhathaṃ*, the householders were to be instructed in looking upon worldly pleasures as evil and retirement as the best course of life (*nekkhamme ānisaṃsaṃ*). Hence it is evident that the ideal held by Buddhism even before the householder was not rebirth in one of the heavens but retirement from the worldly life. In the *Mahāparinibbānasutta*, Buddha is heard to say about the fruits attained by some of his departed *upāsakas*. He said that Sudatta (=Anāthapiṇḍika) and ninety others had become Sakadāgāmi, while Sijātā and 500 others Sotāpanna. Kakudha upāsaka reached the anāgāmi stage, so also did Kāliṅga, Nikaṭa, Kaṭissabho, Tuṭṭha, Santuṭṭha, Bhadda, Subhadda and several others.[1]

The next lower fruits attained by the upāsakas are detailed in the *Janavasabha Sutta*,[2] where it is stated that those who took the *trisaraṇa* and observed the *sīlas* were reborn as Paranimmitavasavatti, Nimmāṇarati, Tusita, Yama, Tāvatiṃsa and Cātummahārājika[3] gods, and that the lowest state in which an upāsaka could be reborn was *Gandhabba*. The merit of observing the uposatha with eight precepts is immense happiness surpassing even that of the kingship of all the sixteen provinces of India. He is reborn as one of the gods of the heavens mentioned above. A man or a woman who has observed the uposatha and earned the least merit will be reborn as a god.[4] It is evident therefore that the fruits earned by an upāsaka ranged from the Anāgāmi stage to rebirth as a *gandhabba*. An advanced upāsaka naturally did not wish to have re-existence however happy it might be. Citta gahapati when in deathbed was tempted by to the gods to wish to have a future existence as a Cakkavatti, but Citta Gahapati convinced them that the life of a Cakkavatti was impermanent and hence it was also not a desirable state.[5]

---

1. *Dīgha*, ii, pp. 92-93, 200-1.
2. *Ibid.*, II, p. 212.
3. Cf. *Aṅguttara*, iv, pp. 252 f.
4. *Aṅguttara*, iv, p. 255.

Tasmā hi nārī ca naro ca sīlavā aṭṭhaṅgupetam upavass'u uposathaṃ puññāni katvāna ṣukhudrayāni aninditā saggam upenti ṭhānan ti.

5. *Saṃyutta*, iv, pp. 301-4.

The upāsakas and upāsikās, though retaining their white dress, aspired for the fruits obtained by the monks and nuns, viz., Sotāpatti, Sakadāgāmi and Anāgāmi. Like the monks they had not the opportunity of following a particular way of life, but still they were held out the hope that by fulfilling the duties prescribed for them they could attain three of the four fruits attained by a monk or nun.

The first fruit attained by a monk is Sotāpatti. It could also be attained by an upāsaka or upāsikā by practising *saddhā*, *sīla suta*, *cāga* and paññā explained above.[1] The condition precedent to the attainment of this fruit is the removal of three hindrances, viz., belief in the existence of a self (*sakkāyadiṭṭhi*),[2] belief in the efficacy of rituals (*sīlabbataparāmāsa*) and lack of faith in the Triratna (*vicikicchā*). There are instances of several upāsakas and upāsikās who attained sotāpatti.[3]

It is rather interesting to read of an instance of a lay-devotee though addicted to drinking attaining the fruit of Sotāpatti. The reason shown is that he had so much faith in the *Triratna* that he could not be reborn in any of the lower planes of existence and was destined to *sambodhi*.[4]

The second fruit attained by a monk is Sakadāgāmi. The conditions precedent to the attainment of this stage was the reduction of attachment (*rāga*), hatred (*dosa*) and delusion (*moha*) to the minimum (*tanutta*). A large number of lay-devotees complied with this condition and attained the Sakadāgāmi stage, i.e., they would come once more to this world, and then attain Nibbāna.

The third fruit attained by a monk is Anāgāmi. To attain this stage one must completely remove *rāga*, *dosa* and *moha*. The usual condition laid down for a lay-devotee is that he is to remove the five impurities of the lower category (*ormabhāgīyas*) to attain this fruit. The five impurities are the three *saṃyojanas*, mentioned above viz., *sakkāyadiṭṭhi*, *sīlabbataparāmāsa* and *vicikicchā*, the other two being *Kāmarāga* and *byāpāda* in other words, *rāga* and *dosa*. By reaching the Anāgāmi stage, the lay-devotee does not return to the world but is reborn only once in one of the heavens to attain Nibbāna (*tatthaparinibbāyī*).

---

1. Detailed in the *Saṃyutta*, ii, p. 681.
2. That the self is identical with one or all of the *khandhas*. See *Saṃyutta*, iv, p. 287.
3. *Saṃyutta*, v, p. 411. In addition to the above five-fold practices, the lay-devotees were recommended to cultivate the following four habits: association with wise men, listening to religious discourses, proper mental exertion (*yoniso manasikara*) and observance of all major and minor rules of morality.
4. *Saṃyutta*, v. p. 375.

The fourth fruit *arhatta* is not attained by any householders, hence it is beyond the range of achievements of a lay-devotees.[1]

In view of the several statements in the Nikāyas about the afterlife of an upāsaka, it is clear that no upāsaka attained arhathood, i.e., Nibbāna. In the *Aggivacchagottasutta*[2] it is explicitly stated that no householder without giving up the householder's life can end his suffering at the time of his death. In other words, he can only be at the most an Anāgāmi, i.e., he must be born once more as a god to attain Nibbāna.

There was a controversy between the Theravādins and the Uttarāpathakas, and recently between Prof. de la Vallée Poussin and Dr. B.C. Law[3] on the point whether a householder could become an arhat (*Gihi 'ssa arahā ti*?).[4] The Uttarāpathakas and Dr. B.C. Law relied on certain passages of the Nikāyas, in which a few householders are mentioned as having become *arhats*. The Uttarāpathakas cited the instances of Yasa Kulaputta, Uttiya gahapati and Setu Māṇava.[5] while Dr. B.C. Law drew his support from the *Aṅguttara Nikāya* (iii, p. 451), in which it is said that Sudatta gahapati (=Anāthapiṇḍika), Citta gahapati, Uggo gahapati and a few other householders realised the immortal (*amataddaso*), i.e. Nibbāna. The remark in the *Majjhima Nikāya*[6] that a householder could realise the excellent truth is discussed in the *Milindapañha* (p. 243), in which Milinda raised the question that if a householder or a recluse could attain the truth by following the right course, there was no necessity for a person to become a monk. Again he questioned (*Milindapañha*, p. 350) if countless householders visualised the truth, what was the good of taking recourse to the ascetic practices (*dhutaṅgas*). Nāgasena gave an evasive answer and dilated on the merits of renunciation and observance of *dhutaṅga* precepts, and avoided the issue by saying that those householders who realised the truth had practised the *dhutaṅgas* in their previous lives.

The passage relied on by Dr. B.C. Law no doubt speaks of the gahapatis having been *amataddaso*, but in the same Nikāya and elsewhere Buddha declared at Nadika that none of the Upāsakas mentioned there became arhats. Nakulapitā and Jivaka became a

---

1. See, Infra.
2. *Majjhima*, i. p. 483: Natthi koci gihī gihisaṃyojanam appahāya kāyassa bhedā dukkhass' antakaro 'ti.
3. *Annals of the Bhandarkar Oriental Institute*, xiv, p. 82.
4. *Kathāvatthu*, iv, 1.
5. *Ibid*.
6. Cf. *Majjhima*, ii, p. 197: gahaṭṭho ārādhako hoti ñeyaṃ dhammaṃ kusalaṃ.

Sotāpanna, Sudatta a Sakadāgāmi[1] Ugga and Citta became Anāgāmis.[2] The Theravādins[3] contended that a householder in the enjoyment of worldly pleasures could not normally be expected to became arhats. In the similar strain Nāgasena stated that on the very day that a householder attained *arhthood*, he must either die or take the yellow robe.[4] Prof. de la Vallée Poussin also held the opinion that a layman, however faithful or virtuous he might be, could not attain Nibbāna.[5] Buddhaghosa explained the anomaly by saying that Yasa, Uttiya and Setu were mere householders in name, in external dress but not spiritually: they were free from all worldly ties though they had not yet discarded the white dress of a householder.[6] The conclusion that should be drawn from the conflicting statements in the Nikāyas about the attainments of an upāsaka[7] and the controversies in the *Kathāvatthu* and the *Milindapañha*, is that normally a householder could not become an arhat, but there were exceptional cases of householders who became so spiritually advanced that they deserved arhathood but the convention was that no householder unless he gave up his household life would be recognised as an arhat. Upāsakas like Citta and Hatthaka, and not *asekhas* (=arhats).[8] They are said to have destroyed the *orambhāgīya* impurities[9] but not the five *uddhambhāgīyas*: viz., *rūparāga, arūparāga, māna, uddhacca,* and *avijja,* and hence, they could not attain *arhathood.*[10]

---

1. See above.
2. *Saṃyutta*, iv. p. 301. Cf. Malalasekera, *Dictionary*, s.v., Citta, Nakulapitā, Jīvaka.
3. *Kathāvatthu*, iv. 1.
4. *Milindapañha*, p. 265.
5. *The way to Nirvāṇa*, p. 150-151.
6. See above.
7. Cf. *Papañcasūdani*, iii, p. 196: Santati the minister, Uggaseno the banker's son, Vitasoka the young boy who attained arhathood while in householder's dress, but householder's dress (*gihiliṅgam*) cannot uphold the merit of an *arhat* and so they must either die or retire on the very day.
8. Cf. *Visuddhimagga*, p. 442: Cittagahapati, Upāligahapati, Dhammika-upāsaka, Khujjuttarā upāsikā acquired *patisambhidā* of the *Sekhabhūmi*.
9. Cf. *Majjhima*, i. pp. 467, 490-1.
10. In the *Aṅguttara* (iv. p. 456), it is stated that one cannot be an arhat without removing *rāga, dosa, moha, kodha, upanāha, makkha, palāsa, issā,* and *macchariya*.

Chapter - 24

Buddhist Psychology

Bratindra Kumar Sengupta

In Buddhism there is a very well-defined psychological study, vying at times with many a modern concept. The complex and intricate internal life of human beings has been sought to be analysed and explained in the Pali *Tipiṭaka*. In *Abhidhamma* texts it is stated that the human mind is based on certain notions, preconceived as well as origination, so that no one state of mind can be a full explanation of any human type. There are, so to say, different designations of human types on the psychological analysis and the consequential metaphysical status of the human individual. In the *Puggalapaññatti*, a Pali canonical text under the *Abhidhamma*, it has been clearly stated at the outset that there are six such designations on the psycho-metaphysical side of analysis.[1] Now, apparently all these six types of designations of the *knowing* individual may not be found to be of a strict scientific division inasmuch as there are over-lappings, e.g., between the *āyatana-paññtti* and the *dhātupaññatti*; yet there are good grounds in each for special kind of stress, as on the *objective* side in the former and on he *mental* side in the latter.

In this psycho-metaphysical analysis of the human individual, the very first *sine qua non* is the doctrine of 'the designation of groups' (*Khandha-paññatti*). In general Buddhist theory of *pañca-skandha* or five-fold aggregate consisting of the inner and the outer worlds in all acts of cognition, this enunciation of the *Khandha-paññatti* as the first 'designation' assumes a significant role in Buddhist psychology of the Idealistic type. The *rūpa* (material form), *vedanā* (sensation),

---

1. Cha paññattiyo:—*khandha-paññatti, āyatana-paññatti, dhātu-paññatti, sacca-paññatti, indriya-paññatti, puggala-paññatti* (*loc. cit.*, Pt. I., P.T.S., ed. R. Morris).

saññā (perception)[1], *saṇkhāra* (confection)[1], and *viññāṇa* (consciousness) have been put under this group, giving a broad classification of the different requisites in an act of cognition. It is well known and admitted almost as a universal rule that the mind is the seat of all cognitional processes. In Buddhist theories of the mind and its processes of *knowing*, it has been generally accepted, in both Hīnayāna and Mahāyāna schools with certain doctrinal modifications, that the mind is the seat of consciousness. This basic recognition of the mind in the psycho-physical and consequential philosophico-metaphysical doctrines of origin and control of mental states and systematisation of knowledge in realising the Ultimate Truth, has been the backbone of Buddhist tradition. Starting from the material form which is out and there, Buddhist writers have given a predominant role to our inner world of the mental processes, culmination through various notions, in the actual psychological re-actions. It is here that the Buddhist theory is not purely psychological, but psycho-physical and ultimately psycho-ethical. It has been a vexed question whether psychology should be studied from an ethical attitude, but it has been nonetheless generally accepted that ethical studies have a great anticipation of psychological analyses. Mrs. Rhys Davids in her *Buddhist Psychology* (a translation of the *Dhammasmgaṇi* under the *Abhidhamma*) has discussed, in the learned Introduction, this question and this attitude in the Buddhist tradition at great length. Psychology is, according to the tradition which is the object of our discussion, pre-eminently suited to an analysis of the human mind in the hope of its exposure to an ethical adjudgment.

If we examine, on a general study, the five-fold *Khanda-paññatti* enumerated and described above, we shall find that the sensory organs have their respective fields and roles in the enumeration of different kinds of 'sensation' (*Vedanā*). It is, therefore, evident that this first 'designation' (*Paññatti*) is mainly a description of the internal states and conditions re-acting, under specific circumstances, on particular external stimuli coming from the objective world. In this regard, Buddhist writers have given us a scientific basis as the starting-point in psychology. The next 'designations' as enumerated in the text, *Puggala-paññatti*, are the gradual exposition of this fundamental hypothesis. The numbers and groupings may appear to be not strictly

1. These two terms 'perception' and 'confection' as equivalents to *saññā* and *saṅkhāra* have been used by B.C. Law in *Designation of Human Types*, P.T.S. It should be noted that *saññā* here does not mean 'name' as applied in the genral *pañca-skandha* theroy of outer designation, as opposed to the inner process which is described in this context.

scientific to modern minds, but that there are different groupings depending on, and elucidating, peculiar points of view in a psychological situation, is undeniably true. The *āyatanapaññatti* is a twelve-fold group and the *dhātu-paññatti* an eighteen-fold group, elucidating the second and the third 'designation' respectively.[1]

These *āyatana* and *dhātu-paññatti* aggregates are enumerated to show that in that Buddhist theory, the psychological processes are sensory, motor and even reflex, depending on the seats or organs and reactions. The *āyatanas* are these seats as well as the specific qualities adhering to the external world that the former are capable to grasp. It is interesting here that even the *manas* or *citta* that is the specific internal conscious state is also included here along with *dhamma* which quality it is capable to grasp. This *dhamma* is the three-fold group without form (*arūpa khandhattayo*) of *vedanā*, *saññā* and *saṅkhāra*.[2] In the *dhātu-paññatti* aggregate are listed the same twelve-fold group *plus* six types of *viññāṇa* belonging to six organs including the mind (*citta*). The *dhātu-paññatti* aggregate is, therefore, enumerated after the *āyatana-paññatti*, for the fact that when specific seats or organs are capable to grasp specific objects in their specific qualities, then the actual grasping through a deeper region, so to say, takes place. This is the *dhātu-paññatti* aggregate which is not merely an aggregate of seats but also of actual *re-acting agents*. Perhaps on that account has the *viññāṇa* (consciousness), that has been specifically included in the first 'designation' of *Khandha*, been once more added to this aggregate to show that sensory processes depend on consciousness for actual psychological results to be achieved. It is, however, an hypothesis worked out from the Idealistic position of Buddhism.

Let us turn a little from the main path to study, in brief, certain other implications which are corollaries. The *citta*,—which we have translated as 'mind' in Western terminology for want of a better equivalent, though imperfectly— is, in the Buddhist tradition, generally of four types. These types of mind, as enumerated and explained, are judged not merely from the psychological point of view, but also, and more so, from the ethico-metaphysical point of view. These are: (1) *Kāmāvacara* — it is the 'mind of desire' having good (*kuśala*), bad

---

1. *rāgañca dosañca pahāya mohaṃ*
   sammappajāno suvimuttacitto
   anupādiyāno idha vā huraṃ vā
   sa bhāgavā sāmaññassa hoti (*Dhammapada*, I/20).

In this verse there is the ethical approach to the analysis of the mind acting on the objective world through *upādāna*.

2. *manopubhaṁgamā dhammā manosṣṭṭhā manomayā: Dhammapada* (I/ I-2).

(*akuśala*), indifferent (*kriyā*) and ripe (*vipāka*) kinds, depending on the nature of our mental propensities; (2) *Rūpāvacara* — it is, the 'mind of sublation' having good (*kuśala*), indifferent (*kriyā*) and ripe (*vipāka*) kinds, possessed by super-human beings residing in higher regions; (3) *Arūpāvacara* — it is the 'mind of trance,' also of three kinds as *Rūpāvacara*, but possessed by still higher Beings residing in *nirākāra* (formless) regions, yet having some *karmic* propensities to manifest; (4) *Lokottara* — it is the 'mind of realisation,' having as its object the bliss of *Nirvāṇa*, and having two kinds depending on the Path and the Result. It is the higher Perfection and the ultimate Goal. Buddha-hood is included in this category, and in nothing else. It is, therefore, evident that all these classes are not purely psychological. Ethical, metaphysical and spiritual evaluations are implicated in the four different kinds of *citta* as briefly enumerated and explained above. But, however lower or higher the *citta* may be, it is admitted generally in the Buddhist tradition that the three-fold formless group (*arūpa khandhattayo*) of *vedanā*, *saññā* and *saṅkhāra* is the resultant of such 'graded minds'. This three-fold group has its origin in mind which again is of lower or higher propensities.

Consciousness, again, in Buddhist tradition is ever-changing. But every consciousness has two elements — one Constant and the other Variable. Now, this constant element is the Form of Consciousness which is reached in an Order of Thought by mind in well-defined Paths (*Vīthi*). The subjective element can rise above the changing processes in its state of 'stream of being' which is free from process of thought (*Vīthi-mutta*), but the objective process-consciousness (*Vīthi-citta*) which is the Matter and the Variable element is ever the functional aspect of the knowing individual. All these varieties of consciousness, however, have three movements of genesis, existence and destruction. The mind, therefore, has an infinite series of thought-processes in the construction of a system of thought though the Form it reaches. The variability of consciousness is the mind's inner process but the constancy of consciousness is its system of Form in the synthetic judgements it forms. The subject, however, in its real nature is 'a stream of being' where thought-processes are capable of being transcended, and the *Vīthi-mutta* subject may stay as the metaphysical entity.[1] It is interesting to compare this analysis of the Buddhist theories of mind and its processes,— the objective data and the thought-construction on them — with the Kantian epistemology and metaphysics. In germinal forms the *Abhidhamma* tradition in Buddhism

1. Cf. *Compendium of Philosophy*— Shwe Zan Aung & Mrs. Rhys Davids, pp. 25 ff.

seems to reflect the much later and much more developed Kantian system. The metaphysical subject, again, is tinged with the transcendental hypothesis here, though not in the Kantian sense, with the pronounced stress on the ideality of the conscious subject.

It remains for us to study the implications of *indriya-paññatti* or 'designation of sense-organs' in the psychological theory of Buddhism. We have discussed above the nature of the *āyatana* and the *dhātu-paññatti* aggregates and shown their separate implications. In this designation of *indriya*, there has been a stress on the functional aspect. In fact, this aggregate is properly to be designated as 'a designation of functions of faculties'. "Indriya" says B.C.Law in his *Designation of Human Types* (p.I.f.n.) "literally means a controlling principle or force." *Indriya-paññatti* is an aggregate of twenty-two such 'principles' comprising the regions from sense-desire to the supramundane. It is, therefore, not merely the actual seats or senses that are included in this aggregate but the 'controlling principles or forces' that are working on for the control of the human body lest it should cease to function.

Buddhist psychology has a vital bearing on the Buddhist theories of morality and spirituality. It is said in the few *gāthās* in the *cittavaggo* of the *Dhammapada* that the *citta* or mind is the most perturbed and therefore the most dangerous possession of the human individual. It is always enticed away to vices, to things of ephemeral consequences, to distant paths of darkness, to *akuśalas* of the lowest form of *kāmāvacara*-state far removed from the higher and higher times of mental development; but it is through meditation of graded varieties (of five kinds), through good and virtuous practice and through inner control over the mind's dissipations that one can achieve peace and tranquillity, and attain to the state of an *Arhat*.

Chapter - 25

The Buddhist Social Ideals

B.G.Gokhale

The social and political world in which Early Buddhism arose was characterized by an element of intense crisis. In its homeland of Magadha there was arising an imperial state which was threatening the very existence of a number of other states both monarchical and oligarchic-republican. Kāsi, Aṅga, Kośala, Avantī, the Vajjis, Mallas, Sākyas, all these and many more, were soon to feel the compelling impact of the rulers of Magadha. Economic life was experiencing a virtual revolution with the development of currency as a medium of exchange and the consequence growth of trade and commerce. Out of this revolution was emerging a new class, the *Gahapati* and *Seṭṭhi*, whose economic influence and political prestige could no longer be ignored. The story narrating how Anāthapiṇḍika bought a plot of land belonging to Prince Jeta is indicative of the position of this new class. Large standing armies replacing the old tribal levies, a new class of professional bureaucrats and a new powerful class of bankers and merchants, these were the characters in the drama of the new society that was in the making. The conflict of ideas was paralleled by a clash of classes and in this "time of troubles" the old norms and values developed by the tribal culture of the invading Aryans were successfully challenged. The new age that was dawning demanded new forms of political organization and a revaluation of norms of social behaviour and formulation of new social goals. The history of Early Buddhism reflects the elements of crisis as also the attempts made to crystalize and express the new social outlook.

The traditional accounts tells us that Siddhārtha saw the four signs prior to his Great Renunciation. These are significantly described as an old man, an ailing man, a dead body and a recluse. It is possible to interpret these as symbols not only of the different phases of an individual's life but also as those of the changing social scene. The first three may be taken as portents of the sense of anxiety from which the old society, now on the verge of a transformation, was suffering while the figure of the Recluse was the traditional answer to the challenge of the times, Siddhārtha himself became a Recluse and practised severe austerities.[1] The Bodhisatta gave up the austerities as futile but continued to pursue the phase of withdrawal from the world. With the Enlightenment and the *Dhammacakkapavattana*, however, came the culmination. Indeed the *Mahābhinikkhamaṇa* can be properly understood only in the context of the *Dhammacakkapavattana* for the two are organic parts of the single process of the making of the Buddha. The Turning of the wheel of Law and the foundation of the Saṅgha were events of great social significance.[2] The whole episode of the Buddha's reluctance to preach the Doctrine and the successful intervention of Brahma Sahampati is significant in its social content. It is the dramatization of the profound conflict between the claims of the traditional ascetic and the demands of the New Man whose ideals and aspirations were to be reflected in Early Buddhism. And the portals were thrown open and Buddhism began its career.

This Early Buddhist movement had to pass through three distinct phases before it could achieve its ultimate social fulfilment. These phases may be described as isolation, association and transformation. The phase of isolation may be called the *Khaggavisāṇa* phase.[3] This was the phase of wandering alone "like the horn of a rhinoceros." This phase persists throughout the history of Early Buddhism as phrases like "a hole-and-corner life is all a home can give, whereas Pilgrimage is in the open, it is hard for a house-keeping man to live the higher life in all its full completeness and full perfection and purity"[4] is almost a stock-phrase in the *Nikāyas*. To a certain extent it also expressed the antagonistic claims of the temporal realm and the realm of the spirit, a sentiment which is common to all great religions of the world. As the *Dhammapada* puts it *aññā hi lābhūpanisā, aññā nibhāṇgāminī*—the Path of gain and the path of Nibbāna are totally different (Verse 75). This early phase, then, was preoccupied with renunciation and seclusion, the phase when monks lived away from all social contacts beyond the most rudimentary and restricted to the

1. See *Majjhima Nikāya*, I, pp. 162-163.

2. See Arnold Toynbee, *A Study of History*, III, pp. 270-271. It is difficuit to agree with all that Toynbee has to say especially when he describes the mental content of Buddha's Enlightenment as nothing short of "spiritual self-annihilation".

3. As in *eko care khaggavisāṇakappo, Sutta Nipāta*, Verse 35ff.

4. *M.N.*, I, p. 240, Chalmers, *Further Dialogues of the Buddha*, I, p. 173

receiving of alms. But mere renunciation and seclusion were but a part of the New Way of Life preached by the Buddha. And the social consequences of a large scale renunciation were not slow in making themselves manifest as the *Mahāvagga* story indicates. Seeing a large number of their men folk adopting the garb of the homeless wanderer the people cried: *vedhavyāya āgato samaṇo Gotama— sabbe Sañjaye netvān kiṁsū dāni nayissati* (the ascetic Gotama has come to deprive our women of their husbands— after having taken away all the Sañjayas, whom shall he take away now?[1]). It also led to an incipient clash with the State when men of the royal service, debtors and others who had social, economic and political obligations to discharge came to be admitted and the Buddha promptly laid down rules forbidding such ordinations.[2]

In the meanwhile a transformation was going on within the body of the Saṅgha itself. Devadatta's Five Demands, whatever the motive behind their presentation, represent the last stand of the old phase. These related to life-long practice of living in the woods, on alms, dressing themselves in cast-off rags, living under trees and abstaining from eating fish or flesh.[3] Demands like these were rightly rejected for they would have isolated the community from the broad surface of popular life. Now the ideal of *khaggavīsaṇa* was being slowly replaced, in the matter of emphasis, by that of *sukhā samghassa sāmaggī, samaggānam tapo sukho*—blessed is the unity of the Saṅgha, blessed is the exertion of the united (*Dhammapada*, verse 194). This change was due, in part, to the development of the Buddhists as a distinct religious community. The insistence on *sāmaggī* may be adequately explained in the changed social composition of the Saṅgha and the change in its social role. Now had begun the phase of the association of the Saṅgha with the society at large and this created the problems of adjustment. The Saṅgha had to define its own social relations and also influence the social ideals of the society at large. The members of the Saṅgha were now in sustained social contact with aristocracy as well as the common people. This social orientation is indicated by the fact that among the categories of proficiencies acquired by certain outstanding monks, such as in the knowledge of the *Suttanta*, *Vinaya* and *Dhamma*, there is also mentioned one of wisdom in worldly lore.[4] And among all the foremost disciples the Venerable Ānanda was the one who had shown the greatest proficiency in maintaining excellent and intimate relations with members of the

1. *Mahā Vagga*, I, 24, 5.
2. See *Ibid.*, I, 40ff.
3. *Culla Vagga*, VII, 3. 15.
4. *Ibid.*, IV, 4, 4

society at large. Oldenberg explains it in material terms as "the external existence of the Church even demanded, that regular relations be maintained between it and the worldly circles, which were favourably disposed to the interests of the Order. Without a laity......an order of mendicants could not be thought of, and the religious movement of Buddhism would have been shut out from contact with the broad surface of popular life".[1] But to describe the association of the Saṅgha with society at large in purely utilitarian and material terms would be to state only a part of the process. For Buddhism had now begun to distinguish the believers from the non-believers in the lay society indicating thereby that the process of the creation of a Buddhist society was already at work. Thus when a monk spent his *Vassa* in a village and if the people of the village had to migrate during that time the monk was required to go with those who were believers what ever their number.[2] The importance of this emergent Buddhist society was duly recognized by giving the laity the right to scrutinize the intellectual accomplishments and moral earnestness of a monk supported on their devoted charity.[3] Certain influential laymen successfully mediated between the Buddha and those monks with whom the Master was displeased;[4] the moral and social pressure of the lay society was duly enlisted in the task of disciplining quarrelsome and recalcitrant groups of monks like the Kosambaka bhikkhus[5]; and an attempt was made to curb the evil schismatic activities of Devadatta by carrying out an act of public denunciation in Rājagaha.[6] Incidents like these, and they are numerous, bring out the increased importance of the society at large in the affairs of the Saṅgha. This awareness of social ties also led to the formulation of such rulers whereby the Saṅgha was required to expel one of its members when, in the opinion of the congregation, his conduct was likely to lead the laity astray.[7] This close identification of spiritual and social interests between the Saṅgha and the laity is very succinctly expressed by Nāgasena when he enumerates the ten qualities of an ideal layman. The ideal layman, according to Nāgasena, "suffers like pain and feels like joy as the Order does".[8] With the statement of such views the process of association was completed and that of transformations was already underway.

1. *Buddha*, p. 382
2. *M.V.*, III, 10
3. *M.N.*, II, p. 172
4. *Ibid.*, I, p. 458
5. *Ibid.*, II, p. 172
6. *M.V.*, X. 5, 1
7. *C.V.*, I, 13, 7
8. *Milinda Pañha*, pp. 94-95

This process of transformation in the role of Buddhism and its Saṅgha was closely associated with the Buddhist view of society. It was readily recognized that society was constantly preoccupied with things (*papañcābhiratā pajā*);[1] that this acquisitive instinct led to conditions of strife, conflict and imbalance.[2] The situation was further complicated by the existence of hierarchies of power, wealth and prestige. By the laws of its own being and nature Buddhism, as an organized way of spiritual life, could not directly initiate a social revolution for then it would have projected itself into the social and economic problems of the times. It has often been argued that the Buddha was no social reformer.[3] In such arguments the Buddha's views about the irrelevance of caste distinction is explained away as doctrinaire discussion. But suttas like *Vasala* in the *Sutta Nipāta* and *Madhura*, *Assalāyana* and *Canki* in the *Majjhima Nikāya* are not just doctrinaire dissertations but have a most direct social content. It is readily agreed that the Saṅgha knew of no caste distinctions but it is parenthetically added that this castelessness of the Saṅgha living in close association with lay community had no effect on that lay community. This is a proposition difficult to accept. The Buddhist position was made quite clear in the many utterances of the Buddha and in the composition of the Order itself and it was that caste as an institution was unacceptable to the Buddhist community. In fact, the whole trend of Buddhist teachings was to create an equalitarian ethos which would cut across tribal lines and the distinctions of caste and race. The Buddha had said: "I assert that lineage does not enter into a man's being either good or bad; nor do good looks or wealth."[4] He had challenged the extravagant claims put forward by the priest-hood. During its third phase of becoming an instrument of social transformation Buddhism had postulated certain new norms and goals of social behaviour. The idea put forward before society now was the creation of a *sappurisa* or an *uttamapurisa*.[5] The basis of this new society were *vissāsa* (mutual trust, co-operation in the place of conflict and acquisitiveness)[6]. *asāhasa* (non-violence), *samatā* (basic equality of all human beings) and *dhamma* (righteousness as an ultimate value). In fact the four pillars of this society were declared to be *sacca* (truth, homogenity, unity through an absence of invidious distinctions based on birth, wealth or family in the matter of social evaluation,) *dhamma*

1. *Dhammapada*, verse 254
2. *M.N.*, II, p. 120
3. See Oldenberg, *Op. cit.*, p. 153. Fick, *Social Organization in North-East India in Buddha's Time* (Trans. by Maitra), p. 32
4. *M.N.*, II p.179.
5. *Dhp.*, Verse 54
6. *Ibid.*, Verse 204

(righteousness, goodness, morality) *dāna* (charity as a way of life rather than a specific set of isolated acts) *asāhasa* (non-violence, violence being the negation of righteousness.)[1] The rule of *dhamma* was to be looked upon as of all-pervasive force, valid as much in the home as in the market-place as indicated in *dhammena mātāpitaro bhareyya, payojaye dhammikam so vaṇijjam* (righteously he should support his parents and righteously he should carry on his trade.)[2] The Five commandments for the laymen namely, abstinence from violence, stealing, falsehood, immorality and drinking intoxicating liquors, were a simple formalization of the four pillars of society and became the basis of Buddhist social ethics. When to these were added Faith in the Buddha, Dhamma and Saṅgha, respect for elders and women,[3] disciplining of the mind in the way of righteousness, the formulation of the Buddhist social ethics was completed. These ideals were postulated as a middle way between the two extremes of aggressiveness resulting in constant preoccupation with acquisitiveness to the exclusion of all other considerations and indulgence leading to dissipation and degradation. Reason, moderation, harmony, a constant awareness of the primacy of righteousness, the ennobling nature of charity as a way of life, compassion and wisdom were the norms which were now constantly put before society. This society was conceived of as a "universal" as distinguished from a tribal society; it was the community of the righteous anywhere and everywhere unencumbered by rules of tribal, regional or caste affiliations.

These were the social ideals that Early Buddhism espoused and put before the society of its times. The role of the Saṅgha was now that of the custodian of the moral and spiritual values of society. The Saṅgha now, in this final phase, became the spiritual preceptor, the personal counseller and the educator of the society within which it lived. It functioned within society though it was not of it. The *Dhamma* had now become both a spiritual and social force. It became an instrument dedicated to the creation of certain values like *samatā* (cf. Aśoka insistence on *daṇḍasamatā* and *vyavahārasamatā*), *dāna sacca* and *dhamma*. These social ideals were of general applicability and cut across divisive lines of caste, tribe and race and thus provided the social cement to fuse the diverse ethnic and cultural elements into a harmonious social group based on certain basic postulates.

---

1. See *Dhp.*, Verses 84, 129, 142, 223, 256, 257
2. *Sutta Nipāta*, Verse 404
3. Cf. the seven conditions of stability as preached to the Vajjis by the Buddha, Mahāparinibbāṇa Sutta, Dīgha Nikāya, S.B.E., XI, pp. 3-5

Chapter - 26

Buddhist Ecclesiastical Punishments

Anukul Chandra Banerjee

Discipline consists in the attenuation of human conduct to a set of laws. For the Buddhist monks this set of law is collected in the Vinaya Piṭaka. It is the foundation of ethical life in Buddhist Saṅgha. Mr. Sukumar Dutta has dealt with this subject in his *Early Buddhist Monachism,*[1] MM. Prof. Vidhusekhar Śāstrī in his notes on some of the terms in his Bengali edition of the *Bhikkhu* and *Bhikkhuṇī Pātimokkha* and MM Prof. Satish Chandra Vidyā-bhūṣaṇa in his edition of the *So-sortharpa.* With the help of these notes, an attempt has been made in this paper to give a running account of the different forms of disciplinary measures embodied in the Vinaya Piṭaka. The measures are classed as major and minor.

Major Disciplinary Measures

I. *Tajjaniya-kamma*—This punishment is meted out to a bhikkhu who is quarrelsome, an idle talker, a maker of schism in the saṅgha or guilty of such other faults including the frequenting of societies of lay people. The punishment consists in an act of reprimand. A bhikkhu against whom a charge of *Tajjaniyakamma* is brought is first warned and reminded, and then charged with the particular offence committed by him. This charge is forthwith brought to the notice of the saṅgha by a competent and learned bhikkhu by means of a motion (*ñatti*) and the saṅgha punish him if he is found guilty of the transgression. The punishment consists in denying the bhikkhu the privileges enjoyed in common with the other members of the saṅgha. He is no longer permitted to ordain novices, grant *nissaya*[2] to neophytes and offer exhortations to nuns. He is not even entitled to occupy the same seat with other bhikkhus. The restrictions remain until revoked by the saṅgha formally.

1. pp. 168-172.
2. See Mhv., I, p. 80.

II. *Nissaya-kamma*—This punishment is inflicted on a bhikkhu who is foolish and incompetent and who does not give proper attention to moral teachings and commits offences repeatedly even while undergoing the punishments of *Parivāsa,* *Mānatta,* Mūl*āya-paṭikassanā.*[1] The punishment consists in placing the guilty bhikkhu under the guidance of another bhikkhu. The procedure for bringing the guilty bhikkhu to task by the saṅgha is the same as described above. A bhikkhu guilty of *Nissayakamma* forfeits his privileges in the saṅgha. The punishment continues until it is revoked by the saṅgha formally. Mr. Dutt says, "this measure is carried out against a bhikkhu who had been repeatedly guilty of saṅghādisesa offences and undergone sentences therefor."

III. *Pabbājaniya-kamma*—The punishment is imposed on a group of bhikkhus who living in an ārāma (monastery) close to a town or a village resort to evil practices, freuent lay societies, cut jokes with women and amuse themselves with different kinds of games which are all prohibited in the teachings of the master. By resorting to this sort of frivolities and frequenting lay societies, they create a scandal and become cause of annoyance to the laity. The procedure for imposing the punishment on the delinquent monk is the same as described above in para I. The punishment consists in driving away those guilty bhikkhus from the place of the commission of offences. The saṅgha in such cases usually go to the spot where the offence is committed and formally inflict the punishment upon them. The punishment lasts until a revocation is made by the saṅgha, the revocation being made only when the monk is found to behave properly and receive exhortations on Dhamma and Vinaya regularly.

IV. *Paṭisāraṇiya-kamma*—This punishment is inflicted upon a bhikkhu who does harm to a faithful and believing householder, brings about loss to the laity, finds fault with the laity and causes division among the lay devotees and does similar other acts. The punishment consists in an act of reconciliation. The procedure for imposing the punishment on the guilty bhikkhu by the saṅgha is the same as described above in para I. The guilty bhikkhu is directed to ask for and obtain pardon of the aggrieved householder. If he fails to obtain pardon of the householder, a companion is then formally selected by the saṅgha to implore the householder personally on his behalf. Now if the companion so selected by the saṅgha fails to obtain pardon of the householder, he is to ask for pardon of the householder for

1. See *infra.*

the delinquent bhikkhu in the name of the saṅgha and even if he be not pardoned, then the guilty bhikkhu is directed to squat on the ground with folded hands, putting robes on his one shoulder and ask pardon of the householder against whom he has committed wrong by confessing his guilt. The punishment lasts until a revocation is made by the saṅgha, the revocation being made only when the guilty bhikkhu is found to behave properly.

Patta-nikkujjana-kamma[1] (the act of overturning the bowl) is a punishment when a householder offends a monk and the monk in return refuses to accept alms from him. The householder on being repentant is allowed to give alms to the offending bhikkhu as an act of expiation.

V. *Ukkhepaniya-kamma*—This punishment is imposed on a bhikkhu on three grounds:—(i) for not confessing a guilt (*āpattiyā* adassane), (ii) for not atoning for a guilt (*āpattiyā* appaṭikamme) and (iii) for not givin up a false doctrine (*pāpikāya diṭṭhiyā appaṭinissagge*). The punishment consists in the forfeiture of certain privileges of a monk. The procedure for the imposition of the punishment by the saṅgha is the same as described above. The guilty monk is denied the privileges of ordaining novices, granting *nissaya*, accepting novices and giving exhortations to nuns. He is no longer entitled to reverence, service and such other privileges. The punishment continues unless a revocation is made by the saṅgha, the revocation being made only when the delinquent monk is found to behave properly and become submissive to the saṅgha. Mr. Dutt says, "with regard to (iii), it is laid down that the bhikkhus should first exhort the guilty bhikkhu to give up the false doctrine (so that his refusal to do so would amount to Pācittiya offence no. 68). Now in Pācittiya 69 it is laid down that a bhikkhu, guilty of Pācittiya offence (68), should be subjected to a social boycott by the bhikkhus."[2]

Minor Disciplinary Measures

I & II. *Mānatta* and *Parivāsa*—These two punishments are imposed on a bhikkhu found guilty of transgressing one of the thirteen Saṅghādisesa rules. The guilty bhikkhu is denied the privileges of the saṅgha as mentioned above. *Mānatta* is imposed when a guilty bhikkhu confesses his guilt whereas *Parivāsa* is inflicted in case of non-confession. There is no prescribed time-limit for *Parivāsa*. It

---

1. *Cullavagga*, V, 20, 6-7.
2. *Early Buddhist Monachism*, p. 171.

remains until a revocation is made by the saṅgha, the revocation being made only when the delinquent bhikkhu is found to have purged himself of all the evils. But *Mānatta* can in no case exceed six days. After a guilty bhikkhu undergoes the *Mānatta* discipline, he is taken back into the saṅghas i.e. rehabilitated. The term for this formality is *Abbhāna*. *Parivāsa* is generally of three types:—

(1) *Paṭicchana-parivāsa*—when a bhikkhu, having committed an offence, knowingly conceals the same, he is then subjected to Parivāsa. But he has to undergo Parivāsa for the number of days he kept the offence concealed.

(2) *Suddhanta-parivāsa*—when a bhikkhu, having committed a number of Saṅghādisesa offences, fails to remember the actual dates as well as the nature of the offences, he is then subjected to Suddhanta-parivāsa and the period of punishment is calculated from the date of his Upasampadā ordination up to the day of imposition of the punishment.[1]

(3) *Samodhāna-parivāsa*—when a bhikkhu while undergoing the punishment of Parivāsa commits a fresh offence, he is then again subjected to Parivāsa, the period of which is the same as the difference of the number of days between the commission of the second offence and the Parivāsa period prescribed for the first offence, whichever is the longer.

Parivāsa for four months is also imposed on bhikkhus who after ordination leave the order and want to rejoin it and on those who formerly belonged to a heretical school.[2]

III. *Mūlāya-paṭikassanā* means re-undergoing the punishment. When a bhikkhu under punishment commits an offence and confesses it, he is directed to undrgo again the punishment which was prescribed for the first offence. Prof. Śāstrī says, "when a bhikkhu is fit for Abbhāna after serving out the sentences of Parivāsa and Mānatta, commits a fresh offence in the meantime, he is then punished by Mūlāya-Paṭikassanā."

IV. *Pakāsaniya-kamma*—This punishment was imposed on Devadatta, cousin of Buddha, for his attempt to make schism in the Buddhist order while he was an active member of the saṅgha. It is an extraordinary punishment carried only against him and is mentioned once only in the whole of the Vinaya Piṭaka.[3]

---

1. taṃ gahetvā gahitadivasato yāva upasampadādivaso tāva rattiyo gaṇetvā parivasitabbaṃ—*Samanta-pāsādikā.*
2. *Mhv.*, I. p. 69.
3. *Cullavagga*, VII, 3. 2.

Chapter - 27

An Aspect of Becoming in Early Buddhism

I.B. Horner

The sixth century B.C. is well known to have been a period which in India was remarkable for a profusion of intellectual activity and curiosity closely combined with a probing into fundamental values concerning Man. The great age of the Vedas was over: their influence had waned, although perhaps it was destined never entirely to cease; their interest, focussed on certain phenomena of nature, and expressed for example in the magnificent hymns to the Sun and the Dawn, was gradually but relentlessly shifted to a growing interest taken by man in Man. This was the work of the Upaniṣads, this is their permanent and incomparable contribution to the world's store of learning. Henceforward man, his soul or self or *ātman* (*attā* in Pāli), its relation to the whole of Reality, its beginning and more especially its ending with the wys of achieving the highest consummation, were to be the problems which the teachers and thinkers, more numerous then than now, attempted to solve.

From among a host of minor leaders propounding theories, enunciating dogmas, setting forth new views on subjects of undeniable importance, the names of all but a few are unknown at the present day to any but students of Indology. Their name was legion, but their views have not stood the test of time. Hence their names are unimportant to the seeker after religion, although they may still possess some historical significance to those whose enquiries lie in this field.

Out of this extraordinarily fertile time of speculative unrest (which was perhaps spread over centuries), out of man's slowly awakening consciousness of self, two "systems" emerged which not only profoundly affected contemporary thought, but down the years have wielded an uninterrupted ascendancy over the lives and thought of millions: the "systems" of Hindus and Buddhists. For these two "systems" (which for lack of a better word I call them) are the teaching of the Early Upaniṣads and the teaching we now call Buddhism. The one was, as it were, a corporate effort, composed almost certainly during a long strech of time, and therefore almost, I may say quite, certainly by more than one thinker. The other was the much modified result of fifty years of ceaseless, tireless ministry, and is usually ascribed to one man, namely Gotama the Buddha.

His teaching, more truly called Śākya than Buddhism, cannot be interpreted aright if it be separated from its historical setting. No great religion has ever sprung out of a void. The working of cause and effect, recognised and enunciated by Śākya, was as active in the production of Primitive Buddhism as in the shaping of its later growth. But Śākya did not arise on the ashes of the static outlook of the Upaniṣads. Looked at historically it arose as the supplement, the complement and the development of the Upaniṣadic standpoint. And this it achieved by the substitution of the concept of Becoming for that of Being. A view of fundamental importance in the Upaniṣ ads, that of man *being* that Highest Reality—epitomised in two phrases now become classical: "That are thou" (*tat tvam asi*) and "I am Brahma" (*ahaṃ Brahma asmi*)—gave way to the Śākyan view that man can train himself to *become* as That.

This doctrine was in Śākya nowhere plainly stated in those words; but it is there nevertheless, impregnating the Śākyan teaching for those who have eyes to sêe, insisting that man can grow, can increase, can be mae to become, can progress further on the Way. The dawnings of this view were not altogether absent from the Upaniṣ ads. I think, but were implied rather than stressed.

From the unreal lead me to the Real,
From darkness lead me to Light,
From death lead me to Non-death

(Bṛhad. I. 3. 28).

is a verse which suggests that however much one might *be* the Real, yet a closer contact with it by means of the *ñāṇamārga* (or way of knowledge) was essential for salvation, which was to be gained, as is here shown, through intellectual apprehension of the Real, through spiritual light, and by the cutting through of the ocean of *saṃsāra* (rebirth). So much then had man to achieve in order that for him Being might become a reality. In Primitive Buddhism it is amply apparent that this process could only be valid, the end could only be assured, if man made himself, his powers and his faculties, become greater and greater still.

The example which I wish to present of the way in which Primitive Buddhism looked at this matter is only one from among many which might have been adduced. It is drawn from the Pātimokkha of the *Vinaya.* The *Vinaya* consists largely of stories of various kinds of wrong behaviour on the part of the monks (*bhikkhu*), and of the rules laid down for the prevention and punishment of occurrences of the same sort in the future. Thus offences against the course of training laid down by the Buddha for the monks are modified. *Vinaya* III opens with three of the very gravest kinds of offence, known as Pārājika offences: those of unchastity, stealing and depriving of life. These are indeed condemned by all civilised communities, valuing as they do safety of person and property.

But the fourth (and last) Pārājika shows, I think, a mode of thought which could only arise in circumstances where the notion that can *become* is an absolutely vital force, commanding if not awe, then a tremendous respect. This Pārājika, well tempered as are all the rules by the quality of mercy, declares that if a monk mistakenly claims a condition of the further-men, unless he does so with undue confidence in himself, with an undue estimate of himself, then he falls into defeat. He is defeated by the course of training, morally he is too weak to support it, he has to leave the Order, there is no hope of rehabilitation for him.

This offence was so gave, ranking as it does with unchastity, stealing and the depriving of life, not because the transgressor showed conceit, not because it was tantamount to lying, although this certainly came in, but above all because the claim put forward was an assumpsion, unjustifiable and unfounded, amounting to theft (*Vin.* III. 90), of conditions (*dhammā*) to be won only by steadfast determination to reach the further (*uttari*), to make the higher become. Those who had truly achieved this are called in Pārājika IV *uttari-manussā*, the further-men—the best men (*seṭṭha-purisā*) according to the commentarial exegesis. It cannot be too much emphasised that the powers won did not surpass those which men were capable of developing, were not superhuman, did not go beyond man's conditions, as various translators have suggested. It was not that the conditions were beyond man in the flesh, beyond his grasp, severed from the spheres in which he could move and discipline himself. It was that there were men here in this world who differed from others in that they were bound to become (*bhabba*), and who hence had gone further on the Way, achieving as they did so certain conditions denied to those who had not travelled so far. They were not devas, nor those reborn in other worlds: they were the further-men, but *men* nevertheless.

Now what are these conditions whose attainment marks off the zealous, ardent monks whose inmost self has striven (*pahitattā*) from those others who cannot for long raise their thoughts above the pleasures of the senses? Pārājika IV has several answers to this question. For example those lax monks who spent a *vassa* (rains) on the banks of the river Vaggamudā thought, and rightly so, that the conditions of the further-men include possession of one or more of the four musings (*jhāna,* Skt. *dhyāna*), attainment of one or more of the four stages of the Way (stream-entry, once-returning, non-returning, arahanship), the mastery of the threefold knowledge, the mastery of the sixfold knowledge. These two knowledges include knowledge of previous rebirths, of destruction of the cankers (*āsava,* Skt. *āsrava*), and of what we should now call telepathy, clairvoyance and clairaudience. The Old Commentary on Pārājika IV adds to these conditions those of freedom, attainment, concentration, making the Way to become (*maggabhāvanā*), realisation of the fruits of the Way, and the destruction of the corruptions (*kilesā*). This last it defines in terms strongly reminiscent of the *Saṃyutta's* definition of both *nirvāṇa* and *arahatta*: destruction of passion, of hatred and of confusion.

Towards the end of Pārājika IV the great disciple Moggallāna is accused by the monks of claiming for himself conditions of the further-men. In alleging that he saw shapes and forms going through the air, that he heard their cries of distress, and that he knew what they had been in previous rebirths, he was undoubtedly claiming these conditions for himself. But he was supported by Gotama, so it is stated, who said that Moggallāna spoke truly and that therefore there was no offence for him. He was a further-man, removed by his own power of endeavour, by his own spiritual development both from the pious, moderate monks, and from the mass of depraved, evil monks, who figure so largely in the Vinaya, and who are accountable for the framing of the Rules. Only in a teaching where such a qualitative difference between *men* was fully recognised, only where spiritual progress with its load of conditions as yet unattained by those lower on the Way was accounted of supreme importance, could the claiming of those conditions by one who did not truly possess them be ranked as one of the four gravest offences, entailing expulsion from the monastic order.

Chapter - 28

The Democratic Attitude of the Buddha

Nand Kishore Prasad

Gotama, the Buddha, neither appealed to the people nor constrained them to adhere to his dhamma and discipline. On the contrary, he proclaimed; "You yourself must strive. The Blessed Ones are (only) preachers."[1] Once requested by Ānanda to lay down instructions concerning the Order, the Blessed one is reported to have said: "Surely Ānanda, should there be any one who harbours the thought 'It is I who will lead the brotherhood, or the Order is dependent upon me,' it is he who should lay down instructions concerning the Order. Now the Tathāgata, Ānanda, things not that the Order is dependent upon him. Why then should he leave instructions in any matter concerning the Order."[2] Furthermore he inspired Ānanda as follows: "......Be ye lamps unto yourselves. Be ye a refuge to yourselves, Betake yourselves to no external refuge,"[3] and his final injunction was "what Dhamma and Vinaya have been promulgated and proclaimed by me, let that be after my demise your teacher."[4]

What we propose to emphasise is that the assertions cited above are almost all democratic is spirit. The same spirit is manifest in the ecclesiastical regulations of the Buddhist Order (Saṅgha). Based on democratic footing, these rules are sufficient to prove that their promulgator was an ardent supporter of democratic ideals. Scholars are almost unanimous that the constitution of the Buddhist Fraternity was republican in nature.[5] But despite the fact, some of the eminent scholars harbour doubt about the Buddha being a zealous democrat. They perceive in him a dictatorial attitude. Thus Prof. Oldenberg

1. *Dp*. Gatha, 276.
2. *DB.*, Part II, p. 107.
3. *Ibid.*, p. 108.
4. *Ibid.*, p. 171.
5. *Buddha*, p. 338; *EMB.*, vol.1, p. 315; *EBJ.*, p. 148 and *HBC.*, p. 155.

remarks that "The authority to frame a law for the community belongs to the Buddha alone......".[1] Similarly Dr. S. Dutt says "that the ideal that there was no leader of the Saṅgha, no one on whom the Saṅgha was dependent, came to the fore after the death of the first master (Satthā)".[2] Dr. N. Dutt is decidedly vehement in his assertion that the Buddha "himself, however, acted more as a dictator than as a constitutional head......".[3] And Buddha by his towering personality no doubt, outshone them all".[4]

Prof. Oldenberg is not unjust in passing such a remark. He is, of course, right so far as the promulgation of the rules is concerned.[5] But regulation and imposition are poles apart. It is indubitable that Buddha laid down instructions for religious life, but he neither advised nor forced any one to have a blind faith in them. His attitude, on the contrary, was always rationalistic. "Test by logic and reason and only then accept any thing, not out of mere regards for the Master' was one of his golden advices given to his followers from time to time. Once he is heard advising the Kālāmas: "So then, Kālāmas, as to my words to you just now: 'Be ye not misled by report or tradition or hearsay. Be not misled by proficiency in the collections, nor by mere logic or inference, nor after considering reasons, nor after reflection on and approval of some theory, nor because it fits becoming, nor out of respect for a recluse (who holds it). But, Kālāmas, when your know yourselves: These things are unprofitable, these things are blameworthy, these things are censured by the intelligent, these things, when performed and undertaken, conduce to loss and sorrow,.........then indeed do ye reject them."[6]

The Buddha's rationalistic attitude is again evidence by the reply given to the query put to the Teacher by the Bhikkhus. On one occasion, the master is reported to have enquired: "Would you monks, knowing thus, seeing thus, speak thus; 'The Lord is oppressive to us, but we speak out of respect to our Teacher?" "No Lord" was the bold reply of the Bhikkhus. He again interrogated them; "Do not you, monks, speak only of that which of yourselves you have known, seen and discerned?" And they expressly admitted it by the phrase" "Yes, Lord"[7].

---

1. *Buddha*, p. 333.
2. *EBM.*, p. 125.
3. *EMB.*, vol. 1, p. 315.
4. *EBJ.*, p. 86.
5. Even this much is not accepted unanimously, See *EBJ.*, p. 85.
6. *BGS.*, vol, 1, p. 173.
7. MLS., Part 1, p. 321.

It is clear that the rules framed by the Buddha were put into practice only after a thorough examination of their suitability and unsuitability to the Saṅgha. Thus Prof. A.J. Bahm seems to be justified when he remarks: "But they should do so only because this appears to them best suited to their needs not because Gotama gave an authoritative command to do so."[1]

Let us come to Dr. S. Dutt. The evidence supplied in support of his assertion has merely a show of truth, for when examined in the light of a similar contradiction referred to in the *Milindapañha*, its implausibility becomes clear. He finds, inconsistency in Buddha's denial of himself as 'managing' the Saṅgha or of the Saṅgha as 'depending' on him, and Assaji's acknowledgment of himself as 'being initiated in the Blessed One's name.'[2] As early as the first century B.C. an apparent contradiction was found by king Milinda in the statements: "Tathāgatassa kho Ānanda na evaṃ hoti 'ahaṃ bhikkhusaṅghaṃ pariharissāmīti' vā 'mamuddesiko bhikkusaṅgho' ti vā" and "so anekasahassaṃ bhikkusaṅghaṃ pariharissati seyyathā pi ahaṃ etarahi anekasataṃ bhikkhusaṅghaṃ pariharāmīti,"[3] made by the Buddha himself in this respect. He put it to Thera Nāgasena for its solution.

Thera Nāgasena replied that the king is partly right and partly wrong in his remark. The contradiction or inconsistency pointed out in the passages is only applicable so far as the conventional truth is concerned. To the Blessed ones, "This is I" or "This is mine," for example, is merely a custom of every day life (*sammutisacca*) rather than a transcendental truth (*paramatthasacca*); for Blessed ones are free from all attachments. They are not helped in any way by their adherents, but their adherents are helped in every way by them. To make it easily comprehensible, he explained it with the help of two similes—one that of the 'earth' (*paṭhavī*) and the other that of the 'mighty rain-cloud' (*mahatimahāmegho*). It is well-known that the earth is a support and shelter for all and the rain provides nourishment to all, but they have no attachment for them. In the same way the Tathāgata is an asylum of righteous life of the beings but it never occurs to him that "These are mine." Thus, "It is not the Tathāgata, O King" observed Thera Nāgasena, "who seeks after a following, but the followers who seek after him."[4] The intention behind Assaji's statement is thus brought out. It is but befitting for a neophyte like Assaji to acknowledge gratitude to his Teacher and to look to him for necessary assistance as

1. *PB.*, p. 140.
2. *EBM.*, p. 69.
3. *MP.*, p. 160.
4. *SBE.*, vol. XXXV, pp. 225-226.

the occasion arose. As such the view that the Order was dependent on the Teacher during his lifetime is untenable.

Instead of applying force to solve any issue of the Order the Buddha always entreated his adherents to tackle it amicably. For instance, the case of dissension in the Church at Kosambi may be cited.[1] The Kosambian monks were divided on certain issue of the Church and the Buddha could not settle it. Seeing the awkward situation, he left the place. To give an authoritative command to the mendicants to obey him would have been the course adopted by a dictator in his place. But he always looked down upon dictatorship because his followers were, in his view, his equals and companions; not his subordinates and inferiors. The sympathetic words uttered by the compassionate Teacher to the Bhikkhus just before his departure from Kosambi bears testimony to this. He advised them to associate with friends who were righteous, mindful, wise and happy and to abandon those who were of the opposite nature. This shows that the Buddha left the question of reconciliation to his followers themselves and thus provided scope for the free exercise of their own wisdom.

"Dictators who remain in office tend to be corrupted and misled by their own power. Their closest advisers become flatterers."[2] The Buddha was regarded as a great Teacher of his time. Many sought to wait on him, others to cajole and flatter him. But he always repudiated and discouraged such ideas: "I have naught to do with homage, Nāgita, nor has homage aught to do with me."[3] On one occasion, when praised by Sāriputta, the Generalissimo of the Dhamma, he ridiculed him with the following words: "You see then, Sāriputta, that you know not the hearts of the Able Awakened ones of the past and of the future. Why therefore are your words so grand and bold? Why do you burst forth into such a song of ecstasy?"[4]

Being conscious of the consequences of dictatorship or supreme authority, the Buddha neither acted himself as a dictator not expected others to do the same in his presence or after his passing away. Consequently, he did never appoint his successor or an Abort of the Brotherhood. The enquiry made of Ānanda by Gopaka Moggallāna testifies to it unmistakably.

"Is there, good Ānanda, even one monk who was designated by the good Gotama saying: 'After my passing this one will be your support (*paṭisaraṇa*),' and to whom you might have recourse now?"

---

1. See Mv, 'Kosambakakkhandhaka'.
2. *CPE.*, vol. IV, 89.
3. *BGS.*, vol. IV, p. 224.
4. *DB.*, Part II, p. 88.

"There is not even one monk, brāhmaṅa, who was designated by the Lord who knew and saw, perfected one, fully Self-Awakened one, saying: 'After my passing this one will be your support,' and to whom we might have recourse now."

"But is there even one monk, Ānanda, who is agreed upon by the order and designated by a number of monks who are elders, saying: 'After the Lord's passing this one will be our support', and to whom you might have recourse now?"

"There is not even one monk, brāhmaṇa, who is agreed upon by the order..............and to whom we might have recourse now."[1]

It also shows that the righteous monks strictly adhered to the admonitions of the Teacher and accordingly did not select or elect their head even after the Great-Decease of the Teacher.

Though the question about the head of the Brotherhood does not arise, for the Lord had already vested the authority in the 'Dhamma and Vinaya': "Yo vo, Ānanda, mayā dhammo ca vinayo ca desito paññatto, so vo mamaccayena satthā,"[2] yet Gopaka-Moggallāna remarked: "Evam appaṭisaraṇe, bho Ānanda, ko hetu sāmaggiyā' ti." Ānanda admitted the same (i.e. Dhamma and Vinaya) as the support of the Brotherhood to Gopaka-Moggallāna: "Na kho mayaṃ, brāhmaṇa, appaṭisaraṇā; sappaṭisaraṇā mayaṃ, brāhmaṇa dhammappaṭsaraṇā'ti."[3]

Several designations namely, Gaṇadhara[4] or the head of a group, Gacchācārya or the teacher of a group and Maṇḍalī-Thera or elderly monk who headed a group etc. of the Jaina Order illustrate distinctly that it adopted autocratic form of administration. In other words it believed in personal authority. The Buddhist Brotherhood, on the other hand, did never conceive of such offices. What is conceived of were Dhammasenāpati, Dhammadhara and Vinayadhara etc., which signify the Generalissimo of the doctrines (Dhamma), the custodian of the doctrines, and the custodian of the ecclesiastical laws (Vinaya) etc. are clearly impersonal. It may be observed thus that Buddha neither outshone the members of the church nor considered himself above all. He stuck to a total avoidance of such ideas. And hence, he preached 'Dhamma and Vinaya' for the welfare of the multitude (*bahujanahitāya bhujansukhāya*) as the regulator of the community which derived its authority directly from them (namely, Dhamma and Vinaya) which are entirely impersonal.[5]

---

1. *MLS.*, vol. III, p. 59-60.
2. *Dn.*, Part II, p. 118.
3. *Mn.*, Part III, pp. 69-70.
4. Lord Mahāvīra had nine Gaṇas but eleven Gaṇadharas, namely Indrabhūyi. Agnibhūti etc. Under these Gaṇadharas were placed all the monks of his Order. See *LM.*, pp. 82-83.
5. See *Buddha*, p. 338.

The problem which attracts our attention next is—How did this novel idea come into the mind of the Buddha? Did it occur spontaneously or did he borrow it from others? A brief analysis of the then social, religious and political conditions as mentioned in the Pāli texts will be undoubtedly of much help in this respect.

It is known to all of us the Lord Mahāvīra was a Licchavi Prince by birth and a contemporary of the Buddha. In spite of his being a preacher from their own clan, the Licchavians preferred the Buddha to Mahāvīra. The influence that the Buddha and his teachings exercised upon the orthodox Licchavis may be due to the fact that he adopted the Licchavian constitution for the confraternity with necessary changes. The matter would have taken an opposite turn if he would not have adopted the republic constitution of the Licchavis. The obvious reason behind it was that they were not ready at all to tolerate subjugation. As a testimony to this, the case of the Vajjiputtakas may be put forward. The Vajjiputtaka-Bhikkhus were all Licchavian. No sooner did they perceive that their independent spirit was under subjugation than they separated themselves from the general body of the Church and formed an independent unit known as the Vajjiputtaka-school.[1]

The democratic set-up of the Buddhist order can best be compared with that of the democratic state. On account of its being a religious unit, the constitution of the Saṅgha cannot be compared with that of the State. But still the influence of King or State on the order can easily be traced. Most often royal life seems to be the background of monastic life as well as of the monastic rules.

Our contention is supported by the reply given by the Buddha to the enquiry made by Vassakāra, the prime Minister of Ajātasattu, King of Magadha. The Buddha related a set of seven conditions of the welfare of a community (*Satta Aparihāniyā Dhammā*), that were inherent in the Vajjis and further remarked, "so long as the Vajjis will practise these *Aparihāniyā Dhammās,* so long may the Vajjis be expected to prosper and not to decline." Thereafter the Buddha prescribed six sets of *Aparihāniyā Dhammās* for the Saṅgha. At least the first set is directly derived from the set pointed out about the Vajjis. The others may be regarded as mere corollaries of it. Citation of at least the first two sets—One said about the Vajjis and the other prescribed for the Bhikkhus, will make the position intelligible.

The seven conditions of the welfare said about the Vajjis:

1. See '*Second Buddhist Council*'.

(1) "So long, Ānanda, as the Vajjians foregather thus often, and frequent the public meetings of their clan;

(2) So long, as the Vajjians meet together in concord and rise in concord, and carry out their undertaking in concord;

(3) So long, as they enact nothing not already established, abrogate nothing that has been already enacted and act in accordance with the ancient institutions of the Vajjians, as established in former days;

(4) So long as they honour and esteem and revere and support the Vajjian elders, and hold it a point of duty to hearken to their words;

(5) So long as no women or girls belonging to their clans are detained among them by force or abduction;

(6) So long as they honour and esteem and revere and support the Vajjian shrines (Caityas) in town or country, and allow not the proper offerings and rites, as formerly given and performed, to fall into destitude;

(7) So long as the rightful protection, defence and support shall be full provided for the Arhantas among them;

So long may the Vajjians be expected not to decline but to prosper."

The seven conditions of the welfare prescribed for the Bhikkhus:

(1) "So long as the Bhikkhus meet together in full and frequent assemblies;

(2) So long as they meet together in concord and rise in concord and carry out in concord the duties of the Order (Saṅgha);

(3) So long as the brethern shall establish nothing that has not already been prescribed, and abrogate nothing that has been already established, and act in accordance with the rules of the Order as now laid down;

(4) So long as the brethern honour and esteem and revere and support the elders of experience and long standing, the fathers and the leaders of the Order and hold it a point of duty to hearken to their words;

(5) So long as the brethren fall not under the influence of the craving, which springing up within them, would give rise to renewed existence;

(6) So long as the brethren delight in a life of solitude:

(7) So long as the brethren so train their minds in self-possession that the good men among their fellow disciples shall come to them, and those who have come shall dwell at ease;

So long may the brethren be expected not to decline, but to prosper.[1]

Prof. E.J. Rapson maintains that certain technical terms namely, *ñatti* or motion, *ubbāhikā* or 'reference to arbitration', etc. found in the Buddhist Vinaya were most probably borrowed from the constitution of the free clans.[2] If this is a fact, then no proof or support is required for the view that the entire system of the administration of the Buddhist Order itself was copied from the existing republican clans. This view is further corroborated by Dr. K.P Jayaswal and Miss Bhagavat.[3] The least possibility for doubt, if there be any, is again removed by Mahāpaṇḍita Rahul Sankrityayana, when he unhesitatingly asserts that the Buddha organised his Order taking the free clans as his ideal.[4]

It has already been asserted that democratic spirit, in some form or other, is patent throughout in the constitution of the Buddhist Church. To prove our thesis we propose to give a brief analysis of (1) the rules regarding communal ownership of the Saṅgha property, (2) the problem of seniority and succession in the Buddhist hierarchy, (3) the freedom of learning the Buddhavacana (Sermons of the Buddha) in one's own language and (4) the place of laity in the Buddhist Saṅgha.

1. Communal Ownership of the Saṅgha-property

In its early days, the Saṅgha owned no property according to Buddhist Theory. A mendicant is advised to be satisfied "with sufficient robes to cherish his body, with sufficient food to keep his body going." With these words he is further compared with a bird: "whitherso ever he may go forth, these things he takes with him as he goes— just as a bird with wings, whitherso ever he may fly, carries his wings with him as he flies[5]". But later on, the multiplication of the members of the Saṅgha and the introduction of a corporate life in a settled Āvāsa (residence) necessitated the acceptance of property by the Order. Consequently, acquisition of gifts became permissible and later on it was considered a 'birth right"[6] of the Saṅgha.

Somehow or other, there was some property owned by the Saṅgha. No one could claim it as his own except the right of using it properly and equally with others. If any one wished to make some offer to an individual member of the Saṅgha, it was to be offered to

---

1. *DB.*, 'The Book of the Great-Decease.'
2. *CHI.*, p. 157.
3. *HP.*, p. 42 and ERJ, p. 127.
4. VAG., p. 23.
5. *DB.*, Part 1, p.81.
6. *EBJ.*, p. 156.

the Saṅgha with special reference to that person[1]. On the admission of a heretic into the Buddhist Order his properties vested in the Saṅgha. The case of Uruvela Kassapa may be taken as an instance in point[2].

After the demise of a Bhikkhu or a Bhikkhunī, the Bhikkhu-Saṅgha or the Bhikkhunī-Saṅgha, as the case may be, was the legal heir to all his or her belongings. It was not to be transferred in any case from Bhikkhu Saṅgha to Bhikkhunī-Saṅgha or vice versa[3]. But the persons who attended him (i.e. the deceased monk or sāmaṇera) during his last sickness were not neglected. In such cases, robes and bowl were to fall in their share and the trifles were to be distributed to the members of the Saṅgha present there[4].

This ideal or communal ownership reaches the climax in the injunction made by the Lord: "so long as they shall divide without partiality, and share in common with their upright companions, all such things as they receive in accordance with the just provisions of the Order, down even to the mere contents of a begging bowl, so long may the brethren be expected not to decline, but to prosper[5]".

2. Problem of Seniority and Succession

Problem of seniority and succession is one of the most significant problems that come before an organisation, of whatever nature it may be. The Buddhist Church was not an exception. Even in the life-time of Lord Buddha the problem arose with regard to individual preferences provided by the Saṅgha.

The main qualifications of the officers of the Buddhist Fraternity were moral integrity, the knowledge of Dhamma and Vinaya and their proper and regular practice. It is evidenced by the rules framed for the guidance of the Saṅgha that "only a learned, competent Bhikkhu who had completed ten years or more may confer ordination and give *Nissaya* (dependance)"[6]; and that "a learned, competent Bhikkhu is allowed to ordain two novices or as many novices as he is able to admonish and instruct to"[7], and that "even a Bhikkhu of less standing is to be authorised instantly to recite the *Pātimokkha*, if all the Theras of an Āvāsa be ignorant"[8]. We notice that regulations were laid down to encourage the novices and to avoid unhealthy competition as well.

1. *Mv.*, p. 231.
2. *Cv.*, p. 233.
3. *Ibid.*, p. 318.
4. *Mv.*, p. 319.
5. *DB.*, Part II, p. 85.
6. *Mv.*, p. 67.
7. *Mv.*, p. 87.
8. *Mv.*, p. 117.

In framing the rules the Buddhist Order showed the keenest foresight and a peculiar psychological approach to human nature. Consequently, it was conscious enough of giving the least opportunity that might cause dissension in the Order at any time to come. One of the causes of cessation of the dependence (*Nissaya*), for example, may be cited. The *Nissaya* ceases if the teacher (Ācariya), and the preceptor (Upajjhāya) of a monk under dependence have come together[1]. It distinctly installed the Upajjhāya at a level higher than the Ācariya.

Moreover, due consideration was given to circumstances beyond one's control. For instance, if a supervisor of the construction of new buildings (*Navakammika*) after taking the charge of the construction of the new buildings becomes incompetent and "if he then admits that he is mad or that his mind is unhinged, or that he is afflicted with bodily pain,......, the office and its privileges are still his"; otherwise the Saṅgha becomes the owners[2].

We should not forget that the framer or rather the framers of the Buddhist Laws after all were human beings, and as such they were in the know of the human short-comings and lapses. Their best effort seems to be to accommodate all such short-comings and lapses without defying the rules of decorum and decency. The rule that if an Ācariya or an Upajjhāya, as the case may be, committed some grave offence, then he should not be denied the right to hold that office instantly, illustrates it. He should be given even due opportunity to undergo the penance or atone for the offence committed by him. Moreover, his pupil must strive in order that the Saṅgha may revoke its sentence and restore him to the office[3].

3. The freedom for learning Buddha-vacana in one's own language

Once, emphasising the unification and oneness of his Order, Lord Buddha is reported to have observed; "Just, O Bhikkhus, as the great rivers—that is to say, the Gaṅgā, the Yamunā, the Aciravatī, the Sarabhū, and the Mahī—when they have fallen into the great ocean, renounce their name and linage and are thenceforth reckoned as the great ocean—just so, O Bhikkhus, do these four castes—the Khattiyas, the Brāhmaṇas, the Vessas, and the Suddas—whem they have gone forth from the world under the doctrine and discipline proclaimed by the Tathāgata, renounce their names and lineage, and enter into the number of the Sakyaputtiya Samaṇas[4]".

---

1. *Mv.*, p. 67.—In Hindu and Jaina tradition Ācārya is installed higher in position than the Upādhyāya.
2. *Cv.*, p. 270.
3. *Mv.*, pp. 46-47.
4. *SBE.*, vol. XX, p. 304.

What is desired to bring to notice is that the members of the Saṅgha had come from different families and different corners of the Jambudvīpa with various dialects as their lingua franca. Naturally, it became not only very difficult but really impracticable for them to learn the Buddha-vacana in the language preached by the Blessed one. Two brothers, Yameḷu and Tekula who had come from Brāhmaṇa family, therefore; proposed to tender the words of the Budddha into Chandas, the Vedic Sanskrit. When the Blessed One was informed he disapproved the proposal and said: "I allow, O Bhikkhus, to learn the words of the Buddha, each in your own language[1]". Though the issue is open to question, yet the intention to avoid imposition is reasonably apparent.

4. Place of laity in the Saṅgha

It is not easy to determine the place of laity in the Buddhist Church, for "No direct mention is made in the Vinaya of laymen associated with the Saṅgha except that the rules regulate the conduct of the Bhikkhus towards laymen, their reception as Upāsakas, etc[2]". Anyhow, Dr. Pachow has shown that for the same offence—offence of false complaint against a Bhikkhu by an Upāsaka or vice versa, the penance or punishment imposed upon the Bhikkhu was to some extent heavier than that imposed upon the Upāsaka[3]. This may be due to various reasons. The Upāsakas were not counted as the full-fledged members of the Order[4], and this may be one of them. In spite of this, the Order was conscious of the fact that its very existence stood on the sympathy and mercy of the lay devotees. Thus the significant position of the lay devotees that they were donors, providers and supporters of the Saṅgha may be another reason. Thus the special latitude granted to the laity by the Saṅgha is justified.

Now it can be taken as an admitted fact that all were on the same footing as regards constitutional rights, privileges and obligations. As such it has rightly been summed up that "The Buddha's administration of the Saṅgha resembled that of a real democratic system[5].

1. *SBE.*, vol. XX, p. 155.
2. *Vp.*, vol.I, Introduction, p. 13, fn, 2.
3. See *JAIOC.*, Legal dealings between the Buddhist Monks and the Laity',
4. *Buddha*, p. 382.
5. *HBC.*, p. 155.

ABBREVIATIONS

Cv	—Cullavagga (Nālandā Devanāgarī Pāli Series).
Dn	—Dighanikāya (Nālandā Devanāgarī Pāli Series).
Mn	—Majjhimanikāya (Nālandā Devanāgarī Pāli Series).
Mv	—Mahāvagga (Nālandā Devanāgarī Pāli Series).
Mp	—Milindapañha (Pāli Text Society)
Vp	—Vinayapiṭaka (Pāli Text Society).
Bgs	—The Book of the Gradual Sayïngs.
DB	—Dialogues of Buddha.
Dp	—Dhammapada (Translated by Dr. S. Radhakrishnan).
Mls	—The Middle Length Sayings.
SBE	—The Sacred Books of the East.
Buddha	—Buddha by Prof. H. Oldenberg.
CHI	—The Cambridge History of India by Prof. E.J.Rapson.
CPE	—Compton's Pictured Encyclopedia.
EBJ	—Early Buddhist Jurisprudence by Miss D.N. Bhagvat.
EBM	—Early Buddhist Monasticism by S. Dutt.
EMB	—Early Monastic Buddhism by N. Dutt.
HBC	—History of Buddhism in Ceylon by Dr. W. Rahula.
HP	—Hindu Polity by Dr. K.P. Jayasawal.
JAIOC	—Journal of All India Oriental Conference, October, 1946.
JMJ	—Jaina Monastic Jurisprudence by Dr. S.B. Deb.
LM	—Lord Mahābīra by Dr. Bool Chanda.
PB	—Philosophy of the Buddha by Prof. A.J. Bahm.
VAG	—Vaishālī Abhinandana Grantha.